NEW JERSEY

ELECTRICIAN'S REFERENCE MANUAL

PREPARED BY

PROMETRIC

Ninth Edition

TABLE OF CONTENTS

4. CONTRACTS

5. PROJECT MANAGEMENT

6. RISK MANAGEMENT

7. SAFETY

8. LABOR LAWS

9. FINANCIAL MANAGEMENT

10. TAX LAWS

11. CONSTRUCTION LIEN LAW

12. GLOSSARY

INTRODUCTION

Your decision to become a licensed electrical contractor is the first step toward establishing a successful career and a potentially rewarding future. Prometric has written the *New Jersey Electrician's Reference Manual* with two goals in mind – to make the electrical construction industry understandable for you as you enter the business world and to clearly present the terms and concepts that will help you prepare to take your licensing examinations.

This *New Jersey Electrician's Reference Manual* is divided into 12 chapters, including a glossary of important legal and industry terms. The chapters are organized into specific content areas that outline the construction process step-by-step and discuss the laws that regulate the business. Each content area includes an easy-to-read description of industry procedures and legal requirements, and for your convenience, we have also included copies of up-to-date governmental rules and regulations.

Chapter 1 highlights organizing and managing a business. It reviews the advantages and disadvantages of various types of business organizations that a company may choose. Also included are some suggestions for managing a business. Finally, the chapter reviews state and federal agencies that regulate business start-ups.

Chapter 2 outlines the requirements of the state licensing laws that electrical contractors must follow to become licensed to do business. The chapter explains how to get licensed. Excerpts from the *New Jersey Electrical Contractors Licensing Act, New Jersey Electrical Contractor Regulations*, the *New Jersey Fire Alarm, Burglar Alarm and Locksmith Licensees and Businesses Administrative Code*, the *Uniform Enforcement Act*, and *N.J.A.C. Uniform Regulations* are reprinted in this chapter.

Chapter 3 describes the process of estimating and bidding construction jobs, and includes hints on preparing accurate, competitive bids.

Chapter 4 explains the technical elements of contracts and how to clearly establish the contractual relationships between the different participants in a construction project.

Chapter 5 presents information on many aspects of managing a construction project.

Chapter 6 defines risk management and how you can protect yourself from liability for injury and damages on the job. It also examines how to reduce financial risk through insurance and bonds.

Chapter 7 reviews safety regulations and gives an overview of the federal Occupational Safety and Health Act (OSHA). It includes a reprint of 29 CFR 1904, *Recording and Reporting Occupational Injuries and Illnesses.*

Chapter 8 describes state and federal labor laws that apply to employers and employees. The chapter also discusses the state's workers' compensation and unemployment compensation laws. Reprinted in this chapter are the *Handy Reference Guide to the Fair Labor Standards Act, ADA: Your Responsibilities as an Employer*, the *Form I-9, Employment Eligibility Verification*, excerpts from New Jersey's *Wage and Hour Regulations, Child Labor Laws*, and the *Employer's Guide to Workers' Compensation in New Jersey.*

Chapter 9 details the accounting and recordkeeping systems necessary to accurately represent the economic health of a business. The chapter includes information on managing business costs.

Chapter 10 outlines tax laws, filing requirements, and payroll reporting responsibilities.

Chapter 11 defines a lien, explains who is entitled to a lien, and gives a general overview of the procedures necessary to file a lien. The *New Jersey Construction Lien Law* is reprinted in this chapter.

Chapter 12 is the glossary. You should refer to it often as a guide to help you understand the everyday technical and legal terms common to the business.

The *New Jersey Electrician's Reference Manual* is intended to be an all-in-one reference book for electrical contractors. Once you have begun your business, you will find that the reference material and outlines will be an invaluable source of answers to your ongoing operational questions. The manual is not intended to provide you with specific legal, accounting, insurance, or other professional assistance. You should always seek out a qualified professional to advise you on current requirements.

Prometric recognizes that a testing program involves people, not just statistics. We are keenly aware of the pressure that taking an examination imposes on candidates. Our goal is to serve both client and candidates in a responsive, professional, and courteous manner. We are proud of our national reputation for providing reliable, responsive, high-quality examination services. We wish you the best of luck in your business.

1

ORGANIZING AND MANAGING A BUSINESS

GETTING ORGANIZED

A contractor who wants to start a successful business needs to create a plan of action. The first step is to set goals. The second step is to develop a business plan.

Goal setting helps a new business owner define what he or she wants to do, why he or she wants to do it, how it is going to be accomplished, and where he or she wants to be in five years. Once these decisions are made, the business plan should be developed.

A written business plan shows how the owner will achieve his or her goals. Be aware that a business plan is an ever-changing document; as the business grows and expands, the plan should be updated. Use it to evaluate problems and find solutions. Then, review it to set revised goals.

In addition to the company's primary goals, the business plan should also address:
- Market possibilities;
- Competition;
- Financial needs (both short term and long term);
- The company's assets and liabilities;
- Growth and profit; and
- Business organization type.

A detailed business plan helps the owner see where he or she is going. It shows when the company should (or should not) expand. It is useful in seeking financial help. A thorough business plan is as important to starting a business as a set of blueprints is to building a structure.

BUSINESS OWNERSHIP TYPES

Sole proprietorships, corporations, general partnerships, and limited partnerships are the most common ways businesses are organized today. State statutes require every business to adopt a business structure. Each type has advantages and disadvantages. Besides clarifying company ownership, much of the difference between the types centers on the degree of personal liability placed on owners. Generally, types that allow greater business freedom require greater personal liability. Those business types with less ownership liability are more highly regulated. Owners should choose a business type based on their level of involvement in management, their financial institution, and the degree of personal liability they are willing to accept.

A. SOLE PROPRIETORSHIP

The sole proprietorship is the simplest and least expensive business type to organize. In a sole proprietorship, one person owns, operates, and leads the business. One owner (proprietor) has sole control and sole responsibility for all the business decisions and actions. Because of their willingness to accept unlimited liability for their company, sole proprietors enjoy the greatest degree of business freedom and the least degree of business regulation.

Except for obtaining a business license, no legal steps are required to organize a sole proprietorship. Owners may operate under their own name or under a chosen business name (for example, ABC Construction) as long as that name does not too closely resemble the name of another business and state laws have been obeyed. States sometimes require that business names be registered with the Secretary of State. In some states, business may only be conducted in the name shown on a person's license. For example, if John Brown's license is obtained in his name (John Brown), then Mr. Brown cannot do business as J. B. Construction.

Companies not organized into other business types, such as partnerships or corporations, are usually considered (for tax and legal purposes) to be operating as sole proprietorships. Because an individual owns the company, profits are considered personal income and are taxed as such – whether or not the profits are actually withdrawn for personal use. The owner raises capital based solely on individual credit, assets, and reputation. The owner is also free to sell or change the business.

Sole proprietorships can be terminated or suspended without taking any legal steps; the owner simply stops doing business. The owner may also, at any later time, simply resume doing business. Company ownership dissolves with the death of the owner.

Although sole proprietorships offer contractors freedom from much business regulation, they are still responsible for obtaining all applicable licenses and abiding by insurance and tax obligations, and rules for contractors, as well as by general business law. A sole proprietor is personally responsible for all financial burdens and business obligations. This liability extends to the owner's personal assets to pay for business debt, even though those personal assets may not have been involved in the business. One common mistake sole proprietors make is to mix business and personal funds.

ADVANTAGES OF A SOLE PROPRIETORSHIP

- It is easy to create.
- The owner has full control and responsibility.
- The owner makes all the decisions.
- Ownership is freely transferable.
- The owner can sell, alter, or exchange all or part of the business.

DISADVANTAGES OF A SOLE PROPRIETORSHIP

- The owner has unlimited personal liability.
- The business terminates upon the death of the owner.
- Personal credit, funds, and property must be used as security for loans.
- Business profits are taxed as ordinary income to the owner.

In summary, sole proprietorships are simple to set up, easy to terminate, and easy to reopen. They offer greater freedom from regulation, organizational simplicity, and the ability to adapt and grow quickly. Operating capital can be difficult to obtain in a sole proprietorship because credit is based on the owner's resources. Proprietorships also require unlimited responsibility and liability from the owner.

B. CORPORATION

A corporation is a unique legal body. Creating a corporation essentially creates an artificial person. This legal person, or corporation, is separate from its owners (shareholders). The primary benefit of forming a corporation is that shareholders have limited liability. Shareholders are generally not liable for debt incurred by the corporation. However, in exchange for reduced ownership liability, corporations are highly regulated.

Corporations may exercise contracts, hold and sell property, sue and be sued, and have financial accounts unattached to their shareholders' personal assets. But corporations must provide a great deal of information about their activities to the state, and, in some cases, to the federal government. These public records are also open to the media and to any member of the public. The legal fees and procedures to create and maintain a corporation can be considerable, though usually not prohibitive.

The steps to begin a corporation vary from state to state. Commonly, filing documents include:
- Articles of incorporation;
- Unique corporate name (usually must include the word corporation, company, or incorporated);
- The purpose of the business;
- The number of shares the company is allowed to issue;
- The name, address, and signature of each incorporator; and
- A filing fee.

The articles of incorporation, corporate by-laws, and state laws control the acts, organizational structures, and financial aspects of all corporations. As long as a corporation abides within these guidelines, the corporation will be granted a charter to operate.

Shareholders elect corporate officers, usually at least a President, Vice-president, Secretary, and Treasurer, to conduct daily business. Corporate officers may also be found to be legally liable for misconduct or neglect.

A corporation continues to "live" even when shareholders or officers do not. A corporation can only be terminated by passing a shareholder motion and submitting it for approval to the state. Annual meetings with recorded minutes are among the many corporate regulations. Disregard of such formalities, and mingling corporate and shareholder assets (called "piercing the veil" that should separate shareholders from the corporation) may result in the corporation being legally considered to be a proprietorship or partnership. This could result in increased shareholder liability and higher taxes.

Shareholders may invest more into the company by buying more company stock. They may also, at any time, reduce their investment by selling their stock. Non-employed shareholders pay taxes only on the corporate profits that are actually paid from the business. These profits are called dividends. Shareholders who are employed by the corporation must pay personal taxes on their take-home wages and on dividends. The corporation also pays taxes on its profits.

When a corporation does business in the state in which it was chartered, it is called a "domestic" corporation. A corporation doing business in another state is considered by that state as a "foreign" corporation. Foreign corporations must abide by the laws of the state in which they operate. Some states require foreign corporations to have a registered agent in their state.

ADVANTAGES OF A CORPORATION
- Limited liability of owners (shareholders).
- Greater ease in raising capital.
- Continuity if one of the owners dies.
- Regarded as separate and distinct from its owners.

- Possible double taxation: the corporation is taxed first on its profits, and then its shareholders are taxed as individuals on any dividends they may receive.
- Start-up procedures, costs, and maintenance of the legal aspects of a corporation are costly and complex.
- Corporations are highly regulated.

Overall, corporations offer ease of multiple ownership, transferring ownership, and management continuity. Limited owner liability and tax incentives enhance company stability and encourage investment and expansion. Corporations are highly regulated, require a separation between non-employed shareholders and management, and must pay corporate taxes on their profits at rates that may be higher than proprietorships or partnerships.

C. GENERAL PARTNERSHIP

Partnerships fall somewhere between a sole proprietorship and a corporation. They are designed to maintain the business freedom of a proprietorship without the regulation of a corporation. A general partnership is a legal association between two or more persons. By pooling resources, a general partnership often provides greater capacity than would be available to each of the partners separately.

Partnerships are often governed by "Articles of Partnership." In the Articles of Partnership, partners select a business name to be registered, specify ownership proportions, designate how profits are distributed, and outline partner duties. Ownership may be equal or in proportion to each partner's contribution to the company. In accordance with the Articles of Partnership, profits or losses are usually distributed in proportion to each partner's percent of ownership. In a general partnership, partners are usually expected to work full time for the partnership.

Like a corporation, partnerships may engage in contracts, own and sell property, and sue and be sued. But owners who work for the partnership are not considered to be employees. They are considered self-employed, similar to sole proprietorships.

Partners are legally responsible to act in good faith for each other, and each has authority to make binding business agreements. Notice given to one partner is considered notice given to all. However, partnerships cannot be sold or mortgaged without the consent of all partners. General partners, like sole proprietors, have unlimited individual liability for the contracts, claims, and debts of the partnership. Partners are liable for any partnership obligations that cannot be met by any other partner. For example: two partners, with a 60 – 40 percent investment, incurred a $100,000 partnership obligation. Each partner, regardless of his investment, is liable for the entire $100,000. Ideally, the obligation would be split according to the investment percentage. However, if one partner became incapacitated and unable to meet his part of the obligation, the other partner would be responsible for the entire amount. A partner's interest can only be sold or transferred with the consent of all partners. In such cases, the new person does not become a partner, but has only the right to receive the partner's profits.

The partnership does not pay an income tax, but it must file an information tax return. Partners are either paid annual salaries or advance payment on anticipated profits, for which they are obligated to pay personal income tax. Partnerships have a certain financial appeal over corporations because income from partnerships is taxed only once – at personal income tax rates – rather than at corporate and personal rates.

A partnership is terminated by the death of any partner, bankruptcy, the withdrawal of any partner, or mutual consent of the partners. Because each partner accepts responsibility for the actions, contracts, and debts of all the others, a person should exercise the utmost judgment in selecting business partners.

ADVANTAGES OF A GENERAL PARTNERSHIP

- Pooling of financial resources.
- Pooling of individual talents.
- Sharing of daily responsibilities, management, ideas, and goals.
- Single taxation.

DISADVANTAGES OF A GENERAL PARTNERSHIP

- General partners have unlimited personal liability.
- A partnership terminates upon the death of a partner, bankruptcy, or through withdrawal of a partner.
- A partnership interest is not transferable without the consent of all the partners.

In summary, general partnerships are easy to form. They offer each partner the right to manage daily business affairs, and they allow individuals to pool their resources in a common effort. Partners have an obligation to work for the mutual benefit of the partnership, and thereby incur unlimited liability for the obligations and debts of all partners. Though partnerships may own property, only the individual partners may sue or be sued. Partnerships do not pay corporate tax. Instead, the individual partners pay personal tax on the profits they receive.

D. LIMITED PARTNERSHIP

A limited partnership may be formed by two or more persons, but at least one person is considered a general partner. A limited partner contributes funds or property to a partnership, but does not provide services or participate in day-to-day management decisions. If one of the limited partners later becomes active in day-to-day management of the partnership, then that partner is no longer a limited partner but becomes one of the general partners with all the rights and responsibilities. Limited partners are treated roughly the same as in a general partnership, both in terms of compensation, authority, and liability. Limited partners are compensated by receiving a proportion of profits equal to their investment. Limited partners are liable only for the amount of their investment.

Limited partnerships are used as a way to raise capital without the general partners having to give over management of the business to investors. Limited partnerships are attractive to investors because this ownership type gives them an opportunity for ownership and profit without having to be involved in the operation of the business.

ADVANTAGES OF A LIMITED PARTNERSHIP

- Limited partners have liability limited to their investment.
- Limited partnership interests are transferable.

DISADVANTAGES OF A LIMITED PARTNERSHIP

- A limited partnership requires formal organization and compliance with state and federal laws.
- Limited partners are excluded from daily management.

In general, limited partnerships have functions and rights similar to general partnerships. The primary exception is the reduced involvement of the limited partner. General partners have unlimited liability for the partnership obligations, while limited partners are at risk only for their contributions. Limited partners often have no particular expertise in the business. Their involvement is limited to investing capital into the company. However, if limited partners do become involved in the management of the business, then the business structure changes and the limited partner may be considered a general partner.

E. Subchapter S or "S" Corporation

Small corporations, usually those with fewer than 35 shareholders and relatively modest revenue volume, are eligible to be categorized as an "S" corporation. As such, they enjoy the privileges of a corporation, such as limited liability and ease of transferability, while having a lowered tax rate.

Regular corporations pay taxes on profit; their shareholders pay personal income tax on dividends. Taxes on corporate profit can be higher or lower than shareholder personal tax rates. An "S" corporation differs from regular corporations in that "S" corporations' profits and losses are taxed like a partnership – directly as shareholders' personal income. This reduces the need to either keep profits in the corporation or pay them out as dividends solely based on which tax rate is lower. The advantage to newer small corporations (that often need to make long-term capital investment) is that they will not be penalized with possibly higher corporate taxes when they keep profits in the company. Conversely, it allows older small corporations (that may have little need for additional capital) to pay out higher dividends without a tax rate loss. This eliminates sinking corporate profits unnecessarily into business projects simply to avoid paying possibly higher personal income taxes.

Overall, the "S" corporation is a modified corporation for small businesses. It has all the rights and regulations of a regular corporation. The fundamental difference is that "S" corporation shareholders may choose to have their profits taxed at either the corporate or individual tax rate. The "S" corporation is designed to reduce the lure for small companies to make business decisions exclusively on the basis of tax rates.

F. Limited Liability Company

The Limited Liability Company (LLC) has the flexibility and tax advantage of a general partnership and the limited liability of a limited partnership or corporation. An LLC consists of two or more members (individuals, corporations, partnerships, estates, trusts, etc.) that join together to do business. An LLC is created when Articles of Organization are filed with the state. The LLC does have greater recordkeeping, public disclosure, and reporting requirements than partnerships or proprietorships.

LLC members, managers, and employees are generally not liable for the obligations or debts of the LLC members. They also enjoy greater management involvement in the business than a limited partnership. Furthermore, the LLC is not restricted only to small companies. LLC profits are divided among members, as stipulated in the Articles of Organization, and are taxed as individual earnings.

G. Joint Ventures

Joint ventures are created when two or more firms join together on a particular project. A joint venture contract requires a common purpose and equal control among parties. Though the joint venture itself becomes a separate business entity, the companies maintain their business type (i.e., sole proprietorships, corporations, or partnerships). Most states also require that all participants in a joint venture be individually licensed to perform any of the tasks of the project. For contractors, this means all parties must be licensed contractors to form a joint venture construction project. Also, contractors' bid bonding limits may or may not increase with a joint venture, depending on state law.

More than three-fourths of contractors in the United States are sole proprietorships. Less than one-fifth are corporations, and only about one in 20 are partnerships. Although the few large contracting firms account for most of the construction industry's dollars, the vast majority of contractors in the United States are self-employed or family owned. While choosing a business organization type that will suit a contractor's needs and resources takes careful analysis and, most likely, expert legal and financial assistance, beginning a contracting business is not necessarily expensive. Figure 1-1 presents a comparison of the features of the predominant business types.

Figure 1-1
Features of Predominant Business Types

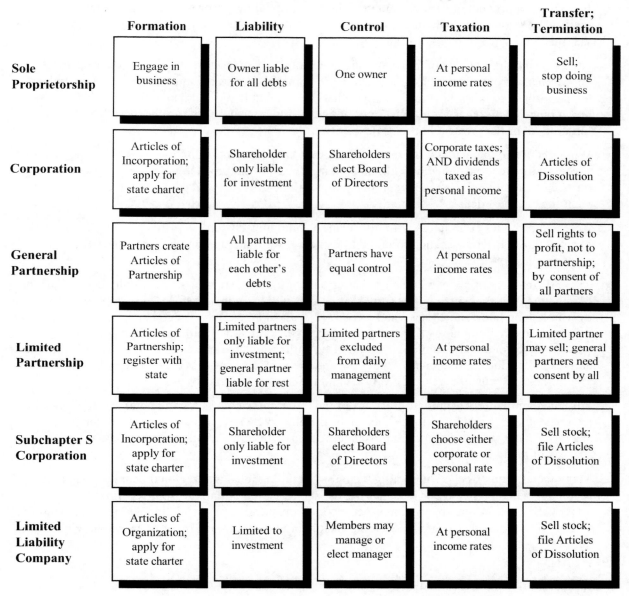

	Formation	Liability	Control	Taxation	Transfer; Termination
Sole Proprietorship	Engage in business	Owner liable for all debts	One owner	At personal income rates	Sell; stop doing business
Corporation	Articles of Incorporation; apply for state charter	Shareholder only liable for investment	Shareholders elect Board of Directors	Corporate taxes; AND dividends taxed as personal income	Articles of Dissolution
General Partnership	Partners create Articles of Partnership	All partners liable for each other's debts	Partners have equal control	At personal income rates	Sell rights to profit, not to partnership; by consent of all partners
Limited Partnership	Articles of Partnership; register with state	Limited partners only liable for investment; general partner liable for rest	Limited partners excluded from daily management	At personal income rates	Limited partner may sell; general partners need consent by all
Subchapter S Corporation	Articles of Incorporation; apply for state charter	Shareholder only liable for investment	Shareholders elect Board of Directors	Shareholders choose either corporate or personal rate	Sell stock; file Articles of Dissolution
Limited Liability Company	Articles of Organization; apply for state charter	Limited to investment	Members may manage or elect manager	At personal income rates	Sell stock; file Articles of Dissolution

MANAGING THE BUSINESS

Creating a realistic, functional, and responsive business is especially vital to a contractor. The hallmark of quality contracting is the ability to organize and direct material and labor in the most efficient ways. Although there are many steps in organizing and managing a business, those that are particularly vital to contractors include:

- Researching;
- Planning;
- Funding;
- Marketing; and
- Accounting.

A. RESEARCHING

The first step in creating a business plan is to research the market and contractors already in business. Even when a product or service is in great demand, research can provide insight into whether the demand will continue or change. Research may point to unmet opportunities or to innovative ways that meet the demand more profitably.

Research should include an objective look at customers. Contractors may target their business to appeal to a narrow or broad base of customers. Some customers are attracted exclusively to high quality; others look for new technology; others want reliable old standards. Contractors may offer a broad range of products and services, attracting customers who want the cheapest deal, the fastest turnaround, or the greatest building flexibility.

While there may be demand from all of these customer types, it is doubtful that a contractor can successfully meet the demand of all, or even most, customers profitably. Customers have varying traits. For example, those who want innovation will be different to deal with than customers who want the cheapest deal.

Research provides contractors with information about how customers differ. Contractors should identify those differences and direct their business toward the traits with which they feel most comfortable working.

These differences apply even when selecting subcontractors, suppliers, and employees. For example, contractors who specialize in fast turnaround times will be more effective with employees who want overtime, long hours, and occasional weeks off, with suppliers who specialize in fast deliveries and won't complain about lack of lead time, and with subcontractors who favor tight scheduling. By matching the contractor's abilities and interests with the related customers' and associates' interests and resources, the contractor will enjoy the entire contracting process more. For these reasons, it is vital to research customer/employee types and traits.

Studying competitors should also be part of the research. A contractor should assess their capabilities, techniques, fees, and reputations. This analysis will show a new business how to differentiate itself. Research can also help a contractor discover reasons why some contracting businesses are more successful than others.

Many factors can affect a contracting business, including local and regional business laws, the skill, cost, and availability of labor, weather trends, etc. Research eliminates some of the risk and guesswork. Research is an ongoing process for all businesses. In such a fluctuating and changing field as contracting, research can be a deciding factor about company profitability and longevity.

B. PLANNING

Once information is collected and analyzed, a business plan that will help the owner to stay focused and on track should be written. A simple business plan would include:

- A specific business concept statement;
- A general timetable of goals; and
- An estimate of costs and revenues.

1. BUSINESS CONCEPT STATEMENT

New businesses often need to set themselves apart from established firms in order to attract work. Contractors can pinpoint where their company will fit in by creating a well-worded concept or mission statement. The mission statement reminds owners, employees, subcontractors, suppliers, and customers exactly what the company wants to do and become.

It is not enough to broadly state: "Smith, Inc. builds good buildings." A better concept statement would be: "Smith, Inc. specializes in providing expert contracting of high technology, luxury homes with 100% customer satisfaction." Another concept statement for a contractor with a different focus might be: "Jones Construction builds more inexpensive apartment buildings on time than anyone in the area."

2. TIMETABLE OF GOALS

Making a timetable of goals helps to identify and put in sequence the many steps in the process of contracting, and to recognize which steps precede profit and company growth. A timetable can also be useful in making decisions when obstacles and complications arise.

Goals may include number of units built, dollar volume, levels of profit, or even how much money each employee should generate per hour. Goals are usually set by time. Rather than setting a goal of earning one million dollars, the goal is better stated: Earn $1,000,000 profit in 10 years. The timetable then breaks down that goal into segments. The first year goal may be $30,000 in profit, the second year goal might be $50,000 in profit, with the third year goal of $100,000, etc.

A timetable of profits forms the basis for annual gross dollar volume goals. Annual volume goals provide a basis for monthly volume goals. Monthly volume goals are then divided into weekly, or even daily, volume goals. Weekly and daily timetables are the foundation of planning resources and contracts.

3. COST/REVENUE ESTIMATE

The purpose of a general cost/revenue estimate is to provide an initial framework of anticipated business expenses and realistic profit potential. The estimate should include both start-up costs and operating costs. Businesses usually do not expect to open at full capacity. Thus, start-up costs may be lower in the beginning, but operating costs will grow as the business volume grows.

A comparison of projected costs versus projected revenues includes a carefully designed price schedule. Find out what competitors are charging. New businesses either need to charge less than their competitors or find ways of making their services attractive enough to customers to justify charging the same or higher rates.

In addition to outlining labor costs, equipment, and supplies, a new business owner needs to estimate the interval from when the business opens until it receives revenue. This cycle can be lengthy, especially for contractors. The cost/revenue estimate need not be extremely detailed, but it should show the amount of funding needed to begin and complete a number of projects.

C. FUNDING

Regardless of what funds a company is owed, what really counts is the money it actually receives. Taking in less than it pays out is called a negative cash flow. Cash flow problems are common in many businesses. The lag time from work completed until payment is received can be more than frustrating; lack of capital is a major reason for business failures.

A company needs to have enough funds on hand to take care of expenses when earned revenue is delayed. Some contractors attend to this problem by requiring upfront payments; others use credit. Many contractors use their personal savings to begin and maintain their businesses. Financial institutions generally loan money only on approved credit and adequate collateral security (real property, equipment, etc.). Banks seldom loan money to start-up businesses.

Other ways of finding capital include taking on a limited partner, selling shares in a corporation, soliciting venture capital (a group of private investors), using charge accounts from vendors and suppliers (often 30 to 90 days), and utilizing leasing agencies (for equipment). Some government agencies provide consultation and advice about finding business capital. In many cases, legal and financial counsel are needed to help contractors protect their company interests.

D. MARKETING

One area of business planning that can make a difference between success and failure is the formation of a marketing plan. Marketing is the ability to identify probable customers and to attract them to a product or service. Businesses seldom can simply open their doors and have customers walk through them. It is more likely that a new business will need a systematic marketing effort. A marketing plan can increase business volume or allow the luxury of choosing more profitable accounts even for those businesses that have adequate sales.

Because professional marketing assistance may be too expensive for new or small businesses, owners commonly create their own marketing plans and advertising with good results. A person can develop an eye for marketing simply by noticing what gets attention. Attention-getting strategies from other fields may improve traditional marketing strategies for contracting.

Traditional marketing for contractors includes professional-quality project signs and a company brochure. Other tactics encompass well-targeted radio, television, and newspaper advertising. Newspapers, community newsletters, and trade journals are often eager to report on new projects, completions, and awards. The important idea is to get the company positive public name recognition.

Marketing includes every contact a contractor has with potential employers. Signs on company vehicles can only provide positive marketing impact if their drivers are courteous. Telephones are helpful if they are promptly and considerately answered. Word-of-mouth advertising is more effective if employees and customers are happy and have something positive to say. Many contractors recognize that local sports team sponsorships, community involvement, and being a good neighbor promotes effective, low-cost marketing.

Effective marketing strategies almost create themselves when owners and employees think of and share all the ways they would like to be approached from the point of view of the customer. Write those ideas down, organize them, and put them in a timetable; this, then, becomes the marketing plan.

E. ACCOUNTING

Some experts say that a business cannot afford to not have an accountant. Still, there is no reason that small business owners cannot do their own books. Business, payroll, and personal taxes require knowledge, but they are not as complicated as is often portrayed. Here are a few guidelines to follow:

- Plan a time every week to enter all business incomes and expenses;
- Designate a place to keep receipts and numbered, two-part invoice forms (filed by month, for at least three years);
- Plan collection procedures and how to react to late-payers and non-payers;
- Keep very good track of all owner withdrawals (pay for the owner) and keep personal and business accounts clearly separate; and
- Develop friendly, cooperative relationships with the bank and with tax collecting agencies.

Make certain the accounting aspects of a business plan establish a commitment to honesty, plainness, and reasonable thoroughness. This is true for all parts of creating a business plan. The time involved is worth the effort. Many books, some simple, some comprehensive, are available that address the process step by step.

F. Management Functions

The successful business owner/manager must carefully plan, organize, and guide the activities and resources of the business. This is imperative if the business is to be profitable. Included in the functions of the competent and efficient manager are planning, organizing, supervising employees, controlling results, standardizing tasks, delegating responsibility, and communicating effectively.

Planning means taking a look ahead at business opportunities. Planning time is well spent, since it can be used to forecast and solve problems before issues arise. Having a plan prevents delays and redoing work.

Organizing is a skill closely related to planning. It identifies issues, prioritizes work, and assigns tasks to personnel most capable of handling the work.

Supervising employees is one of the most important functions of a manager. The employee must be motivated to accept and work toward the company goals. Individuals respond to many different motivating factors, so finding the right one for each individual is challenging. In general, it is best for the owner to avoid reprimands, and instead, praise the actions he or she wants repeated. Employees will respond positively if they feel that their contributions are significant and appreciated. The innovative manager helps the employees feel satisfaction in their work.

Controlling results requires the manager to follow through with the plans so the desired result is achieved. Assigned tasks are verified, and if results vary from the original plan, steps must be taken to make corrections.

Standardizing tasks involves creating a structure of ways to do work. When an effective method or procedure is discovered, it should be documented and become a standard for other similar tasks. This will save time in planning.

Delegating responsibility involves assigning work to all the members of the organization. Make sure the employees have responsibility and authority to do their tasks, and hold them accountable for outcomes.

Communicating is a two-way process that must be clear and complete in order to be effective. Communicating involves listening and responding as well as giving information. Good communicating is the key to a successful business. It is critical in all parts of the organization. Communication between management and employees can express plans and directions, uncover effective ways of working, keep everyone on task, and raise morale.

How to Get Started

A. Marketing and Business Assistance

The U.S. Small Business Administration (SBA) offers a number of services to individuals who want to start a business. By accessing the SBA Web site at www.sba.gov, individuals can get online training on how to start a small business, financial assistance information, small business management counseling, and review publications written for small business owners. The Web site also lists the regional and district SBA offices that individuals can contact for guidance and support.

The SBA also partners with SCORE, a nonprofit association dedicated to educating entrepreneurs and helping small businesses start, grow, and succeed. SCORE publishes material on business plans, loan package guidelines, recordkeeping, and automation systems. SCORE's Web site is www.score.org/index.html.

Local libraries or college and university libraries are good places to begin the information-gathering process. They offer a variety of general and specific business references on numerous topics (including lists of other contractors and suppliers) and step-by-step handbooks about the entire process.

B. COMPLYING WITH GOVERNMENTAL REGULATIONS

1. BOARD OF EXAMINERS OF ELECTRICAL CONTRACTORS

To do business as an electrical contractor in New Jersey, an individual must first obtain a license and a business permit. The State Board of Examiners of Electrical Contractors licenses and regulates electrical contractors; registers qualified journeyman electricians; and is responsible for granting exemptions from licensure to persons or businesses engaged in telecommunications wiring in New Jersey. Chapter 2 of this manual has more details on the licensing laws and regulations that electrical contractors must follow. Contact the Board at:

Board of Examiners of Electrical Contractors
Division of Consumer Affairs
P. O. Box 45006
Newark, NJ 07101
973.504.6410
www.njconsumeraffairs.gov/electric/

The State Board of Examiners of Electrical Contractors also supervises the New Jersey Fire Alarm, Burglar Alarm and Locksmith Advisory Committee, which governs the licensing and practice of fire and burglar alarm installers and locksmiths. Contact the Advisory Committee at:

Fire Alarm, Burglar Alarm and Locksmith Advisory Committee
Division of Consumer Affairs
P. O. Box 45042
Newark, NJ 07101
973.504.6245
www.state.nj.us/lps/ca/fbl/

Additionally, a business owner should contact the municipality and county in which the business is located to determine if there are any local regulations to which the business must adhere or any permits required for the business to operate.

2. REQUIRED BUSINESS REGISTRATIONS

The state of New Jersey's Business Action Center (BAC) acts as a one-stop shop for individuals who want to start a business in New Jersey. Individuals can find out about the BAC's services by going online to **www.state.nj.us/njbusiness/starting/** or by calling 866.534.7789.

Depending on the type of business being operated, an owner will need to take one or two steps for a business to be properly registered in New Jersey.

Step 1 – Registering a New Business Entity. If the business is a legal entity such as a corporation, limited partnership, or limited liability company, the owner must file formation or authorization documents for the public record with the state of New Jersey. General partnerships and sole proprietors are not subject to this first step.

An owner must register a new business entity with the Division of Commercial Recording, New Jersey Department of Treasury. This may be done online at **www.NewJerseyBusiness.gov** and clicking on the "Starting a Business" tab; or by contacting the Division directly at:

New Jersey Division of Commercial Recording
P. O. Box 308
333 West State Street
Trenton, NJ 08625-0308
866.534.7789

Step 2 – Registering the Business for Tax Purposes. All businesses must complete this step by filing an Application for Registration (Form NJ-REG) with the New Jersey Division of Revenue to be registered for tax and employer purposes. There is no fee for registration, but the application must be filed at least five business days prior to starting business.

Filing Form NJ-REG ensures that the business is registered under the correct tax identification number and that the business owner receives the proper returns and notices. If the business is subject to the entity formation/authorization filing in Step 1 above, both the business entity and tax registration filings may be submitted together. The NJ-REG, however, must be filed within 60 days of filing the new business entity if the registrations are submitted separately.

Once the business is registered, it will be assigned a 12-digit New Jersey Tax Identification number that will appear on all preprinted forms received from the Division. The first nine digits of the number usually correspond to the business' Federal Employer Identification Number. This number should be included on all checks and correspondence that are sent to the Division.

An owner must register for tax and employer purposes online at **www.NewJerseyBusiness.gov** and clicking on the "Starting a Business" tab; or by contacting the Division directly at:

New Jersey Division of Revenue
Client Registration Bureau
PO Box 628
Trenton, NJ 08646
866.534.7789
www.nj.gov/treasury/revenue/

3. REGISTERING A TRADE NAME

To register a trade name for partnerships and a sole proprietorship, contact the county clerk of the county in which the business will be located. If doing business under a person's own name, registration is desired, but not required. If trading under any name other than the owner's own name, registration is required by law.

Registration of a trade name in a county generally protects the trade name from use by other businesses in that county. Frequently, businesses that prefer not to incorporate simply register their business name in each of New Jersey's 21 counties. However, if another business incorporates under that business trade name and adds "Inc." to that trade name, the original business name may not be protected.

To review current business names already on file in the state for free, go to **www.state.nj.us/treasury/revenue/checkbusiness.htm**. For assistance with checking on the availability of a name, call 609.292.9292. Fees will apply for telephone assistance.

4. INTERNAL REVENUE SERVICE

A business that has employees must register with the Internal Revenue Service (IRS) to obtain an Employer Identification Number (EIN), which is also known as a Federal Tax Identification Number. The EIN is used by businesses for reporting and paying employment withholding and business taxes. To obtain the forms to apply for an EIN or to apply online, go to the IRS Web site **www.irs.gov/businesses/index.html**.

5. EMPLOYEE-RELATED ISSUES

If a business has at least one employee, it is required to comply with employer insurance requirements.

Unemployment insurance. A business with at least one employee must register with the Division of Employer Accounts, New Jersey Department of Labor and Workforce Development, PO Box 913, Trenton, NJ 08625-0390; http://lwd.state.nj.us/labor/index.html. More detailed information about unemployment insurance in New Jersey may be found in Chapter 8.

Workers' compensation insurance. All employers must provide workers' compensation insurance for their employees. In New Jersey, the Department of Labor and Workforce Development, Division of Workers' Compensation, is responsible for ensuring that New Jersey employers not covered by federal programs, obtain appropriate workers' compensation insurance coverage for their employees. To apply for coverage, a business owner should contact his or her insurance provider, or the Compensation Rating and Inspection Bureau at: 60 Park Place, Newark, NJ 07102; 073.622.6014. Chapter 8 has more specific information about workers' compensation coverage.

2

LICENSING

LICENSING IN GENERAL

The primary reason that New Jersey licenses electrical contractors is to protect public health, safety, and welfare. State laws accomplish these goals by preventing unqualified people from practicing a given profession or occupation. Licensing is also a formal and legal way of defining a profession and includes all those who meet the predetermined standards necessary for giving the public some assurance that the people they are hiring are knowledgeable and qualified to some extent. Licensing bodies serve society by:

- Screening applicants to ensure that they possess those minimum qualifications necessary for safe practice;
- Providing a mechanism for investigating charges of incompetence or impropriety; and
- Setting standards of practice and codes of conduct. These standards give the public a basis for determining acceptable quality in workmanship, service, and conduct.

A governmental agency that will first investigate charges of a licensee's incompetence or failure to perform work and then will take appropriate disciplinary action, helps to protect the profession from incompetent, unethical, or dishonest practitioners. It also serves notice on others that the regulatory agency will not tolerate practitioners whose activities may be harmful to the public.

LICENSING ELECTRICAL CONTRACTORS IN NEW JERSEY

Standards for licensure are set forth by New Jersey state laws and regulations. These laws and regulations represent the judgment of the legislature and licensing board as to what minimum qualifications an applicant must possess in order to be licensed. The language in licensing laws tends to be broad, leaving the regulating agency responsible for filling in specific details through the rule-making process.

The New Jersey Board of Examiners of Electrical Contractors, under the Department of Law & Public Safety, Division of Consumer Affairs, is responsible for determining the licensure qualifications and licensing examination content under New Jersey laws and regulations.

> **Board of Examiners of Electrical Contractors**
> Division of Consumer Affairs
> P. O. Box 45006
> Newark, NJ 07101
> 973.504.6410
> www.njconsumeraffairs.gov/electric/

Besides passing an examination, the law specifies minimum qualifications for education, training, and experience. It may also require that applicants meet citizenship, residency, or good moral character requirements. In some cases a bond or financial information is required.

A. LICENSING PROCEDURES

To be eligible to take the electrical contractor licensing examination, an applicant must:

- Be over 21 years of age.
- Hold a high school diploma or equivalency certificate.
- Have at least five years of practical hands-on experience working with tools in the installation, alteration, or repair of wiring for electric light, heat or power in compliance with the National Electrical Code. "Practical hands-on experience" does not include time spent in supervising, engaging in the practice of engineering, estimating and performing other managerial tasks.
- In the alternative, the applicant may satisfy the practical hands-on experience requirement by:
    - Completing a four-year apprenticeship program approved by both a Federal agency and a Federally certified State agency and having at least one year of practical hands-on experience; **or**
    - Satisfying the eligibility requirements for a qualified journeyman electrician and completing at least one year of practical hands-on experience; **or**
    - Earning a bachelor's degree in electrical engineering and completed two years of practical hands-on experience; **or**
    - Working in the field of electrical contracting for at least five years immediately preceding the date of application.
- Submit a completed application for examination, on a form provided by the Board.
- Submit the appropriate application fee.

After the Board has reviewed all required application materials, including work experience certification forms signed by employers and school completion certificates, the Board will send a letter that informs the applicant whether he or she is eligible to take the licensing examination. The applicant is then required to submit an application for examination 120 days prior to the examination date.

B. PRESSURE SEAL REQUIREMENTS

At the time of the issuance of the license, the Board shall furnish a pressure seal to the licensed electrical contractor. The cost of the pressure seal must be paid for by the licensed electrical contractor to whom it is issued. The licensed electrical contractor is required to impress the seal upon all applications for electrical inspection permits.

The pressure seal remains the property of the Board and must be returned to the Board if the electrical contractor's license is suspended or revoked as a result of either a disciplinary order or a failure to pay licensing fees, if the contractor registers the license as inactive with the Board, if the license was terminated, or if the contractor resigned from his or her position as a qualifying licensee for a business.

C. BONDING

Any person engaged in the business of electrical contracting in the State of New Jersey must obtain a bond in favor of the State of New Jersey in the sum of $1,000.00. The bond must be executed by a surety company authorized to transact business in the State of New Jersey and approved by the Department of Banking and Insurance. The bond shall be for the term of 24 months and must be renewed upon expiration for the ensuing 24 months.

D. CHANGE OF ADDRESS OR NAME

Every licensed electrical contractor and business permit holder must notify the Board, in writing, of any changes in his or her residence or business address within 10 days after the change. A licensee must immediately notify the Board of any change in the name of the electrical contracting business in which he or she is engaged as the qualifying licensee.

E. IDENTIFICATION OF LICENSEES

The Board furnishes a wallet-size identification card to every licensee at the time of the triennial renewal. The licensee is required to present this identification card upon request when applying for electrical permits.

All commercial vehicles used by state-licensed electrical contractors must be marked on both sides in lettering at least three-inches high with the name of the licensee and the words "Electrical Contractor License Number" followed by the license number of the qualifying licensee, and the words "Electrical Contractor business permit number" followed by the business permit number of the business permit holder.

Business correspondence, invoices, and stationery must show the name of the licensed contractor, license number, business permit number, and the business address of the qualifying licensee.

F. RENEWAL OF LICENSE

Licenses need to be renewed triennially (every three years). The Board sends a notice of renewal to each licensee at least 60 days prior to the expiration of the license. The licensee must submit a renewal application to the Board, along with the renewal fee, prior to the date the license expires. Failure to renew a license within 30 days after the expiration date will result in suspension of the license without a hearing. Each applicant for renewal must also submit proof that the required continuing education credits have been completed during the prior triennial period.

G. CONTINUING EDUCATION REQUIREMENTS

Each applicant for triennial license renewal is required to complete, during the preceding triennial period, a minimum of 34 credit hours of continuing education. Of those 34 hours, a minimum of 10 hours must be in a course of study relating to the most recent edition of the National Electrical Code, with one of those 10 hours pertaining to applicable State statutes and rules. The remaining 24 credit hours should be obtained in the following areas: installation, erection, repair or alteration of electrical equipment for the generation, transmission or utilization of electrical energy; supervisory responsibilities; and any other subjects relevant to electrical contracting and electrical construction. The Board maintains a list of all approved continuing education programs, courses, and lecturers. A copy of this list is available to licensees upon request.

The Board may waive continuing education requirements on an individual basis for reasons of hardship, such as illness, disability, or military duty. Any licensee seeking a waiver of the continuing education requirements must apply to the Board in writing detailing the specific reasons for requesting the waiver.

Upon triennial license renewal, a licensee shall attest that he or she has completed the required number of continuing education courses. Falsification of any information submitted on the renewal application may require an appearance before the Board and may subject a licensee to disciplinary action.

FIRE ALARM, BURGLAR ALARM AND LOCKSMITH ADVISORY COMMITTEE

The Fire Alarm, Burglar Alarm and Locksmith Advisory Committee, under the supervision of the Board of Examiners of Electrical Contractors, is responsible for regulating the licensing and practice of fire and burglar alarm installers and locksmiths. The law creating the Advisory Committee, *Chapter 31A Fire Alarm, Burglar Alarm and Locksmith Licensees and Businesses,* is reprinted in this chapter.

For more information about these rules, regulations, and standards, contact:

Fire Alarm, Burglar Alarm and Locksmith Advisory Committee
Division of Consumer Affairs
P. O. Box 45042
Newark, NJ 07101
973.504.6245
www.state.nj.us/lps/ca/fbl/

A. LICENSING PROCEDURES

1. ALARM BUSINESS APPLICANTS

An applicant seeking licensure to engage in the **alarm business** shall:

- Be at least 18 years of age.
- Be of good moral character, and not have been convicted of a crime of the first, second, or third degree within 10 years prior to the filing of the application.
- Meet qualifications established by the board, in consultation with the committee, regarding experience, continuing education, financial responsibility and integrity.
- Successfully complete:
  - an examination approved by the board, in consultation with the committee; **or**
  - 40 hours of technical training that has been approved by the board, in consultation with the committee.
- Submit a completed application to engage in the alarm business, on a form provided by the Board, in consultation with the committee, which includes a passport-size photograph, the name, age, residence, present and previous occupations of the applicant and, in the case of a business firm engaged in the alarm business, of each member, officer or director thereof, the name of the municipality and the location therein by street number or other appropriate description of the principal place of business and the location of each branch office.
- Present, together with the application, a list of all criminal offenses of which the applicant has been convicted, including the date and place of each conviction, the name under which the applicant was convicted, if other than that on the application, and fingerprints of both hands taken on standard fingerprint cards by a state or municipal law enforcement agency.
- Submit the appropriate application fee.

2. LOCKSMITH APPLICANTS

An applicant seeking licensure as a **locksmith** shall:

- Be at least 18 years of age.
- Be of good moral character, and not have been convicted of a crime of the first, second, or third degree within 10 years prior to the filing of the application.
- Present evidence to the board of having successfully completed any training and continuing education requirements established by the board, in consultation with the committee.
- Successfully complete a written examination approved by the board, in consultation with the committee.

- Submit a completed application to engage in locksmithing services, on a form provided by the Board, in consultation with the committee, which includes a passport-size photograph, the name, age, residence, and present and previous occupations of the applicant.
- Present, together with the application, a list of all criminal offenses of which the applicant has been convicted, including the date and place of each conviction, the name under which the applicant was convicted, if other than that on the application, and fingerprints of both hands taken on standard fingerprint cards by a state or municipal law enforcement agency.
- Submit the appropriate application fee.

B. CHANGE OF ADDRESS

If the address shown on the most recently issued license changes, a licensee should notify the Committee in writing no later than 30 days following the change. Failure to notify the Committee of any change of address may result in disciplinary action.

C. IDENTIFICATION OF LICENSEES

Every licensee and every employee or other person engaged in the unsupervised installation, servicing, or maintenance of burglar alarm, fire alarm, or electronic security systems shall, at all times during working hours, display an identification card issued by the Board. Identification cards are issued for a three-year period corresponding to the triennial renewal of the license.

A licensee shall be able to substantiate the truthfulness of any material, objective assertion, or representation made in an advertisement. Advertisements regarding fees shall be limited to those that contain a fixed or a stated range of fees for specifically described burglar alarm, fire alarm, or locksmithing services.

All advertisements and professional representations, including advertisements in a classified directory, business cards, and professional stationery should include the:
- Name and license number of the licensee;
- Words "Burglar Alarm license number" or "Fire Alarm license number" or "Locksmith license number" as applicable; and
- Street address and telephone number of the business office.

All commercial vehicles used in the burglar alarm business, fire alarm business, or locksmithing services business must be marked on both sides of the vehicle, in lettering as close to three-inches high as possible, with the licensee's business name; the appropriate wording for the business category along with the relevant license; and the name of the municipality from which the licensee practices or where the licensee has a principal office.

D. RENEWAL OF LICENSE

All licenses issued by the Committee are for a three-year period. The Committee sends a notice of renewal to all licensees at least 60 days prior to the date of license expiration. To renew a license, a licensee must submit a license renewal application and the license renewal fee prior to the expiration of the current license.

If the licensee does not renew his or her license prior to its expiration date, the licensee may renew it within 30 days of its expiration by submitting a renewal application, the license renewal fee, and a late fee.

A license that is not renewed within 30 days of its expiration is automatically suspended. An individual who continues to practice with a suspended license shall be deemed to be engaged in unlicensed practice.

E. CONTINUING EDUCATION REQUIREMENTS

At the time of triennial license renewal, a licensee will need to provide verification of having completed the 36 required continuing education credits in the specified areas of education. The holder of multiple licenses issued by the Committee may apply a maximum of 12 credits obtained in satisfaction of the 36 credits required for one license toward satisfaction of the 36 continuing education credits required for his or her second and third Committee-issued license(s), if applicable.

A licensee shall complete a minimum of two continuing education credits per triennial registration period in the Barrier Free Subcode, two continuing education credits in the New Jersey Uniform Construction Code, exclusive of the Barrier Free Subcode, two continuing education credits in the Americans with Disabilities Act Code, and two continuing education credits in industrial safety.

A licensee seeking renewal of a burglar alarm license shall complete a minimum of three credits of continuing education per triennial registration period in smoke detection systems. A maximum of 12 credits in continuing education courses can be in subjects related to business and/or law. The balance of continuing education credits should be in trade-related subjects.

The Committee maintains a list of all approved continuing education programs, courses, and lecturers. A copy of this list is available to licensees upon request.

NEW JERSEY STATUTES

TITLE 45: PROFESSIONS AND OCCUPATIONS

CHAPTER 5A: ELECTRICAL CONTRACTORS LICENSING ACT

45:5A-1. Short title

This act may be cited as "The Electrical Contractors Licensing Act of 1962."

45:5A-2. Definitions

For the purpose of this act, unless otherwise indicated by the context:

(a) "Act" means this act and the rules and regulations adopted under it;

(b) "Board" means the Board of Examiners of Electrical Contractors created by section 3 of this act;

(c) "Department" means the Department of Law and Public Safety;

(d) "Electrical contractor" means a person who engages in the business of contracting to install, erect, repair or alter electrical equipment for the generation, transmission or utilization of electrical energy;

(e) "Person" means a person, firm, corporation or other legal entity.

(f) "Alarm business" means the installation, servicing or maintenance of burglar alarm, fire alarm or electronic security systems, or the monitoring or responding to alarm signals when provided in conjunction therewith. "Installation," as used in this definition, includes the survey of a premises, the design and preparation of the specifications for the equipment or system to be installed pursuant to a survey, the installation of the equipment or system, or the demonstration of the equipment or system after the installation is completed, but does not include any survey, design or preparation of specifications for equipment or for a system that is prepared by an engineer licensed pursuant to the provisions of P.L.1938, c.342 (C.45:8-27 et seq.), or an architect licensed pursuant to the provisions of chapter 3 of Title 45 of the Revised Statutes, if the survey, design, or preparation of specifications is part of a design for construction of a new building or premises or a renovation of an existing building or premises, which renovation includes components other than the installation of a burglar alarm, fire alarm or electronic security system, and further does not include the design or preparation of specifications for the equipment or system to be installed that are within the practice of professional engineering as defined in subsection (b) of section 2 of P.L.1938, c.342 (C.45:8-28);

(g) "Burglar alarm" means a security system comprised of an interconnected series of alarm devices or components, including systems interconnected with radio frequency signals, which emits an audible, visual or electronic signal indicating an alarm condition and providing a warning of intrusion, which is designed to discourage crime;

(h) "Business firm" means a partnership, corporation or other business entity engaged in the alarm business or locksmithing services;

(i) "Committee" means the Fire Alarm, Burglar Alarm, and Locksmith Advisory Committee created by section 3 of P.L.1997, c.305 (C.45:5A-23);

(j) "Electronic security system" means a security system comprised of an interconnected series of devices or components, including systems with audio and video signals or other electronic systems, which emits or transmits an audible, visual or electronic signal warning of intrusion and provides notification of authorized entry or exit, which is designed to discourage crime;

(k) "Fire alarm" means a security system comprised of an interconnected series of alarm devices or components, including systems interconnected with radio frequency signals, which emits an audible, visual or electronic signal indicating an alarm condition and which provides a warning of the presence of smoke or fire. "Fire alarm" does not mean a system whose primary purpose is telecommunications with energy control, the monitoring of the interior environment being an incidental feature thereto;

(l) "Licensed locksmith" means a person who is licensed pursuant to the provisions of section 7 of P.L.1997, c.305 (C.45:5A-27);

(m) "Licensee" means a person licensed to engage in the alarm business or provide locksmithing services pursuant to the provisions of section 7 of P.L.1997, c.305 (C.45:5A-27);

(n) "Locksmithing services" means the modification, recombination, repair or installation of mechanical locking devices and electronic security systems for any type of compensation and includes the following: repairing, rebuilding, recoding, servicing, adjusting, installing, manipulating or bypassing of a mechanical or electronic locking device, for controlled access or egress to premises, vehicles, safes, vaults, safe doors, lock boxes, automatic teller machines or other devices for safeguarding areas where access is meant to be limited; operating a mechanical or electronic locking device, safe or vault by means other than those intended by the manufacturer of such locking devices, safes or vaults; or consulting and providing technical advice regarding selection of hardware and locking systems of mechanical or electronic locking devices and electronic security systems; except that "locksmithing services" shall not include the installation of a prefabricated lock set and door knob into a door of a residence;

(o) "Qualified journeyman electrician" means a person registered pursuant to P.L.1962, c.162 (C.45:5A-1 et seq.) or P.L.2001, c.21 (C.45:5A-11.1 et al.), as a qualified journeyman electrician by the board.

45:5A-3. Board of examiners; creation; membership; qualifications; terms; vacancies
There is created a Board of Examiners of Electrical Contractors in the Department of Law and Public Safety consisting of 7 members, hereinafter referred to as the "board." The members of such board shall be citizens of the State appointed by the Governor, with the advice and consent of the Senate. They shall be appointed initially for the following terms: Three members for terms of 1 year from July 1, 1962, 2 members for terms of 2 years from July 1, 1962, and 2 members for terms of 3 years from July 1, 1962. Thereafter members shall be appointed for terms of 3 years and until the appointment and qualification of their successors. The Governor shall fill any vacancy in said board for the unexpired portion of the term. No more than 4 members of the board shall be members of the same political party. Three members of the board shall be qualified electrical contractors with experience of not less than 10 years as an electrical contractor, one shall be a qualified electrical inspector, with experience of not less than 5 years as an electrical inspector, one shall be a qualified journeyman employed in the electrical construction industry for not less than 5 years. One shall be a public member not associated with the electrical industry, and one shall be a licensed professional engineer with experience of not less than 5 years in the electrical industry.

45:5A-4. Compensation; traveling expenses
Each member of the board shall receive $25.00 for each day of actual service in attending meetings of the board at which business is transacted and in addition shall be entitled to be reimbursed for his necessary traveling expenses; provided, such compensation in 1 fiscal year shall not exceed $1,000.00 per member.

45:5A-5. Organization of board; appointment of assistants; incurring of expenses
At the meeting for organization after the first appointment of said board members thereof shall choose from among their number a chairman, who shall preside at all meetings of the board, and a secretary who need not be a member of the board. The chairman and secretary so chosen shall be subject to the approval of the Attorney General. The chairman and secretary shall hold office for 1 year and until their successors are chosen. Vacancies in the office of chairman or secretary between regular appointments shall be filled by the board, with the approval of Attorney General. The board is authorized to appoint, with the approval of the Attorney General such clerical assistants as may be required. The board, with the approval of the Attorney General, shall fix the compensation of the secretary and the clerical assistants, within the limits of available appropriations and subject to applicable civil service provisions. The board shall be authorized to incur such other expenses, within available appropriations therefor, as may be required to carry out its purpose and function. All moneys received by said board shall be remitted to the State Treasury.

45:5A-6. Rules and regulations
The board may adopt and amend all rules and regulations not inconsistent with the Constitution and laws of the State which may be reasonably necessary for the proper performance of its duties and the purposes of this act and for the conduct of the proceeding before it.

45:5A-8. Record of proceedings; register of license applications; contents
The Board of Examiners of Electrical Contractors shall keep a record of its proceedings and a register of all applications for licenses and business permits, which register shall show: (a) the name, age and residence of each applicant, (b) the date of the application, (c) the place of business of such applicant, (d) the qualifications of the applicant, (e) whether or not an examination was required, (f) whether the applicant was rejected, (g) whether a license or business permit was granted, (h) the date of the action of the board and (i) such other information as may be deemed necessary by the board.

45:5A-9. Necessity of business permit and license; qualifications; examinations; fees

(a) On or after July 1, 1963, no person shall advertise, enter into, engage in or work in business as an electrical contractor, unless such person has secured a business permit and such person or an officer, partner or employee who is or will be actively engaged in the business for which a business permit is sought has obtained a license from the board in accordance with the provisions of this act, and such licensee shall assume full responsibility for inspection and supervision of all electrical work to be performed by the permittee in compliance with recognized safety standards. A licensee shall not be entitled to qualify more than one person for a business permit.

Any single act or transaction shall constitute engaging in the business of electrical contracting within the meaning of this chapter.

(b) Except as otherwise provided in section 10, no person shall be granted an electrical contractor's license unless he shall first establish his qualifications therefor and shall take and pass the examination for electrical contractors. An applicant for such examination shall have been employed or engaged in the business of electrical construction and installation or have equivalent practical experience for a period of not less than five years preceding the time of such application, or shall otherwise establish to the satisfaction of board that the applicant has the necessary educational background and experience to qualify to take the examination for a license.

The examination shall be so designed as to establish the competence and qualification of the applicant to perform and supervise the various phases of electrical contracting work. Any applicant who shall fail to pass such examination shall not be eligible to retake an examination until six months from the date of such failure.

(c) An applicant for an examination for a license shall apply to the board for permission to take such examination upon forms provided by the board and shall provide the board with such information as shall be necessary to establish his qualifications to take the examination. The applicant for an initial examination shall pay a fee to the board of $25.00. An applicant for re-examination shall pay a fee to the board of $15.00. Such fees shall not be refundable.

45:5A-9.1 Electrical contractors, letter of credit, liability insurance required

Every person who holds a business permit for electrical work pursuant to P.L. 1962, c.162 (C.45:5A-1 et seq.) shall:

a.   Secure, maintain and file with the board proof of a bank letter of credit covering the electrical work done pursuant to that business permit or a certificate of general liability insurance from an insurance company authorized and licensed to do business in this State covering the electrical work done pursuant to that business permit. The minimum amount of the bank letter of credit shall be $300,000 for property damage and bodily injury to or death of one or more persons and the minimum amount of general liability insurance shall be $300,000 for the combined property damage and bodily injury to or death of one or more persons in any one accident or occurrence; and

b.   File with the board its Federal Tax Identification number.

Every proof of a bank letter of credit or certificate of insurance required to be filed with the board pursuant to this section shall provide that cancellation of the bank letter of credit or insurance shall not be effective unless and until at least 10 days' notice of intention to cancel has been received in writing by the board.

45:5A-11. Issuance of licenses and business permits by board

The board shall receive all applications for licenses or business permits filed by persons seeking to enter upon or continue in the electrical contracting business as herein defined within this State and upon proper qualification of such applicant shall issue the license or permit applied for.

45:5A-11.1. Registration as qualified journeyman electrician

The board shall register as a qualified journeyman electrician an applicant who:

a.   Holds a current valid license to practice electrical contracting by the board; or

b.   Has acquired sufficient practical experience working with tools in the installation, alteration or repair of wiring for electric light, heat or power, as determined by the board, and has successfully completed an appropriate number of classroom hours of related instruction, as determined by the board, which requirement of practical experience shall not include time spent in supervising, engineering, estimating and other managerial tasks; or

c.   Has demonstrated to the satisfaction of the board that he has met the requirements of subsection b. of this section through alternative means.

45:5A-11.2. Application for registration as qualified journeyman electrician

On and after the effective date of P.L.2001, c.21 (C.45:5A-11.1 et al.), any person desiring to register as a qualified journeyman electrician shall make application to the board to be so registered and shall pay all the fees required in connection therewith, which fees shall be established, prescribed or changed by the board to the extent necessary to defray all proper expenses incurred by the board to administer the provisions of this act. Fees shall not be fixed at a level, however, that will raise amounts in excess of the amount estimated to be so required.

45:5A-11.3. Register of applications

The board shall keep a register of all applications by individuals registering as qualified journeymen electricians, which register shall include the following information: name, address, telephone number, the age of the applicant; the date of the application; the place of business of the applicant; whether the applicant was accepted or rejected, and in the case of a rejection, the reasons for that action; the registration number, if issued; the date of action of the board; and any other information the board deems necessary.

45:5A-11.4. Continuing education required for license renewal

a.   The board shall require each qualified journeyman electrician, other than a qualified journeyman electrician licensed to practice electrical contracting issued by the board, as a condition for triennial license renewal pursuant to section 1 of P.L.1972, c.108 (C.45:1-7), to complete a 10-hour course of study relating to the most recent edition of the National Electrical Code.

b.   The board shall approve all programs of education for the 10-hour course of study established pursuant to subsection a. of this section and the instructors for those courses.

45:5A-11.5. Waiver of continuing education requirements

The board may, in its discretion, waive requirements for continuing education under this act on an individual basis for reasons of hardship such as illness or disability, retirement of the certificate of registration or other good cause.

45:5A-11.6. Renewal cycle for registration

Notwithstanding any other law, rule or regulation to the contrary, the renewal cycle for registration as a qualified journeyman electrician shall be the same as that for licensed electrical contractors.

45:5A-12. Examinations; notice

The board shall prescribe the conditions of examination of, and subject to the provisions of this act, shall give examinations to all persons who are, under the provisions of this act, required to take such examinations. The scope of such examinations shall cover such matters as the provisions of nationally recognized electrical installation safety standards and the theoretical and practical application of the same encountered in electrical work. It shall hold a minimum of 4 examinations each year at such time and place within the State as the board shall designate. Public notice shall be given of the time and place of all examinations. In the conduct of the examination the board shall prescribe a standard form of examination which may be revised from time to time as circumstances require. Said examinations shall give ample opportunity for all applicants to be thoroughly and carefully examined, may be written or practical, or both, and shall be supervised by 3 or more of the examiners, but no license shall be granted except by the board.

45:5A-13. Initial license or business permit; renewals; fees; applications; duration of license or permit; re-examination

Before a license or business permit shall issue fees shall be paid for same in the following amounts: (a) for initial license–$75.00, (b) for renewal–$25.00, (c) for initial business permit or renewal thereof–$12.50.

A person seeking issuance or renewal of any business permit shall file with the board an application in writing upon forms prescribed by the board. The application shall designate the person who possesses a license issued pursuant to the provisions of this act and shall contain such other information as the board may prescribe. The application shall be accompanied by the proper fee.

If the applicant is a natural person, the application shall be signed and sworn to by the applicant. If the applicant is a partnership or other business association, the application shall be signed and sworn to by all natural persons composing such partnership or business association. If the applicant is a corporation, the application shall be signed and sworn to by the president and secretary thereof.

A person seeking issuance or renewal of any license shall file with the board an application in writing upon forms prescribed by the board, containing such information as the board shall be required to maintain the register provided for in section 8 of this act and to establish the qualifications of the applicant. The application shall be signed and sworn to by the applicant and shall be accompanied by the proper fee.

The license and business permit periods shall be from July 1 to June 30 of the following year and licenses and business permits shall be renewed on or before July 1 of each year. Renewal shall be governed by the standards applicable to initial issuance. The board may require a re-examination upon failure to apply for a renewal within 30 days of the date of the expiration of any license. Any license expiring while the holder thereof is outside the continental limits of the United States in connection with any project undertaken by the Government of the United States, or while in service of the Armed Forces of the United States shall be renewed without further examinations upon payment of the prescribed fee at any time within 4 months after such person's return to the United States or discharge from the armed forces.

45:5A-13.1. Continuing education requirements for electrical contractors

The Board of Examiners of Electrical Contractors shall require each electrical contractor, as a condition for triennial license renewal pursuant to section 1 of P.L.1972, c.108 (C.45:1-7), to complete 34 credits of continuing education requirements imposed by the board pursuant to sections 2 and 3 of this act.

45:5A-13.2. Responsibilities of board as to courses and programs

   a.   The board shall:

   (1)   Establish standards for continuing electrical contracting education regarding the subject matter and content of continuing education courses;

   (2)   Approve educational programs offering credit towards the continuing electrical contracting education requirements; and

   (3)   Approve other equivalent educational programs including, but not limited to, programs provided by electrical contracting associations and other relevant professional and technical associations, and shall establish procedures for the issuance of credit upon satisfactory proof of the completion of these programs.

   b.   In the case of education courses and programs, each hour of instruction shall be equivalent to one credit.

45:5A-13.3. Contents of educational course of study

The educational course of study required of licensed electrical contractors for each triennial registration period shall include 34 hours of continuing education as follows:

   a.   A 10-hour course of study relating to the most recent edition of the National Electrical Code, nine hours of which shall pertain to the code and one hour of which shall pertain to applicable State statutes and regulations; and

   b.   Twenty-four hours of instruction approved by the board covering one or more of the following subjects:

   (1)   Installation, erection, repair or alteration of electrical equipment for the generation, transmission or utilization of electrical energy;

   (2)   Transmission or utilization of electrical energy;

   (3)   Job estimating, management and business practices;

   (4)   Supervisory responsibilities required of licensees pursuant to the laws of this State; and

   (5)   Any other subject relevant to electrical contracting and construction as determined by the board.

45:5A-13.4. Waiver of continuing education requirement

The board may, in its discretion, waive requirements for continuing education under this act on an individual basis for reasons of hardship such as illness or disability, retirement of the license or other good cause.

45:5A-13.5. Continuing education credits not required under certain circumstances

The board shall not require completion of continuing education credits for initial registrations. The board shall not require completion of continuing education credits for any registration periods commencing within 12 months of the effective date of this act. The board shall require completion of continuing education credits on a pro rata basis for any registration periods commencing more than 12 but less than 36 months following the effective date of this act.

45:5A-13.6. Carryover of credit hours permitted under certain circumstances

In the event an electrical contractor completes a number of continuing education credit hours in excess of the number required by the board pursuant to section 1 of this act, the board shall allow a maximum of eight credit hours to be carried over to satisfy the electrical contractor's continuing education requirement for the next triennial licensure period, but these credit hours shall not be applicable thereafter.

45:5A-13.7. Differential in registration fees for non-members

The board shall permit any electrical contracting association or other professional or technical association offering a continuing electrical contracting education program approved by the board pursuant to section 2 of this act to impose a reasonable differential in registration fees for courses upon licensed electrical contractors who are not members of that association.

45:5A-14. Death or disability of qualifying representative; continuance of business

No person shall be denied the privilege of continuing business as an electrical contractor in the event of death, illness, or other physical disability of the representative thereof who qualified the person for a business permit for at least 6 months following the date of such death, illness or other physical disability; provided that said business is conducted under such qualified supervision as the board deems adequate.

45:5A-15. Transferability of license or business permit

No license or business permit issued under this act shall be assigned or transferable.

45:5A-17. Powers of municipalities; violations of municipal ordinances

(a) This act shall not deny to any municipality the power to inspect electrical work or equipment or the power to regulate the standards and manner in which electrical work shall be done but no municipality shall require any business permit holder or electrical contractor licensed under this act to obtain a municipal license or business permit to engage in the business of electrical contracting in such municipality.

(b) Any licensee or business permit holder who willfully fails to comply with any municipal ordinance concerning the inspection of electrical work shall be guilty of a violation of this act.

45:5A-18. Exempt work or construction

Electrical work or construction which is performed on the following facilities or which is by or for the following agencies shall not be included within the business of electrical contracting so as to require the securing of a business permit under this act:

(a) Minor repair work such as the replacement of lamps and fuses.

(b) The connection of portable electrical appliances to suitable permanently installed receptacles.

(c) The testing, servicing or repairing of electrical equipment or apparatus.

(d) Electrical work in mines, on ships, railway cars, elevators, escalators or automotive equipment.

(e) Municipal plants or any public utility as defined in R.S.48:2-13, organized for the purpose of constructing, maintaining and operating works for the generation, supplying, transmission and distribution of electricity for electric light, heat, or power.

(f) A public utility subject to regulation, supervision or control by a federal regulatory body, or a public utility operating under the authority granted by the State of New Jersey, and engaged in the furnishing of communication or signal service, or both, to a public utility, or to the public, as an integral part of a communication or signal system, and any agency associated or affiliated with any public utility and engaged in research and development in the communications field.

(g) A railway utility in the exercise of its functions as a utility and located in or on buildings or premises used exclusively by such an agency.

(h) Commercial radio and television transmission equipment.

(i) Construction by any branch of the federal government.

(j) Any work with a potential of less than 10 volts.

(k) Repair, manufacturing and maintenance work on premises occupied by a firm or corporation, and installation work on premises occupied by a firm or corporation and performed by a regular employee who is a qualified journeyman electrician registered pursuant to section 3 of P.L.2001, c.21 (C.45:5A-11.1).

(l) Installation, repair or maintenance performed by regular employees of the State or of a municipality, county, or school district on the premises or property owned or occupied by the State, a municipality, county, or school district; provided that a regular employee of the State, municipality, county or school district performing this work is a qualified journeyman electrician registered pursuant to section 3 of P.L.2001, c.21 (C.45:5A-11.1), or holds any civil service title with a job description which includes electrical work pursuant to the "Civil Service Act," N.J.S.11A:1-1 et seq., or regulations adopted pursuant thereto, or any employee of a State authority who has completed an apprenticeship training program approved by the United States Department of Labor, Bureau of Apprenticeship Training, that deals specifically with electrical work, and is of a minimum duration of three years.

Any regular employee of the State, or of a municipality, county or school district who has submitted his registration application to the board for registration as a qualified journeyman electrician shall be permitted to continue to perform work pursuant to this subsection until such time as the board acts upon his application. Any applicant whose registration application is not approved by the board shall no longer be permitted to perform electrical work pursuant to this subsection.

(m) The maintaining, installing or connecting of automatic oil, gas or coal burning equipment, gasoline or diesel oil dispensing equipment and the lighting in connection therewith to a supply of adequate size at the load side of the distribution board.

(n) Work performed by a person on a dwelling that is occupied solely as a residence for himself or for a member or members of his immediate family.

(o) (Deleted by amendment, P.L.1997, c.305).

(p) Any work performed by a landscape irrigation contractor which has the potential of not more than 30 volts involving the installation, servicing, or maintenance of a landscape irrigation system as this term is defined by section 2 of this amendatory and supplementary act. Nothing in this act shall be deemed to exempt work covered by this subsection from inspection required by the "State Uniform Construction Code Act", P.L. 1975, c.217 (C.52:27D-119 et seq.) or regulations adopted pursuant thereto.

(q) Any work performed by a person certified pursuant to sections 1 through 10 of P.L.2001, c.289 (C.52:27D-25n through C.52:27D-25w) that is not branch circuit wiring. For the purposes of this subsection, "branch circuit wiring" means the circuit conductors between the final overcurrent device protecting the circuit and one or more outlets. A certificate holder shall be deemed to have engaged in professional misconduct for the purposes of section 8 of P.L.1978, c.73 (C.45:1-21) for violating the provisions of this subsection.

(r) Any work performed by an alarm business, as that term is defined by section 2 of P.L.1985, c.289 (C.45:5A-18.1), licensed pursuant to P.L.1997, c.305 (C.45:5A-23 et seq.) that is not branch circuit wiring. For the purposes of this subsection, "branch circuit wiring" means the circuit conductors between the final overcurrent device protecting the circuit and one or more outlets. A licensee shall be deemed to have engaged in professional misconduct for the purposes of section 8 of P.L.1978, c.73 (C.45:1-21) for violating the provisions of this subsection.

The board may also exempt from the business permit provisions of the act such other electrical activities of like character which in the board's opinion warrant exclusion from the provisions of this act.

45:5A-18.1. Definitions
As used in this amendatory and supplementary act:

a. "Alarm business" means a partnership, corporation or other business entity engaged in the installation, servicing or maintenance of burglar or fire alarm systems, or the monitoring or responding to alarm signals when provided in conjunction therewith. "Installation" includes the survey of a premises, the design and preparation of the specifications for the equipment or system to be installed pursuant to a survey, the installation of the equipment or system, or the demonstration of the equipment or system, or the demonstration of the equipment or system after the installation is completed but does not include any survey, design or preparation of specifications for equipment or for a system which is prepared by an engineer licensed pursuant to the provisions of P.L.1938, c.342 (C45:8-27 et seq.), or an architect licensed pursuant to the provisions of R.S. 45:3-1 et seq., if the survey, design or preparation of specifications is part of a design for construction of a new building or premises or a renovation of an existing building or premises, which renovation includes components other than the installation of a burglar or fire alarm system.

b. "Burglar alarm" means a security system comprised of an interconnected series of alarm devices or components including systems interconnected with radio frequency signals which emits an audible, visual or electronic signal indicating an alarm condition and providing a warning of intrusion, which is designed to discourage crime.

c. "Fire alarm" means a security system comprised of an interconnected series of alarm devices or components including systems interconnected with radio frequency signals which emits an audible, visual or electronic signal indicating an alarm condition and provides a warning of the presence of smoke or fire; except that "fire alarm" does not mean a system whose primary purpose is telecommunications with energy control, the monitoring of the interior environment being an incidental feature thereto.

d. "Landscape irrigation contractor" means a person engaged in the installation, servicing, or maintenance of a landscape irrigation system.

e. "Landscape irrigation system" means any assemblage of components, materials or special equipment which is designed, constructed and installed for controlled dispersion of water from any safe suitable source, including properly treated wastewater, for the purpose of irrigating landscape vegetation or the control of dust and erosion on landscape areas, including integral pumping systems or integral control systems for the manual, semiautomatic, or automatic control of the operation of these systems.

45:5A-19. Bond of contractor

In addition to such other bonds as may otherwise be required, any person engaged in the business of electrical contracting under the provisions of this act shall not undertake to do any electrical work in the State of New Jersey or any political subdivision thereof unless and until he shall have entered into bond in favor of the State of New Jersey in the sum of $1,000.00, executed by a surety company authorized to transact business in the State of New Jersey, approved by the Department of Banking and Insurance, and to be conditioned on the faithful performance of the provisions of this act. The board shall, by rule and regulation, provide who shall be eligible to receive the financial protection afforded by said bond. The aforesaid bond shall be for the term of 24 months and must be renewed upon expiration for the ensuing 24 months.

45:5A-21. Disorderly person

Any person advertising or engaging in the business of electrical contracting without having a business permit from the board is a disorderly person.

45:5A-23. "Fire Alarm, Burglar Alarm and Locksmith Advisory Committee"

a. There is created within the Division of Consumer Affairs in the Department of Law and Public Safety, under the Board of Examiners of Electrical Contractors, a "Fire Alarm, Burglar Alarm and Locksmith Advisory Committee." The committee shall consist of 15 members who are residents of this State as follows:

(1) Two members shall have been engaged in the alarm business in this State on a full-time basis for at least five consecutive years immediately preceding their appointments, shall be members of the New Jersey Burglar and Fire Alarm Association and, except for the members first appointed, shall be licensed under the provisions of section 7 of this act;

(2) Five members shall be municipal officials, and shall include (a) a fire prevention officer; (b) a crime prevention officer; (c) a fire sub-code official; (d) a building inspector; and (e) a chief of police who is a member of the New Jersey Association of Chiefs of Police;

(3) One member shall be a representative of the Division of State Police;

(4) One member shall have been engaged in the alarm business in this State on a full-time basis for at least five consecutive years immediately preceding appointment, shall be a member of the Automatic Fire Alarm Association of New Jersey and, except for the member first appointed, shall be licensed under the provisions of section 7 of this act;

(5) Two members shall have been engaged as practicing locksmiths on a full-time basis for at least five consecutive years immediately preceding appointment, shall be members of a duly recognized professional locksmith association in New Jersey and, except for the members first appointed, shall be licensed as locksmiths under the provisions of section 7 of this act;

(6) One member shall have been engaged in the alarm business in this State on a full-time basis, shall be a member of both the New Jersey Burglar and Fire Alarm Association and a duly recognized professional locksmith association and, except for the member first appointed, be licensed under the provisions of section 7 of this act;

(7) One member shall have been engaged as a practicing locksmith in this State on a full-time basis for at least five consecutive years immediately preceding appointment, shall be a member of both the New Jersey Burglar and Fire Alarm Association and a duly recognized professional locksmith association and, except for the member first appointed, be licensed under the provisions of section 7 of this act;

(8) One member shall be a member of the International Brotherhood of Electrical Workers, A.F.L.-C.I.O; and

(9) One member shall be a public member who meets the requirements pertaining to public members set forth in subsection b. of section 2 of P.L.1971, c.60 (C.45:1-2.2).

b. The Governor shall appoint each member for a term of three years, except that of the members first appointed, five shall serve for terms of three years, five shall serve for terms of two years, and five shall serve for terms of one year.

c. Any vacancy in the membership of the committee shall be filled for the unexpired term in the manner provided for the original appointment. No member of the committee may serve more than two successive terms in addition to any unexpired term to which he has been appointed.

d. The committee shall annually elect from among its members a chair and vice-chair. The committee shall meet at least four times a year and may hold additional meetings as necessary to discharge its duties. In addition to such meetings, the committee shall meet at the call of the chair, the board, or the Attorney General.

e. Members of the committee shall be compensated and reimbursed for actual expenses reasonably incurred in the performance of their official duties and reimbursed for expenses and provided with office and meeting facilities and personnel required for the proper conduct of the committee's business.

f. The committee shall make recommendations to the board regarding rules and regulations pertaining to professional training, standards, identification and record-keeping procedures for licensees and their employees, classifications of licensure necessary to regulate the work of licensees, and other matters as necessary to effectuate the purposes of this act.

45:5A-24. Powers, duties of board

The board shall have the following powers and duties, or may delegate them to the committee:

a. To set standards and approve examinations for applicants for a fire alarm, burglar alarm or locksmith license and issue a license to each qualified applicant;

To administer the examination to be taken by applicants for licensure;

c. To determine the form and contents of applications for licensure, licenses and identification cards;

d. To adopt a code of ethics for licensees;

e. To issue and renew licenses and identification cards;

f. To set the amount of fees for fire alarm, burglar alarm and locksmith licenses, license renewal, applications, examinations and other services provided by the board and committee, within the limits provided in subsection b. of section 11 of this act;

g. To refuse to admit a person to an examination or refuse to issue or suspend, revoke, or fail to renew the license of a fire alarm, burglar alarm, or locksmith licensee pursuant to the provisions of P.L.1978, c. 73 (C.45:1-14 et seq.);

h. To maintain a record of all applicants for a license;

i. To maintain and annually publish a record of every licensee, his place of business, place of residence and the date and number of his license;

j. To take disciplinary action, in accordance with P.L.1978, c. 73 (C.45:1-14 et seq.) against a licensee or employee who violates any provision of this act or any rule or regulation promulgated pursuant to this act;

k. To adopt standards and requirements for and approve continuing education programs and courses of study for licensees and their employees;

l. To review advertising by licensees; and

m. To perform such other duties as may be necessary to effectuate the purposes of this act.

45:5A-25 Requirements for advertising alarm business.

a.   No person shall advertise that he is authorized to engage in, or engage in the alarm business, or otherwise engage in the installation, service or maintenance of burglar alarm, fire alarm or electronic security systems unless he satisfies the requirements of this act.

b.   No person shall represent himself as qualified to provide, or otherwise provide locksmithing services unless he is licensed as a locksmith in accordance with the provisions of this act.

45:5A-26 Application for license as alarm business, locksmithing

(a)   Application for a license to engage in the alarm business or to provide locksmithing services, as the case may be, shall be made to the board in the manner and on the forms as the board, in consultation with the committee may prescribe.

(1)   An application to engage in the alarm business shall include the name, age, residence, present and previous occupations of the applicant and, in the case of a business firm engaged in the alarm business, of each member, officer or director thereof, the name of the municipality and the location therein by street number or other appropriate description of the principal place of business and the location of each branch office.

(2)   An application to engage in locksmithing services shall include the name, residence and principal business address of the applicant, or in the case of an employee, the principal business address of his employer.

b.   Every applicant shall submit to the board, together with the application, his photograph, in passport size, a list of all criminal offenses of which he has been convicted, setting forth the date and place of each conviction and the name under which he was convicted, if other than that on the application, and fingerprints of his two hands taken on standard fingerprint cards by a State or municipal law enforcement agency. Before approving an application, the board shall submit the fingerprints of the applicant to the Division of State Police in the Department of Law and Public Safety, for comparative analysis. The board is authorized to exchange fingerprint data with and receive criminal history record information from the Division of State Police and the Federal Bureau of Investigation for use in making the determinations required by this act. The applicant shall bear the cost for the criminal history record check. No license shall be issued to any applicant whose license has been revoked under the provisions of this act within five years of the date of filing of an application.

c.   If an applicant files with the board fingerprints of a person other than the applicant, he shall be guilty of a crime of the fourth degree and shall have his license application denied or license revoked.

d.   The board may require other information of the applicant and, if the applicant is proposing to qualify a business firm, of the business firm to determine the professional competence and integrity of the concerned parties.

45:5A-27. Requirements for licensure

a.   An applicant seeking licensure to engage in the alarm business shall:

(1)   Be at least 18 years of age;

(2)   Be of good moral character, and not have been convicted of a crime of the first, second or third degree within 10 years prior to the filing of the application;

(3)   Meet qualifications established by the board, in consultation with the committee, regarding experience, continuing education, financial responsibility and integrity; and

(4)   Establish his qualifications to perform and supervise various phases of alarm installation, service and maintenance as evidenced by successful completion of an examination approved by the board, in consultation with the committee, except that any person engaged in the alarm business on the effective date of this act and filing an application within 120 days following the effective date of this act, shall not be required to submit evidence of the successful completion of the examination requirement if that person shows proof of having completed 40 hours of technical training prior to the effective date of this act, which training has been approved by the board, in consultation with the committee. No examination or training requirement shall apply to any person providing evidence of having been engaged in the alarm business for at least one year prior to the effective date of this act.

b.   An applicant seeking licensure as a locksmith shall:

(1)   Be at least 18 years of age;

(2) Be of good moral character, and not have been convicted of a crime of the first, second or third degree within 10 years prior to the filing of the application;

(3) Present evidence to the board of having successfully completed any training and continuing education requirements established by the board, in consultation with the committee; and

(4) Successfully complete a written examination approved by the board, in consultation with the committee to determine the applicant's competence to engage in locksmithing services, except that no examination requirement shall apply to any person engaged in locksmithing services who has practiced locksmithing services for at least one year prior to the effective date of this act and who files an application within 120 days following the effective date of this act.

45:5A-27.1. Ineligibility for license to engage in fire alarm business

Any person certified to engage in the fire protection contractor business pursuant to P.L.2001, c.289 (C.52:27D-25n et al.) whose certificate of certification is not in good standing with the Commissioner of Community Affairs shall not be eligible for a license to engage in the fire alarm business under the provisions of section 1 of P.L.1995, c.213 (C.45:5A-9.1).

45:5A-28. Nonapplicability of act

The provisions of this act regarding the practice of locksmithing services shall not apply to:

a. The activities of any person performing public emergency services for a governmental entity if that person is operating under the direction or control of the organization by which he is employed;

b. The activities of any sales representative who is offering a sales demonstration to licensed locksmiths;

c. The activities of any automotive service dealer or lock manufacturer, or their agent or employee, while servicing, installing, repairing, or rebuilding locks from a product line utilized by that dealer or lock manufacturer;

d. The activities of any member of a trade union hired to install any mechanical locking device as part of a new building construction or renovation project; and

e. The activities of any person using any key duplicating machine or key blanks, except for keys marked "do not duplicate" or "master key."

45:5A-29 Exemptions from licensing requirement.

a. Telephone utilities and cable television companies regulated by the Board of Regulatory Commissioners pursuant to Title 48 of the Revised Statutes and persons in their employ while performing the duties of their employment are exempt from the requirement of obtaining a license to engage in the alarm business pursuant to this act.

b. Electrical contractors regulated by the Board of Examiners of Electrical Contractors pursuant to P.L.1962, c.162 (C.45:5A-1 et seq.) and persons in their employ while performing the duties of their employment are exempt from the requirement of obtaining a license to engage in the alarm business pursuant to this act.

c. Any person who is certified to engage in the fire protection equipment business or who holds a fire protection contractor business permit pursuant to P.L.2001, c.289 (C.52:27D-25n et al.) and persons in their employ are exempt from the requirement of obtaining a license to engage in the fire alarm business pursuant to this act.

45:5A-30. Issuance of locksmith license

Notwithstanding any other provision of this act to the contrary, the board shall, upon application with submission of satisfactory proof and payment of the prescribed fee, within six months following the effective date of this act, issue a locksmith license to:

a. Any person who has successfully completed a locksmith apprentice program which has been approved by the Bureau of Apprenticeship and Training of the United States Department of Labor; or

b. Any person who has been engaged full-time in the practice of locksmithing services for at least three years immediately prior to the date of his application for a locksmith's license.

45:5A-31. Issuance of license to persons engaged in alarm business, locksmithing; duration; renewal; fees.

a. Licenses shall be issued to qualified applicants seeking licensure to engage in the alarm business or as a locksmith for a three-year period, upon payment of a licensing fee. License renewals shall be issued for a three-year period upon the payment of a renewal fee. A renewal application shall be filed with the board at least 45 days prior to expiration of a license. A license issued pursuant to this act shall not be transferable.

b.   Fees shall be established, prescribed or changed by the board, in consultation with the committee, to the extent necessary to defray all proper expenses incurred by the committee, the board and any staff employed to administer the provisions of this act, except that fees shall not be fixed at a level that will raise amounts in excess of the amount estimated to be so required. All fees and any fines imposed under this act shall be paid to the board and shall be forwarded to the State Treasurer and become part of the General Fund.

45:5A-32. Requirements for licensee.

a.. No licensee qualified under the provisions of this act shall engage in the alarm business or in the practice of locksmithing services, unless the licensee:

(1) Maintains at least one business office within the State or files with the board a statement, duly executed and sworn to before a person authorized by the laws of this State to administer oaths, containing a power of attorney constituting the board the true and lawful attorney of the licensee upon whom all original process in an action or legal proceeding against the licensee may be served and in which the licensee agrees that the original process that may be served upon the board shall be of the same force and validity as if served upon the licensee and that the authority thereof shall continue in force so long as the licensee engages in the alarm business or in the practice of locksmithing services, as the case may be, in this State;

(2) Clearly marks the outside of each installation and service vehicle to be used in conjunction with the alarm business with the alarm business name or the outside of each installation and service vehicle to be used in conjunction with locksmithing services with the locksmithing service's name;

(3) Maintains an emergency service number attended to on a 24-hour basis and responds appropriately to emergencies on a 24-hour basis when engaged in the alarm business; and

(4) Retains at all times general liability insurance in an amount determined by the board, in consultation with the committee, and insurance coverage or a surety bond in favor of the State of New Jersey in the sum of $10,000, executed by a surety company authorized to transact business in the State of New Jersey and which is approved by the Department of Banking and Insurance, and which is to be conditioned on the faithful performance of the provisions of this act. The board shall by rule or regulation provide who shall be eligible to receive the financial protection afforded by that bond and the bond shall be in full force and effect for the term of the license issued.

b.   Except in the case of an employee licensed as a locksmith, no licensed locksmith shall engage in locksmithing services unless that licensee maintains at least one business office within the State.

45:5A-33. Display of identification card.

a.   Every licensee and every employee or other person engaged in the unsupervised installation, servicing or maintenance of burglar alarm, fire alarm or electronic security systems shall, at all times during working hours, display an identification card issued by the board. The identification card shall contain the following information:

(1) the name, photograph and signature of the person to whom the card has been issued;

(2) the business name and address and license number of the licensee;

(3) the expiration date of the card; and

(4) that other information the board deems appropriate for identification purposes.

b.   Identification cards shall be issued for a three-year period which, in the case of a licensee, shall correspond to the term of the license period of the licensee. Application for renewal of an identification card for other than a licensee shall be made by the person named on the card at least 45 days prior to the expiration date of the card. The information provided on the identification card shall at all times be current, and the named holder of the card shall advise the board of any changes and file for issuance of an updated card within five days following occurrence of a change, which card shall be issued for the unexpired term of the original card.

c.   Identification cards shall not be transferable in the event of a change in employment.

45:5A-34. Requirements for employees of licensee.

No person shall be employed by a licensee to install, service or maintain a burglar alarm, fire alarm or electronic security system or, except in the case of a licensee, shall otherwise engage in the installation, service or maintenance thereof:

a.   unless the person is of good moral character; or

b.   where the work is to be performed other than under the field supervision of a licensee or a person qualified pursuant to the provisions of this section, unless the person shall have at least three years of practical experience and shall have successfully completed a course of study or a competency examination prescribed by the board, in consultation with the committee; except that an employee employed in the installation, servicing or maintenance of burglar alarm, fire alarm or electronic security systems by a license applicant filing an application within 120 days of the effective date of this act and identified as an employee on the application, shall not be required to satisfy the competency requirements of this subsection, until the first renewal of the employee's identification card.

45:5A-35. Responsibilities of licensee relative to employees.

a.   A licensee shall be responsible for any unlawful or unprofessional conduct by an employee, except that the conduct shall not be a cause for suspension or revocation of a license, unless the board determines that the licensee had knowledge thereof, or there is shown to have existed a pattern of unlawful or unprofessional conduct.

b.   Within 30 days of employing a person in connection with an alarm business or as a locksmith, a licensee shall notify the board and shall provide the board with the employee's photograph, in passport size, fingerprints of the employee's two hands taken on standard fingerprint cards by a State or municipal law enforcement agency, a list of all criminal offenses, supplied by the employee, of which the employee has been convicted, setting forth the date and place of each conviction, and the name under which the employee was convicted, if other than that given in the written notification to the board and, if the work of the employee is not to be directly supervised, evidence of practical experience and professional competence in accordance with the requirements of subsection b. of section 14 of this act.

c.   If a licensee knowingly falsifies any information required by the board, the licensee shall be guilty of a crime of the fourth degree and shall have his license revoked.

d.   After confirming the information provided on an employee with the Division of State Police in the Department of Law and Public Safety and conducting other investigations as necessary, if the board determines that an employee is subject to the requirements of section 14 of this act and fails to satisfy those requirements, the board shall advise the licensee immediately of the employee's unfitness. The board is authorized to exchange fingerprint data with and receive criminal history record information from the Division of State Police and the Federal Bureau of Investigation for use in making the determinations required by this act. The employer shall bear the cost for the criminal history record check pursuant to this section. Employees hired by an alarm business through a recognized trade union on a temporary basis not to exceed six months or one project, whichever is greater, are exempt from the requirements of this act.

45:5A-36. Municipality, county prohibited from regulating locksmiths, alarm businesses.

No municipality or county shall enact an ordinance or resolution or promulgate any rules or regulations relating to the licensing or registration of locksmiths or alarm businesses. The provisions of any ordinance or resolution or rules or regulations of any municipality or county relating to the licensing or registration of locksmiths or alarm businesses are superseded by the provisions of this act. Nothing in this section shall be construed, however, to prohibit municipal regulation of door-to-door vendors or salespersons of burglar alarm, fire alarm or electronic security systems nor shall anything in this section be construed to prohibit or restrict municipal consideration of alarm business service proposals in consent proceedings under the "Cable Television Act," P.L.1972, c. 186 (C.48:5A-1 et seq.).

45:5A-37. Licensure from other jurisdictions

If the board, after consultation with the committee, determines that an applicant holds a valid license from another jurisdiction which requires equal or greater experience and knowledge requirements, the board may accept evidence of that license as meeting the experience and knowledge requirements of this act for a person engaged in the alarm business or in the practice of locksmithing services.

45:5A-38. Rules, regulations.

The board, after consultation with the committee, shall adopt rules and regulations pursuant to the "Administrative Procedure Act," P.L.1968, c. 410 (C.52:14B-1 et seq.) necessary to effectuate the purposes of this act.

Updated through 7/8/09.

NEW JERSEY PERMANENT STATUTES
TITLE 45: PROFESSIONS AND OCCUPATIONS
CHAPTER 1: UNIFORM ENFORCEMENT ACT

45:1-1. Persons entitled to practice, etc. under former laws unaffected

Any person now entitled to practice any profession or to engage in any occupation, governed or regulated by the provisions of this title by virtue of any prior law, shall continue to be entitled to practice or engage in the same, notwithstanding the enactment of this title, and the validity of any license or other authorization to practice any such profession or to engage in any such occupation, heretofore issued to any person under any prior law, or of any proceeding pending to obtain such a license or authorization shall not be affected by the enactment of this title but all such persons shall in all other respects be subject to the provisions of this title.

45:1-2.1 Applicability of act.

The provisions of this act shall apply to the following boards and commissions: the New Jersey State Board of Accountancy, the New Jersey State Board of Architects, the New Jersey State Board of Cosmetology and Hairstyling, the Board of Examiners of Electrical Contractors, the New Jersey State Board of Dentistry, the State Board of Mortuary Science of New Jersey, the State Board of Professional Engineers and Land Surveyors, the State Board of Marriage and Family Therapy Examiners, the State Board of Medical Examiners, the New Jersey Board of Nursing, the New Jersey State Board of Optometrists, the State Board of Examiners of Ophthalmic Dispensers and Ophthalmic Technicians, the Board of Pharmacy, the State Board of Professional Planners, the State Board of Psychological Examiners, the State Board of Examiners of Master Plumbers, the New Jersey Real Estate Commission, the State Board of Court Reporting, the State Board of Veterinary Medical Examiners, the Radiologic Technology Board of Examiners, the Acupuncture Examining Board, the State Board of Chiropractic Examiners, the State Board of Respiratory Care, the State Real Estate Appraiser Board, the State Board of Social Work Examiners, the State Board of Examiners of Heating, Ventilating, Air Conditioning and Refrigeration Contractors, the State Board of Physical Therapy Examiners, the Orthotics and Prosthetics Board of Examiners, the New Jersey Cemetery Board, the State Board of Polysomnography, the New Jersey Board of Massage and Bodywork Therapy, the Genetic Counseling Advisory Committee and any other entity hereafter created under Title 45 to license or otherwise regulate a profession or occupation.

45:1-2.2 Membership of certain boards and commissions; appointment, removal, quorum

a.   All members of the several professional boards and commissions shall be appointed by the Governor in the manner prescribed by law; except in appointing members other than those appointed pursuant to subsection b. or subsection c., the Governor shall give due consideration to, but shall not be bound by, recommendations submitted by the appropriate professional organizations of this State.

b.   In addition to the membership otherwise prescribed by law, the Governor shall appoint in the same manner as presently prescribed by law for the appointment of members, two additional members to represent the interests of the public, to be known as public members, to each of the following boards and commissions: the New Jersey State Board of Accountancy, the New Jersey State Board of Architects, the New Jersey State Board of Cosmetology and Hairstyling, the New Jersey State Board of Dentistry, the State Board of Mortuary Science of New Jersey, the State Board of Professional Engineers and Land Surveyors, the State Board of Medical Examiners, the New Jersey Board of Nursing, the New Jersey State Board of Optometrists, the State Board of Examiners of Ophthalmic Dispensers and Ophthalmic Technicians, the Board of Pharmacy, the State Board of Professional Planners, the State Board of Psychological Examiners, the New Jersey Real Estate Commission, the State Board of Court Reporting, the State Board of Social Work Examiners, and the State Board of Veterinary Medical Examiners, and one additional public member to each of the following boards: the Board of Examiners of Electrical Contractors, the State Board of Marriage and Family Therapy Examiners, the State Board of Examiners of Master Plumbers, and the State Real Estate Appraiser Board. Each public member shall be appointed for the term prescribed for the other members of the board or commission and until the appointment of his successor. Vacancies shall be filled for the unexpired term only. The Governor may remove any such public member after hearing, for misconduct, incompetency, neglect of duty or for any other sufficient cause.

No public member appointed pursuant to this section shall have any association or relationship with the profession or a member thereof regulated by the board of which he is a member, where such association or relationship would prevent such public member from representing the interest of the public. Such a relationship includes a relationship with members of one's immediate family; and such association includes membership in the profession regulated by the board. To receive services rendered in a customary client relationship will not preclude a prospective public member from appointment. This paragraph shall not apply to individuals who are public members of boards on the effective date of this act.

It shall be the responsibility of the Attorney General to insure that no person with the aforementioned association or relationship or any other questionable or potential conflict of interest shall be appointed to serve as a public member of any board regulated by this section.

Where a board is required to examine the academic and professional credentials of an applicant for licensure or to test such applicant orally, no public member appointed pursuant to this section shall participate in such examination process; provided, however, that public members shall be given notice of and may be present at all such examination processes and deliberations concerning the results thereof, and, provided further, that public members may participate in the development and establishment of the procedures and criteria for such examination processes.

    c.   The Governor shall designate a department in the Executive Branch of the State Government which is closely related to the profession or occupation regulated by each of the boards or commissions designated in section 1 of P.L.1971, c.60 (C.45:1-2.1) and shall appoint the head of such department, or the holder of a designated office or position in such department, to serve without compensation at the pleasure of the Governor as a member of such board or commission.

    d.   A majority of the voting members of such boards or commissions shall constitute a quorum thereof and no action of any such board or commission shall be taken except upon the affirmative vote of a majority of the members of the entire board or commission.

45:1-2.3. Qualification; rights and duties.
Such additional members:

    a.   Need not meet the educational and professional requirements for membership on such boards or commissions as provided in the several statutes establishing such boards and commissions; and

    b.   Shall be voting members subject to the same rights, obligations and duties as other members of their respective boards and commissions.

45:1-2.4. Effect of act on term of member in office.
Nothing in this act shall affect the right of a board or commission member in office on the effective date of this act to continue to serve for the term for which he was appointed.

45: 1-2.5. Compensation and reimbursement of expenses of members; executive secretaries; compensation and terms; office and meeting places
With respect to the boards or commissions designated in section 1 of P.L.1971, c.60 (C.45:1-2.1), except as otherwise provided in subsection d. of this section, and notwithstanding the provisions of any other law:

    a.   The officers and members shall be compensated on a per diem basis in the amount of $25.00 or an amount to be determined by the Attorney General, with the approval of the State Treasurer, but not to exceed $100.00 per diem or $2,500.00 annually, and shall be reimbursed for actual expenses reasonably incurred in the performance of their official duties. Such moneys shall be paid according to rules and regulations promulgated by the Attorney General.

    b.   The executive secretary shall receive such salary as shall be determined by the appointing authority within the limits of available appropriations and shall serve at its pleasure. Any such executive secretary who holds a certificate, license or registration issued by the board or commission by which he is employed shall not during such employment be permitted to engage in any profession or occupation regulated by the board or commission.

    c.   The head of the department to which such board or commission is assigned shall maintain within any public building, whether owned or leased by the State, suitable quarters for the board's or commission's office and meeting place, provided that no such office or meeting place shall be within premises owned or occupied by an officer or member of such board or commission.

    d.   The compensation schedule for members of boards and commissions provided in subsection a. of this section shall not apply to the members of the New Jersey Real Estate Commission, who shall be compensated pursuant to R.S.45:15-6 or to members of the State Board of Medical Examiners who shall receive compensation of $150 per diem.

45:1-2.6. Inapplicability of act to rights under civil service or any pension law or retirement system
Nothing in this act shall deprive any person of any tenure rights or of any right or protection provided him by Title 11 of the Revised Statutes, Civil Service, or any pension law or retirement system.

45:1-3 Expenses of boards paid from income; surplus paid to state treasurer; accounts
Each member of the boards mentioned in section 45:1-2 of this title shall be entitled to his actual traveling and other expenses incurred in the performance of his duties, which sum shall be paid from the license fees and other sources of income of such boards. Such boards shall also be entitled to expend from their income such sums as shall be necessary to defray all proper expenses incurred by them in the performance of their duties, including the compensation of any of their officers or agents whom they are authorized to compensate. Such boards, if authorized to collect an annual registration or license fee from persons licensed by them, may retain in their treasuries the fees so collected and use the same for the purpose of defraying the expenses of securing evidence against and prosecuting persons violating the provisions of the laws with the enforcement of which they are charged, or, in case the revenue of the boards from other sources shall be insufficient to pay the salary of their secretaries and their other expenses, such fees may be expended for such purposes. Such boards shall be entitled to retain, in addition to the above, at least one hundred dollars in their treasuries for the purpose of preparing and holding their examinations. On or before October thirty-first in each year such boards shall pay to the state treasurer all moneys remaining in their treasuries, except as above stated, which sum, when so paid, shall form a part of the state fund. Such boards shall keep accurate accounts of their receipts and expenditures, which accounts shall be subject to audit by the state comptroller.

45:1-3.1. Applicability of act.
The provisions of this act shall apply to the following boards and commissions: the New Jersey State Board of Accountancy, the New Jersey State Board of Architects, the New Jersey State Board of Cosmetology and Hairstyling, the Board of Examiners of Electrical Contractors, the New Jersey State Board of Dentistry, the State Board of Mortuary Science of New Jersey, the State Board of Professional Engineers and Land Surveyors, the State Board of Marriage and Family Therapy Examiners, the State Board of Medical Examiners, the New Jersey Board of Nursing, the New Jersey State Board of Optometrists, the State Board of Examiners of Ophthalmic Dispensers and Ophthalmic Technicians, the Board of Pharmacy, the State Board of Professional Planners, the State Board of Psychological Examiners, the State Board of Examiners of Master Plumbers, the State Board of Court Reporting, the State Board of Veterinary Medical Examiners, the Radiologic Technology Board of Examiners, the Acupuncture Examining Board, the State Board of Chiropractic Examiners, the State Board of Respiratory Care, the State Real Estate Appraiser Board, the New Jersey Cemetery Board, the State Board of Social Work Examiners, the State Board of Examiners of Heating, Ventilating, Air Conditioning and Refrigeration Contractors, the State Board of Physical Therapy Examiners, the State Board of Polysomnography, the Orthotics and Prosthetics Board of Examiners, the New Jersey Board of Massage and Bodywork Therapy, the Genetic Counseling Advisory Committee and any other entity hereafter created under Title 45 to license or otherwise regulate a profession or occupation.

45:1-3.2 Charges for examinations; licensures and other services; establishment or change by rule; standards
Notwithstanding the provisions of Title 45 of the Revised Statutes or any other law to the contrary, any board or commission named in section 1 of this supplementary act may by rule establish, prescribe or change the charges for examinations, licensures and other services it performs, which rule shall first be approved by the head of the department to which such board or commission is assigned and shall be adopted in accordance with the provisions of the "Administrative Procedure Act," P.L.1968, c. 410 (c. 52:14B-1).

Any board's or commission's charges established, prescribed or changed pursuant to this section shall be established, prescribed or changed to such extent as shall be necessary to defray all proper expenses incurred by the board or commission in the performance of its duties but such charges shall not be fixed at a level that will raise amounts in excess of the amount estimated to be so required.

45:1-3.3 Administrative fees
The Director of the Division of Consumer Affairs may by rule establish, prescribe, or modify administrative fees charged by boards in accordance with the "Administrative Procedure Act," P.L.1968, c.410 (C.52:14B-1 et seq.). For purposes of this section, "administrative fees" are charges assessed to licensees, registrants or holders of certificates, as the case may be, for board functions that are not unique to a particular board but are uniform throughout all boards. Administrative fees include, but are not limited to, fees for a duplicate or replacement license, certification or registration, late renewal fee, license reinstatement fee, and the fee for processing change of address.

45:1-4. Salary of secretary.

The secretary of each of the boards mentioned in section 45:1-2 of this title, whether or not a member thereof, shall be entitled to receive such reasonable salary or compensation for his services as secretary as shall be fixed by such boards, which shall be paid by the boards from their receipts, unless an appropriation is made for the expenses of such boards, in which case the same shall be paid from such appropriation.

45:1-7 Issuance of certain licenses or certificates of registration

Notwithstanding any of the provisions of Title 45 of the Revised Statutes or of any other law to the contrary, all professional or occupational licenses or certificates of registration, except such licenses or certificates issued to real estate brokers or salesmen pursuant to chapter 15 of Title 45, which prior to the effective date of this act were issued for periods not exceeding one year and were annually renewable, shall, on and after the effective date of this act, be issued for periods of two years and be biennially renewable, except that licenses and business permits issued to electrical contractors and certificates of registration issued to qualified journeymen electricians pursuant to chapter 5A of Title 45 shall be issued for periods of three years and be triennially renewable; provided, however, the boards or commissions in charge of the issuance or renewal of such licenses or certificates may, in order to stagger the expiration dates thereof, provide that those first issued or renewed after the effective date of this act, shall expire and become void on a date fixed by the respective boards or commissions, not sooner than six months nor later than 29 months, after the date of issue.

The fees for the respective licenses and certificates of registration issued pursuant to this act for periods of less or greater than one year shall be in amounts proportionately less or greater than the fees established by law.

45:1-7.1 Applicability of act; renewals; reinstatements

a.   Notwithstanding any other act or regulation to the contrary, the provisions of this section and sections 6 and 7 of P.L.1999, c.403 (C.45:1-7.2 and C.45:1-7.3) shall apply to every holder of a professional or occupational license or certificate of registration or certification issued or renewed by a board specified in section 2 of P.L.1978, c.73 (C.45:1-15), who seeks renewal of that license or certificate.

b.   Every holder of a professional or occupational license or certificate of registration or certification, issued or renewed by a board specified in section 2 of P.L.1978, c.73 (C.45:1-15), who seeks renewal shall submit a renewal application and pay a renewal fee prior to the date of expiration of the license or certificate of registration or certification. If the holder does not renew the license or certificate prior to its expiration date, the holder may renew it within 30 days of its expiration date by submitting a renewal application and paying a renewal fee and a late fee. Any professional or occupational license or certificate of registration or certification not renewed within 30 days of its expiration date shall be suspended without a hearing.

c.   Any individual who continues to practice with an expired license or certificate of registration or certification after 30 days following its expiration date shall be deemed to be engaged in unlicensed practice of the regulated profession or occupation, even if no notice of suspension has been provided to the individual.

d.   A professional or occupational license or certificate of registration or certification suspended pursuant to this section may be reinstated within five years following its date of expiration upon submission of a renewal application and payment of an additional reinstatement fee. An applicant seeking reinstatement of a license or certificate suspended pursuant to this section more than five years past its expiration date shall successfully complete the examination required for initial licensure, registration or certification and submit a renewal application and payment of an additional reinstatement fee.

e.   A board specified in section 2 of P.L.1978, c.73 (C.45:1-15) shall send a notice of renewal to each of its holders of a professional or occupational license or certificate of registration or certification, as applicable, at least 60 days prior to the expiration of the license or certificate. If the notice to renew is not sent at least 60 days prior to the expiration date, no monetary penalties or fines shall apply to the holder for failure to renew.

45:1-7.2 Reinstatement of license, registration, certification

A board may reinstate the professional or occupational license or certificate of registration or certification of an applicant whose license or certificate has been suspended pursuant to section 5 of P.L.1999, c.403 (C.45:1-7.1), provided that the applicant otherwise qualifies for licensure, registration or certification and submits the following upon application for reinstatement:

a.   Payment of all past delinquent renewal fees;

b.   Payment of a reinstatement fee;

c.   An affidavit of employment listing each job held during the period of suspended license, registration or certification which includes the names, addresses, and telephone numbers of each employer; and

d.   If applicable, satisfactory proof that the applicant has maintained proficiency by completing the continuing education hours or credits required for the renewal of an active license or certificate of registration or certification.

45:1-7.3 Active, inactive options on renewal applications

a.   Renewal applications for all professional or occupational licenses or certificates of registration or certification shall provide the applicant with the option of either active or inactive renewal. A renewal applicant electing to renew as inactive shall not engage in professional or occupational practice within the State.

b.   An applicant who selects the inactive renewal option shall remain on inactive status for the entire renewal period unless, upon application to the board, the board permits the inactive applicant to return to active status provided such applicant presents satisfactory proof that he has maintained proficiency by completing the continuing education hours or credits required for the renewal of an active license, registration or certification, if applicable. The continuing education hours or credits shall be completed by the applicant within three years prior to the date of application for the return to active status, unless otherwise provided by board rule.

45:1-8. Contractors; application of s. 45:1-9
The provisions of this act apply to the following classes of contractors:

a.   Tree experts, certified pursuant to P.L.1940, c.100 (C. 13:1-28 et seq.1);

b.   Home repair contractors, licensed pursuant to P.L.1960, c.41 (C. 17:16C-62 et seq.);

c.   Electrical contractors, licensed pursuant to P.L.1962, c.162 (C. 45:5A-1 et seq.);

d.   Master plumbers, licensed pursuant to P.L.1968, c. 362 (C. 45:14C-1 et seq.);

e.   Well drillers, licensed pursuant to P.L.1947, c.377 (C. 58:4A-5 et seq.); and

f.   Any class of contractors who hereafter are licensed by the State.

45:1-9. Indication of license or certificate number on contracts, bids and advertisements
Any contractor licensed by the State shall indicate his license or certificate number on all contracts, subcontracts, bids and all forms of advertising as a contractor.

45:1-11. Violations; penalty
Any person violating this act shall be guilty of a misdemeanor.

45:1-14. Legislative findings and declarations; liberal construction of act
The Legislature finds and declares that effective implementation of consumer protection laws and the administration of laws pertaining to the professional and occupational boards located within the Division of Consumer Affairs require uniform investigative and enforcement powers and procedures and uniform standards for license revocation, suspension and other disciplinary proceedings by such boards. This act is deemed remedial, and the provisions hereof should be afforded a liberal construction.

45:1-15. Application of act.
The provisions of this act shall apply to the following boards and all professions or occupations regulated by, through or with the advice of those boards: the New Jersey State Board of Accountancy, the New Jersey State Board of Architects, the New Jersey State Board of Cosmetology and Hairstyling, the Board of Examiners of Electrical Contractors, the New Jersey State Board of Dentistry, the State Board of Mortuary Science of New Jersey, the State Board of Professional Engineers and Land Surveyors, the State Board of Marriage and Family Therapy Examiners, the State Board of Medical Examiners, the New Jersey Board of Nursing, the New Jersey State Board of Optometrists, the State Board of Examiners of Ophthalmic Dispensers and Ophthalmic Technicians, the Board of Pharmacy, the State Board of Professional Planners, the State Board of Psychological Examiners, the State Board of Examiners of Master Plumbers, the State Board of Court Reporting, the State Board of Veterinary Medical Examiners, the State Board of Chiropractic Examiners, the State Board of Respiratory Care, the State Real Estate Appraiser Board, the State Board of Social Work Examiners, the State Board of Examiners of Heating, Ventilating, Air Conditioning and Refrigeration Contractors, the State Board of Physical Therapy Examiners, the State Board of Polysomnography, the Professional Counselor Examiners Committee, the New Jersey Cemetery Board, the Orthotics and Prosthetics Board of Examiners, the Occupational Therapy Advisory Council, the Electrologists Advisory Committee, the Acupuncture Advisory Committee, the Alcohol and Drug Counselor Committee, the

Athletic Training Advisory Committee, the Certified Psychoanalysts Advisory Committee, the Fire Alarm, Burglar Alarm, and Locksmith Advisory Committee, the Home Inspection Advisory Committee, the Interior Design Examination and Evaluation Committee, the Hearing Aid Dispensers Examining Committee, the Landscape Architect Examination and Evaluation Committee, the Perfusionists Advisory Committee, the Physician Assistant Advisory Committee, the Audiology and Speech-Language Pathology Advisory Committee, the New Jersey Board of Massage and Bodywork Therapy, the Genetic Counseling Advisory Committee and any other entity hereafter created under Title 45 to license or otherwise regulate a profession or occupation.

45:1-15.1. Rules, regulations
Consistent with their enabling acts, P.L.1978, c.73 (C.45:1-14 et seq.) and the "Administrative Procedure Act," P.L.1968, c.410 (C.52:14B-1 et seq.), the boards and others set forth in section 2 of P.L.1978, c.73 (C.45:1-15) are authorized to adopt rules and regulations to serve the public health, safety and welfare.

45:1-15.2. Professional, occupational licenses, registrations, expiration date for individuals with certain types of military service; delayed.
Any license issued by a professional or occupational board designated in section 2 of P.L.1978, c.73 (C.45:1-15), and any registration issued under the "New Jersey Controlled Dangerous Substances Act," P.L.1970, c.226 (C.24:21-1 et al.), shall not expire while the licensee or registrant is an active member of the Armed Forces of the United States and shall be extended for up to 120 days after his or her return from active service. Any late renewal fees, reinstatement fees and other reinstatement requirements shall be waived by the applicable professional or occupational board or the Division of Consumer Affairs upon application by the licensee or registrant within 120 days after he or she returns from active service. If the license or registration is renewed during the 120-day period after his or her return from active service, and the licensee or registrant submits documentation verifying his or her active military service, the licensee or registrant shall only be responsible for normal fees and activities relating to renewal of the license or registration and shall not be charged any additional costs, such as, but not limited to, late fees or delinquency fees.

As used in this section, "active member" means an individual or member of an organized unit ordered into active service in the Armed Forces of the United States by reason of membership in a reserve component of the Armed Forces of the United States or any branch of the Armed Forces of the United States.

45:1-16. Definitions
As used within this act the following words or terms shall have the indicated definition unless the contest clearly indicates otherwise.

"Board" means any professional or occupational licensing board designated in section 2 of this act.

"Director" means the Director of the Division of Consumer Affairs in the Department of Law and Public Safety.

"Person" means any natural person or his legal representative, partnership, corporation, company, trust, business entity or association, and any agent, employee, salesman, partner, officer, director, member, stockholder, associate, trustee or cestuis que trust thereof.

45:1-17. Powers of Attorney General to implement act and administer law enforcement activities of boards
In implementing the provisions of this act and administering the law enforcement activities of those professional and occupational boards located within the Division of Consumer Affairs, the Attorney General may:

(a) After advice to the board or boards in question of his intent to proceed under this section, and the specific action he intends to take, and the failure of such board or boards to take steps in accordance with the advice of the Attorney General within 30 days of receipt of such advice, promulgate rules and regulations consistent with the provisions of this act and the Administrative Procedure Act, P.L. 1968, c. 410 (C. 52:14B-1 et seq.) governing the procedure for administrative hearings before all boards within the Division of Consumer Affairs. Such rules and regulations shall govern administrative complaints, answers thereto, issuance of subpoenas, appointment of hearing examiners, adjournments, submission of proposed findings of fact and conclusions of law, the filing of briefs, and such other procedural aspects of administrative hearings before the boards as the Attorney General may deem necessary; provided, however, nothing herein authorized shall be construed to require the Attorney General to promulgate rules regarding prehearing investigative procedures.

(b) After advice to the board or boards in question of his intent to proceed under this section, and the specific action he intends to take, and the failure of such board or boards to take steps in accordance with the advice of the Attorney General within 30 days of receipt of such advice, promulgate substantive rules and regulations consistent with the provisions of any statute governing the activities of any licensing agency, board or committee located within the Division of Consumer Affairs, which shall be limited to disciplinary matters and arbitrary restrictions on initial licensure. In addition to promulgating such rules and regulations, the Attorney General may direct that any proposed or existing regulation be amended, abandoned or repealed. Prior to the final adoption of any regulation affecting the activities of any professional or occupational licensing agency, board or committee located within the division and prior to the issuance of any directive to amend, abandon or repeal any regulation, the Attorney General or his designee shall first consult with the agency, board or committee whose activities are affected regarding the proposed action.

(c) After a full consideration of all relevant facts and the applicable law, may direct the initiation of any appropriate enforcement action by a professional or occupational licensing board or set aside, modify or amend, as may be necessary, any action or decision of a licensing agency, board or committee located within the Division of Consumer Affairs; provided, however, no such action shall be directed by the Attorney General in reviewing the action or decision of any agency, board or committee unless such action or decision is contrary to applicable law.

45:1-18. Investigative powers of boards, director or Attorney General

Whenever it shall appear to any board, the director or the Attorney General that a person has engaged in, or is engaging in any act or practice declared unlawful by a statute or regulation administered by such board, or when the board, the director or the Attorney General shall deem it to be in the public interest to inquire whether any such violation may exist, the board or director through the Attorney General, or the Attorney General acting independently, may exercise any of the following investigative powers:

a.   Require any person to file on such form as may be prescribed, a statement or report in writing under oath, or otherwise, as to the facts and circumstances concerning the rendition of any service or conduct of any sale incidental to the discharge of any act or practice subject to an act or regulation administered by the board;

b.   Examine under oath any person in connection with any act or practice subject to an act or regulation administered by the board;

c.   Inspect any premises from which a licensed profession or occupation is conducted;

d.   Examine any goods, ware or item used in the rendition of any professional or occupational service;

e.   Examine any record, book, document, account or paper prepared or maintained by or for any professional or occupational licensee in the regular course of practicing such profession or engaging in such occupation or any individual engaging in practices subject to an act or regulation administered by the board. Nothing in this subsection shall require the notification or consent of the person to whom the record, book, account or paper pertains, unless otherwise required by law;

f.   For the purpose of preserving evidence of an unlawful act or practice, pursuant to an order of the Superior Court, impound any record, book, document, account, paper, goods, ware, or item used, prepared or maintained by or for any board licensee in the regular course of practicing such profession or engaging in such occupation or any individual engaging in a practice or activity subject to an act or regulation administered by the board. In such cases as may be necessary, the Superior Court may, on application of the Attorney General, issue an order sealing items or material subject to this subsection; and

g.   Require any board licensee, permit holder or registered or certified person to submit to an assessment of skills to determine whether the board licensee, permit holder or registered or certified person can continue to practice with reasonable skill and safety.

In order to accomplish the objectives of this act or any act or regulation administered by a board, the Attorney General may hold such investigative hearings as may be necessary and the board, director or Attorney General may issue subpoenas to compel the attendance of any person or the production of books, records or papers at any such hearing or inquiry.

45:1-19. Failure or refusal to file statement or report, refuse access to premises or failure to obey subpoena; penalty

If any person shall fail or refuse to file any statement or report or refuse access to premises from which a licensed profession or occupation is conducted in any lawfully conducted investigative matter or fail to obey a subpoena issued pursuant to this act, the Attorney General may apply to the Superior Court and obtain an order:

a.   Adjudging such person in contempt of court; or

b.   Granting such other relief as may be required; or

c.   Suspending the license of any such person unless and until compliance with the subpoena or investigative demand is effected.

45:1-20. Compelling testimony or production of book, paper or document; immunity from prosecution

If any person shall refuse to testify or produce any book, paper, or other document in any proceeding under this act for the reason that the testimony or evidence, documentary or otherwise, required of him may tend to incriminate him, convict him of a crime, or subject him to a penalty or forfeiture, and shall, notwithstanding, be directed to testify or to produce such book, paper, or document by the Attorney General, he shall comply with such direction.

A person who is entitled by law, to, and does assert such privilege, and who complies with such direction of the Attorney General shall not thereafter be prosecuted or subjected to any penalty or forfeiture in any criminal proceeding which arises out of and relates to the subject matter of the proceeding. No person so testifying shall be exempt from prosecution or punishment for perjury or false swearing committed by him in giving such testimony or from any civil or administrative action arising from such testimony.

45:1-21. Refusal to license or renew, grounds

A board may refuse to admit a person to an examination or may refuse to issue or may suspend or revoke any certificate, registration or license issued by the board upon proof that the applicant or holder of such certificate, registration or license:

a.   Has obtained a certificate, registration, license or authorization to sit for an examination, as the case may be, through fraud, deception, or misrepresentation;

b.   Has engaged in the use or employment of dishonesty, fraud, deception, misrepresentation, false promise or false pretense;

c   Has engaged in gross negligence, gross malpractice or gross incompetence which damaged or endangered the life, health, welfare, safety or property of any person;

d.   Has engaged in repeated acts of negligence, malpractice or incompetence;

e.   Has engaged in professional or occupational misconduct as may be determined by the board;

f.   Has been convicted of, or engaged in any acts constituting, any crime or offense involving moral turpitude or relating adversely to the activity regulated by the board. For the purpose of this subsection a judgment of conviction or a plea of guilty, non vult, nolo contendere or any other such disposition of alleged criminal activity shall be deemed a conviction;

g.   Has had his authority to engage in the activity regulated by the board revoked or suspended by any other state, agency or authority for reasons consistent with this section;

h.   Has violated or failed to comply with the provisions of any act or regulation administered by the board;

i.   Is incapable, for medical or any other good cause, of discharging the functions of a licensee in a manner consistent with the public's health, safety and welfare.

j.   Has repeatedly failed to submit completed applications, or parts of, or documentation submitted in conjunction with, such applications, required to be filed with the Department of Environmental Protection;

k.   Has violated any provision of P.L.1983, c.320 (C.17:33A-1 et seq.) or any insurance fraud prevention law or act of another jurisdiction or has been adjudicated, in civil or administrative proceedings, or a violation of P.L.1983, c.320 (C.17:33A-1 et seq.) or has been subject to a final order, entered in civil or administrative proceedings, that imposed civil penalties under that act against the applicant or holder;

l.   Is presently engaged in drug or alcohol use that is likely to impair the ability to practice the profession or occupation with reasonable skill and safety. For purposes of this subsection, the term "presently" means at this time or any time within the previous 365 days;

m.   Has prescribed or dispensed controlled dangerous substances indiscriminately or without good cause, or where the applicant or holder knew or should have known that the substances were to be used for unauthorized consumption or distribution;

n.   Has permitted an unlicensed person or entity to perform an act for which a license or certificate of registration or certification is required by the board, or aided and abetted an unlicensed person or entity in performing such an act;

o.   Advertised fraudulently in any manner.

The division is authorized, for purposes of facilitating determinations concerning licensure eligibility, to require the fingerprinting of each applicant in accordance with applicable State and federal laws, rules and regulations. Each applicant shall submit the applicant's name, address, and written consent to the director for a criminal history record background check to be performed. The division is authorized to receive criminal history record information from the State Bureau of Identification in the Division of State Police and the Federal Bureau of Investigation. Upon receipt of such notification, the division shall forward the information to the appropriate board which shall make a determination regarding the issuance of licensure. The applicant shall bear the cost for the criminal history record background check, including all costs of administering and processing the check, unless otherwise provided for by an individual enabling act. The Division of State Police shall promptly notify the division in the event an applicant or licensee, who was the subject of a criminal history record background check pursuant to this section, is convicted of a crime or offense in this State after the date the background check was performed.

For purposes of this act:

"Completed application" means the submission of all of the information designated on the checklist, adopted pursuant to section 1 of P.L.1991, c.421 (C.13:1D-101), for the class or category of permit for which application is made.

"Permit" has the same meaning as defined in section 1 of P.L.1991, c.421 (C.13:1D-101).

L.1978,c.73,s.8; amended 1991, c.420, s.1; 1997, c.151, s.10; 1999, c.403, s.2; 2003, c.199, s.31.

45:1-21.1. Information on DEP application compliance, seminar attendance

a.   A board obtaining information from the Department of Environmental Protection pursuant to section 1 of P.L.1991, c.418 (C.13:1D-110) on the compliance of a member of a regulated profession with the requirements for completed applications of the department, shall annually develop a detailed written summary of the information gathered by the department pursuant to P.L.1991, c.418 (C.13:1D-110) regarding compliance with the department's requirements for completed applications and attendance records for continuing education seminars required to be filed with the department pursuant to section 2 of P.L.1991, c.419 (C.13:1D-117).

b.   Any reasonable costs incurred in preparation of the report required pursuant to this section may be included in the charges authorized pursuant to P.L.1974, c.46 (C.45:1-3.2).

c.   Information required to be compiled by a board pursuant to this section, shall be deemed to be public records subject to the requirements of P.L.1963, c.73 (C.47:1A-1 et seq.).

45:1-21.2 Suspension of certain licenses, registrations, certifications for failure to repay student loans.

The director or a board shall suspend, as appropriate, after a hearing, the license, registration or certification of any person who has been certified by a lender or guarantor and reported to the director or the board, as the case may be, for nonpayment or default of a State or federal direct or guaranteed educational loan. The license, registration or certification shall not be reissued until the person provides the director or board with a written release issued by the lender or guarantor stating that the person has cured the default or is making payments on the loan in accordance with a repayment agreement approved by the lender or guarantor. If the person has continued to meet all other requirements for licensure, registration or certification during the suspension, reinstatement shall be automatic upon receipt of the notice and payment of any reinstatement fee the director or the board may impose.

45:1-21.3 Violation of the responsibility to make 911 calls, forfeiture of license, authorization to practice.

A health care professional licensed or otherwise authorized to practice as a health care professional pursuant to Title 45 of the Revised Statutes who violates the provisions of section 3 of P.L.2003, c.191 (C.30:6D-5.3) shall, in addition to being liable to a civil penalty pursuant to section 4 of P.L.2003, c.191 (C.30:6D-5.4), be subject to revocation of that individual's professional license or other authorization to practice as a health care professional by the appropriate licensing board in the Division of Consumer Affairs in the Department of Law and Public Safety, after appropriate notice and opportunity for a hearing.

45:1-21.4 Certain information relative to address of certain applicants, licensees; nondisclosure.

Notwithstanding any other law, rule or regulation to the contrary, the director or a board shall not disclose to the public information indicating the place of residence of any applicant for or holder of a license, registration or certification without the consent of the applicant or holder, except for such disclosure to a federal or State regulatory authority or a law enforcement or judicial authority.

45:1-22. Additional, alternative penalties

In addition or as an alternative, as the case may be, to revoking, suspending or refusing to renew any license, registration or certificate issued by it, a board may, after affording an opportunity to be heard:

a.   Issue a letter of warning, reprimand, or censure with regard to any act, conduct or practice which in the judgment of the board upon consideration of all relevant facts and circumstances does not warrant the initiation of formal action;

b.   Assess civil penalties in accordance with this act;

c.   Order that any person violating any provision of an act or regulation administered by such board to cease and desist from future violations thereof or to take such affirmative corrective action as may be necessary with regard to any act or practice found unlawful by the board;

d.   Order any person found to have violated any provision of an act or regulation administered by such board to restore to any person aggrieved by an unlawful act or practice, any moneys or property, real or personal, acquired by means of such act or practice; provided, however, no board shall order restoration in a dollar amount greater than those moneys received by a licensee or his agent or any other person violating the act or regulation administered by the board;

e.   Order any person, as a condition for continued, reinstated or renewed licensure, to secure medical or such other professional treatment as may be necessary to properly discharge licensee functions.

f.   Order any person, as a condition for continued, reinstated or renewed licensure, to submit to any medical or diagnostic testing and monitoring or psychological evaluation which may be required to evaluate whether continued practice may jeopardize the safety and welfare of the public;

g.   Order any person, as a condition for continued, reinstated or renewed licensure, to submit to an assessment of skills to determine whether the licensee can continue to practice with reasonable skill and safety, and to take and successfully complete educational training determined by the board to be necessary;

h.   Order any person, as a condition for continued, reinstated or renewed licensure, to submit to an assessment of skills to determine whether the licensee can continue to practice with reasonable skill and safety, and to submit to any supervision, monitoring or limitation on practice determined by the board to be necessary.

A board may, upon a duly verified application of the Attorney General that either provides proof of a conviction of a court of competent jurisdiction for a crime or offense involving moral turpitude or relating adversely to the regulated profession or occupation, or alleges an act or practice violating any provision of an act or regulation administered by such board, enter a temporary order suspending or limiting any license issued by the board pending plenary hearing on an administrative complaint; provided, however, no such temporary order shall be entered unless the application made to the board palpably demonstrates a clear and imminent danger to the public health, safety and welfare and notice of such application is given to the licensee affected by such order. If, upon review of the Attorney General's application, the board determines that, although no palpable demonstration of a clear and imminent danger has been made, the licensee's continued unrestricted practice pending plenary hearing may pose a risk to the public health, safety and welfare, the board may order the licensee to submit to medical or diagnostic testing and monitoring, or psychological evaluation, or an assessment of skills to determine whether the licensee can continue to practice with reasonable skill and safety.

In any administrative proceeding commenced on a complaint alleging a violation of an act or regulation administered by a board, such board may issue subpoenas to compel the attendance of witnesses or the production of books, records, or documents at the hearing on the complaint.

45:1-23. Summary proceeding in Superior Court; injunction; orders necessary to prevent unlawful practice or remedy past unlawful activity

Whenever it shall appear to a board, the director or the Attorney General that a violation of any act, including the unlicensed practice of the regulated profession or occupation, or regulation administered by such board has occurred, is occurring, or will occur, the Attorney General, in addition to any other proceeding authorized by law, may seek and obtain in a summary proceeding in the Superior Court an injunction prohibiting such act or practice. In any such proceeding the court may assess a civil penalty in accordance with the provisions of this act, order restoration to any person in interest of any moneys or property, real or personal acquired by means of an unlawful act or practice and may enter such orders as may be necessary to prevent the performance of an unlawful practice in the future and to fully remedy any past unlawful activity. In any action brought pursuant to this section, the court shall not suspend or revoke any license issued by a board.

45:1-24. Failure to pay penalties; enforcement

Upon the failure of any person to comply within 10 days after service of any order of a board directing payment of penalties or restoration of moneys or property, the Attorney General or the secretary of such board may issue a certificate to the Clerk of the Superior Court that such person is indebted to the State for the payment of such penalty and the moneys or property ordered restored. A copy of such certificate shall be served upon the person against whom the order was entered. Thereupon the clerk shall immediately enter upon his record of docketed judgments the name of the person so indebted and of the State, a designation of the statute under which the penalty is imposed, the amount of the penalty imposed, and the amount of moneys ordered restored, a listing of property ordered restored, and the date of the certification. Such entry shall have the same force and effect as the entry of a docketed judgment in the Superior Court, and the Attorney General shall have all rights and remedies of a judgment creditor in addition to exercising any other available remedies. Such entry, however, shall be without prejudice to the right of appeal to the Appellate Division of the Superior Court from the board's order.

An action to enforce the provisions of any order entered by a board or to collect any penalty levied thereby may be brought in any municipal court or the Superior Court in summary manner pursuant to the "penalty enforcement law" (N.J.S. 2A:58-1 et seq.) and the rules of court governing the collection of civil penalties. Process in such action shall be by summons of warrant, and in the event that the defendant fails to answer such action, the court shall issue a warrant for the defendant's arrest for the purpose of bringing such person before the court to satisfy any order entered.

45:1-25. Violations; penalties.

    a.   Any person who engages in any conduct in violation of any provision of an act or regulation administered by a board shall, in addition to any other sanctions provided herein, be liable to a civil penalty of not more than $10,000 for the first violation and not more than $20,000 for the second and each subsequent violation. For the purpose of construing this section, each act in violation of any provision of an act or regulation administered by a board shall constitute a separate violation and shall be deemed a second or subsequent violation under the following circumstances:

        (1) an administrative or court order has been entered in a prior, separate and independent proceeding;

        (2) the person is found within a single proceeding to have committed more than one violation of any provision of an act or regulation administered by the board; or

        (3) the person is found within a single proceeding to have committed separate violations of any provision of more than one act or regulation administered by a board.

    b.   In lieu of an administrative proceeding or an action in the Superior Court, the Attorney General may bring an action in the name of any board for the collection or enforcement of civil penalties for the violation of any provision of an act or regulation administered by such board. Such action may be brought in summary manner pursuant to the "Penalty Enforcement Law of 1999" P.L.1999, c.274 (C.2A:58-10 et seq.) and the rules of court governing actions for the collection of civil penalties in the municipal court where the offense occurred. Process in such action may be by summons or warrant and in the event that the defendant in such action fails to answer such action the court shall, upon finding an unlawful act or practice to have been committed by the defendant, issue a warrant for the defendant's arrest in order to bring such person before the court to satisfy the civil penalties imposed. In any action commenced pursuant to this section, the court may order restored to any person in interest any moneys or property acquired by means of an unlawful act or practice.

    c.   Any action alleging the unlicensed practice of a profession or occupation shall be brought pursuant to this section or, where injunctive relief is sought, by an action commenced in the Superior Court.

    d.   In any action brought pursuant to this act, a board or the court may order the payment of costs for the use of the State, including, but not limited to, costs of investigation, expert witness fees and costs, attorney fees and costs, and transcript costs.

45:1-26. Repeal of inconsistent acts and parts of acts

All acts and parts of acts inconsistent with this act are hereby superseded and repealed.

Updated through 9/16/09.

NEW JERSEY ADMINISTRATIVE CODE

TITLE 13, CHAPTER 31: ELECTRICAL CONTRACTORS REGULATIONS

SUBCHAPTER 1.   GENERAL RULES AND REGULATIONS

13:31-1.1 Board Meetings; quorum

(a) Regular Board meetings shall be held in accordance with a schedule that is published yearly and filed with the Secretary of State.

(b) Special meetings may be held at the request of a Board member or called by the Chairman with publication of appropriate notice pursuant to the requirements of the Open Public Meetings Act.

(c) A majority of the voting members of the Board shall constitute a quorum thereof and no action of the Board shall be taken except on the affirmative vote of a majority of the members of the entire Board.

(d) In the absence of the chairman, members shall select one of the members attending the meeting to serve as chairman for that meeting.

13:31-1.2 Definitions

The following words and terms, when used in this chapter, shall have the following meanings, unless the context clearly indicates otherwise:

"Act" means the Electrical Contractor Licensing Act of 1962, P.L. 1962, c.162, N.J.S.A. 45:5A-1 et seq.

"Apprentice" means a person who is enrolled in a four-year apprenticeship program approved by both a Federal agency and a Federally certified state agency.

"Board" means the Board of Examiners of Electrical Contractors established pursuant to N.J.S.A. 45:5A-3.

"Business permit holder" means an electrical contractor who has obtained a business permit pursuant to N.J.S.A. 45:5A-9.

"Licensee" means a person who has satisfied the requirements of N.J.A.C. 13:31-2.1 and 2.2 and has been issued a license as an electrical contractor by the Board pursuant to N.J.S.A. 45:5A-9.

"Minor repair work" shall include, without limitation, the replacement of lamps and fuses operating at less than 150 volts to ground with like or similar lamps or fuses.

"Qualified journeyman electrician" means:

1. A person who has a current license to practice electrical contracting issued by the Board;

2. A person who has acquired 8,000 hours of practical hands-on experience working with tools in the installation, alteration or repair of wiring for electric light, heat or power and who has had a minimum of 576 classroom hours of instruction in the installation, alteration or repair of wiring for electric light, heat or power. "Practical hands-on experience," as used in this definition, does not include time spent supervising, engaging in the practice of engineering, estimating or performing other managerial tasks; or

3. A person who can demonstrate that he or she has gathered the required experience through alternative means.

"Qualifying licensee" means a licensee who has satisfied the requirements of N.J.A.C. 13:31-2.1 and 2.2 and whose license qualifies a business permit holder to engage in the business of electrical contracting in the State of New Jersey.

"Regular employee" as used in N.J.S.A. 45:5A-18(l) means an individual who receives a regular salary for the performance of functions which include those associated with the installation, repair and maintenance of electrical work for the State, county, municipality, or school district which occupies the premises on which such work is done.

13:31-1.3 Bonds

An action may be maintained on the bond required by N.J.S.A. 45:5A-19 by any person injured, aggrieved or damaged through the failure of the obligor to perform the duties prescribed for electrical contractors under the provisions of N.J.S.A. 45:5A-1, et seq. or any rule of the Board.

13:31-1.4 Compliance with laws.

Electrical contractors and business permit holders shall comply with all general and special Federal, State and municipal laws, ordinances and regulations pertaining to the business of electrical contracting and those employed or engaged therein. Violations of any such Federal, State and municipal laws, ordinances and regulations may be deemed occupational misconduct within the meaning of N.J.S.A. 45:1-21(e) and may subject the licensee to disciplinary actions as set forth at N.J.S.A. 45:1-21 et seq.

13:31-1.5 Identification of licensees, permittee and qualified journeyman electricians; vehicles; stationery; advertising.

(a) All commercial vehicles utilized in the practice of licensed electrical contracting shall be visibly marked on both sides with the following information:

1. The name of the licensed electrical contractor in lettering at least three inches in height.

2. The words "Electrical Contractor license number" or "Electrical Contractor Lic.#" followed by the license number of the qualifying licensee and the words "Electrical Contractor business permit number" or "Electrical Contractor Bus. Permit #" followed by the business permit number of the business permit holder in lettering at least three inches in height; and

3. The name of the owner or lessee of the vehicle and the municipality from which the licensee practices or where the licensee has a principal office in lettering at least three inches in height.

    i. Where available space for lettering is limited, either by design of the vehicle or by the presence of other legally specified identification markings, making strict compliance with (a)1, 2 or 3 above impractical, the size of the lettering shall be as close to three inches high as possible within the limited space, provided the name is clearly visible and readily identifiable.

(b) All business correspondence and stationery shall display the following information:

1. The name of the licensed contractor;

2. The words "Electrical Contractor license number" or Electrical Contractor Lic.#" followed by the license number of the qualifying licensee and the words "Electrical Contractor business permit number" or "Electrical Contractor Bus. Permit #" followed by the business permit number of the business permit holder; and

3. The business address, including the street name and number, of the qualifying licensee.

(c) All advertising shall include the following information:

1. The name of the licensed electrical contractor;

2. The words "Electrical Contractor license number" or "Electrical Contractor Lic. #" followed by the license number of the qualifying licensee and the words "Electrical Contractor business permit number" or "Electrical Contractor Bus. Permit #" followed by the business permit number of the business permit holder; and

3. The business address, including the street name and number, of the qualifying licensee.

(d) Every licensed electrical contractor whose name, office address, place of practice, license number or business permit number appears or is mentioned in any advertisement of any kind or character shall be presumed to have caused, permitted or approved the advertising and shall be personally responsible for its content and character.

(e) No licensee shall perform electrical contracting work without having in his possession a business permit identification as provided in N.J.S.A. 45:5A-9.

13:31-1.6 Fee schedule

(a) The following fees shall be charged by the Board:

1. Application fee (non-refundable) $100.00

2. Initial license fee:

    i. If paid during the first year of a triennial renewal period 150.00

    ii. If paid during the second year of a triennial renewal period 100.00

    iii. If paid during the third year of a triennial renewal period 50.00

3. Triennial license renewal 150.00

4. Late renewal fee (within 30 days) 50.00
5. Reinstatement fee 100.00
6. Initial business permit:
    i.   If paid during the first year of a triennial renewal period 75.00
    ii.   If paid during the second year of a triennial renewal period 50.00
    iii. If paid during the third year of a triennial renewal period 25.00
7. Triennial business permit renewal 75.00
8. Late renewal fee, permit 25.00
9. Initial/replacement seal press 25.00
10. Duplicate license/business permit fee 25.00
11. Replacement wall license/business permit 40.00
12. Verification of licensure 25.00
13. Qualified journeyman electrician registration fee:
    i.   If paid during the first year of a triennial renewal period 60.00
    ii.   If paid during the second year of a triennial renewal period 40.00
    iii. If paid during the third year of a triennial renewal period 20.00
14. Qualified journeyman electrician registration renewal 60.00
15. Telecommunications wiring exemption-application fee and issuance of
    identification card (non-refundable) 120.00
16. Continuing education sponsor fee 100.00

13:31-1.7 Continuing education requirements

(a) Upon triennial license renewal, a licensee shall attest that he or she has completed courses of continuing education of the types and number of credits specified in (b), (c), (d) and (e) below. Falsification of any information submitted on the renewal application may require an appearance before the Board and may subject a licensee to disciplinary action as set forth at N.J.S.A. 45:1-21 et seq.

(b) Each applicant for triennial license renewal shall be required to complete, during the preceding triennial period, except as provided in (b)1 below, a minimum of 34 credit hours of continuing education.

1. Licensees shall not be required to complete the continuing education requirements for the triennial registration period in which they initially received licensure;

2. A licensee who completes more than the minimum continuing education credits set forth above in any triennial registration period may carry no more than eight of the additional credits into a succeeding triennial period;

3. Any continuing education credits completed by the licensee in compliance with an order or directive from the Board as set forth in (j) below shall not be used to satisfy the minimum continuing education requirements as set forth in this section.

(c) A licensee, who is not exempt pursuant to (b)1 above, shall complete a minimum of a 10 hour course of study relating to the most recent edition of the National Electrical Code, nine hours of which shall pertain to the code and one hour of which shall pertain to applicable State statutes and rules. A licensee shall obtain the balance of continuing education credits in the following areas:

1. Installation, erection, repair or alteration of electrical equipment for the generation, transmission or utilization of electrical energy

2. Transmission or utilization of electrical energy.

3. Job estimating, management and business practices;

4. Supervisory responsibilities as set forth in N.J.A.C. 13:31Ã'1.13; and

5. Any other subjects relevant to electrical contracting and electrical construction.

(d) A licensee may obtain continuing education credits from the following:

1.   Successful completion of continuing education courses or programs approved by the Board pursuant to (h) below. The Board shall approve only such continuing education courses and programs as are available and advertised on a reasonable nondiscriminatory basis to all persons practicing electrical contracting in the State and are directly related to the practice of electrical contracting in the State of New Jersey, except that an electrical contracting association or other professional or technical association offering continuing education programs or courses may impose a reasonable differential in program or course registration fees for licensees who are not members of that association. The Board shall maintain a list of all approved programs, courses and lecturers at the Board office and shall furnish this information to licensees upon request;

2.   Participation in instructional activities such as developing curriculum for a new program or course and/or teaching a new program or course, provided the program or course is directly related to the practice of electrical contracting in the State of New Jersey. "New" means that the licensee has never taught or developed curriculum for that course or program in any educational setting;

3.   Authorship of a textbook or manual or a chapter of a textbook or manual directly related to the practice of electrical contracting in the State of New Jersey, provided the textbook or manual, as published, is at least 7,500 words in length; and

4.   Authorship of a published article related to the practice of electrical contracting in the State of New Jersey, provided the article, as published, is at least 250 words in length.

(e)   Credit for continuing education shall be granted as follows for each triennial registration period:

1.   Attendance at continuing education programs and courses approved by the Board: one credit for each hour of attendance at an approved program or course. Credit shall not be granted for programs or courses that are less than one instructional hour long. Credit shall not be granted for more than eight instructional hours obtained in one day. Completion of an entire program or course or segment of program or course instruction shall be required in order to receive any continuing education credit;

2.   Participation in instructional activities: one credit per hour of program or course instruction to a maximum of 15 credits per triennial registration period;

3.   Authorship of a textbook or manual or a chapter of a textbook or manual: five continuing education credits per textbook or manual or chapter of a textbook or manual, to a maximum of 10 credits per triennial registration period; and

4.   Authorship of a published article: two continuing education credits per published article, to a maximum of eight credits per triennial registration period.

(f)   The Board may perform audits on randomly selected licensees or upon any licensee who is the subject of a complaint received by the Board or who is the subject of any Board investigation to determine compliance with continuing education requirements. A licensee shall maintain the following documentation for a period of six years after completion of the credits and shall submit such documentation to the Board upon request.

1.   For attendance at programs or courses approved by the Board: a certificate of completion from the sponsor;

2.   For publication of manual, textbook, or article: the published item, including the date of publication; and

3.   For developing curriculum or teaching a course or program: documentation, including a copy of the curriculum, location, date and time of course, duration of course by hour, and letter from sponsor confirming that the licensee developed or taught the course or program.

(g)   The Board may waive the continuing education requirements of this section on an individual basis for reasons of hardship, such as severe illness, disability, or military service, or for retirement of the license.

1.   A licensee seeking a waiver of the continuing education requirements shall apply to the Board in writing at least 90 days prior to license renewal and set forth in specific detail the reasons for requesting the waiver. The licensee shall provide the Board with such supplemental materials as will support the request for waiver.

2.   A waiver of continuing education requirements granted pursuant to this subsection shall only be effective for the triennial period in which such waiver is granted. If the condition(s) which necessitated the waiver persist(s) into the next triennial period, a licensee shall apply to the Board for the renewal of such waiver for the new triennial period.

(h) All sponsors of continuing education programs or courses shall:

1. Obtain Board approval, in each triennial period, prior to representing that any course, seminar or program fulfills the requirements of this section;

2. Submit the following for each course or program offered, for evaluation by the Board:

    i. A detailed description of course content and the hours of instruction; and

    ii. A curriculum vitae of each lecturer, including specific background which qualifies the individual as a lecturer in the area of instruction;

3. Monitor the attendance at each approved course and furnish to each enrollee a verification of attendance which shall include at least the following information:

    i. The title, date and location of program or course offering;

    ii. The name and license number of attendee;

    iii The number of the hours attended; and

    iv. The name and signature of officer or responsible party;

4. Solicit program or course evaluations from both participants and the instructors; and

5. Submit a fee pursuant to N.J.A.C. 13:31-1.6 for each submission of course or program offering(s) for which Board approval is sought, per triennial period. A sponsor shall submit any changes to an approved course or program offering, including changes to course content, hours of instruction, or course lecturer, to the Board for review. A sponsor shall submit the fee set forth at N.J.A.C. 13:31-1.6 upon submission of such changes.

(i) Sponsors of continuing education programs or courses shall not:

1. Teach the 10 hour course of study on the National Electrical Code set forth in (c) above prior to the January following the publication of the most recent edition of the National Electrical Code; and

2. Conduct a continuing education course or program with more than 75 participants.

(j) The Board may direct or order a licensee to complete continuing education credits:

1. As part of a disciplinary or remedial measure in addition to the required 34 hours of continuing education; or

2. To correct a deficiency in the licensee's continuing education requirements.

13:3 1.8 Notification of change of address or business name; service of process; termination or resignation of qualified licensee.

(a) Every licensee and business permit holder shall give notice to the Board of any change of his or her address of record within 10 days of such change. For purposes of this section, "address of record" means an address designated by a licensee or business permit holder which is part of the public record and which may be disclosed upon request. "Address of record" may be a licensee or business permit holder's home, business or mailing address, but shall not be a post office box.

(b) Service of an administrative complaint or other process initiated by the Board, the Attorney General or the Division of Consumer Affairs at the licensee or business permit holder's address of record shall be deemed adequate notice for the commencement of any inquiry or disciplinary proceeding against the licensee or business permit holder.

(c) A licensee who has been terminated or has resigned from his or her position as a qualifying licensee for a business shall immediately notify the Board of such termination or resignation.

(d) A licensee shall immediately notify the Board of any change in the name of the electrical contracting business in which he or she is engaged as the qualifying licensee.

SUBCHAPTER 2.   LICENSURE AND BUSINESS PERMIT REQUIREMENTS

13:31-2.1 Qualifications of applicants.

(a) Applicants for examination for a license as an electrical contractor shall present proof satisfactory to the Board that the applicant:

1. Is over the age of 21 years;

2.   Holds a high school diploma or equivalency certificate; and

3.   Has had, immediately preceding the submission of the application, at least five years of practical hands-on experience working with tools in the installation, alteration, or repair of wiring for electric light, heat or power, which work shall have been done in compliance with the National Electrical Code. "Practical hands-on experience" shall not include time spent in supervising, engaging in the practice of engineering, estimating and performing other managerial tasks. In the alternative, the applicant may satisfy the practical hands-on experience requirement by having:

   i.   Completed a four-year apprenticeship program approved by both a Federal agency and a Federally certified State agency and at least one year of practical hands-on experience as defined in (a)3 above. A certificate of completion issued by the apprenticeship program and a certification by an employer regarding the additional year of practical hands-on experience shall be submitted with the application for the electrical contractor's examination; or

   ii.   Satisfied the eligibility requirements for a qualified journeyman electrician as set forth in N.J.A.C. 13:31-5.1 and completed at least one year of practical hands-on experience as defined in (a)3 above. The applicant shall submit proof of having satisfied the eligibility requirements of a qualified journeyman electrician in N.J.A.C. 13:31-5.1 and a certification by an employer regarding the additional year of practical hands-on experience;

   iii.   Earned a bachelor's degree in electrical engineering and completed two years of practical hands-on experience as defined in (a)3 above. The applicant shall submit a copy of his or her diploma and a certification by an employer regarding the additional two years of practical hands-on experience; or

   iv.   Worked in the field of electrical contracting for at least five years immediately preceding the date of application. The applicant shall submit a certification by an employer establishing that the applicant has at least five years of practical hands-on experience as defined in (a)3 above.

13:31-2.2 Examinations

(a)   The Board examination shall be the National Electrical Contractor Licensing Examination developed by Thomson Prometric, LLC.

(b)   An applicant must obtain a passing grade on the National Electrical Contractor Licensing Examination. Any applicant who fails to pass the Board examination shall not be eligible to retake the examination for six months from the date of such failure.

(c)   An applicant shall complete all required application forms and questionnaires supplied by the Board. Examinations shall be held at least four times a year. Information about scheduled examinations and deadlines for submissions of completed applications including appropriate fees may be obtained from the Board offices at Post Office Box 45006, Newark, New Jersey 07101.

13:31-2.3 License renewal; suspension; reinstatement

(a)   A licensee shall renew his or her license for a period of three years from the last expiration date. The licensee shall remit a renewal application to the Board, along with the renewal fee set forth in N.J.A.C. 13:31-1.6, prior to the date of license expiration. A licensee who submits a renewal application within 30 days following the date of license expiration shall submit the renewal fee, as well as the late fee set forth in N.J.A.C. 13:31-1.6. A licensee who fails to submit a renewal application within 30 days of license expiration shall have his or her license suspended without a hearing.

(b)   A licensee who continues to engage in the practice of electrical contracting with a suspended license shall be deemed to be engaging in the unauthorized practice of electrical contracting and shall be subject to the penalties set forth in N.J.S.A. 45:1-25 et seq.

(c)   A licensee who has had his or her license suspended pursuant to (a) above may apply to the Board for reinstatement within five years following the date of license expiration. A licensee applying for reinstatement shall submit a renewal application, all past delinquent renewal fees and the reinstatement fee set forth in N.J.A.C. 13:31-1.6, as well as evidence of having completed all continuing education credits for the current triennial registration period within three years prior to the date of application for reinstatement, consistent with the requirements set forth in N.J.A.C. 13:31-1.7.

(d)   A licensee who has had his or her license suspended pursuant to (a) above who is applying for reinstatement more than five years following the date of license expiration shall submit a renewal application, all past delinquent renewal fees and the reinstatement fee set forth in N.J.A.C. 13:31-1.6, and shall retake and pass the National Electrical Contractor Licensing Examination.

(e) The Board shall send a notice of renewal to each licensee, at least 60 days prior to the expiration of the license. If the notice to renew is not sent 60 days prior to the expiration date, no monetary penalty or fines shall apply to the holder for any unlicensed practice during the period following the licensure expiration, not to exceed the number of days short of 60 before the renewals were issued.

13:31-2.4 Inactive license status

A licensee may, upon application to the Board, renew his or her license by choosing inactive status. A licensee electing to renew his or her license as inactive shall not engage in the practice of electrical contracting for the entire triennial registration period. An inactive licensee may resume the practice of electrical contracting upon application to the Board, which shall include the submission of the renewal fee set forth in N.J.A.C. 13:31-1.6 and evidence of having completed the continuing education requirements for the current triennial registration period within three years prior to the date of application for the return to active status, as set forth in N.J.A.C. 13:31-1.7.

SUBCHAPTER 3. STANDARD OF PRACTICE

13:31-3.1 Worker's compensation

(a) Business permit holders shall obtain the worker's compensation insurance required by the laws of this State covering employees employed by the business permit holder or his subcontractor. Business permit holders shall maintain on file a certificate of insurance evidencing such coverage.

(b) Business permit holders shall ensure that all temporary employees working under the supervision of the permit holders have obtained the required worker's compensation coverage.

13:31-3.2 Work standards and inspections

(a) Every licensee who performs or supervises the installation, erection, repair or alteration of electrical equipment for the generation, transmission or utilization of electrical energy subject to The Electrical Contractors Licensing Act of 1962, N.J.S.A. 45:5A-1 et seq., shall ensure that the work performed is in conformity with the standards of the State Uniform Construction Code Act, N.J.S.A. 52:27D-119 et seq., and its implementing rules set forth in the Uniform Construction Code, N.J.A.C. 5:23, in effect at the time work is performed.

(b) Every licensee who performs or supervises work described in (a) above shall secure permits when required and, within a reasonable time after completion of the work, secure an inspection of the completed work when required to ensure conformity with the State Uniform Construction Code Act, N.J.S.A. 52:27D-119 et seq., and its implementing rules set forth in the Uniform Construction Code, N.J.A.C. 5:23.

(c) Every licensee shall be responsible for correcting, within a reasonable time and at no additional charge to the customer, any Code violation discovered in the work performed or supervised by the licensee.

(d) Failure to comply with (a), (b) or (c) above may be deemed occupational misconduct within the meaning of N.J.S.A. 45:1-21(e) and may subject the licensee to disciplinary action as set forth in N.J.S.A. 45:1-21 et seq.

13:31-3.3 Pressure seal and signature requirements

(a) At the time of the issuance of the license or as soon thereafter as deemed appropriate, the Board shall furnish a pressure seal to every licensed electrical contractor. The cost of the pressure seal, as set forth in N.J.A.C. 13:31-1.6, shall be paid for by the licensed electrical contractor to whom it is issued. The pressure seal shall be used exclusively by the licensed electrical contractor in the conduct of his or her practice. The licensed electrical contractor shall be required to impress the pressure seal upon all applications for electrical inspection by the appropriate duly licensed State inspection agency and shall sign all applications for electrical permits. The pressure seal shall remain the property of the Board and shall be returned to the Board as provided in (c) below.

(b) No person, other than the electrical contractor to whom the license and business permit shall have been issued by the Board, shall have the right to use the pressure seal. Any violation of this provision shall subject the person wrongfully using the pressure seal, and the licensee who willfully or negligently allows such unlicensed and unauthorized person to use said seal to such penalties and sanctions or disciplinary action as shall be imposed by the Board pursuant to authority granted by N.J.S.A. 45:5A-1 et seq., 45:1-14 et seq. and 45:1-21 et seq.

(c) A licensee whose license is suspended or revoked as a result of either a disciplinary order or a failure to pay licensing fees, or who has registered with the Board as inactive pursuant to N.J.A.C. 13:31-2.4, or who has been terminated or has resigned from his or her position as a qualifying licensee for a business, shall immediately return to the Board the previously issued official pressure seal. A licensee seeking a new pressure seal following the return of a previously issued pressure seal to the Board shall remit the fee set forth in N.J.A.C. 13:31-1.6 for the issuance of the new pressure seal.

(d) If the person whose license qualified a business entity to engage in electrical contracting is rendered incapable of fulfilling his or her professional duties due to death, illness or other condition, the licensee or such other individual who may lawfully act for the business entity may delay returning the official pressure seal for at least six months provided that:

  1.   The Board is immediately notified in writing of the name of a new electrical contractor licensed by the Board, or a qualified journeyman electrician registered with the Board pursuant to N.J.A.C. 13:31-5.1, or other person with substantially equivalent experience who shall qualify the business entity during the interim period provided by this subsection; and

  2.   The business entity complies with all the provisions of the Electrical Contractors Licensing Act of 1962 and all regulations adopted thereafter.

(e) During this six month period, the business entity may complete work in progress and may contract for new work provided that all such electrical work is performed or supervised by the person whose name is provided to the Board pursuant to (d)1 above.

(f) The Board may, for good cause shown, extend by six months the interim period during which electrical contracting may be performed provided that the conditions set forth in (d) above are satisfied.

(g) By the end of either the initial six-month period or the additional six-month extension period, the pressure seal issued by the Board to the individual licensee, qualified journeyman electrician or other qualified person cited in (d) above shall be returned to the Board consistent with N.J.S.A. 45:5A-14.

13:31-3.4. Supervision of electrical work

(a) The qualifying licensee shall assume full responsibility for the inspection and supervision of all electrical work, other than electrical activities exempt pursuant to N.J.S.A. 45:5A-18, to be performed by the business permit holder in compliance with N.J.A.C. 13:31-1.4 and the State Uniform Construction Code Act, N.J.S.A. 52:27D-119 et seq., and its implementing rules set forth in the Uniform Construction Code, N.J.A.C. 5:23.

(b) The qualifying licensee shall:

  1.   Supervise the installation, erection, repair or alteration of electrical equipment for the generation, transmission or utilization of energy, other than electrical activities exempt pursuant to N.J.S.A. 45:5A-18, to ensure that such work is performed in compliance with N.J.A.C. 13:31-1.4 and with the State Uniform Construction Code Act, N.J.S.A. 52:27D-119 et seq., and its implementing rules set forth in the Uniform Construction Code, N.J.A.C. 5:23, in effect at the time that the work is performed.

  2.   Personally inspect the work of employees pursuant to (d) below;

  3.   Ensure that electrical workers are afforded the degree of personal on-site supervision commensurate with their level of competence and the complexity of the work to be performed pursuant to (d) below; and

  4.   Be present, on a regular and continuous basis, at the principal office of the business permit holder, where the business permit holder maintains a New Jersey office, or at work sites of electrical work performed in New Jersey, where the business permit holder does not maintain a New Jersey office.

(c) Every 10 employees who are performing electrical work at either one job site or who are performing electrical work at several jobs at different sites simultaneously shall be supervised, pursuant to (d) below, by a qualifying licensee or by a licensee or qualified journeyman electrician.

(d) qualifying licensee, licensee or qualified journeyman electrician shall provide the following supervision:

  1.   If the employee performing the work has less than three and one half years experience working under the State Uniform Construction Code Act, N.J.S.A. 52:27D-119 et seq., and its implementing rules set forth in the Uniform Construction Code N.J.A.C. 5:23, the qualifying licensee, licensee or qualified journeyman electrician shall ensure constant on-site supervision of the employee; or

  2.   If the employee performing the work has more than three and one half years experience working under the State Uniform Construction Code Act, N.J.S.A. 52:27D-119 et seq., and its implementing rules set forth

in the Uniform Construction Code, 5:23, the qualifying licensee, licensee or qualified journeyman electrician shall provide the employee with a verbal or written work order specifying the type of work to be performed, and at the conclusion of the job, the employee shall confirm that the work order has been completed.

(e) A qualifying licensee who violates any provision of this section shall be deemed to have engaged in occupational misconduct within the meaning of N.J.S.A. 45:1-21(e) and shall be subject to disciplinary action as set forth at N.J.S.A. 45:1-21 et seq.

13:31-3.5 Joint ventures; subcontracting of electrical work

(a) Where two or more persons form a joint venture for the purpose of contracting to perform electrical work in New Jersey, each party to the joint venture shall hold a business permit issued by the Board to engage in electrical contracting in New Jersey.

(b) The term "persons," as used in (a) above, is defined to mean individuals, corporations, partnerships or other business entities.

(c) An electrical contractor holding a business permit issued by the Board may only subcontract electrical work to a person or persons holding a business permit issued by the Board.

(d) An electrical contractor holding a business permit shall not subcontract electrical work to be performed by unlicensed persons. This provision shall not be interpreted to prohibit an electrical contractor holding a business permit from assigning electrical work to be performed by his or her unlicensed employees.

(e) The term "employee," as used in (d) above, is defined to mean persons hired to work on an ongoing and continuous basis, whose remuneration is reported on a Form W-2 to the Internal Revenue Service, and whose work is supervised pursuant to the provisions of N.J.A.C. 13:31-3.4.

13:31-3.6 Identification card required

(a) At the time of triennial renewal of the license and/or business permit, the Board shall furnish a wallet size identification card to every licensee. The card shall be used exclusively by the licensee in the conduct of his or her practice. A licensee who willfully or negligently allows an unlicensed or an unauthorized person to use his or her identification card shall be deemed to have engaged in occupational misconduct and shall be subject to disciplinary action as shall be imposed by the Board pursuant to authority granted by N.J.S.A. 45:5A-1 et seq., 45:1-14 et seq. and 45:1-21 et seq. The licensee shall be required to present the identification card upon request to the appropriate duly licensed inspection agency upon all applications for electrical permits.

(b) Use of an identification card by any person other than the licensee to whom it is issued or his duly authorized agent acting on the licensee's behalf shall be deemed to be the use or employment of dishonesty, fraud, deception, misrepresentation or false pretense. Such conduct shall be unlawful and may be grounds for the suspension or revocation of the license of the unauthorized user if he or she is already licensed by the Board or may result in other disciplinary action against such unauthorized user by the Board pursuant to N.J.S.A. 45:1-21 et seq. With respect to an unlicensed user, such conduct shall be grounds for the refusal to issue a State license at any point in the future or any other action permitted by law pursuant to the provisions of N.J.S.A. 45:1-14 et seq., including a finding that such person has engaged in the unlicensed practice of electrical contracting.

13:31-3.7 Unconscionable pricing

(a) A licensee of the State Board of Examiners of Electrical Contractors shall not charge an excessive fee for services. A fee is excessive when, after a review of the facts, a licensee of ordinary prudence and familiarity with local market rates would recognize that the price is so high as to be manifestly unconscionable or overreaching under the circumstances. The Board shall consider the following factors in determining whether a fee is excessive:

1. The time and effort required;

2. The novelty or difficulty of the job;

3. The skill required to perform the job properly;

4. Any special conditions placed upon the performance of the job by the person or entity for which the work is being performed;

5. The experience, reputation and ability of the licensee to perform the services;

6. The cost of materials; and

7. The price customarily charged in the locality for similar services.

(b) It shall constitute occupational misconduct within the meaning of N.J.S.A. 45:1-21(e) to charge an excessive price for services.

13:31-3.8 Activities requiring licensure and business permit

(a) The following words and terms, when used in this section, shall have the following meaning unless the context indicates otherwise.

"Service point" means the point of connection between the facilities of the public utility serving a customer and the premises wiring.

"Premises wiring" interior and exterior wiring, including power, lighting, control and signal circuit wiring, together with all of their associated hardware, fittings and wiring devices, both permanently and temporarily installed, that extends from the service point of utility conductors or source of power such as a battery, a solar photovoltaic system, or a generator, transformer or converter windings, to the outlets. Premises wiring does not include wiring internal to appliances, fixtures, motors, controllers, motor control centers, and similar equipment.

(b) Installing, maintaining or servicing wiring for the supplying of power from the service point on a customer's premises to an appliance or other equipment used by the customer for the purpose of light, heat or power, shall be performed only by a licensee holding a business permit, except as provided in N.J.S.A. 45:5A-18 and (c) below.

(c) Installing, maintaining or servicing wiring for the supplying of power from the service point on a customer's premises to an appliance or other equipment used by the customer for the purpose of light, heat or power may be performed by an employee of a public utility offering services that relate to an end user's premises wiring and determined by the Board of Public Utilities to be competitive, provided that the employee has obtained a license from the Board or is working under the supervision of such a licensee and the utility has obtained a business permit from the Board pursuant to N.J.S.A. 45:5A-9.

SUBCHAPTER 4 LICENSURE EXEMPTIONS

13:31-4.1 Limited telecommunications wiring exemption

(a) Pursuant to N.J.S.A. 45:5A-18, the Board may grant an exemption from the license and business permit requirements of N.J.S.A. 45:5A-9(a) to a business engaged in telecommunications wiring.

(b) For purposes of this subsection, "telecommunications wiring" wiring within a premises, either inside or outside a building for voice and/or data transmission at voltage(s) compatible with the system being installed and connected to an FCC recognized communication network at the point of connection provided by the public utility providing communication services to the customer. It shall also include the interconnection of data wiring between computers and/or terminals.

(c) An applicant for a telecommunications wiring exemption shall provide the following to the Board:

1. The full name and address of the applicant together with the nature of the business entity (for example, corporation, partnership or individual proprietorship) and the names and addresses of the owners, partners and/or officers of the entity;

2. A certification that the applicant is familiar with and is in full compliance with Part 68 of the Federal Communications Commission regulations (47 C.F.R. section 68.1 et seq.) concerning installation of telecommunications wiring and any other applicable Federal regulations;

3. A certification that the applicant is familiar with and will comply with applicable National Electrical Code requirements, including, but not limited to, Article 800 (communication circuits) and the State Uniform Construction Code Act, N.J.S.A. 52:27D-119 et seq., and its implementing rules set forth in the Uniform Construction Code, N.J.A.C. 5:23, and that the applicant will be responsible for obtaining any required local permits and inspections for all work;

4. A certification that the applicant shall not perform the following work unless or until an electrical contractor's business permit is obtained from the Board:

    i. Wiring defined by the National Electrical Code as service conductors (the conductors from the service point to the service disconnecting means), feeder (all circuit conductors between the service equipment, the source of a separately derived system, or other power supply source and the final branch-circuit overcurrent device), and branch circuit (the circuit conductors between the final overcurrent device protecting the circuit and the outlets(s)). Wiring between power supplies integral with telecommunication equipment and the telecommunication equipment is not intended to be prohibited.

ii. Telecommunications wiring from telecommunications equipment to power operated controlled equipment; or

iii. Installation of work in hazardous/classified areas as defined by Article 500 of the National Electrical Code. Classified areas are those in which hazardous liquids, vapors, gases, dusts and fiber are normally present (Division 1 locations) or may be present due to maintenance or equipment malfunction (Division 2 locations); and

5. A certification that the business shall not subcontract telecommunications wiring work to a person or business entity not having a business permit or a telecommunications wiring exemption issued by the Board.

(d) The application shall be accompanied by a processing fee set forth in N.J.A.C. 13:31-1.6.

(e) The Board may require a personal interview with the applicant.

(f) If the applicant meets Board requirements for exemption as set forth in this subsection, the Board shall issue a letter and an identification card designating the business as exempt.

(g) The exempt entity shall notify the Board in writing of any change of address within 10 days of the address change.

(h) The exempt entity shall notify the Board in writing of any change in name, ownership or form of ownership within 30 days of such change.

(i) After an opportunity to be heard pursuant to the Administrative Procedure Act, N.J.S.A. 52:14B-1 et seq., a telecommunications wiring exemption may be revoked on a showing that the exempt entity has engaged in the unlicensed practice of electrical contracting involving non-exempt electrical work; or that the exempt entity has a history of failure to pass local inspections or to obtain required permits; or for any reason which may serve as a basis to suspend, revoke or deny a license to engage in electrical contracting as more particularly set forth in N.J.S.A. 45:1-21 et seq.

(j) Nothing in this section shall preclude a licensed electrical contractor from performing telecommunications wiring.

13:31-4.2 Limited well drillers or pump installers exemption

(a) Well drillers or pump installers licensed pursuant to N.J.S.A. 58:4A-4.1 et seq., are exempt from the license and business permit requirements of N.J.S.A 45:5A-9(a) for work involving the installation, servicing, or maintenance of well or water pumps.

1. Such work includes any exterior wiring from the well or water pump to the outside of the building and any interior wiring from the exterior wall terminating at the load side terminals of the pump controller, pressure switch or disconnecting means for the pump which must be no more than 10 feet from the point where the exterior wiring enters the building.

2. Nothing in this section shall be deemed to exempt such work from permits and inspections required by the State Uniform Construction Code Act, N.J.S.A. 52:27D-119 et seq. and its implementing rules set forth in the Uniform Construction Code, N.J.A.C. 5:23.

13:31-4.3 Testing, servicing or repairing of electrical equipment or apparatus exemption

(a) For purposes of this section, the following words and terms shall have the following meanings, unless the context clearly indicates otherwise:

"Ballast" means a component of an electric-discharge lamp used to obtain the necessary circuit conditions for starting and operating the electric-discharge lamp.

"Branch circuit" means the circuit conductor between the final overcurrent device protecting the circuit and the outlet(s).

"Electrical equipment or apparatus" means utilization equipment, other than electric signs, that are connected to a branch circuit.

"Servicing or repairing" means restoration or improvement of electrical equipment or apparatus by replacing a component of the electrical equipment or apparatus that is worn or broken such that the electrical equipment or apparatus, once serviced or repaired, conforms to the manufacturer's original specifications. "Servicing or repairing" shall not be construed to permit the replacement of ballasts.

"Testing" means procedures used to determine proper operation of electric equipment or apparatus or to isolate non-functioning components of such equipment or apparatus.

"Utilization equipment" means equipment that utilizes electric energy for electronic, electromechanical, chemical, heating, lighting or similar purpose.

(b) Pursuant to N.J.S.A. 45:5A-18(c), testing, servicing or repairing of electrical equipment or apparatus, consistent with the provisions of this section, shall be exempt from the license and business permit requirements of N.J.S.A. 45:5A-9(a).

Updated through 12/15/08.

NEW JERSEY ADMINISTRATIVE CODE

TITLE 13, CHAPTER 31A: FIRE ALARM, BURGLAR ALARM AND LOCKSMITH LICENSEES AND BUSINESSES

SUBCHAPTER 1.   GENERAL PROVISIONS

13:31A-1.1 Purpose and scope

(a) The rules in this chapter implement the provisions of P.L. 1997, c.305, amending and supplementing the provisions of P.L. 1962, c.162, N.J.S.A. 45:5A-1 et seq., The Electrical Contractors Licensing Act, which created the Fire Alarm, Burglar Alarm and Locksmith Advisory Committee under the Board of Examiners of Electrical Contractors pursuant to N.J.S.A. 45:5A-23 et seq.

(b) Except as set forth in (c) below, this chapter shall apply to the following:

1. All applicants seeking licensure to engage in burglar alarm or fire alarm businesses as defined in N.J.A.C. 13:31A-1.2;

2. All applicants seeking licensure to engage in locksmithing services as defined in N.J.A.C. 13:31A-1.2;

3. Licensees engaged in the burglar alarm or fire alarm business or in the provision of locksmithing services in the State of New Jersey;

4. Persons who monitor burglar alarms and/or fire alarms and who, as part of the response to an alarm signal, send an agent to the premises to investigate the alarm signal or to reset the alarm system; and

5. Persons who send agents, in response to an alarm signal, to investigate the alarm signal or to reset the alarm system, after they have been notified by an alarm business or by a company that monitors the alarm, unless such persons are licensed by the State Police pursuant to the Private Detective Act set forth in N.J.S.A. 45:19-8 et seq.

(c) The provisions of this chapter shall not apply to:

1. Telephone utilities and cable television companies regulated by the Board of Public Utilities pursuant to N.J.S.A. 48:5A-1 et seq. and 48:17-8 et seq., and employees of such companies while performing the duties of their employment, as set forth in N.J.S.A. 45:5A-29(a).

2. Electrical contractors licensed by the Board pursuant to N.J.S.A. 45:5A-1 et seq., and their employees while performing the duties of their employment, as set forth in N.J.S.A. 45:5A-29(b).

3. Persons certified to engage in the fire protection contractor business by the Department of Community Affairs, or persons who hold fire protection contractor business permits issued by the Department of Community Affairs, pursuant to N.J.S.A. 52:27D-25n et seq., P.L. 2001, c.289 and their employees while performing the duties of their employment, as set forth in N.J.S.A. 45:5A-29(c).

4. Employees hired by an alarm business through a recognized trade union on a temporary basis which shall not exceed six months or one project, whichever is greater, as set forth in N.J.S.A. 45:5A-35(d).

5. The following individuals when engaged in the provisions of locksmithing services, as set forth in N.J.S.A. 45:5A-28;

    i. A person performing public emergency services for a governmental entity if that person is operating under the direction or control of the governmental entity;

    ii. A sales representative who offers a sales demonstration to licensed locksmiths;

    iii. An automobile service dealer or lock manufacturer, or their agents or employees, while servicing, installing, repairing or rebuilding locks from a product line utilized by that dealer or lock manufacturer;

    iv. A member of a trade union hired to install any mechanical locking device as part of a new building construction or renovation project; and

    v. A person using any key duplication machine or key blanks, except for keys marked "do not duplicate," "master key" or any other words or terms which depict restricted duplication of keys.

6. Engineers licensed pursuant to N.J.S.A. 45:8-27 et seq., who engage in the survey, design or preparation of specifications for equipment or for a system, if the survey, design or preparation of the specifications is part of a design for the construction of a new building or premises or a renovation of an

existing building or premises, which renovation includes components other than the installation of a burglar alarm, fire alarm or electronic security system. Licensed engineers engaged in the design or preparation of specifications for the equipment or system to be installed that are within the practice of professional engineering as defined in N.J.S.A. 45:8-28(b), shall also be exempt from the provisions of the Act.

7. Architects licensed pursuant to N.J.S.A. 45:3-1 et seq., who engage in the survey, design or preparation of specifications for equipment or for a system, if the survey, design or preparation of the specifications is part of a design for the construction of a new building or premises or a renovation of an existing building or premises, which renovation includes components other than the installation of a burglar alarm, fire alarm or electronic security system; and

8. Persons who monitor burglar alarms and/or fire alarms and whose only response to an alarm signal is to provide notification of the alarm signal to the person designated as the responsible party for the premises or to a third party.

(d) This chapter shall supercede any ordinance, resolution, rule or regulation of any municipality or county relating to the licensure or registration of burglar alarm, fire alarm or locksmith businesses.

(e) Notwithstanding (d) above, pursuant to N.J.S.A. 45:5A-36, this chapter shall not prohibit municipal regulation of door-to-door vendors or salespersons of burglar alarm, fire alarm, or electronic security systems or locksmithing services, nor shall it prohibit municipal consideration of alarm business service proposals in consent proceedings under the Cable Television Act, P.L.

13:31A-1.2 Definitions

The following words and terms, when used in this chapter, shall have the following meanings, unless the context clearly indicates otherwise:

"Act" means P.L. 1997, c.305, amended and supplemented the Electrical Contractors Licensing Act, P.L. 1962, c.162, N.J.S.A. 45:5A-1 et seq.

"Access control system" means a system that provides access to authorized persons and may record and report which persons entered or exited a facility or areas within a facility, which doors or areas were accessed while persons are within a facility, and the time that such activity occurred. "Access control systems" may include the use of keys, access cards, locks, card readers, biometric identification devices, recorders, printers and control devices. "Access control systems" may be independent systems or may be integrated with other electronic security systems.

"Board" means the Board of Examiners of Electrical Contractors established pursuant to N.J.S.A. 45:5A-3.

"Burglar alarm" means a security system comprised of an interconnected series of alarm devices or components, including systems interconnected with radio frequency signals, which emits an audible, visual or electronic signal indicating an alarm condition and providing a warning of intrusion, which is designed to discourage crime.

"Burglar alarm business" means the installation, servicing or maintenance of burglar alarms or electronic security systems, or the monitoring or responding to alarm signals when provided in conjunction with the installation, servicing or maintenance of burglar alarms or electronic security systems. "Burglar alarm business" shall also include the installation, servicing or maintenance of smoke detection systems in one and/or two family detached, residential dwellings.

"Business firm" means a partnership, corporation or other business entity engaged in the burglar alarm business, fire alarm business, or the provision of locksmithing services.

"Business license" means the authorization to provide fire alarm, burglar alarm, electronic security system or locksmithing services.

"Business qualifier" means a licensee who has satisfied the experience requirements set forth in N.J.A.C. 13:31A-2.1 or 3.1, who authorizes the holder of a business license to provide fire alarm, burglar alarm, electronic security system or locksmithing services.

"Commissioning" means to perform a system verification in order to test the system for service readiness.

"Committee" means the Fire Alarm, Burglar Alarm and Locksmith Advisory Committee established pursuant to N.J.S.A. 45:5A-23.

"Closed circuit television" or "CCTV" means a video security system that may include video cameras, IP (Internet Protocol) cameras, monitors, switches, camera enclosures, controls and other related devices. "Closed circuit television" may be an independent system or may be integrated with other electronic security systems.

"Division" means the New Jersey Division of Consumer Affairs in the Department of Law and Public Safety.

"Electronic security system" means a security system comprised of an interconnected series of devices or components, including systems with audio and video signals or other electronic systems, which emits or transmits an audible, visual or electronic signal warning of intrusion and provides notification of authorized entry or exit, which is designed to discourage crime. "Electronic security systems" include access control systems, CCTV systems, intercom systems and other electronic monitoring devices.

"Employee" means any person engaged in the burglar alarm business, fire alarm business, or the provision of locksmithing services who performs installation, servicing or maintenance of burglar alarms or fire alarms, or who performs locksmithing services for the business qualifier, other than an independent contractor.

"Fire alarm" means a security system comprised of an interconnected series of alarm devices or components, including systems interconnected with radio frequency signals, which emits an audible, visual or electronic signal indicating an alarm condition and which provides a warning of the presence of smoke or fire. "Fire alarm" does not include an energy management system whose primary purpose is telecommunications with energy control, the monitoring of the interior environment being an incidental feature thereto.

"Fire alarm business" means the installation, servicing or maintenance of fire alarms or electronic security systems, or the monitoring or responding to alarm signals when provided in conjunction with fire alarms or electronic security systems in any facility.

Installation" means the survey of a premises, the design and preparation of the specifications for the equipment or system to be installed pursuant to a survey, the installation of the equipment or system, or the demonstration of the equipment or system after the installation is completed.

"Intercom system" means an audio security communication system containing control circuitry that may include a feature designed to selectively release electronically secured doors.

"Licensed locksmith" means a person who is licensed pursuant to N.J.S.A. 45:5A-27 and the provisions of this chapter.

"Licensee" means a person licensed to engage in the burglar alarm business, the fire alarm business, or the provision of locksmithing services pursuant to N.J.S.A. 45:5A-27 and the provisions of this chapter.

"Locksmithing services" means the modification, recombination, repair or installation of mechanical locking devices and electronic security systems for any type of compensation and includes repairing, rebuilding, recoding, servicing, adjusting, installing, manipulating or bypassing of a mechanical or electronic locking device, for controlled access or egress to premises, vehicles, safes, vaults, safe doors, lock boxes, automatic teller machines, or other devices for safeguarding areas where access is meant to be limited. Locksmithing services also means operating a mechanical or electronic locking device, safe or vault by means other than those intended by the manufacturer of such locking devices, safes or vaults, and consulting and providing technical advice regarding selection of hardware and locking systems of mechanical or electronic locking devices and electronic security systems. "Locksmithing services" does not include the installation of a prefabricated lock set and door knob into a door of a resident.

"Person" means a person, firm, corporation or other legal entity.

"Smoke detection system" means an electronic system consisting of a control unit (which may be a component of a combination fire/burglar control panel), smoke detector(s), heat detector(s), if required, audible appliance(s) and battery back-up, as utilized in one and/or two family detached, residential dwellings.

"Verification" means the testing of a system with sufficient thoroughness so as to ascertain that every primary and secondary operation coincides with each appropriate initiating device or zone's activation ensuring correct system operation.

13:31A-1.3 Office of the Committee
The office of the Committee shall be maintained at 124 Halsey Street, Newark, New Jersey. The mailing address of the Committee is PO Box 45042, Newark, New Jersey. The telephone number of the Committee is (973) 504-6245.

13:31A-1.4 Fees

(a) The following fees shall be charged by the Committee:

1. Initial application fee $150.00

2. Application fee for second/and/or third license issued by the Committee $100.00

3. Initial license fee:

   i. If paid during the first year of a triennial renewal period $120.00

   ii. If paid during the second year of a triennial renewal period $80.00

   iii. If paid during the third year of a triennial renewal period $40.00

4. Initial Business License fee (100 or more employees):

   i. If paid during the first year of a triennial renewal period $150.00

   ii. If paid during the second year of a triennial renewal period $100.00

   iii. If paid during the third year of a triennial renewal period $50.00

5. Initial Business License fee (less than 100 employees):

   i. If paid during the first year of a triennial renewal period $75.00

   ii. If paid during the second year of a triennial renewal period $50.00

   iii. If paid during the third year of a triennial renewal period $25.00

6. Triennial license renewal fee $120.00

7. Triennial business license renewal fee (100 or more employees) $150.00

8. Triennial business license renewal fee (less than 100 employees) $75.00

9. Inactive renewal fee .... (to be established by the Director)

10. Late renewal fee (within 30 days of renewal date) ....
.... (to be established by rule by the Director)

11. Reinstatement fee (more than 30 days after renewal date)...
.... (to be established by rule by the Director)

12. Employee listing fee $75.00

13. Employee listing renewal fee $50.00

14. Reciprocity license fee $120.00

15. Continuing education program sponsor fee $100.00

13:31A-1.5 License renewal; inactive status

(a) The Committee shall send a notice of renewal to all licensees at least 60 days prior to the date of license expiration. If the notice to renew is not sent at least 60 days prior to the license expiration date, no monetary penalties or fines shall apply to a licensee for any unlicensed practice during the period following licensure expiration, not to exceed the number of days short of 60 before the renewals were issued.

(b) All licensees shall be issued by the Committee for a three-year period. A licensee who seeks renewal of the license shall submit a license renewal application and the license renewal fee set forth in N.J.A.C. 13:31A-1.4 prior to the expiration of the current license.

(c) Renewal applications shall provide the applicant with the option of either active or inactive status. A licensee electing inactive status shall pay the inactive licensee fee set forth in N.J.A.C. 13:31A-1.4 and shall not engage in the burglar alarm business, the fire alarm business, or the provision of locksmithing services.

(d) If the licensee does not renew his or her license prior to its expiration date, the licensee may renew it within 30 days of its expiration by submitting a renewal application, a license renewal fee and a late fee, as set forth in N.J.A.C. 13:31A-1.4.

(e) A license that is not renewed within 30 days of its expiration shall be automatically suspended. An individual who continues to practice with a suspended license shall be deemed to be engaged in unlicensed practice.

13:31A-1.6 Change of license status; inactive to active

A licensee, upon application to the Committee, may change from inactive to active status upon payment of the renewal fee set forth in N.J.A.C. 13:31A-1.4, and upon submission of a certification verifying the completion of the continuing education requirements set forth in N.J.A.C. 13:31A-1.12 for the current renewal period within three years prior to the date of application.

13:31A-1.7 Reinstatement of suspended license

(a) An individual whose license has been automatically suspended for nonpayment of a triennial license renewal fee shall be reinstated by the Committee, provided the applicant otherwise qualifies for licensure pursuant to N.J.A.C. 13:31A-2.1 or 3.1, and submits a completed reinstatement application and one of the following to the Committee:

  1. A certification or licensure in good standing from any other state or jurisdiction in which the applicant has engaged in the burglar alarm or fire alarm business or in the provision of locksmithing services during the period the license was suspended in this State;

  2. A certification by the applicant stating that he or she has engaged in the burglar alarm or fire alarm business, or in the provision of locksmithing services, in a state or jurisdiction which does not require certification or licensure, during the period the license was suspended in this State; or

  3. A certification stating that the applicant has not engaged in the burglar alarm or fire alarm business or in the provision of locksmithing services in this or any other jurisdiction during the period the license was suspended in this State.

(b) An individual who has engaged in the burglar alarm or fire alarm business or in the provision of locksmithing services in the manner described in (a)1 or 2 above shall submit written verification, on a form provided by the Committee, from all of the applicant's employers. The verification shall document dates of employment from the date the New Jersey license was suspended to the date of application for reinstatement, and the name, address and telephone number of each employer.

(c) An individual whose license has been automatically suspended for a period of between two and five years shall complete the continuing education requirements, as set forth in N.J.A.C. 13:31A-1.12, for each renewal period the license was suspended.

(d) An individual whose license has been automatically suspended for a period of five or more years shall take the examination required for initial licensure, set forth in N.J.A.C. 13:31A-2.3 or 3.2.

(e) Prior to reinstatement, an applicant shall pay a reinstatement fee and all past delinquent triennial renewal fees pursuant to N.J.A.C. 13:31A-1.4.

13:31A-1.8 Change of address; service of process

(a) A licensee shall notify the Committee in writing of any change of address from that registered with the Committee and shown on the most recently issued license. Such notice shall be sent to the Committee by certified mail, return receipt requested, not later than 30 days following the change of address. Failure to notify the Committee of any change of address may result in disciplinary action in accordance with N.J.S.A. 45:1-21(h).

(b) Service of an administrative complaint or other Committee-initiated action at a licensee's address which is on file with the Committee shall be deemed adequate notice for the purposes of N.J.A.C. 1:1-7.1 and the commencement of any disciplinary proceedings.

(c) A licensee shall, within 30 days of receiving notice of disciplinary action taken against the licensee in any state, territory or jurisdiction, report to the Committee in writing of such notification and provide a copy of the notification and the underlying documentation of the disciplinary action.

13:31A-1.9 Suspension, revocation or refusal to issue or renew license

(a) The Committee may, pursuant to the provisions of N.J.S.A. 45:1-14 et seq., the Act and this chapter, deny admittance to the fire alarm, burglar alarm or locksmith licensing examinations, deny, refuse to renew, suspend or revoke a license or issue a civil penalty under this section, upon proof that an applicant or licensee:

  1. Has obtained a license through fraud, deception or misrepresentation;

  2. Has engaged in the use or employment of dishonesty, fraud, deception, misrepresentation, false promise or false pretense;

  3. Has engaged in gross negligence, gross malpractice or gross incompetence which damaged or endangered the life, health, welfare, safety or property of any person;

  4. Has engaged in repeated acts of negligence, malpractice or incompetence;

  5. Has engaged in professional misconduct as outlined in N.J.A.C. 13:31A- 1.15;

6.　Has been convicted of, or engaged in acts constituting, any crime in the first, second or third degree, or any crime relating adversely to the burglar alarm or fire alarm business or the provision of locksmithing services within 10 years prior to the filing of the application;

7.　Has been convicted of the fourth degree offense of engaging in the unlicensed practice of electrical contracting;

8.　Has had the authority to engage in the burglar alarm or fire alarm business or the provision of locksmithing services revoked or suspended by any other state, agency or authority for reasons consistent with this subsection;

9.　Has had an application to engage in the installation or maintenance of fire protection equipment denied by the Department of Community Affairs, pursuant to N.J.S.A. 52:27D-25n et seq.;

10.　Has violated or failed to comply with the provisions of any law or regulation administered by the Committee;

11.　Is incapable, for medical or other good cause, of discharging the functions of a licensee in a manner consistent with the public health, safety and welfare;

12.　Has violated any provisions of the New Jersey Insurance Fraud Prevention Act, N.J.S.A. 17:33A-1 et seq., or any insurance fraud prevention act of another jurisdiction, or has been adjudicated, in civil or administrative proceedings, of violating N.J.S.A. 17:33A-1 et seq., or has been subject to a final order, entered in civil or administrative proceedings, that imposes civil penalties under that act against the applicant or the licensee;

13.　Is presently engaged in drug or alcohol use that is likely to impair the ability to engage in the burglar alarm or fire alarm business or the provision of locksmithing services with reasonable skill and safety. For purposes of this subsection, the term "presently" means at this time or any time within the previous 365 days;

14.　Has permitted an unlicensed person or entity to perform an act for which a license is required by the Committee or the Board, or aided and abetted an unlicensed person or entity in performing such an act; or

15.　Advertised fraudulently in any manner.

(b)　In addition to the consequences listed in (a) above, the Committee may impose additional or alternative penalties pursuant to N.J.S.A. 45:1-14 et seq. for violations of any provision of the Act and this subchapter.

(c)　In addition to the express consequences of (a) and (b) above, the Committee may enforce consequences arising from actions taken by other statutory authorities.

(d)　The denial, refusal to issue or renew, suspension or revocation of a license, and/or the issuance of a civil penalty under this section may be ordered by a decision of a majority of the Committee after notice and an opportunity to be heard in accordance with the Administrative Procedure Act, N.J.S.A 52:14B-1 et seq. and the Uniform Administrative Procedure Rules, N.J.A.C. 1:1.

(e)　An application may be made to the Committee for reinstatement of a revoked license if the revocation has been in effect for at least one year. The reinstatement shall be granted upon an affirmative vote by a majority of the Committee.

13:31A-1.10　Qualifications for licensure for applicants licensed in other states

(a)　Any person with a valid registration, certification or license to engage in the burglar alarm or fire alarm business or the provision of locksmithing services issued by another state or possession of the United States or the District of Columbia may, upon the submission of a Committee-provided application and the payment of the fee set forth in N.J.A.C. 13:31A-1.4, be issued a license to engage in the burglar alarm or fire alarm business or the provision of locksmithing services in the State, whichever is applicable, provided that:

1.　The experience and knowledge requirements in such other jurisdictions are equal or greater to those required by New Jersey at the time of application, as set forth in N.J.A.C. 13:31A-2.1 or 3.1;

2.　The applicant submits an application for licensure by reciprocity to the Committee;

3.　The applicant submits verification from all states in which he or she holds a registration, certification or license to engage in the burglar alarm or fire alarm business or in the provision of locksmithing services, whichever is applicable, establishing that such registrations, certifications or licenses are in good standing;

4.　The applicant successfully completes the burglar alarm, fire alarm or locksmith examination, whichever is applicable, as set forth in N.J.A.C. 13:31A-2.3 or 3.2;

5.   The applicant successfully completes, within three years immediately preceding the date of application, two hours of training in the Barrier Free Subcode, N.J.A.C. 5:23-7, two hours of training in the New Jersey Uniform Construction Code, N.J.A.C. 5:23, exclusive of the Barrier Free Subcode, two hours of training in the Americans with Disabilities Act Code, 36 CFR 1191, and two hours of training in industrial safety; and

6.   The applicant submits his or her fingerprints for the purpose of permitting a criminal history records check.

(b)   Notwithstanding (a) above, an applicant for licensure by reciprocity may be denied a license to engage in the burglar alarm or fire alarm business or the provision of locksmithing services in the State pursuant to the provisions of N.J.A.C. 13:31A-1.9.

13:31A-1.11   Waiver

Any applicant for licensure or any licensee engaged in the burglar alarm business, the fire alarm business, or the provision of locksmithing services desiring a waiver or release from the express requirements of any provision of this chapter may make such request, in writing, to the Committee. The applicant or licensee shall describe the conditions or reasons for the proposed waiver, including the reference of the specific rule which necessitates the proposal. A waiver shall be granted only by the Committee, in writing, for good cause and then only when the waiver does not contravene the purposes of the Act.

13:31A-1.12   Continuing education requirements

(a)   Upon triennial license renewal, a licensee shall attest that he or she has completed courses of continuing education of the types and number of credits specified in (b), (c), (d) and (e) below. Falsification of any information submitted on the renewal application may require an appearance before the Committee and may result in penalties and/or suspension of the license pursuant to N.J.S.A. 45:1-21 et seq.

(b)   Each applicant for triennial license renewal shall complete during the preceding triennial period, except as provided in (b)1 below, a minimum of 36 credits of continuing education. Applicants who hold multiple licenses issued by the Committee shall complete 36 credits of continuing education for each license held, except as provided in (b)3 below.

1.   Applicants shall not be required to complete continuing education requirements for the triennial registration period in which they initially received licensure.

2.   A licensee who completes more than the minimum continuing education credits set forth above in any triennial registration period may carry no more than eight of the additional credits into a succeeding triennial period.

3.   The holder of multiple licenses issued by the Committee may apply a maximum of 12 credits obtained in satisfaction of the 36 credits required for one license pursuant to this section toward satisfaction of the 36 continuing education credits required for his or her second and third Committee-issued license(s), if applicable.

4.   Any continuing education credits completed by the licensee in compliance with an order or directive from the Board as set forth in (i) below may not be used to satisfy the minimum continuing education requirements as set forth in this section.

(c)   A licensee shall complete a minimum of two continuing education credits in the Barrier Free Subcode, N.J.A.C. 5:23-7, two continuing education credits in the New Jersey Uniform Construction Code, N.J.A.C. 5:23, exclusive of the Barrier Free Subcode, two continuing education credits in the Americans with Disabilities Act Code, 36 CFR 1191 and two continuing education credits in industrial safety per triennial registration period. A licensee seeking renewal of a burglar alarm license shall complete a minimum of three credits of continuing education per triennial registration period in smoke detection systems. A licensee may take a maximum of 12 credits per triennial registration period in continuing education courses related to business and/or law. A licensee shall obtain the balance of continuing education credits in trade-related subjects.

(d)   A licensee may obtain continuing education credits from the following:

1.   Successful completion of continuing education courses or programs approved by the Committee pursuant to (h) below. The Committee shall approve only such continuing education courses and programs as are available and advertised on a reasonable nondiscriminatory basis to all persons providing burglar alarm, fire alarm or locksmithing services in the State and are related to the provision of such services in

the State of New Jersey. The Committee shall maintain a list of all approved programs, courses and lectures at the Committee office and shall furnish this information to licensees upon request.

2.   Participation in instructional activities, such as developing curriculum for a new program or course and/or teaching a new program or course, provided the program or course is related to the provision of burglar alarm, fire alarm or locksmithing services in the State of New Jersey. "New" means that the licensee has never taught or developed curriculum for that course or program in any educational setting, except as provided below.

i.   A licensee shall receive continuing education credit for teaching Committee-approved continuing education courses related to the Barrier Free Subcode, the New Jersey Uniform Construction Code, the Americans with Disabilities Act Code and industrial safety, pursuant to (c) above, irrespective of whether the licensee has previously taught the course.

ii.   A licensee who teaches such a course shall be deemed to have satisfied the continuing education credit requirements set forth in (c) above in Barrier Free Subcode, New Jersey Uniform Construction Code, Americans with Disabilities Act Code or industrial safety, as applicable to the course taught, for the triennial licensing period during which the course was taught.

3.   Authorship of a textbook or manual directly related to the provision of burglar alarm, fire alarm or locksmithing services in the State of New Jersey, provided the textbook or manual, as published, is at least 7,500 words in length; and

4.   Authorship of a published article related to the provision of burglar alarm, fire alarm or locksmithing services in the State of New Jersey, provided the article, as published, is at least 250 words in length.

(e) Credit for continuing education shall be granted as follows for each triennial registration period:

1.   Attendance at continuing education programs and courses approved by the Committee: one credit for each hour of attendance at an approved program or course. Credit shall not be granted for programs or courses that are less than one instructional hour long. Credit shall not be granted for more than eight instructional hours obtained in one day. Completion of an entire program or course or segment of program or course instruction shall be required in order to receive any continuing education credit;

2.   Participation in instructional activities: one credit per hour of program or course instruction to a maximum of 15 credits per triennial registration period;

3.   Authorship of a textbook or manual: five continuing education credits per textbook or manual, to a maximum of 10 credits per triennial registration period; and

4.   Authorship of a published article: two continuing education credits per published article, to a maximum of eight credits per triennial registration period.

(f) The Committee shall perform audits on randomly selected licensees to determine compliance with continuing education requirements. A licensee shall maintain the following documentation for a period of six years after completion of the credits and shall submit such documentation to the Committee upon request:

1.   For attendance at programs or courses approved by the Committee: a certificate of completion from the sponsor;

2.   For publication of a manual, textbook, or article: the published item, including the date of publication; and

3.   For developing curriculum or teaching a course or program: documentation, including a copy of the curriculum, location, date and time of course, duration of course by hour, and letter from the sponsor confirming that the licensee developed or taught the course or program.

(g) The Board may waive the continuing education requirements of this section on an individual basis for reasons of hardship, such as severe illness, disability, or military service.

1.   A licensee seeking a waiver of the continuing education requirements shall apply to the Committee in writing at least 90 days prior to license renewal and set forth in specific detail the reasons for requesting the waiver. The licensee shall provide the Committee with such supplemental materials as will support the request for waiver.

2.   A waiver of continuing education requirements granted pursuant to this subsection shall only be effective for the triennial period in which such waiver is granted. If the condition(s) which necessitated the

waiver persists into the next triennial period, a licensee shall apply to the Committee for the renewal of such waiver for the new triennial period.

(h) All sponsors of continuing education programs or courses shall:

1. Obtain Committee approval, in each triennial period, prior to representing that any course, seminar or program fulfills the requirements of this section. All sponsors who have received certification from the International Association for Continuing Education and Training (IACET) shall be pre-approved by the Committee for trade-related subjects and shall not be required to comply with the requirements of (h)2 and 5 below, except that such sponsors shall be required to submit a detailed description of course content and hours of instruction for each course, seminar or program offered.

2. Submit the following for each course or program offered, for evaluation by the Committee:

   i. Detailed description of course content and the hours of instruction; and

   ii. Curriculum vitae of each lecturer, including specific background which qualifies the individual as a lecturer of repute in the area of instruction.

3. Monitor the attendance at each approved course and furnish to each enrollee a verification of attendance, which shall include at least the following information:

   i. Title, date and location of program or course offering;

   ii. Name and license number of attendee;

   iii. Number of hours attended; and

   iv. Name and signature of officer or responsible party;

4. Solicit program or course evaluations from both participants and the instructors; and

5. Submit a fee pursuant to N.J.A.C. 13:31A-1.4 for each submission of course or program offering(s) for which Committee approval is sought.

(i) The Committee may direct or order a licensee to complete additional continuing education credits:

1. As part of a disciplinary or remedial measure in addition to the required 36 hours of continuing education credit; or

2. To correct a deficiency in the licensee's continuing education requirements.

13:31A-1.13 Advertising

(a) The following words and terms, when used in this section, shall have the following meanings, unless the context clearly indicates otherwise:

"Advertisement" means an attempt, directly or indirectly, by publication, dissemination, or circulation in print, electronic or other media, to induce any person or entity to purchase or enter into an agreement to purchase burglar alarm, fire alarm or locksmithing services or goods related thereto.

"Electronic media" means radio, television, telephone, internet, and other electronic means of communication.

"Print media" means business cards, newspapers, magazines, periodicals, professional journals, telephone directories, circulars, handbills, flyers, billboards, signs, direct mail, match covers and other items disseminated by means of the printed word.

"Range of fees" means a statement of fees containing an upper and lower limit on the fees charged for services or goods offered by a licensee under this subchapter.

(b) A licensee shall be able to substantiate the truthfulness of any material, objective assertion or representation set forth in an advertisement.

(c) A licensee who is a principal, partner or officer of a firm or entity identified in an advertisement for the provision of burglar alarm, fire alarm or locksmithing services, goods or devices shall be responsible for the form and content of any advertisement disseminated by or on behalf of a person employed by the firm.

(d) A licensee shall ensure that an advertisement does not misrepresent, suppress, omit or conceal a material fact. Omission, suppression or concealment of a material fact includes directly or indirectly obscuring a material fact under circumstances where the licensee knows or should know that the omission is improper or prohibits a prospective client from making a full and informed judgment on the basis of the information set forth in the advertisement.

(e) A licensee shall include the following in all advertisements and professional representations, other than an office entry sign, including advertisements in a classified directory, business cards and professional stationery:

    1. The name and license number of the licensee;

    2. The words "Burglar Alarm Business License Number" or "Burglar Alarm Business Lic. #," "Fire Alarm Business License Number" or "Fire Alarm Business Lic. #" or "Locksmith Business License Number" or "Locksmith Business Lic. #," or any combination thereof, as applicable; and

    3. The street address and telephone number of the business office.

(f) All commercial vehicles used in the burglar alarm business, the fire alarm business, or the provision of locksmithing services shall be marked on both sides with the following information:

    1. The business name of the licensee in lettering at least three inches in height;

    2. The words "Burglar Alarm Business License Number" or "Burglar Alarm Business Lic. #," "Fire Alarm Business License Number" or "Fire Alarm Business Lic. #" or "Locksmith Business License Number" or "Locksmith Business Lic. #" or any combination thereof, as applicable, along with the relevant number; and

    3. The name of the municipality from which the licensee practices or where the licensee has a principal office, in lettering at least three inches in height.

        i. Where available space for lettering is limited, either by design of the vehicle or by the presence of other legally specified identification markings, making strict compliance with (f)3 above impractical, the size of the lettering shall be as close to three inches high as is possible within the limited space, provided the name is clearly visible and readily identifiable.

(g) Advertisements regarding fees shall be limited to those which contain a fixed or a stated range of fees for specifically described burglar alarm, fire alarm or locksmithing services.

(h) A licensee who advertises a fee or range of fees shall include the following disclosures in any such advertisement:

    1. All relevant and material variables and considerations which are ordinarily included in the advertised services so that the fee will be clearly understood by prospective clients. In the absence of such disclosures, the stated fees shall be presumed to include everything ordinarily required for the advertised services;

    2. The additional services contemplated and the fee to be charged therefor. In the absence of such disclosures, the licensee shall be prohibited from charging an additional fee for the advertised service; and

    3. The period during which the advertised fee will remain in effect. In the absence of such disclosure, the advertisement shall be deemed to be effective for 30 days from the date of its publication.

(i) The advertisement of any specific fee shall not preclude the licensee from decreasing the fee or waiving the fee in individual circumstances.

(j) A licensee shall not offer a professional service which the licensee knows or should know is beyond his or her ability or expertise to perform.

(k) A licensee shall not advertise by using any technique or communication which appears to intimidate, exert undue pressure or unduly influence a prospective client.

(l) An advertisement containing a lay or an expert testimonial shall be based upon the testimonial giver's personal knowledge or experience obtained from a relationship with the licensee or upon the testimonial giver's direct personal knowledge of the subject matter of the testimonial.

(m) Prior to using the testimonial, the licensee shall obtain a signed, notarized statement and release indicating the testimonial giver's willingness to have his or her testimonial used in the advertisement.

(n) A layperson's testimonial shall not attest to any technical matter beyond the layperson's competence to comment upon.

(o) An expert testimonial shall be rendered only by an individual possessing specialized expertise sufficient to allow the rendering of a bona fide statement or opinion.

(p) A licensee shall be able to substantiate any statement of fact appearing in a testimonial.

(q) Where a licensee directly or indirectly provides compensation to a testimonial giver, the fact of such compensation shall be conspicuously disclosed in a legible and readable manner in any advertisement in the following language or its substantial equivalent: COMPENSATION HAS BEEN PROVIDED FOR THIS TESTIMONIAL.

(r) A licensee shall retain for a period of three years from the date of initial publication or dissemination, a copy of every advertisement appearing in print or electronic media. The licensee shall indicate on all advertisements in his or her possession the date and place of publication or dissemination.

(s) Documentation relating to the use of testimonials shall be retained for a period of three years from the date of the last use. Documentation shall include:

1. The name, address and telephone number of the testimonial giver;

2. The type and amount or value of compensation; and

3. The notarized statement and release required pursuant to (m) above.

13:31A-1.14 Standards of practice

(a) All licensees engaged in the burglar alarm or fire alarm business or in the provision of locksmithing services shall comply with the following standards of practice:

1. A licensee shall comply with all applicable Federal, State and local laws and codes;

2. A licensee shall determine and document the identity of a client prior to commencing any work. All correspondence, contracts and bills shall be addressed to the client, unless expressly directed otherwise, in writing, by the client;

3. A licensee shall provide a client with a written contract, work order, invoice or its equivalent, for any services provided to the client;

4. Any licensee who performs or supervises the installation, erection, repair or alteration of burglar alarm, fire alarm or locksmithing equipment and systems pursuant to the Act, consistent with the provisions of N.J.A.C. 13:31A-2.8 or 3.7, shall ensure that work so performed conforms to the standards of the New Jersey Uniform Construction Code in effect at the time the work is performed;

5. A licensee who performs or supervises work described in 4 above shall secure a construction permit and inspection of the completed work in conformity with the New Jersey Uniform Construction Code, N.J.S.A. 52:27D-119 et seq., and the Uniform Construction Code, N.J.A.C. 5:23, if applicable;

6. A licensee shall correct any code violation generated by the work performed or supervised by the licensee, within a reasonable amount of time and at no additional charge to a client; and

7. A licensee shall ensure the confidentiality of information obtained from a client and shall not disclose information relating to the provision of burglar alarm, fire alarm or locksmithing services to the client without the consent of the client, unless compelled to disclose such information to a law enforcement agency by statute, regulation or court order.

(b) A licensee who fails to comply with the requirements of (a) above shall be deemed to be engaged in professional misconduct within the meaning of this section and N.J.S.A. 45:1-21, and shall be subject to the penalties set forth in N.J.S.A. 45:1-25.

13:31A-1.15 Protected practices

(a) A licensee shall be deemed to have engaged in professional misconduct and shall be subject to the penalties set forth in N.J.S.A. 45:1-21 et seq., for engaging in any of the activities set forth in N.J.S.A. 45:1-21 and any of the following prohibited acts or practices:

1. Acting for his or her client or employer in professional matters otherwise than as a faithful agent or trustee, including demanding any remuneration other than his or her stated recompense for services rendered;

2. Disregarding the safety, health and welfare of the public in the performance of his or her professional duties, including preparing, signing or sealing of plans, surveys or specifications which are not of a safe design and/or not in conformity with accepted standards. If the client or employer insists on such conduct, the licensee shall notify the proper authorities and withdraw from further service on the project;

3. Engaging in any activity which involves the licensee in a conflict of interest. A licensee shall:

    i. Inform his or her client or employer of any business connection, interest or circumstances which might be deemed as influencing his or her judgment or the quality of his or her services to the client or employer; and

ii.   Not accept compensation or remuneration, financial or otherwise, from more than one interested party for the same service or for services pertaining to the same work, unless there has been full disclosure to and consent by all interested parties;

4.   Failing to keep a client reasonably informed about the status of a matter and promptly comply with reasonable requests for information;

5.   Failing to notify the Committee of the suspension or revocation of his or her license in another jurisdiction; or

6.   Installing, servicing or maintaining branch circuit wiring. For purposes of this section, "branch circuit" means the circuit conductors between the final overcurrent device protecting the circuit and the outlet(s).

SUBCHAPTER 2. LOCKSMITH LICENSURE

13:31A-2.1 Requirements for locksmith licensure
(a) An applicant seeking licensure as a locksmith shall:

1.   Be at least 18 years of age;

2.   Be of good moral character pursuant to N.J.S.A. 45:5A-27;

3.   Not have been convicted of a crime of the first, second or third degree within 10 years prior to the filing of the application for licensure;

4.   Hold a high school diploma or equivalency certificate;

5.   Have successfully completed the locksmithing examination set forth in N.J.A.C. 13:31A-2.3; and

6.   Have immediately preceding the submission of the application:

i.   At least three years of practical hands-on experience in the provision of locksmithing services. For purposes of this section, three years means a 36-month period, with at least 20 working days per month, during which the applicant has been engaged in the full-time provision of locksmithing services as defined in N.J.A.C. 13:31A-1.2, equal to a minimum of 5,040 hours; or

ii.   Completed a two-year apprenticeship program in the provision of locksmithing services approved by the Bureau of Apprenticeship and Training of the United States Department of Labor; and

7.   Have three years immediately preceding the submission of the application successfully completed two hours of training in the Barrier Free Subcode, N.J.A.C. 5:23-7, two hours of training in the New Jersey Uniform Construction Code, N.J.A.C. 5:23, exclusive of the Barrier Free Subcode, two hours of training in the Americans with Disabilities Act Code, 36 CFR 1191 and two hours of training in industrial safety.

13:31A-2.2 Reserved
Repealed by R.2007 d.73, effective March 5, 2007

13:31A-2.3 Locksmithing examination; re-examination
(a) All applicants for a license to provide locksmithing services shall obtain a passing score on the locksmith examination.

(b) An applicant taking the locksmithing examination for the first time shall take all sections of the examination. An applicant who fails to receive a passing score on any section(s) of the examination shall retake the failed section(s) as provided below:

1.   An applicant shall retake the failed section(s) of the examination within 24 months of the date of the first examination.

2.   If an applicant fails to obtain a passing score on the remaining section(s) during the second examination, the applicant shall not be eligible to retake the remaining section(s) of the examination for six months following the date of reexamination; and

3.   If the applicant fails to obtain a passing score on the remaining section(s) during the third examination, the applicant shall forfeit all passing scores received on any section(s) and shall be required to retake all sections of the examination.

13:31A-2.4 Reserved
Repealed by R.2007 d.73, effective March 5, 2007

13:31A-2.5 Application for locksmith licensure; individual and business firm

(a) All applications by individuals seeking a locksmith license shall include the following information and materials:

1.   The name, date of birth, and principal business address of the applicant, or if the applicant is an employee, the principal business address of the employer;

2.   Two, two-inch by two-inch passport-size photographs of the applicant;

3.   A list of all criminal offenses of which the applicant has been convicted, including the date and place of each conviction and the name under which he or she was convicted, if other than the name on the application;

4.   The applicant's fingerprints provided in such manner as directed by the Division;

5.   A copy of the applicant's high school diploma or equivalency certificate, or if a copy cannot be provided, a certification from the applicant verifying that he or she holds a high school diploma or equivalency certificate;

6.   An affidavit from the applicant's previous employer verifying that the applicant has satisfied the experience requirements set forth in N.J.A.C. 13:31A-2.1. If an applicant cannot obtain an affidavit from his or her previous employer, the applicant may submit copies of the applicant's W2 form to verify the experience requirements set forth in N.J.A.C. 13:31A-2.1; and

7.   A certified check or money order payable to the Committee in the amount of the application fee set forth in N.J.A.C. 13:31A-1.4. Payment for the criminal history records check shall be in the amount and by the means set forth in the application.

(b) Upon review of the materials in (a) above, the Committee shall advise the applicant that he or she is eligible to take the locksmith examination.

(c) All applications by business firms seeking a locksmith business license shall include the following information and materials:

1.   The name, date of birth, residence, present and previous occupations of the business qualifier and each member, officer or director of the business firm, the address of the principal place of business of the firm and the location of all branch offices, if applicable;

2.   The fingerprints of all persons provided pursuant to (c)1 above, provided in such manner as directed by the Division;

3.   Evidence of general liability insurance and insurance coverage or a surety bond as provided in N.J.A.C. 13:31A-2.6; and

4.   A certified check or money order in the amount of the application fee set forth in N.J.A.C. 13:31A-1.4.

(d) If an individual or business firm seeking licensure to engage in the provision of locksmithing services files with the Committee fingerprints of a person other than those specified in the application, the application shall be denied and the applicant shall be guilty of a fourth degree crime.

(e) If an individual or business firm seeking licensure to engage in the provision of locksmithing services falsifies any information contained in the application as required pursuant to (a) and (c) above, the applicant shall be denied a license pursuant to the provisions of N.J.A.C. 13:31A-1.9.

13:31A-2.6 Locksmith business license holder requirements

(a) A locksmith business license holder shall:

1.   Maintain at least one business office within the State or file with the Committee a statement, duly executed and sworn to before a person authorized by the laws of New Jersey to administer oaths, containing a power of attorney constituting the Committee as the true and lawful attorney of the licensee upon whom all original process in an action or legal proceedings against the licensee may be served and in which the licensee agrees that the original process that may be served upon the Committee shall be of the same force and validity as if served upon the licensee and that the authority thereof shall continue in force so long as the licensee engages in the practice of locksmithing in the State;

2.   Clearly mark the outside of each installation and service vehicle to be used in conjunction with the locksmithing service, as set forth in N.J.A.C. 13:31A-1.13;

3.   If the locksmith business license holder is engaged in the provision of electronic security system services, maintain an emergency service number attended to on a 24-hour basis and response appropriately

to emergencies on a 24-hour basis. For purposes of this section, "attended to" means that the main business telephone number or another telephone number designated and advertised by the business as an emergency service telephone number is answered on a 24-hour pay per day basis. For purposes of this section "responds appropriately" means that within 24 hours, any person calling to request service shall be provided with the date and time when such service, if necessary, will be rendered; and

4.   Retain and maintain during the term of the license general liability insurance in the amount of $500,000, and insurance coverage or a surety bond in favor of the State of New Jersey in the sum of $10,000, executed by a surety company authorized to transact business in the State of New Jersey which is approved by the Department of Banking and Insurance, and which is conditioned on the faithful performance of the provisions of the Act and the rules of this subchapter.

   i.   An action may be maintained on the bond required by (a)4 above by any person injured, aggrieved or damaged through the failure of the obligor to perform the duties prescribed for locksmith license holders under the provisions of the Act and the rules of this subchapter.

(b) A locksmith business license holder shall be responsible for any unlawful or unprofessional conduct by an employee in the course of his or her employment. Such conduct shall be cause for suspension or revocation of the employer's license if it is established that the licensee had knowledge of the unlawful or unprofessional conduct, or that there existed a pattern of unlawful or unprofessional conduct.

(c) A locksmith business license holder who employs a person in connection with the provision of locksmithing services shall notify the Committee, in writing, within 30 days of such employment and shall provide the Committee with:

1.   A two-inch by two-inch passport-size photograph of the employee;

2.   A list of all criminal offenses of which the employee has been convicted, including the date and place of each conviction and the name under which the employee was convicted, if other than the name on the written notification provided to the Committee;

3.   The employee's fingerprints provided in such manner as directed by the Division;

4.   Evidence of practical experience and professional competence as set forth in N.J.A.C. 13:31A-2.7, if the work of the employee is not directly supervised; and

5.   A certified check or money order payable to the Committee in the amount of the employee listing fee set forth in N.J.A.C. 13:31A-1.4. Payment for the criminal history records check shall be in the amount and by the means set forth in the application. The employer shall bear the cost of the records check.

(d) If the Committee determines that the evidence of practical experience and professional competency provided pursuant to (c)4 above fails to satisfy the requirements of N.J.A.C. 13:31A-2.7, the Committee shall advise the licensee of the employee's unfitness to engage in the provision of locksmithing services.

13:31A-2.7 Locksmith employees

(a) Any person employed by a locksmith licensee to perform locksmithing services shall be of good moral character.

(b) Any person employed by a licensee to perform locksmithing services while unsupervised shall:

1.   Have at least three years of practical hands-on experience in the provision of locksmith services as defined in N.J.A.C. 13:31A-1.2; and

2.   Have successfully completed a total of four hours of training in the Barrier Free Subcode, N.J.A.C. 5:23-7, the New Jersey Uniform Construction Code, N.J.A.C. 5:23, exclusive of the Barrier Free Subcode, and the Americans with Disabilities Act Code, 36 C.F.R. § 1191, four hours of training in basic electronics and four hours of training in trade related subjects, or have successfully passed a competency examination administered by the Committee, or have obtained a Certified Registered Locksmith rating by the Associated Locksmiths of America (ALOA), or have obtained a Certified Institutional Locksmith rating by the Institutional Locksmiths' Association (ILA).

(c) A person employed by a locksmithing business who performs locksmithing services while unsupervised shall not be required to satisfy the competency requirements of (b) above until January 31, 2011.

13:31A-2.8 Supervision of locksmith employees

(a) The business qualifier shall assume full responsibility for the inspection and supervision of all locksmithing services performed by the business firm, and shall ensure compliance with all applicable Federal, State and local laws and codes.

(b) The business qualifier shall:

1. Supervise the provision of locksmithing services to ensure that such work is performed in compliance with all applicable Federal, State and local laws and codes;

2. Personally inspect the work of employees pursuant to (d) and (e) below;

3. Ensure that employees are afforded the degree of personal on-site supervision commensurate with their level of competence and the complexity of the work to be performed pursuant to (d) and (e) below; and

4. Be present, on a regular and continuous basis, at the principal office of the business firm, where the business license holder maintains a New Jersey office, or at work sites of locksmithing services performed in New Jersey, where the business license holder does not maintain a New Jersey office pursuant to N.J.A.C. 13:31A-2.6(a).

(c) Every 10 employees who are performing locksmithing services at either one job site or who are performing such work at several jobs at different sites simultaneously shall be supervised, pursuant to (d) below, by the business qualifier, a licensee or a supervising employee who is permitted to perform locksmithing services while unsupervised pursuant to N.J.A.C. 13:31A-2.7(b).

(d) The business qualifier, a licensee or a supervising employee shall indirectly supervise an employee performing the functions listed in (d)1 through 5 below, and shall ensure that the work has been completed. For purposes of this section, "indirect supervision" means that the business qualifier, the licensee or the supervising employee shall be reachable either in person or by electronic means to provide consultation to the employee. Indirect supervision shall be required for the following functions:

1. Opening existing locks;

2. Making keys for existing locks;

3. Repairing or recombining existing locks;

4. Installing mechanical security hardware on doors that are not designated as emergency exits; and

5. Performing the survey of a premises, the design and preparation of specifications, and the demonstration of electronic security systems.

(e) If an employee is performing any locksmithing services, other than the work specified in (d) above, the business qualifier, the licensee or the supervising employee shall directly supervise the employee and shall ensure a final inspection of the work upon completion. For purposes of this section, "direct supervision" means that the business qualifier, the licensee or the supervising employee shall provide constant on-site supervision of the employee.

(f) A business qualifier who violates any provision of this section shall be deemed to have engaged in professional misconduct within the meaning of N.J.A.C. 13:31A-1.14 and N.J.S.A. 45:1-21(e) and shall be subject to the provisions of N.J.S.A. 45:1-21.

13:31A-2.9 Identification cards

(a) While engaged in the provision of locksmithing services, all licensed locksmiths, employees or other persons shall display an identification card issued by the Committee which shall contain the following information:

1. The name, photograph, date of birth and signature of the person to whom the identification card has been issued;

2. The business name, business address and business license number of the business license holder, and if the cardholder is a licensee, his or her license number; and

3. The expiration date of the card.

(b) All identification cards shall be issued for a three-year period. All identification cards issued to licensees shall be renewed on a triennial basis which corresponds to the triennial renewal of licenses issued by the Committee, subject to the payment of the fee set forth in N.J.A.C. 13:31A-1.4.

(c)   A licensee shall present the identification card issued by the Committee to all appropriate Federal, State or local agencies in order to obtain applications for permits and inspections, if required, for all work performed by the business firm.

(d)   All employees or other persons holding identification cards shall apply for renewal of the identification card at least 45 days prior to the expiration date of the card and shall pay the fee set forth in N.J.A.C. 13:31A-1.4 for renewal of employee listing. Any employer who permits an employee to work without a valid identification card shall be deemed to have engaged in professional misconduct within the meaning of N.J.A.C. 13:31A-1.14 and N.J.S.A. 45:1-21(e) and shall be subject to the provisions of N.J.S.A. 45:1-21.

(e)   All identification card holders shall advise the Committee of any changes to the information contained on the identification card and shall apply to the Committee for an updated identification card within five days of the occurrence of any change. The updated identification card shall be issued for the unexpired term of the original identification card.

(f)   Identification cards shall not be transferable. Upon termination of employment, identification cards shall be immediately returned to the Committee. Upon change in employment, identification cards shall be returned to the Committee and application for a new identification card shall be made to the Committee.

(g)   A photocopy of an application for an identification card shall serve as temporary identification for an applicant and shall be displayed by the applicant until the issuance of the identification card. The photocopy of the application shall be clearly marked with the word "COPY." The temporary identification shall be valid for no longer than 60 days from the date of application for the identification card and the applicant shall work under direct supervision until the identification card is issued by the Committee.

SUBCHAPTER 3. BURGLAR ALARM OR FIRE ALARM LICENSURE

13:31A-3.1 Requirements for burglar alarm or fire alarm licensure

(a)   All applicants seeking licensure to engage in the burglar alarm or fire alarm business shall:

1.   Be at least 18 years of age;

2.   Be of good moral character pursuant to N.J.S.A. 45:5A-27;

3.   Not have been convicted of a crime of the first, second or third degree within 10 years prior to the filing of the application for licensure;

4.   Not have been convicted of the fourth degree offense of engaging in the unlicensed practice of electrical contracting.

5.   Hold a high school diploma or equivalency certificate;

6.   Have successfully completed the burglar alarm or fire alarm examination, as applicable to the field in which the applicant is seeking licensure, set forth in N.J.A.C. 13:31A-3.2; and

7.   Have immediately preceding the submission of the application, at least four years of experience in burglar alarm or fire alarm business, which shall be satisfied by one of the following:

i.   Proof that the applicant has completed at least four years of practical hands-on experience, which shall include a minimum of 6,720 hours, working with tools in the installation, alteration, or repair of wiring for fire alarms, burglar alarms, and/or electronic security systems and proof that the applicant has completed 80 hours of technical courses applicable to the field in which the applicant is seeking licensure. The 80 hours of technical courses shall include two hours of training in the Barrier Free Subcode, N.J.A.C. 5:23-7, two hours of training in the New Jersey Uniform Construction Code, N.J.A.C. 5:23, exclusive of the Barrier Free Subcode, two hours of training in the Americans with Disabilities Act Code, 36 C.F.R. § 1191, two hours of training in industrial safety, and 72 hours of training in trade-related subjects. "Practical hands-on experience" shall not include time spent supervising, engaging in the practice of engineering, estimating and performing other managerial tasks relevant to the alarm business. The applicant shall submit a certification by an employer verifying the applicant's practical hands-on experience;

ii.   Proof of having earned a bachelors degree in electrical engineering and having completed one year of practical hands-on experience, as defined in (a)7i above, which shall include a minimum of 1,680 hours. The applicant shall submit a copy of his or her diploma and a certification by an employer verifying the applicant's one year of practical hands-on experience; or

iii.   Proof of having completed a minimum of one-year course in the study of trade-related electronics at a technical school and having completed three years of practical hands-on experience, as defined in (a)7i above, which shall include a minimum of 5,040 hours. The applicant shall submit a copy of his or her diploma or certificate of completion and a certification by an employer(s) verifying the applicant's three years of practical hands-on experience.

13:31A-3.2   Burglar alarm or fire alarm examination; reexamination

(a)   All applicants for a license to engage in the burglar alarm or fire alarm business shall obtain a passing score on the burglar alarm examination or the fire alarm examination, respectively, pursuant to N.J.A.C. 13:31A-3.1.

(b)   An applicant taking the burglar alarm or fire alarm examination for the first time shall be required to take all sections of the examination. An applicant who fails to receive a passing score on any section(s) of the examination shall retake the failed section(s) as provided below:

1.   An applicant shall retake the failed section(s) of the examination within 24 months of the date of the first examination;

2.   If an applicant fails to obtain a passing score on the remaining section(s) during the second examination, the applicant shall not be eligible to retake the remaining section(s) of the examination for six months following the date of reexamination; and

3.   If the applicant fails to obtain a passing score on the remaining section(s) during the third examination, the applicant shall forfeit all passing scores received on any section(s) and shall be required to retake all sections of the examination.

13:31A-3-3   Reserved

Repealed by R.2007 d.73, effective March 5, 2007.

13:31A-3.4   Application for burglar alarm for fire alarm licensure; individual and business firm

(a)   All applications for individuals seeking licensure to engage in the alarm business shall include the following information and materials:

1.   The name, date of birth, residence, and present and previous occupations of the applicant;

2.   Two, two-inch by two-inch passport-size photographs of the applicant;

3.   A list of all criminal offenses of which the applicant has been convicted, including the date and place of each conviction and the name under which he or she was convicted, if other than the name on the application;

4.   The applicant's fingerprints provided in such manner as directed by the Division;

5.   A copy of the applicant's high school diploma or equivalency certificate, or if a copy cannot be provided, a certification from the applicant verifying that he or she holds a high school diploma or equivalency certificate;

6.   An affidavit from the applicant's previous employer verifying that the applicant has satisfied the experience requirements set forth in N.J.A.C. 13:31A-3.1. If an applicant cannot obtain an affidavit from his or her previous employer, the applicant may submit copies of the applicant's W2 form to verify the experience requirements set forth in N.J.A.C. 13:31A-3.1;

7.   Evidence of having successfully completed the technical training courses set forth in N.J.A.C. 13:31A-3.1; and

8.   A certified check or money order payable to the Committee in the amount of the application fee set forth in N.J.A.C. 13:31A-1.4. Payment for the criminal history records check shall be in the amount and by the means set forth in the application.

(b)   Upon review of the materials in (a) above, the Committee shall advise the applicant that he or she is eligible to take the burglar alarm or the fire alarm examination.

(c)   All applications by business firms seeking a burglar alarm or fire alarm business license shall include the following information and materials:

1.   The name, date of birth, residence, present and previous occupations of the business qualifier and each member, officer or director of the business firm, the address of the principal place of business of the firm and the location of all branch offices, if applicable;

2. The fingerprints of all persons provided pursuant to (c)1 above, provided in such manner as directed by the Division;

3. Evidence of general liability insurance and insurance coverage or a surety bond as provided in N.J.A.C. 13:31A-3.5; and

4. A certified check or money order payable to the Committee in the amount of the application fee set forth in N.J.A.C. 13:31A-1.4.

(d) If an individual or business firm seeking licensure to engage in the burglar alarm or fire alarm business files with the Committee fingerprints of a person other than those specified in the application, the application shall be denied and the applicant shall be guilty of a fourth degree crime.

(e) If an individual or business firm seeking licensure to engage in the burglar alarm or fire alarm business falsifies any information contained in the application as required pursuant to (a) and (c) above, the applicant shall be denied a license pursuant to the provisions of N.J.A.C. 13:31A-1.9.

13:31A-3.5 Burglar alarm or fire alarm business license holder requirements

(a) A burglar alarm or fire alarm business license holder shall:

1. Maintain at least one business office within the State or file with the Committee a statement, duly executed and sworn to before a person authorized by the laws of New Jersey to administer oaths, containing a power of attorney constituting the Committee as the true and lawful attorney of the licensee upon whom all original process in an action or legal proceedings against the licensee may be served and in which the licensee agrees that the original process that may be served upon the Committee shall be of the same force and validity as if served upon the licensee and that the authority thereof shall continue in force so long as the licensee engages in the burglar alarm or fire alarm business in the State;

2. Clearly mark the outside of each installation and service vehicle to be used in conjunction with the burglar alarm or fire alarm business, as set forth in N.J.A.C. 13:31A-1.13, with the name of the burglar alarm or fire alarm business, the name of the owner, lessee or lessor of the vehicle and the name of the municipality in which the owner, lessee or lessor has its principal place of business pursuant to N.J.S.A. 39:4-46. The sign or name plate used to comply with this requirement shall not be less than three inches high;

3. Maintain an emergency service number attended to on a 24-hour basis and respond appropriately to emergencies on a 24-hour basis when engaged in the burglar alarm or fire alarm business. For purposes of this section "attended to" means that the main business telephone number or another telephone number designated and advertised by the business as an emergency service telephone number is answered on a 24-hour per day basis. For purposes of this section "responds appropriately" means that within 24 hours, any person calling to request service shall be provided with the date and time when such service, if necessary, will be rendered; and

4. Retain and maintain during the term of the license general liability insurance in the amount of $1,000,000, and insurance coverage or a surety bond in favor of the State of New Jersey in the sum of $10,000, executed by a surety company authorized to transact business in the State of New Jersey which is approved by the Department of Banking and Insurance, and which is conditioned on the faithful performance of the provisions of the Act.

    i. An action may be maintained on the bond required by (a)4 above by any person injured, aggrieved or damaged through the failure of the obligor to perform the duties prescribed for burglar alarm or fire alarm license holders under the Act and the rules of this subchapter.

(b) A burglar alarm or fire alarm business license holder shall be responsible for any unlawful or unprofessional conduct by an employee in the course of his or her employment. Such conduct shall be cause for suspension or revocation of the employer's license if it is established that the licensee had knowledge of the unlawful or unprofessional conduct, or that there existed a pattern of unlawful or unprofessional conduct.

(c) A burglar alarm or fire alarm business license holder who employs a person in connection with a burglar alarm or fire alarm business shall notify the Committee, in writing, within 30 days of such employment and shall provide the Committee with the following information and materials:

1. A two-inch by two-inch passport-size photograph of the employee;

2.   A list of all criminal offenses of which the employee has been convicted, including the date and place of each conviction and the name under which the employee was convicted, if other than the name on the written notification provided to the Committee;

3.   The employee fingerprints provided in such manner as directed by the Division;

4.   Evidence of practical experience and professional competence as set forth in N.J.A.C. 13:31A-3.6, if the work of the employee is not directly supervised; and

5.   A certified check or money order payable to the Committee in the amount of the employee listing fee set forth in N.J.A.C. 13:31A-1.4. Payment for the criminal history records check shall be in the amount and by the means set forth in the application. The employer shall bear the cost of the records check.

(d)   If the Committee determines that the evidence of practical experience and professional competency provided pursuant to (c)4 above fails to satisfy the requirements of N.J.A.C. 13:31A-3.6, the Committee shall advise the licensee of the employee's unfitness to engage in the burglar alarm or fire alarm business.

13:31A-3.6 Burglar alarm or fire alarm employees

(a)   Any person employed by a burglar alarm or fire alarm business licensee to install, service or maintain a burglar alarm or fire alarm, shall be of good moral character.

(b)   Any person employed by a licensee to perform installation, servicing or maintenance of a burglar alarm or fire alarm while unsupervised shall:

1.   Have at least three years of practical experience, as defined in N.J.A.C. 13:31A-3.1; and

2.   Have successfully completed two hours of training in the Barrier Free Subcode, N.J.A.C. 5:23-7, two hours of training in the New Jersey Uniform Construction Code, N.J.A.C. 5:23, exclusive of the two hours of training in the Barrier Free Subcode, two hours of training in the Americans with Disabilities Act Code, 36 C.F.R. § 1191, two hours of training in industrial safety, and 32 hours of training in trade-related subjects relevant to the field, or shall have successfully passed a competency examination administered by the Committee.

(c)   A person employed by a burglar alarm or fire alarm business who performs installation, servicing or maintenance of burglar alarms or fire alarms while unsupervised shall not be required to satisfy the competency requirements of (b) above until January 31, 2011.

13:31A-3.7 Supervision of burglar alarm or fire alarm business employees

(a)   The business qualifier shall assume full responsibility for the inspection and supervision of all burglar alarm or fire alarm services performed by the business firm in compliance with all applicable, Federal, State and local laws and codes.

(b)   The business qualifier shall:

1.   Supervise the provision of burglar alarm or fire alarm services to ensure that such work is performed in compliance with all applicable Federal, State and local laws and codes;

2.   Personally inspect the work of employees pursuant to (d) and (e) below;

3.   Ensure that employees are afforded the degree of personal on-site supervision commensurate with their level of competence and the complexity of the work to be performed pursuant to (d) and (e) below; and

4.   Be present, on a regular and continuous basis, at the principal office of the business firm, where the business license holder maintains a New Jersey office, or at work sites of burglar alarm or fire alarm work performed in New Jersey, where the business license holder does not maintain a New Jersey office pursuant to N.J.A.C. 13:31A-3.5(a).

(c)   Every 10 employees who are performing burglar alarm or fire alarm services at either one job site or who are performing such work at several jobs at different sites simultaneously shall be supervised, pursuant to (d) below, by the business qualifier, a licensee or a supervising employee who is permitted to perform installation, servicing or maintenance of burglar alarm or fire alarms while unsupervised pursuant to N.J.A.C. 13:31A-3.6(b).

(d)   The business qualifier, a licensee or a supervising employee shall indirectly supervise an employee performing any of the functions listed in (d)1 through 6 below, and shall ensure that the work has been completed. For purposes of this section, "indirect supervision" means that the business qualifier, the licensee or the supervising employee shall be reachable either in person or by electronic means to provide consultation to the employee. Indirect supervision shall be required for the following functions:

1.   The inspection and testing of burglar alarm, fire alarm or electronic security systems;

2.   The repair or replacement of any component of a burglar alarm, fire alarm or electronic security system with an identical component;

3.   The cleaning and calibration of burglar alarm, fire alarm or electronic security systems or any component thereof;

4.   Any work performed by an employee who is certified by the product manufacturer to perform work on a particular product;

5.   The installation of rough wiring that is subject to inspection by the licensee; and

6.   The survey of a premises, the design and preparation of specifications, and the demonstration of burglar alarm, fire alarm or electronic security systems.

(e)   If an employee is performing any burglar alarm, fire alarm or electronic security system work, other than the work specified in (d) above, the business qualifier, the licensee or the supervising employee shall directly supervise the employee and shall ensure a final inspection of the work upon completion. For purposes of this section, "direct supervision" means that the business qualifier, licensee or supervising employee shall provide constant on-site supervision of the employee.

(f)   A business qualifier who violates any provision of this section shall be deemed to have engaged in professional misconduct within the meaning of N.J.A.C. 13:31A-1.14 and N.J.S.A. 45:1-21(e) and shall be subject to the provisions of N.J.S.A. 45:1-21.

13:31A-3.8 Identification cards

(a)   While engaged in the provision of burglar alarm or fire alarm services, all burglar alarm or fire alarm business licensees, employees or other persons shall display an identification card issued by the Committee which shall contain the following information:

1.   The name, date of birth, photograph and signature of the person to whom the identification card has been issued;

2.   The business name, business address and business license number of the business license holder, and if the cardholder is a licensee, his or her license number; and

3.   The expiration date of the card.

(b)   All identification cards shall be issued for a three-year period. All identification cards issued to licensees shall be renewed on a triennial basis which corresponds to the triennial renewal of licenses issued by the Committee, subject to the payment of the fee set forth in N.J.A.C. 13:31A-1.4.

(c)   A licensee shall present the identification card issued by the Committee to all appropriate Federal, State or local agencies in order to obtain applications for permits and inspections, if required, for all work performed by the burglar alarm or fire alarm business.

(d)   All employees or other persons holding identification cards shall apply for renewal of the identification card at least 45 days prior to the expiration date of the card and shall pay the fee set forth in N.J.A.C. 13:31A-1.4 for renewal of employee listing. Any employer who permits an employee to work without a valid identification card shall be deemed to have engaged in professional misconduct within the meaning of N.J.A.C. 13:31A- 1.14 and N.J.S.A. 45:1-21(e) and shall be subject to the provisions of N.J.S.A. 45:1-21.

(e)   All identification card holders shall advise the Committee of any changes to the information contained on the identification card and shall apply to the Committee for an updated identification card within five days of the occurrence of any change. The updated identification card shall be issued for the unexpired term of the original identification card.

(f)   Identification cards shall not be transferable. Upon termination of employment, identification cards shall be immediately returned to the Committee. Upon change in employment identification cards shall be returned to the Committee and application for a new identification card shall be made to the Committee.

(g)   A photocopy of an application for an identification card shall serve as temporary identification for an applicant and shall be displayed by the applicant until the issuance of the identification card. The photocopy of the application shall be clearly marked with the word "COPY." The temporary identification shall be valid for no longer than 60 days from the date of application for the identification card and the applicant shall work under direct supervision until the identification card is issued by the Committee.

Updated through 10/5/09

NEW JERSEY ADMINISTRATIVE CODE

TITLE 13, CHAPTER 45C: UNIFORM REGULATIONS

SUBCHAPTER 1. LICENSEE DUTY TO COOPERATE AND TO COMPLY WITH BOARD ORDERS

13:45C-1.1 Applicability, scope and definitions

(a) This subchapter shall apply to all licensees of any board, committee or sub-unit within the Division of Consumer Affairs.

(b) For the purpose of this subchapter, "licensee" shall mean any licensee, permittee, certificate holder or registrant of:

1. The Division of Consumer Affairs;

2. Any professional or occupational licensing board, committee, or other subunit of a board or committee located within the Division; or

3. The Legalized Games of Chance Control Commission.

13:45C-1.2 Licensee's duty to cooperate in investigative inquiries

(a) A licensee shall cooperate in any inquiry, inspection or investigation conducted by, or on behalf of, a board, the Director or the licensee's licensing agency into a licensee's conduct, fitness or capacity to engage in a licensed profession or occupation where said inquiry is intended to evaluate such conduct, fitness or capacity for compliance with applicable statutory or regulatory provisions.

(b) A licensee's failure to cooperate, absent good cause or bona fide claim of a privilege not identified in N.J.A.C. 13:45C-1.5 as unavailable, may be deemed by the board, the Director, or the licensing agency to constitute professional or occupational misconduct within the meaning of N.J.S.A. 45:1-21(e) or the agency's enabling act and thus subject a licensee to disciplinary action pursuant to N.J.S.A. 45:1-21(h) or the agency's enabling act.

13:45C-1.3 Specific conduct deemed failure to cooperate

(a) The following conduct by a licensee may be deemed a failure to cooperate and, therefore, professional or occupational misconduct and grounds for disciplinary action including, but not limited to, suspension or revocation of licensure:

1. The failure to timely respond to an inquiry to provide information in response to a complaint received concerning licensee conduct;

2. The failure to timely provide records related to licensee conduct;

3. The failure to attend any scheduled proceeding at which the licensee's appearance is directed. In the event that a licensee elects to retain counsel for the purpose of representation in any such proceeding, it shall be the licensee's responsibility to do so in a timely fashion. The failure of a licensee to retain counsel, absent a showing of good cause therefore, shall not require an adjournment of the proceeding;

4. The failure to timely respond or to provide information requested pursuant to a demand under N.J.S.A. 45:1-18 or other applicable law or to provide access to any premises from which a licensed profession or occupation is conducted. Included within this paragraph shall be the failure to respond to any demand for statement or report under oath, the failure to permit the examination of any goods, ware or item used in the rendition of the professional or occupational service and the failure to grant access to records, books or other documents utilized in the practice of the occupation or profession;

5. The failure to answer any question pertinent to inquiry made pursuant to N.J.S.A. 45:1-18 or other applicable law unless the response to said question is subject to a *bona fide* claim of privilege;

6. The failure to make proper and timely response by way of appearance or production of documents to any subpoena issued pursuant to N.J.S.A. 45:1-18 or as may otherwise be provided by law; or

7. The failure to provide to the Board, the Director or the licensing agency timely notice of any change of address from that which appears on the licensee's most recent license renewal or application.

13:45C-1.4 Failure to comply with Board orders as professional or occupational misconduct
The failure of a licensee to comply with an order duly entered and served upon the licensee or of which the licensee has knowledge shall be deemed professional or occupational misconduct.

13:45C-1.5 Unavailability of privileges in investigative or disciplinary proceedings

(a) In any investigative inquiry conducted pursuant to N.J.S.A. 45:1-18 or in any disciplinary proceeding conducted pursuant to N.J.S.A. 45:1-21, or as may otherwise be authorized by law, the physician-patient privilege, psychologist-patient privilege, marriage and family therapist-client privilege, professional counselor-client privilege, associate counselor-client privilege, social worker-client privilege and the alcohol and drug counselor-client privilege shall be unavailable.

(b) Any statements or records otherwise subject to a claim of the stated privileges which may be obtained by the Board, its agent or the Attorney General pursuant to N.J.S.A. 45:1-18 shall remain confidential and shall not be disclosed unless so ordered by a court of competent jurisdiction, the appropriate licensing board or the Office of Administrative Law in a contested case.

13:45C-1.6 Maintenance of and access to statements, records or other information that is subject to a privilege declared unavailable

(a) Any statements, records or other information acquired which may be subject to any privilege declared unavailable in this subchapter shall be maintained in a secure place and manner by:

1. The evidence custodian within the Division of Consumer Affairs, Enforcement Bureau;

2. The professional or occupational licensing board and the committee or other subunit of a board or committee located within the Division which has a direct connection with, or a need for access to, the matter to which the statements, records or other information pertain; or

3. A Deputy Attorney General.

(b) Except as may be otherwise ordered as provided in the subchapter, access to statements, records or other information shall be afforded only to employees and agents of, and experts or other consultants retained by, the Attorney General, the Enforcement Bureau, or the Board or other subunit of the Division having a direct connection with, or a need for access to, the matter to which the statement, records or other information pertain.

(c) The statements, records or other information may be retained for the period of time during which an investigation remains open or until the completion of all administrative or judicial proceedings relating thereto, at which time they may be returned to the licensee or other person from whom they were obtained. In the absence of such licensee or other person, the statements, records or other information may be returned to the patient, where appropriate.

Updated through 2/21/06.

NEW JERSEY ADMINISTRATIVE CODE

TITLE 13, CHAPTER 45A: ADMINISTRATIVE RULES OF THE DIVISION OF CONSUMER AFFAIRS

SUBCHAPTER 16: HOME IMPROVEMENT PRACTICES

13:45A-16.1 Purpose and Scope

(a) The purpose of the rules in this subchapter is to implement the provisions of the Consumer Fraud Act, N.J.S.A. 56:8-1 et seq., by providing procedures for the regulation and content of home improvement contracts and establishing standards to facilitate enforcement of the requirements of the Act.

(b) The rules in this subchapter shall apply to all sellers as defined in N.J.A.C. 13:45A-16.1A, and to all home improvement contractors as defined in N.J.A.C. 13:45A-17.2 whether or not they are exempt from the provisions of N.J.A.C. 13:45A-17.

13:45A-16.1A   Definitions

The following words and terms, when used in this subchapter, shall have the following meanings unless the context indicates otherwise.

"Home improvement" means the remodeling, altering, painting, repairing, renovating, restoring, moving, demolishing, or modernizing of residential or noncommercial property or the making of additions thereto, and includes, but is not limited to, the construction, installation, replacement, improvement, or repair of driveways, sidewalks, swimming pools, terraces, patios, landscaping, fences, porches, windows, doors, cabinets, kitchens, bathrooms, garages, basements and basement waterproofing, fire protection devices, security protection devices, central heating and air conditioning equipment, water softeners, heaters, and purifiers, solar heating or water systems, insulation installation, siding, wall-to-wall carpeting or attached or inlaid floor coverings, and other changes, repairs, or improvements made in or on, attached to or forming a part of the residential or noncommercial property, but does not include the construction of a new residence. The term extends to the conversion of existing commercial structures into residential or noncommercial property and includes any of the above activities performed under emergency conditions.

"Home improvement contract" means an oral or written agreement between a seller and an owner of residential or noncommercial property, or a seller and a tenant or lessee of residential or noncommercial property, if the tenant or lessee is to be obligated for the payment of home improvements made in, to, or upon such property, and includes all agreements under which the seller is to perform labor or render services for home improvements, or furnish materials in connection therewith.

"Residential or non-commercial property" means a structure used, in whole or in substantial part, as a home or place of residence by any natural person, whether or not a single or multi-unit structure, and that part of the lot or site on which it is situated and which is devoted to the residential use of the structure, and includes all appurtenant structures.

"Sales representative" means a person employed by or contracting with a seller for the purpose of selling home improvements.

"Seller" means a person engaged in the business of making or selling home improvements and includes corporations, partnerships, associations and any other form of business organization or entity, and their officers, representatives, agents and employees.

13:45A-16.2 Unlawful practices

(a) Without limiting any other practices which may be unlawful under the Consumer Fraud Act, N.J.S.A. 56:8-1 et seq., utilization by a seller of the following acts and practices involving the sale, attempted sale, advertisement or performance of home improvements shall be unlawful hereunder:

1.   Model home representations: Misrepresent or falsely state to a prospective buyer that the buyer's residential or noncommercial property is to serve as a "model" or "advertising job", or use any other prospective buyer lure to mislead the buyer into believing that a price reduction or other compensation will be received by reason of such representations;

2. Product and material representations: Misrepresent directly or by implication that products or materials to be used in the home improvement:

    i.   Need no periodic repainting, finishing, maintenance or other service;

    ii. Are of a specific or well-known brand name, or are produced by a specific manufacturer or exclusively distributed by the seller;

    iii. Are of a specific size, weight, grade or quality, or possess any other distinguishing characteristics or features;

    iv. Perform certain functions or substitute for, or are equal in performance to, other products or materials;

    v.   Meet or exceed municipal, state, federal, or other applicable standards or requirements;

    vi. Are approved or recommended by any governmental agency, person, firm or organization, or that they are the users of such products or materials;

    vii. Are of sufficient size, capacity, character or nature to do the job expected or represented;

    viii. Are or will be custom-built or specially designed for the needs of the buyer; or

    ix. May be serviced or repaired within the buyer's immediate trade area, or be maintained with replacement and repair parts which are readily available.

3. Bait selling:

    i.   Offer or represent specific products or materials as being for sale, where the purpose or effect of the offer or representation is not to sell as represented but to bait or entice the buyer into the purchase of other or higher priced substitute products or materials;

    ii. Disparage, degrade or otherwise discourage the purchase of products or materials offered or represented by the seller as being for sale to induce the buyer to purchase other or higher priced substitute products or materials;

    iii. Refuse to show, demonstrate or sell products or materials as advertised, offered, or represented as being for sale;

    iv. Substitute products or materials for those specified in the home improvement contract, or otherwise represented or sold for use in the making of home improvements by sample, illustration or model, without the knowledge or consent of buyer;

    v.   Fail to have available a quantity of the advertised product sufficient to meet reasonably anticipated demands; or

    vi. Misrepresent that certain products or materials are unavailable or that there will be a long delay in their manufacture, delivery, service or installation in order to induce a buyer to purchase other or higher priced substitute products or materials from the seller.

4. Identity of seller:

    i.   Deceptively gain entry into the prospective buyer's home or onto the buyer's property under the guise of any governmental or public utility inspection, or otherwise misrepresent that the seller has any official right, duty or authority to conduct an inspection;

    ii. Misrepesent that the seller is an employee, officer or representative of a manufacturer, importer or any other person, firm or organization, or a member of any trade association, or that such person, firm or organization will assume some obligation in fulfilling the terms of the contract;

    iii. Misrepresent the status, authority or position of the sales representative in the organization he represents;

    iv. Misrepresent that the sales representative is an employee or representative of or works exclusively for a particular seller; or

    v.   Misrepresent that the seller is part of any governmental or public agency in any printed or oral communication including but not limited to leaflets, tracts or other printed material, or that any licensing denotes approval by the governmental agency.

5. Gift offers:

    i.   Offer or advertise any gift, free item or bonus without fully disclosing the terms or conditions of the offer, including expiration date of the offer and when the gift, free item or bonus will be given; or

    ii.   Fail to comply with the terms of such offer.

6. Price and financing:

    i.   Misrepresent to a prospective buyer that an introductory, confidential, close-out, going out of business, factory, wholesale, or any other special price or discount is being given, or that any other concession is made because of a market survey or test, use of materials left over from another job, or any other reason;

    ii.   Misrepresent that any person, firm or organization, whether or not connected with the seller, is especially interested in seeing that the prospective buyer gets a bargain, special price, discount or any other benefit or concession;

    iii. Misrepresent or mislead the prospective buyer into believing that insurance or some other form of protection will be furnished to relieve the buyer from obligations under the contract if the buyer becomes ill, dies or is unable to make payments;

    iv. Misrepresent or mislead the buyer into believing that no obligation will be incurred because of the signing of any document, or that the buyer will be relieved of some or all obligations under the contract by the signing of any documents;

    v.   Request the buyer to sign a certificate of completion, or make final payment on the contract before the home improvement is completed in accordance with the terms of the contract;

    vi. Misrepresent or fail to disclose that the offered or contract price does not include delivery or installation or that other requirements must be fulfilled by the buyer as a condition to the performance of labor, services, or the furnishing of products or materials at the offered or contract price;

    vii. Mislead the prospective buyer into believing that the down payment or any other sum constitutes the full amount the buyer will be obligated to pay;

    viii. Misrepresent or fail to disclose that the offered or contract price does not include all financing charges, interest service charges, credit investigation costs, building or installation permit fees, or other obligations, charges, cost or fees to be paid by the buyer;

    ix. Advise or induce the buyer to inflate the value of the buyer's property or assets, or to misrepresent or falsify the buyer's true financial position in order to obtain credit; or

    x.   Increase or falsify the contract price, or induce the buyer by any means to misrepresent or falsify the contract price or value of the home improvement for financing purposes or to obtain additional credit.

7. Performance:

    i.   Deliver materials, begin work, or use any similar tactic to unduly pressure the buyer into a home improvement contract, or make any claim or assertion that a binding contract has been agree upon where no final agreement or understanding exists;

    ii.   Fail to begin or complete work on the date or within the time period specified in the home improvement contract, or as otherwise represented, unless the delay is for any reason of labor stoppage; unavailability of supplies or materials, unavoidable casualties, or any other cause beyond the seller's control. Any changes in the dates or time periods state in a written contract shall be agreed to in writing; or

    iii. Fail to give timely written notice to the buyer of reasons beyond the seller's control for any delay in performance, and when the work will begin or be completed.

8. Competitors:

    i.   Misrepresent that the work of a competitor was performed by the seller;

    ii.   Misrepresent that the seller's products, materials or workmanship are equal to or better than those of a competitor; or

    iii. Use or initiate the trademarks, trade names, labels or other distinctive marks of a competitor.

9. Sales representations:

    i.   Misrepresent or mislead the buyer into believing that a purchase will aid or help some public, charitable, religious, welfare or veterans' organization, or misrepresent the extent of such aid or assistance;

ii.   Knowingly fail to make any material statement of fact, qualification or explanation causes an advertisement, announcement, statement or representation to be false, deceptive or misleading; or

iii.   Misrepresent that the customer's present equipment, material, product, home or a part thereof is dangerous or defective, or in need of repair or replacement.

10.   Building permits:

i.   No seller contracting for the making of home improvements shall commence work until he is sure that all applicable state or local building and construction permits have been issued as required under state laws or local ordinances; or

ii.   Where midpoint or final inspections are required under state laws or local ordinances, copies of inspection certificates shall be furnished to the buyer by the seller when construction is completed and before final payment is due or the signing of a completion slip is requested by the buyer.

11.   Guarantees or warranties:

i.   The seller shall furnish the buyer a written copy of all guarantees or warranties made with respect to labor services, products or materials furnished in connection with home improvements. Such guarantees or warranties shall be specific, clear and definite and shall include any exclusions or limitations as to their scope or duration. Copies of all guarantees or warranties shall be furnished to the buyer at the time the seller presents his bid as well as at the time of execution of the contract except that separate guarantees or warranties of the manufacturer of products or materials may be furnished at the time such products or materials are installed.

12.   Home improvement contract requirements-Written requirement: All home improvement contracts for a purchase price in excess of $500.00, and all changes in the terms and conditions thereof shall be in writing. Home improvement contracts which are required by this subsection to be in writing, an all changes in the terms and conditions thereof, shall be signed by all parties thereto, and shall clearly and accurately set forth in legible form and in understandable language all terms and conditions of the contract, including, but not limited to, the following:

i.   The legal name and business address of the seller, including the legal name and business address of the sales representative or agent who solicited or negotiated the contract for the seller;

ii.   A description of the work to be done and the principal products and materials to be used or installed in performance of the contract. The description shall include, where applicable, the name, make, size, capacity, model, and model year of principal products or fixtures to be installed, and the type, grade, quality, size or quantity of principal building or construction materials to be used, a description of such products or materials shall be clearly set forth in the contract;

iii.   The total price or other consideration to be paid by the buyer, including all finance charges. If the contract is one for time and materials, the hourly rate for labor and all other terms and conditions of the contract affecting price shall be clearly stated;

iv.   The dates or time period on or within which the work is to begin and be completed by the seller;

v.   A description of any mortgage or security interest to be taken in connection with the financing or sale of the home improvement; and

vi.   A statement of any guarantee or warranty with respect to any products, materials, labor or services made by the seller.

13.   Disclosures and obligations concerning preservation of buyers' claims and defenses:

i.   If a person other than the seller is to act as the general contractor or assume responsibility for performance of the contract, the name and address of such person shall be disclosed in the oral or written contract, except as otherwise agreed, and the contract shall not be sold or assigned without the written consent of the buyer;

ii.   No home improvement contract shall require or entail the execution of any note, unless such note shall have conspicuously printed thereon the disclosures required by either State law (N.J.S.A. 17:16C-64.2 (consumer note)) or Federal law (16 C.F.R. section 433.2) concerning the preservation of buyers' claims and defenses.

SUBCHAPTER 17. HOME IMPROVEMENT CONTRACTOR REGISTRATION

13:45A-17.1 Purpose and scope

(a) The purpose of the rules in this subchapter is to implement the provisions of the Consumer Fraud Act, N.J.S.A. 56:8-1 et seq. as amended by P.L. 2004, c.16 (N.J.S.A. 56:8-136 et seq.) by providing procedures for the regulation of home improvement contractors and establishing standards to facilitate enforcement of the requirements of the Act. The rules establish the Division's registration procedures for those persons who fall under the requirements of this law.

(b) These rules shall apply to home improvement contractors in this State unless otherwise exempt under N.J.A.C. 13:45A-17.4.

13:45A-17.2 Definitions

The following words and terms, as used in this subchapter, shall have the following meanings, unless the context clearly indicates otherwise:

"Advertise" means to communicate to the public by means of any print, electronic or any other media, including, but not limited to, newspapers, magazines, periodicals, journals, circulars, flyers, business cards, signs, radio, telephone, facsimile machine, television, computer or the Internet. "Advertise" includes having a person's name in a classified advertisement or directory in this State under any classification of home improvement as defined in this section but does not include simple residential alphabetical listings in standard telephone directories.

"Director" means the Director of the Division of Consumer Affairs.

"Division" means the Division of Consumer Affairs in the Department of Law and Public Safety.

"Employee" means employee as defined in N.J.A.C. 18:35-7.1.

"Home improvement" means the remodeling, altering, painting, repairing, renovating, restoring, moving, demolishing, or modernizing of residential or noncommercial property or the making of additions thereto, and includes, but is not limited to, the construction, installation, replacement, improvement, or repair of driveways, sidewalks, swimming pools, terraces, patios, landscaping, fences, porches, windows, doors, cabinets, kitchens, bathrooms, garages, basements and basement waterproofing, fire protection devices, security protection devices, central heating and air conditioning equipment, water softeners, heaters, and purifiers, solar heating or water systems, insulation installation, siding, wall-to-wall carpeting or attached or inlaid floor coverings, and other changes, repairs, or improvements made in or on, attached to or forming a part of the residential or noncommercial property, but does not include the construction of a new residence. The term extends to the conversion of existing commercial structures into residential or noncommercial property and includes any of the above activities performed under emergency conditions.

"Home improvement contract" means an oral or written agreement for the performance of a home improvement between a contractor and an owner of residential or noncommercial property, or a contractor and a tenant or lessee of residential or noncommercial property, if the tenant or lessee is to be obligated for the payment of home improvements made in, to, or upon such property, and includes all agreements under which the contractor is to perform labor or render services for home improvements, or furnish materials in connection therewith.

"Home improvement contractor" or "contractor" means a person engaged in the business of making or selling home improvements and includes corporations, partnerships, associations and any other form of business organization or entity, and their officers, representatives, agents and employees.

"Residential or non-commercial property" means a structure used, in whole or in substantial part, as a home or place of residence by any natural person, whether or not a single or multi-unit structure, and that part of the lot or site on which it is situated and which is devoted to the residential use of the structure, and includes all appurtenant structures.

13:45A-17.3 Registration required

(a) On or after December 31, 2005, unless exempt under N.J.A.C. 13:45A-17.4:

1. No person shall engage in the business of making or selling home improvements in this State unless registered with the Division in accordance with this subchapter; and

2. No person shall advertise indicating that the person is a contractor in this State unless the person is registered with the Division in accordance with this subchapter.

(b) Unless exempt under N.J.A.C. 13:45A-17.4, contractors hired by other contractors to make or sell any home improvements shall register with the Division in accordance with this subchapter.

(c) Officers and employees of a registered home improvement contractor shall not be required to register separately from the registered business entity provided that the officers and employees sell or make home improvements solely within their respective scopes of performance for that registered business entity.

(d) Officers and employees of a home improvement contractor that is exempt under N.J.A.C. 13:45A-17.4 shall not be required to register provided that the officers and employees sell or make home improvements solely within their respective scopes of performance for that exempt business entity.

13:45A-17.4 Exemptions

(a) The following persons are exempt from the registration requirements of this subchapter:

1. Any person registered pursuant to "the New Home Warranty and Builders' Registration Act," P.L. 1977, c.467 (N.J.S.A. 46:3B-1 et seq.), but only in conjunction with the building of a new home as defined in N.J.A.C. 5:25- 1.3;

2. Any person performing a home improvement upon a residential or non-commercial property owned by that person, or by the person's family;

3. Any person performing a home improvement upon a residential or non-commercial property owned by a bona fide charity or other non-profit organization;

4. Any person regulated by the State as an architect, professional engineer, landscape architect, land surveyor, electrical contractor, master plumber, locksmith, burglar alarm business, fire alarm business, or any other person in any other related profession requiring registration, certification, or licensure by the State, who is acting within the scope of practice of that profession;

5. Any person employed by a community association or cooperative corporation who is making home improvements within the person's scope of employment at the residential or non-commercial property that is owned or leased by the community association or cooperative corporation;

6. Any public utility as defined under N.J.S.A. 48:2-13;

7. Any person licensed as a home financing agency, a home repair contractor or a home repair salesman pursuant to N.J.S.A. 17:16C-77, provided that the person is acting within the scope of such license; and

8. Any home improvement retailer with a net worth of more than $50,000,000 or any employee of such home improvement retailer who is making or selling such home improvements within the person's scope of employment of the home improvement retailer.

13:45A-17.5 Initial and renewal applications

(a) Each home improvement contractor required to be registered under this subchapter shall initially register with the Division by submitting the following on forms provided by the Director:

1. The name and street address of each place of business of the home improvement contractor and any fictitious or trade name to be used by the home improvement contractor;

2. The type of business organization;

3. The name, residence and business street address of each officer, director, principal and person with an ownership interest of 10 percent or more in the home improvement contractor business, including the percentage of ownership held;

4. The name and number of any professional or occupational license, certificate or registration issued by this State or any other governmental entity to any officer, director, principal or person with an ownership interest of 10 percent or more in the home improvement contractor business;

5. Whether the entity, any officer, director, principal or person with an ownership interest of 10 percent or more in the home improvement contractor business has been adjudged liable in an administrative or civil action involving any of the situations in (a)5i through vi below. For the purposes of this paragraph, a judgment of liability in an administrative or civil action shall include, but not be limited to, any finding or admission that the entity, officer, director, principal or person with an ownership interest of 10 percent or more in the home improvement contractor business engaged in an unlawful practice or practices related to any of the named situations in (a)5i through vi below regardless of whether that finding was made in the context of an injunction, a proceeding resulting in the denial, suspension or revocation of a license, certification or registration, consented to in an assurance of voluntary compliance or any similar order or

legal agreement with any State or Federal agency. As described above, this paragraph covers the following situations:

    i.   Obtained any registration, certification or license by fraud, deception or misrepresentation;

    ii.   Engaged in the use or employment of dishonesty, fraud, deception, misrepresentation, false promise or false pretense;

    iii.   Engaged in gross negligence, gross malpractice or gross incompetence;

    iv.   Engaged in acts of negligence, malpractice or incompetence involving selling or making a home improvement; and

    v.   Engaged in professional or occupational misconduct;

6.   Whether the entity, any officer, director, principal or person with an ownership interest of 10 percent or more in the home improvement contractor business has been convicted of any crime involving moral turpitude or any crime relating adversely to selling or making home improvements. For the purpose of this paragraph, a plea of guilty, non vult, nolo contendere or any other such disposition of alleged criminal activity shall be deemed a conviction;

7.   Whether the entity, any officer, director, principal or person with an ownership interest of 10 percent or more in the home improvement contractor business has had their authority to engage in the activity regulated by the Director revoked or suspended by any other state, agency or authority;

8.   Whether the entity, any officer, director, principal or person with an ownership interest of 10 percent or more in the home improvement contractor business has violated or failed to comply with the provisions of any act, regulation or order administered or issued by the Director;

9.   Whether the entity, any officer, director, principal or person with an ownership interest of 10 percent or more in the home improvement contractor business believes they are unable to meet the requirements of the Contractors' Registration Act, N.J.S.A. 56:8-136 et seq. or rule in this subchapter for medical or any other good cause to the detriment of the public's health, safety and welfare; and

10.   The name and street address of an agent in the State of New Jersey for service of process.

(b) In addition to the information required in (a) above, the applicant shall include the following with the initial application:

1.   A properly completed disclosure statement that complies with the requirements of N.J.A.C. 13:45A-17.6;

2.   Proof of the home improvement contractor's commercial general liability insurance policy in a minimum amount of $500,000 per occurrence that complies with the requirements of N.J.A.C. 13:45A-17.12; and

3.   The initial registration fee in the amount specified in N.J.A.C. 13:45A-17.14.

(c) A registered home improvement contractor shall include the following with the annual renewal application:

1.   A completed renewal application that will be on a form specified by the Director;

2.   Proof of the home improvement contractor's commercial general liability insurance policy in a minimum amount of $500,000 per occurrence that complies with the requirements of N.J.A.C. 13:45A-17.12;

3.   The renewal registration fee in the amount specified in N.J.A.C. 13:45A-17.14; and

4.   If the completed renewal application is received by the Division after the renewal application's due date as specified on the renewal application, the late fee in the amount specified in N.J.A.C. 13:45A-17.14.

13:45A-17.6 Disclosure statement

(a) Each applicant shall file a disclosure statement with the Director stating whether it or any of its officers, directors, principals or persons with an ownership interest of 10 percent or more in the home improvement contractor business has been convicted of any violations of the following provisions of the "New Jersey Code of Criminal Justice," Title 2C of the New Jersey Statutes, or the equivalent under the laws of any other jurisdiction:

1.   Any crime of the first degree;

2.   Any crime which is a second or third degree crime and is a violation of chapter 20 or 21 of Title 2C of the New Jersey Statutes; or

3.   Any other crime which is a violation of N.J.S.A. 2C:5-1 or 2C:5-2 (conspiracy), N.J.S.A. 2C:11-2 (criminal homicide), N.J.S.A. 2C:11-3 (murder), N.J.S.A. 2C:11-4 (manslaughter), N.J.S.A. 2C:12-1 (assault), N.J.S.A. 2C:12-3 (terroristic threats), N.J.S.A. 2C:13-1 (kidnapping), N.J.S.A. 2C:14-2 (sexual assault), subsection a. or b. of N.J.S.A. 2C:17-1 (arson and related offenses), subsection a. or b. of N.J.S.A. 2C:17-2 (causing or risking widespread injury or damage), N.J.S.A. 2C:15-1 (robbery), N.J.S.A. 2C:18-2 (burglary), N.J.S.A. 2C:20-4 (theft by deception), N.J.S.A. 2C:20-5 (theft by extortion), N.J.S.A. 2C:20-7 (receiving stolen property), N.J.S.A. 2C:20-9 (theft by failure to make required disposition of property received), N.J.S.A. 2C:21-2 (criminal simulation), N.J.S.A. 2C:21-2.1 (fraud relating to driver's license or other document issued by governmental agency to verify identity or age; simulation), N.J.S.A. 2C:21-2.3 (fraud relating to motor vehicle insurance identification card; production or sale), N.J.S.A. 2C:21-3 (frauds relating to public records and recordable instruments), N.J.S.A. 2C:21-4 (falsifying or tampering with records), N.J.S.A. 2C:21-6 (fraud relating to credit cards), N.J.S.A. 2C:21-7 (deceptive business practices), N.J.S.A. 2C:21-12 (defrauding secured creditors), N.J.S.A. 2C:21-14 (receiving deposits in a failing financial institution), N.J.S.A. 2C:21-15 (misapplication of entrusted property and property of government of financial institution), N.J.S.A. 2C:21-19 (wrongful credit practices and related offenses), N.J.S.A. 2C:27-2 (bribery in official and political matters), N.J.S.A. 2C:27-3 (threats and other improper influence in official and political matters), N.J.S.A. 2C:27-5 (retaliation for past official action), N.J.S.A. 2C:27-9 (public servant transacting business with certain persons), N.J.S.A. 2C:27-10 (acceptance or receipt of unlawful benefit by public servant for official behavior), N.J.S.A. 2C:27-11 (offer of unlawful benefit by public servant for official behavior), N.J.S.A. 2C:28-1 (perjury), N.J.S.A. 2C:28-2 (false swearing), N.J.S.A. 2C:28-3 (unsworn falsification to authorities), N.J.S.A. 2C:28-4 (false reports to law enforcement officials), N.J.S.A. 2C:28-5 (tampering with witnesses and informants; retaliation against them), N.J.S.A. 2C:28-6 (tampering with or fabricating physical evidence), N.J.S.A. 2C:28-7 (tampering with public records or information), N.J.S.A. 2C:28-8 (impersonating a public servant or law enforcement officer), N.J.S.A. 2C:30-2 (official misconduct), N.J.S.A. 2C:30-3 (speculating or wagering on official action or information), N.J.S.A. 2C:35-5 (manufacturing, distributing or dispensing a controlled dangerous substance), N.J.S.A. 2C:35-10 (possession, use or being under the influence or failure to make lawful disposition of a controlled dangerous substance), N.J.S.A. 2C:37-2 (promoting gambling), N.J.S.A. 2C:37-3 (possession of gambling records), or N.J.S.A. 2C:37-4 (maintenance of a gambling resort).

13:45A-17.7 Duty to update information

(a)   Whenever any information required to be included in the application changes, or if additional information should be added after the filing of the application, the applicant or registered home improvement contractor, as appropriate, shall provide that information to the Director, in writing, within 20 calendar days of the change or addition. Whenever any other information filed with the Director pursuant to the Contractors' Registration Act, N.J.S.A. 56:8-136 et seq., or this subchapter has changed, the applicant or registered home improvement contractor, as appropriate, shall provide that information to the Director, in writing, within 20 calendar days of the change or addition.

(b)   Whenever any information required to be included in the disclosure statement changes, or if additional information should be added after the filing of the statement, the applicant or registered home improvement contractor, as appropriate, shall provide that information to the Director, in writing, within 30 calendar days of the change or addition.

13:45A-17.8 Requirement to cooperate

Home improvement contractor applicants seeking to register with the Division and registered home improvement contractors shall have the continuing duty to provide any assistance or information; to produce any records requested by the Director; and to cooperate in any inquiry, investigation or hearing conducted by the Director.

13:45A-17.9 Refusal to issue, suspension or revocation of registration; hearing; other sanctions

(a)   The Director may refuse to issue or renew, or may suspend or revoke any registration issued by the Division upon proof that an applicant or registrant or any of its officers, directors, principals or persons with an ownership interest of 10 percent or more in the home improvement contractor business:

1.   Has obtained any registration, certification or license by fraud, deception or misrepresentation;

2.   Has engaged in the use or employment of dishonesty, fraud, deception, misrepresentation, false promise or false pretense;

3.   Has engaged in gross negligence, gross malpractice or gross incompetence;

4.   Has engaged in repeated acts of negligence, malpractice or incompetence involving selling or making a home improvement;

5.   Has engaged in professional or occupational misconduct;

6.   Has been adjudged liable in an administrative or civil action involving any finding or admission which would provide a basis for discipline pursuant to (a)1 through 5 above regardless of whether that finding was made in the context of an injunction, a proceeding resulting in the denial, suspension or revocation of a license, certification or registration, consented to in an assurance of voluntary compliance or any similar order or legal agreement with any State or Federal agency;

7.   Has been convicted of any crime involving moral turpitude or any crime relating adversely to selling or making home improvements. For the purpose of this paragraph, a plea of guilty, non vult, nolo contendere or any other such disposition of alleged criminal activity shall be deemed a conviction;

8.   Has had his or her authority to engage in the activity regulated by the Director revoked or suspended by any other state, agency or authority for reasons consistent with this section;

9.   Has violated or failed to comply with N.J.S.A. 56:8-136 et seq. or any provision of this subchapter or the provisions of any act, regulation or order administered or issued by the Director; or

10.   Is unable to meet the requirements of the Contractors' Registration Act, N.J.S.A. 56:8-136 et seq., or rule in this subchapter for medical or any other good cause to the detriment of the public's health, safety and welfare.

(b)   Information contained in the application required pursuant to N.J.A.C. 13:45A-17.5 and information contained in the disclosure statement required to be filed pursuant to N.J.A.C. 13:45A-17.6 may be used by the Director as grounds for denying, suspending or revoking a registration. An applicant whose registration is denied or a home improvement contractor whose registration is suspended or revoked based upon information contained in the application or disclosure statement or any amendments thereto shall be afforded an opportunity to be heard pursuant to the Administrative Procedure Act, N.J.S.A. 52:14B-1 et seq., and the Uniform Administrative Procedure Rules, N.J.A.C. 1:1, upon written request to the Director within 30 days of the notice of denial, suspension or revocation which shall contain the basis for such action. In any matter in which the provisions of the Rehabilitated Convicted Offenders Act, N.J.S.A. 2A:168A-1 et seq., apply, the Director shall comply with the requirements of that Act.

(c)   Except as provided in (b) above, prior to refusing to issue or renew or suspending or revoking a home improvement contractor registration or assessing a penalty, the Director shall notify the applicant or registrant and provide an opportunity to be heard.

(d)   In addition to assessing a monetary penalty for any violation of this subchapter, the Director may revoke a registration or suspend the registration for a period of time dependent upon the seriousness of the violation.

(e)   Nothing contained in this subchapter shall limit the Director from imposing any additional fees, fines, penalties, restitution or any other sanctions as permitted under the Consumer Fraud Act, N.J.S.A. 56:8-1 et seq.

13:45A-17.10   Reinstatement of suspended registration

A registration that is suspended by the Director may be reinstated upon the contractor satisfying the conditions for reinstatement as determined by the Director and paying all outstanding fees, fines, penalties and restitution, including the payment of the reinstatement fee specified in N.J.A.C. 13:45A-17.14.

13:45A-17.11   Ownership and use of registration number; replacement and duplicate certificates

(a)   Each registration number and certificate containing such registration number issued by the Director to a home improvement contractor remain the property of the State of New Jersey. If the Director suspends, fails to renew, or revokes a registration, the home improvement contractor shall immediately return all registration certificates to the Director and shall remove the registration number from all vehicles, advertising and anything else on which the registration number is displayed or otherwise communicated.

(b)   The Director shall issue a replacement certificate upon payment of the replacement certificate fee as set forth in N.J.A.C. 13:45A-17.14 and receipt by the Director of an affidavit or certified statement attesting that the original was either lost, destroyed, mutilated or is otherwise no longer in the custody of and cannot be recovered by the certificate holder.

(c)   The Director shall issue a duplicate certificate to a registered contractor upon payment of the duplicate certificate fee as set forth in N.J.A.C. 13:45A-17.14 and receipt by the Director of an affidavit or certified statement that the registered contractor has multiple places of business in which the contractor must display a certificate. A registered contractor may not possess more registration certificates than the number of places of business utilized by the contractor.

(d) A registered home improvement contractor shall prominently display:

1. The original registration certificate or a duplicate registration certificate issued by the Division at each place of business; and

2. The contractor's registration number on all advertisements distributed within this State, on business documents, contracts and correspondence with consumers of home improvement services in this State.

(e) All commercial vehicles registered in this State and leased or owned by a registrant and used by the registrant for the purpose of providing home improvements, except for vehicles leased or rented by a registrant to a customer of that registrant, shall be marked on both sides with the following information:

1. The name of the registered home improvement contractor in lettering at least one inch in height; and

2. "HIC reg. #" followed by the registration number of the registrant in lettering at least one inch in height.

(f) As of November 4, 2008, any invoice, contract or correspondence given by a registrant to a consumer shall prominently contain the toll-free telephone number provided by the Division pursuant to (b) of N.J.S.A. 56:8-149 and shall be displayed in all caps in at least 10-point bold-face type as follows: FOR INFORMATION ABOUT CONTRACTORS AND THE CONTRACTORS' REGISTRATION ACT, CONTACT THE NEW JERSEY DEPARTMENT OF LAW AND PUBLIC SAFETY, DIVISION OF CONSUMER AFFAIRS AT 1-888-656-6225.

13:45A-17.12 Mandatory commercial general liability insurance

(a) On or after December 31, 2005 every registered home improvement contractor shall secure and maintain in full force and effect during the entire term of registration a commercial general liability insurance policy and shall file with the Director proof that such insurance is in full force and effect.

(b) The insurance policy required to be filed with the Director shall be a commercial general liability insurance policy, occurrence form, and shall provide a minimum coverage in the amount of $500,000 per occurrence. On or after December 31 2005, every registered contractor engaged in home improvements whose commercial general liability insurance policy is canceled or nonrenewed shall submit to the director a copy of the certificate of commercial general liability insurance for a new or replacement policy which meets the requirements of (a) above before the former policy is no longer effective.

(c) The proof of insurance required by (a) above shall be a certificate provided by the insurer containing the insured's name, business street address, policy number, term of the insurance, and information assuring that the policy conforms with (b) above.

(d) A home improvement contractor who either does not renew or otherwise changes the contractor's commercial general liability policy shall submit a copy of the certificate of commercial general liability insurance for the new policy before the former policy is no longer effective.

13:45A-17.13 Requirements of certain home improvement contracts

In addition to the requirements of a home improvement contract pursuant to N.J.A.C. 13:45A-16.2, every home improvement contract in which a person required to be registered as a home improvement contractor is a party shall comply with the provisions of N.J.S.A. 56:8-151.

13:45A-17.14 Fees

(a) The Division shall charge the following non-refundable home improvement contractor registration fees:

1. Initial registration fee $90.00

2. Renewal registration fee $75.00

3. Late fee $25.00

4. Reinstatement fee $50.00

5. Replacement or duplicate certificate fee $20.00

Updated through 8/4/08.

3
ESTIMATING AND BIDDING

OVERVIEW

Construction estimating is the process of anticipating and accounting for all costs involved in a building project. Estimating and bidding make up the first step in the process of winning a contract to perform a project.

Contractors use the estimate as the basis for their bid. A bid should be low enough to attract an offer, but high enough to assure project completion and profit. For these reasons, expert estimating is vital to contractor success.

Careful estimating is necessary for an accurate bid. Done correctly, the estimating process lays a solid foundation for all subsequent phases of project management. Estimating is vital to project profitability. A number of factors make accurate estimating a challenge. Those factors include construction site, labor, and material equipment cost variability.

The estimate is a projection, or forecast, of all the costs required to complete a specific project. Those costs include:

- Materials;
- Labor;
- Equipment;
- Subcontractors;
- Overhead; and
- Profit.

A. MATERIAL COSTS

Materials are defined as anything supplied or installed by the contractor that becomes part of the final project, such as concrete, fasteners, lumber, steel, or drywall.

Delivery, material inspection, and storage costs are part of material costs. Material costs do not include installation, service, or progress inspections. Some contractors prepurchase and stock materials; however, most contractors purchase and have materials delivered by suppliers just before they are needed. A bidding contractor may wish to collect written statements from suppliers to ensure that once the project is awarded the materials will be available.

B. LABOR COSTS

Estimating labor costs is one of the most difficult aspects of the estimating process. Some estimators average all labor costs (direct labor, indirect labor, regular hours, and overtime hours) pertaining to a work item into a single hourly rate. Others account for these costs separately.

Direct labor costs are those basic hourly wages incurred while actually installing, building, or modifying a work item. Indirect labor costs are those labor costs beyond wages, including employee taxes, unemployment insurance, workers' compensation, vacation pay, health insurance, etc. Indirect labor costs range from 20 to 50% of the wage rate. Estimators often add this percentage to the direct labor costs. Indirect labor costs are sometimes referred to as labor burden.

An hourly cost can be developed for each job classification by adding direct and indirect labor costs. Together with productivity estimates, indexes can be used to formulate production rates. For example, if an average mason lays 100 blocks per hour, and the average labor cost is $20 per hour, then the mason's production rate estimate is $.20 per block. If the total number of blocks to be laid is known for the entire project, this production rate can be used to easily estimate the project masonry labor expense.

Of course, because of numerous possible variations, a mason may or may not be able to average 100 blocks per hour. If overtime is needed or if weather or unforeseen conditions slow productivity, the estimate may be low. This reemphasizes the need to thoroughly understand the project specifications, job-site working conditions, as well as the abilities of one's labor force.

C. EQUIPMENT COSTS

Equipment is generally understood to be all tools (large and small) that are purchased or rented by the contractor to complete a project. Hand tools, cords, and hoses to forklifts, graders, and cranes should all be considered equipment. Equipment costs also include all operating expenses such as, fuel, oil, filters, tires, equipment repair, storage, delivery, finance costs, insurance, and taxes.

If the life span of a piece of equipment is expected to be the same length as the project, then the cost of the entire piece can be used in the estimate. When equipment is rented or leased for use in several projects, the equipment cost is estimated by applying the rental/lease rates according to the time the equipment is used in the project. Equipment cost guides have been established by the federal government and by the Associated General Contractors of America (AGC).

As with labor costs, equipment is typically assigned hourly costs. These costs can also be included in production rates. For example, if a loader costs $40 per hour (without labor) and loads an average of 400 cubic yards per hour, then the equipment production rate would be $.10 per cubic yard. If the total number of cubic yards to be loaded is known, then the loader cost for the project can be estimated. This calculation presumes that the loader will maintain continuous productivity. Equipment breakdowns, scheduling problems, inclement weather, and any number of problems can affect the actual productivity per hour.

D. SUBCONTRACTORS

Many portions of a construction project will be performed by subcontractors. The general contractor must send out requests for subcontractor bids for those parts of the work. Although a general contractor may prefer the work of one subcontractor over another, the general contractor should nonetheless request several bids. Subcontractors go through an estimating process similar to the general contractor. It is therefore imperative that bidding subcontractors are provided with both a general scope of the project and with every aspect of the subcontracted job. Requests for subcontractor bids must be sent soon enough for the subcontractor to respond in time for the general contractor to include this information in the bid.

E. COMPANY OVERHEAD

Overhead is typically divided into company overhead and project overhead. Company (or general) overhead includes business expenses such as:

- Office rent;
- Office electricity;
- Office supplies;
- Office furniture;
- Company communication equipment (computers, telephones, fax machines);
- Advertising, accounting, billing, and legal expenses;
- Travel expenses (company vehicles, business trips);
- Office-related labor (secretaries, bookkeepers, maintenance); and
- General liability insurance.

While these expenses are not directly related to a particular project, every project must absorb some of the company overhead. An estimator must include a reasonable proportion of company overhead into the bid – roughly 3 to 10% of the estimate, depending on the size and number of jobs in progress.

F. PROJECT OVERHEAD

Project (or job) overhead includes those expenses that directly relate to the project but are not included as construction labor. A few examples are:

- Bonds and insurance;
- Legal fees related to the bid and contract;
- Consultants' fees for surveying, building layout, or testing;
- Project finance costs;
- Project management salaries (foremen, superintendents);
- Schedules, reports, and shop drawings;
- Electricity, telephone, water, and sanitary facilities for the project;
- Salaries and fees for site personnel (security guards, timekeepers, flaggers, safety personnel, and surveyors);
- Temporary lighting, heating, barricades, signs, and fences; and
- Mobilization costs, garbage removal, and site cleanup, etc.

Project overhead costs commonly range from 5 to 15%, depending on the size of the job. Estimating project overhead differs from company overhead. Rather than using a percentage, a more accurate method is to list and estimate actual costs.

G. PROFIT

Depending on the nature of the project, the company's need for the work, and the competitive environment, an estimate will include a profit range from 5 to 30% or more. This by no means assures that the estimated profit margin will be achieved. Because of the many unforeseeable variances in a project, contractors recognize the need to figure in a sensible contingency fund cushion. Still, in order to win the bid, the bidder must walk the fine line between offering the lowest bid and making a reasonable profit.

BIDDING PROCESS

The estimating and bidding process varies from contractor to contractor. Private builders set their own procedures, while public projects usually follow mandated bidding rules. The first step in the estimating/bidding process is to become aware that a project is open to bid.

Private builders have no obligation to advertise for bids. Negotiated contracts are common, as is invitational bidding. Private owners may invite as many or as few contractors to bid as they want. In larger cities, project reporting services disseminate information on known projects. Contractors in areas without a project reporting service may subscribe to national services (such as Dodge Reports) that monitor and report significant projects in the contractor's locale. Private builders who use competitive bidding are more likely to use these reporting services.

Public projects are legally obligated to advertise for bids. Typically, these advertisements are found in the classified sections of local and regional newspapers and trade magazines. The ad, or invitation to bid, will contain the project description, location, and name of the authorizing agency. Any special rules, the steps for obtaining the project documents, and the place and date to apply must be included in the advertisement. An approximate cost or cost range of the project is included as well as any required fees or deposits. Federal agencies post their project advertisements, called presolicitation notices, in public places and send them to interested and/or known contractors.

In many cases, contractors must qualify to bid on public building projects. Pre-qualification may be required before being permitted to bid. Post-qualifications are those that must be demonstrated after a bid is awarded. Usually, post-qualification requirements are addressed in a written addendum included with the bid. Pre- or post-qualification considerations may include:

- Licensing;
- Finances;
- Capacity;
- Experience;
- Training;
- Employees;
- Jobs in process; and
- References.

Bidding for public projects must be uniform and fair to all parties. A possible exception is that public agencies may set aside some projects based on minority, gender, social status, or company size. In any case, a set of uniform application/bidding policies is created. Those policies are spelled out in the Instructions to Bidders document. Failing to abide by those rules, not completing the proper forms, or missing the specified dates can result in a contractor's bid being rejected.

PROJECT DOCUMENTS

The second step in the estimating and bidding process is to obtain the project documents. Project documents, sometimes referred to as plans and specifications, are the legal and informational documents that encompass the project. They are prepared by architects, engineers, and attorneys for the owners. These documents are available (often for a small fee) to interested bidders.

The Construction Specifications Institute (CSI) is an international organization that has developed a coding system used to describe material and activities that go into a project. Many architects use CSI as a method for organizing the specification booklet that accompanies project plans. For additional information, refer to the CSI Format listing at the end of this chapter.

Project documents define every phase of the project, including:

- Surety bond forms;
- General conditions;
- Supplementary conditions;
- Drawings;
- Specifications;
- Allowances;
- Supplements; and
- Addenda.

Surety bonds are guarantees backed by an insurance company. Contractors deal with several types of bonds (covered in Chapter 6). Two bonds that are usually submitted with the bid are the bid (or proposal) bond and the contract (or performance) bond.

A **bid bond**, also called a proposal bond, is a guarantee backed by an insurance company that the successful bidder will enter into the project contract for the agreed-upon price. In lieu of a bond, owners may require a certified check as bid security. Many contractors use bonds to avoid tying up their capital in bid securities. Bid bonds are returned to unsuccessful bidders shortly after bid opening and to the successful bidder when the contract is signed. A **contract bond** (performance bond) is a guarantee that the selected contractor will properly perform and complete the project according to the plans and specifications.

General conditions outline the roles of the owner, contractor, architect, and engineer. **Supplementary conditions** provide additions or modifications to the general conditions for the specific project. **Drawings** show the physical aspects of the project, including dimensions, quantity, size, and location of each item that is part of the project. For large projects, separate drawings are prepared for the architectural, electrical, mechanical, and plumbing parts of the project.

Specifications describe how a project is to be built, including materials to be used and quality of workmanship. They often refer to a standard specification format developed by the Construction Specifications Institute (CSI). Specifications sometimes limit the use of products or materials to certain manufacturers.

Allowances are funds that must be allotted directly to a special item in the project. Allowances eliminate the need for contractors to produce estimates on highly specific or unique work. An example would be a $2,000 allowance for a carved teakwood executive office door. **Supplements** include soil reports, feasibility studies, or other documents that provide additional information about the project, but are not part of the legal contract documents.

Sometimes design or writing errors slip through and need to be corrected or modified. **Addenda** are additions or clarifications that are made to the project after it has been released for bidding, but before bids are received. Addenda are often responses to bidders' questions.

METHODS OF ESTIMATING

The next step in the process is to decide which estimating method will be used. There are several general methods to estimate a construction job. The two primary methods are the Detailed Survey (Lump Sum) Estimate and the Unit Price Estimate.

Regardless of the estimating method used, contractors need to understand the difficulty of forecasting accurate costs in the highly variable domain of construction. Job sites are not the same. Materials, labor, delivery, weather, and other factors make estimating a challenge. Specialized computer programs may help increase the accuracy of estimating. The creation of national and regional uniform cost indexes may help as well. One such source is the Standard Estimating Practices manual published by the American Society of Professional Estimators (ASPE).

Many contractors adopt or modify existing estimating methods to create a method with which they are comfortable and to which they can apply their experience.

A. DETAILED SURVEY METHOD

The Detailed Survey (or Lump Sum) Estimate is an accurate estimating method that lists all materials and labor needed for a project and assigns a specific price to each item or function. This type of estimate requires that a quantity survey, or takeoff, be made.

A quantity survey (takeoff) is a complete listing of all materials and items of work needed in the project. Many builders provide a general estimate of project needs. However, neither builder nor the architects/engineers are required to do so. A contractor cannot presume that general quantities in bidding documents are accurate or complete. For this reason, estimators complete their own quantity survey (takeoff) based on the drawings and specifications. The takeoff begins by making a list of all the materials and items of work necessary for the project. The results are then categorized and transferred to a summary sheet. The summary sheet guides the contractor in estimating overall materials, labor, equipment, and overhead costs. The overall costs and profit form the project estimate and bid. The following is an example of the Detailed Survey Method.

Assume a contractor is estimating and bidding the installation of 200 feet of underground piping. The costs to be included in the estimate are material, labor, equipment rental, permits, supervision, project overhead, and general overhead.

The contractor's first step is to prepare a material takeoff (quantity survey) from the project drawings and specifications. Vendor quotes are then obtained for the materials to be used (sales taxes are included with material costs).

Equipment needs are determined, and rental quotes are obtained from vendors.

Next, the contractor does a detailed labor study and estimates the labor costs for each phase of the operation. Project overhead requirements, including salaries for supervision, are determined, and estimated costs are added.

The contractor then determines what portion of general overhead costs should be applied to this project. This amount is added to the estimate.

After all these costs have been determined, a decision must be made (usually based on the total costs) about what the profit should be. This figure is added to the estimate. The resulting amount constitutes the quantity survey (lump sum) bid price.

B. UNIT PRICE ESTIMATE

Some construction projects do not work well with a detailed survey (lump sum) bid. They may require a unit price bid, or a bid broken down into several segments or units. The Unit Price Estimate consists of assigning costs to each unit of construction. A quantity survey is performed, but all units are kept separate. For example, in a multibasement project, a separate unit price is estimated for the excavating unit; forming unit; pouring unit, and so forth. Each unit price covers its share of material, labor, overhead (project and company), and profit costs. The bid will show costs for each unit of the project.

Unit price estimating is particularly useful on jobs where specific quantities are difficult to determine. The bid tabulation in the contract documents sometimes requires jobs to be bid per unit price, so that flexibility is possible.

For example, in an excavation project requiring the removal and hauling of an undetermined amount of fill material, the amount of work to be done is not defined. The contractor would estimate an all-inclusive rate to excavate and haul one cubic yard (unit). This rate would include equipment rental and maintenance costs, labor costs, fixed overhead costs, and profit. Once the cost of excavating one cubic yard of fill material is determined, the contractor could estimate this type of job regardless of how many units were involved.

STEPS IN COMPLETING AN ESTIMATE

A thorough estimate involves following many steps in their proper sequence. A sample Estimating Flow Chart (Figure 3-1) shows the general sequence of steps required to complete a cost estimate.

Figure 3-1. Estimating Flow Chart

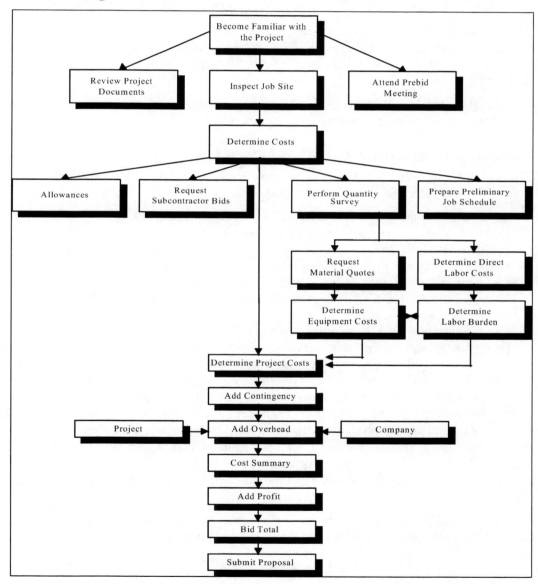

A. BECOME FAMILIAR WITH THE PROJECT

1. REVIEW PROJECT DOCUMENTS

In order to be able to adequately prepare cost data for a project, it is necessary to read and interpret the project documents and to understand *exactly* the scope of the work. The estimator needs to understand all bidding instructions, proposal forms, alternates, etc. The specification booklet must be studied thoroughly, for it contains much information that is *not* in the blueprints. Material suppliers should be consulted if technical specifications call for unfamiliar items or refer to standard specifications not accessible to the contractor.

The estimator must become familiar with building codes and regulations applicable to this job and will review the requirements for submittals, quality control, and material testing.

It will be necessary to review the contract and bond forms and gain a specific understanding of the legal and financial obligations that will be entered into. It may also be necessary to seek assistance from an accountant, bonding company, insurance agent, or attorney to understand these documents.

Any questions will be directed to the architect or engineer. After the project is assigned, questions may cause delays and confusion, and may cost money.

2. CONDUCT ENVIRONMENTAL ASSESSMENT

The environmental aspects of a project can have a serious impact on the project cost and schedule. A careful assessment should be part of the contractor's prebid investigation.

- Part of the site inspection should cover environmentally sensitive areas. The cost of restrictions when working near bodies of water, wetlands, protected trees and animals must be factored into the bid.
- Subsurface investigation should include a search for signs of any old dumping sites, buried fuel tanks, or any other contamination that would require extra cleanup and disposal costs. Even the uncovering of archeological or significant historical remains can disrupt a project if not anticipated.
- Clearing must be done in compliance with local Tree Ordinances. They often require protection of trees during construction and replacement of any trees removed. Local burning ordinances may determine whether trees can be burned on site or removed for off-site disposal. This can affect the clearing budget by many thousands of dollars.
- Earthwork and all subsequent construction must be in compliance with local, state, or federal erosion control laws. Erosion control measures all have initial costs and must be maintained through the life of the project. Budgets and overhead must allow for both.
- Inspections and approvals by environmental agencies at all levels must be factored into the project schedule. These might involve aspects of the project such as specialized equipment or the final acceptance of erosion control measures and are often distinct from the building inspections.

Even if a contractor has no direct responsibility for an environmental problem, the potential for delay and litigation make including them in the prebid investigation essential.

3. Inspect the Job Site

The estimator must be familiar with the general and unique aspects of the job site. Differing conditions will invariably affect the project cost. The following types of information should be determined from the site visit:

- Project location;
- Probable weather conditions;
- Site access and security restrictions;
- Space and staging limitations;
- Condition of existing buildings or other nearby structures;
- Availability of electricity, water, telephone, and other utility services;
- Surface topography, trees, and drainage;
- Subsurface soil, water, and rock; and
- Special safety or traffic control requirements.

If the contractor is building onto existing structures, the condition of those structures must be considered. The contractor must be particularly aware of problems that may arise from tying onto existing electrical lines, sewage, water, and mechanical connections, and efforts that will be necessary to maintain service to nearby buildings during disruption of these lines. The person conducting the job-site inspection should be experienced in all aspects of construction, and preferably in estimating. The contractor may desire to record the visit with a camcorder or camera, with tape and sight measurements, and with notes or sketches. A written job-site report can be prepared to help clarify the conditions at the site for future reference.

4. Attend Prebid Meetings

Prebid meetings with the owner help to clarify any procedures or specifications that are subject to modification. Often on larger projects, a prebid meeting is held by the owner to explain the project to all bidders.

B. Determine Costs

1. Set Aside Allowances

Allowances do not need to be estimated, and can be set aside for later inclusion into the bid. A common allowance item is specialized or unique lighting fixtures.

2. Determine the Work that will be Subcontracted and Obtain Subcontract Bids

In many cases subcontractors perform part of the project work. Equipment and materials will also be provided by others. Subcontractors and suppliers should be contacted early in the process so they will have adequate time to provide bid information. Their bids must also be accurate, complete, and timely to provide the estimator enough time to complete the overall bid before the deadline.

Enough bidders need to be invited to bid in order to ensure a competitive cost for the item. The contractor must verify that the bidders are qualified and licensed to do the work for which they are bidding. All subcontractors must estimate performing the work at the quality level expected throughout the entire project. Otherwise, the low bid may be based on either a lower amount of work or poorer quality of work.

3. PREPARE A COMPLETE, ACCURATE QUANTITY SURVEY

The estimator should prepare a complete, accurate quantity survey (takeoff). The quantity survey (takeoff) is a complete listing of all the materials and items of work that will be required.

Plans and working drawings should be used to make a comprehensive list of all the materials needed. Quantities for each work item listed on the takeoff worksheet should be determined. The labor and equipment required for each work item or unit of material can then be estimated.

The takeoff of an individual item is complete when the item has been listed in appropriate pricing units on the takeoff sheet and the computations have been checked. A systematic method of grouping similar items reduces the possibility of omitting items from the takeoff. Most estimators have references to aid them in completing quantity surveys. Computer programs are also available to assist in this effort. On large projects, a number of takeoff specialists may use the CSI format to track their areas of expertise.

Job-costing data from previous projects may be used to establish labor, material, equipment, and overhead costs for the project being bid. Costs are adjusted to reflect current wage rates, location, and special conditions of this project. Job costing is keeping detailed records of all costs associated with each job. It is important for the successful contractor to develop a checklist that includes every aspect not only of the current project being bid, but also of any conceivable project that may be bid in the future. The more detailed the checklist, the more complete and accurate the estimate. Information gained from job costing can be used as a guide for future estimating, and it also provides a means to monitor labor productivity and supervisory ability on the current job. Job costing also assists the contractor in figuring amounts due in progress payments and provides individual project profit/loss performance data.

After the quantity survey (take off) is complete, each item is classified and totaled onto a summary sheet. The summary sheet lists the total material and labor needed for each task item and is a basis to estimate overall costs. Missing any task items results in estimating mistakes and bids that are too low or high. Such bids lead to unprofitable jobs or loss of prospective jobs.

a. COMPUTE LABOR COSTS

The estimator begins by breaking the job down into individual tasks and assigning labor hours to each task. The more time spent analyzing and developing a task list, the more accurate this part of the estimate will be. Nonproductive items such as on-the-job tool maintenance, scaffold erection and take-down, cleanup, coffee breaks, safety and coordination meetings, superintendent time, and a contingency for the occasional mistake that will have to be redone are included.

Labor market research to become familiar with exactly what crews must be paid should be conducted. The estimator must determine whether union or federal pay scales are required. If a contractor is unsure about pay scales or the time required for a specific task, this is the time to find out.

b. COMPUTE MATERIAL AND EQUIPMENT COSTS

Every piece of material that will be used on the job should be estimated. A contingency for waste and warpage of lumber and other applicable difficulties is usually included. At least three suppliers should provide bids. Daily, weekly, and monthly rates on rental equipment should be obtained. If it is a large project, an outright purchase of needed equipment may be more cost effective than leasing or renting.

4. PREPARE A PRELIMINARY JOB SCHEDULE

The building process confirms the phrase, "time is money." Time (scheduling) needs to be considered carefully in project costs.

Although detailed scheduling is usually done after the cost estimate is complete, a preliminary schedule is needed to estimate labor, equipment, and project overhead costs. These are the cost categories most affected by construction scheduling. Estimated labor unit costs are projections of how many hours it takes workers to complete the project at a specific cost per hour. Equipment costs and many job-site overhead items are measured in units of time (hours, days, weeks, or months). Any difference between the time actually required and the time budgeted in the estimate results in a cost overrun or underrun.

Historical records may be used as a basis for an estimate of the time required to complete individual segments of work. For example, a contractor knows from historical records that a certain sized house can be framed by a certain crew in three weeks (15 days). Adjusting for any wage change, the contractor can easily compute the cost of this portion of the work.

The order of tasks in the schedule is important. An efficient sequence cuts job time and reduces special costs such as temporary facilities, use of staging areas, and equipment costs. If tasks can be scheduled at the same time, overhead costs may be reduced, making the bid more competitive.

Overtime pay affects actual costs and should be included in the cost estimate. If overtime is needed to meet project deadlines, labor costs are increased. On the other hand, job-site overhead is usually based on calendar days, so overtime labor will get the job done more quickly and thus reduce job-site overhead.

C. CALCULATE PROJECT COSTS

To determine project costs, a contractor summarizes material and equipment costs from the quantity survey. To this the contractor adds direct labor costs and labor burden. Project allowances and subcontractor bids are also included at this time.

D. ADD OVERHEAD

Contractors compute project and company overhead costs then add them to the estimate. General overhead costs are those that cannot be attributed to any one project. Even though they are general in nature, these costs can often be estimated in the same way as other project costs because they include material costs, labor costs, or equipment costs. These costs are usually incurred by a company whether or not it is working on a project, and they must be built into every project performed.

E. ADD PROFIT

A company must make a profit to survive and grow. A contract bid must include a certain percentage of markup for profit. Profit is usually estimated as a percentage of the total job cost. The percentage of profit added depends on the type of project and the nature of the market. The amount of profit markup can be affected by a number of variables:

- Size and complexity of the project;
- Location of the project;
- How many other contractors are bidding on the project;
- The economic climate of the area;
- The amount of expertise the project will require and if a company has that expertise; and
- The contractor's level of interest in taking the job.

F. ADD CONTINGENCY

Because of the many variables and risks in a project, contractors often include a contingency value. Contingency rates depend on the confidence in one's estimate and contracting ability, as well as the degree of uncertainty of factors influencing project completion (such as the weather, labor, project complexity, or political unrest).

G. TOTAL BID

Most specification booklets contain a bid sheet that must be submitted as the formal proposal. This bid sheet includes the name of the project, the contractor's name, the bid amount (stated both in words and in figures), allowances, and the contractor's signature. An example of an estimate showing what comprises each element is provided in Figure 3-2.

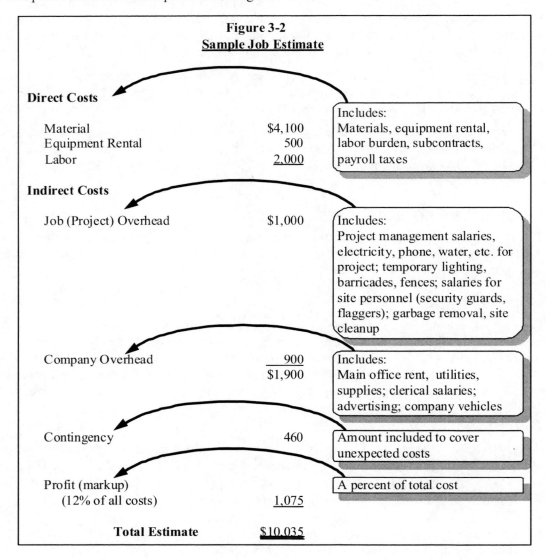

Figure 3-2
Sample Job Estimate

Direct Costs

		Includes:
Material	$4,100	Materials, equipment rental,
Equipment Rental	500	labor burden, subcontracts,
Labor	2,000	payroll taxes

Indirect Costs

Job (Project) Overhead $1,000

Includes:
Project management salaries, electricity, phone, water, etc. for project; temporary lighting, barricades, fences; salaries for site personnel (security guards, flaggers); garbage removal, site cleanup

Company Overhead   900
             $1,900

Includes:
Main office rent, utilities, supplies; clerical salaries; advertising; company vehicles

Contingency   460

Amount included to cover unexpected costs

Profit (markup)
(12% of all costs)   1,075

A percent of total cost

Total Estimate $10,035

VALID BID PROPOSALS

A valid bid is based on a valid cost estimate. If the cost estimate is not valid and an inexact proposal is submitted, the contractor is placing the company at risk. A valid bid proposal usually includes:

- Accurate material quantities;
- Adequate allowances;
- Accurate and complete quantifying of work items;
- Competitive and current material cost quotes;
- Complete, competitive subcontract bids;
- Realistic labor productivity estimates for current wage rates;
- Satisfactory budgets for equipment, tools, and job-site overhead;
- Reasonable contingency amount for unknown factors affecting cost; and
- Sufficient markup for service, risk, and profit.

Overall, the bid must be "responsive" or in other words, it must respond exactly to the specified work, without contractor-imposed provisions. Owners who feel that a contractor is not responsive to their needs, may reject even the low bid. For this reason, bidders must be certain that their proposals are tailored to the project.

Bids are generally accepted or rejected within 30 to 90 days from the bid closing date. Usually the owner or architect has the right to reject any or all bids. Owners may, at their discretion, overlook any technical deficiencies in a bid.

It should be noted that bid rigging, or price fixing, is both a crime and a civil violation. Contractors who conspire together to win or share bids by bid rigging are subject to criminal prosecution and civil penalties up to three times the amount of any damages.

COMMON ERRORS TO AVOID IN ESTIMATING

The worst type of error in construction cost estimating is leaving out an item of work. On a lump-sum bid and contract, the contractor is obligated to do all of the work, even if costs for part of the project are omitted in the estimate bid and contract to build.

Ensuring that all items have been included in the takeoff portion of the estimate is perhaps the most difficult part of the estimate, and it requires careful attention. Any items that may be difficult or unusual in any way should be underlined, checked, or circled.

A marker or colored pencil can be used to check off each item on the plans as they are taken off. Although the check-off process is primarily used to prevent double counting, it also reduces the chance of omissions. A systematic check-off facilitates reviewing plans at the end of the takeoff. The estimator should pay particular attention to unchecked items that may have been missed. In order to prevent error, the estimator should keep takeoff sheets neat and orderly.

Another common error is leaving out the cost of work that has been taken off but is not estimated on the summary sheet when the estimate or bid is completed. The best way of eliminating this is through a comprehensive system to control the estimate summary process. A complete list of work/cost items from the takeoff sheets should be transferred to the cost estimate summary sheet before completing the estimate or bid. The cost estimate should be checked for completeness before the bid is submitted. A difficult error to detect is transposed or reversed numbers in the measurement, quantity determination, or cost extensions. To eliminate transposed figures, each entry should be checked at the time it is made.

All computations required for the quantity takeoff and cost estimate should be figured on a calculator with a paper tape or on a computer so that errors can be traced, and calculations can be compared to the worksheets they were taken from. Another person should review the estimate sheets and check calculations to verify that numbers were transferred and computed correctly.

Using standard forms and procedures on each bid will minimize the chance for mistakes and will produce data that a contractor will be able to use to bid other jobs. Accuracy in cost estimating cannot be overemphasized. When cost estimates are inaccurate due to overestimation of costs or quantities, the bid will not be competitive.

ESTIMATOR'S ROLE

The role of the estimator is important because a successful building business depends on complete, accurate, and consistent cost estimates. Many companies employ a specialist to prepare the cost estimates. This person's full-time work is to bid jobs. A new contractor who is starting a business will probably perform the estimating function. Although the size of the job, the amount of materials needed, and the number of labor hours required may be smaller, the same estimating steps should be followed.

The estimator's role is to develop, in advance, an accurate budget to buy all of the parts and pieces of work to be done. The estimator must know the building process and all the work items and materials required for each project, as well as how to apply the cost factors involved in completing each step in the building process.

Even though cost control minimizes waste, loss, and inefficiency in the building process, such control cannot, by itself, assure a profit on a building project. The original cost estimate must, on an item-by-item basis, provide an adequate budget to purchase the materials and to do the work required.

TIPS FOR COMPETITIVE BIDDING

It is difficult to succeed in bidding against contractors who underprice their work. If possible, a contractor should find out who else is bidding before a cost estimate is prepared. In some cases, a contractor may choose to forego the bid. Owners know that an exceptionally low bid may either be the result of estimating error or an unrealistic bidder. A competitive bid is one that is realistic in every cost category: material, subcontracts, labor costs, equipment costs, job-site overhead, contingency cost, and markup.

A competitive material cost estimate must include the most competitive price within the quality range required. This is accomplished only after thoroughly collecting material cost information. Bidders should use payment discounts in pricing materials and then purchase those materials at the available discount.

Contractors in the same area usually buy materials from the same or competing vendors. With accurate material quantities, the total material cost for two contractors should be, within a reasonable variance, the same. A contractor must ensure that material costs are based on the grades or quality of materials called for in the specifications.

Contractors must try to receive bid proposals from as many subcontractors as possible. However, subcontractors who do the best work may or may not offer the lowest bid. General contractors must use their best judgment as to which subcontractors give the most value for their pay.

The labor cost estimate is also subject to judgment and interpretation. Wage rates in an area are usually similar, but higher wages may lead to higher productivity. The labor unit costs used in the bid are productivity estimates based on historical labor cost records. A contractor should avoid being overly optimistic in estimating labor productivity.

Rental rates used in equipment cost estimates must be reasonable if a competitive bid is to result. Some contractors lower or eliminate their rental rates to gain a competitive edge. Although this may assist in the competitive aspect of the bid, it can result in a loss of profit when the project is built. Realistic rates and amount of time needed should be used to estimate the equipment cost portion of a bid, including pick-up and delivery costs.

The competitive bidder should limit the job-site overhead estimate to only the items for which actual costs must be recovered and not list items for which no costs will be incurred. Contractor historical job site overhead cost records are the best source for estimating these costs.

SUMMARY

Construction estimating is the process of forecasting costs. The more accurate the forecast, the better a contractor can make bidding decisions. A contractor should have the ability to recognize potential problems in the estimating process. Contractors with experience in estimating, bidding, and project completion will likely have an advantage over less-experienced bidders.

Many tools have been developed for contractors to generate successful estimates. Those tools include well-trained estimators, standardized indexes for labor and equipment, estimating computer programs, trustworthy material suppliers and subcontractors, and standardized forms and bidding processes. The art of winning profitable jobs is founded not only on accuracy and thoroughness but especially on good judgment.

November 2004

Division Numbers and Titles

PROCUREMENT AND CONTRACTING REQUIREMENTS GROUP

Division 00   Procurement and Contracting Requirements

SPECIFICATIONS GROUP

GENERAL REQUIREMENTS SUBGROUP

Division 01   General Requirements

FACILITY CONSTRUCTION SUBGROUP

Division 02   Existing Conditions

Division 03   Concrete

Division 04   Masonry

Division 05   Metals

Division 06   Wood, Plastics, and Composites

Division 07   Thermal and Moisture Protection

Division 08   Openings

Division 09   Finishes

Division 10   Specialties

Division 11   Equipment

Division 12   Furnishings

Division 13   Special Construction

Division 14   Conveying Equipment

Division 15   Reserved

Division 16   Reserved

Division 17   Reserved

Division 18   Reserved

Division 19   Reserved

FACILITY SERVICES SUBGROUP

Division 20   Reserved

Division 21   Fire Suppression

Division 22   Plumbing

Division 23   Heating, Ventilating, and Air Conditioning

Division 24   Reserved

Division 25   Integrated Automation

Division 26   Electrical

Division 27   Communications

Division 28   Electronic Safety and Security

Division 29   Reserved

SITE AND INFRASTRUCTURE SUBGROUP

Division 30   Reserved

Division 31   Earthwork

Division 32   Exterior Improvements

Division 33   Utilities

Division 34   Transportation

Division 35   Waterway and Marine Construction

Division 36   Reserved

Division 37   Reserved

Division 38   Reserved

Division 39   Reserved

PROCESS EQUIPMENT SUBGROUP

Division 40   Process Integration

Division 41   Material Processing and Handling Equipment

Division 42   Process Heating, Cooling, and Drying Equipment

Division 43   Process Gas and Liquid Handling, Purification, and Storage Equipment

Division 44   Pollution Control Equipment

Division 45   Industry-Specific Manufacturing Equipment

Division 46   Reserved

Division 47   Reserved

Division 48   Electrical Power Generation

Division 49   Reserved

4

CONTRACTS

OVERVIEW

A contract is a mutually understood agreement that contains an offer to perform a service or provide a product, an acceptance of the offer, and a show of faith (called consideration) by giving each other some kind of service, payment, or deposit. Construction contracts for even small projects can be very detailed.

A construction contract is a means to assign risks, rights and responsibilities, and compensation between the owner and the contractor. Though a legal contract requires a mutually understood agreement, a contractor will gain little benefit or sympathy by stating, after the fact, that a signed contract was unclear, not well understood, or not read thoroughly. The law presumes that licensed contractors understand what they agree to in writing.

When disputes arise, judicial bodies are likely to interpret construction contracts strictly by the letter, or in other words, by what is written rather than by what may have been said or supposedly mutually understood. In the construction field, contracts tend to be lengthy in order to insure clarity.

ELEMENTS OF A VALID CONTRACT

To be legally valid, a written contract must include:

- A mutual understanding;
- An offer to provide a product or perform work;
- An acceptance (signed and dated); and
- Consideration.

A valid contract requires at least two parties, both of which must be above the age of majority and mentally competent. Contracts are not valid if they pertain to any illegal activity.

Contracts usually do not need to be in writing to be valid and enforceable. Oral agreements are usually perfectly legal and valid, but they may be difficult to enforce because the parties often forget what they said or what they meant. In many states, Statutes of Fraud mandate that contracts involving real property that last more than one year, or exceed $500 in value, are not legally binding unless they are in writing. Although oral contracts may, in some cases, be legal, a smart contractor will always use a written contract.

Owners and contractors should identify themselves with their full legal names as well as identifying their complete registered business or corporate name. If any of the parties to the contract are doing business under an assumed personal or business name, that name should be disclosed. Persons should express the capacity in which they are functioning (proprietorship, partner, corporate officer, member of a limited liability company, etc.).

Consideration is anything of value, such as a payment, exchanged between parties to show good faith in the contract. In the case of construction contracts, the consideration of the owner usually consists of money exchanged for the contractor's services.

A few legal guidelines of contract interpretation that have evolved over the years include:

- Written agreements prevail over oral agreements;
- Later agreements prevail over earlier agreements;
- Words prevail over numbers;
- Special clauses prevail over general clauses;
- Specifications prevail over drawings;
- Handwritten agreements prevail over machine printed agreements; and
- Ambiguousness is interpreted against the party that wrote it.

Regardless of whether standard or custom contract forms are used, all parties must carefully examine the contract and all its provisions. This assessment will help to avoid misunderstandings and possibly even considerable expense.

Because it is presumed that all contract documents complement each other, it is not necessary to reestablish every detail of the work in every document where previously stated information applies. Contracts typically offer details only once and then are cross-referenced when needed.

Most contracts contain an integration clause, or the notation that the forms and documents constitute the whole agreement. This clause rejects any and all representations not specifically contained in the written agreement.

A construction contract may contain many documents to make it more understandable. These documents often contain numerous clauses, specifications, and provisions. They will likely include highly detailed professional and legal language that may require expert counsel.

STANDARD CONTRACT FORMS

Standard contract forms have been developed by a number of private and public organizations. Most contractors use these forms because they help to eliminate misunderstanding. Standard contract forms contain legally tested wording. Builders, architects, engineers, and attorneys are familiar with and use these forms.

The most common forms for private projects are the comprehensive contract package offered by the American Institute of Architects (AIA). The AIA is the source of this standard contract because owners have traditionally relied on architects to prepare construction contract documents. The Associated General Contractors (AGC) endorses AIA construction contract documents. The AGC has developed additional contract documents covering management, cost plus, and design/build contracts. Contracts prepared and used by government agencies vary widely. The use of forms created by government agencies is no guarantee of legality, modernness, or comprehensiveness.

THE STANDARD FORM OF AGREEMENT

The Standard Form of Agreement is a form that joins all the estimating/bidding documents and other contract documents into one formal, legal agreement. The Agreement usually includes provisions from the other documents by stating that it "incorporates" them "by reference." It establishes the general project scope, time of expected completion, project responsibilities, price of the project, terms of payment, insurance and bonding details, etc. The Agreement is quite brief compared to the other contract documents. It is usually separate from the other contract documents and is often the only contract document signed by both parties.

The written acceptance must include a specific reference to the offer, a clear and unconditional acceptance of that offer, the date of acceptance, and the signature of the contractor and the owner.

The Agreement should include the:

- Owner's name and address;
- Contractor's name and address;
- Nature, general description, and scope of the project;
- Address and general description of the property;
- Starting and completion dates;
- Identification of drawings and specifications;
- Contract amount and payment arrangements; and
- Plainly worded offer.

In addition to the Standard Form of Agreement, construction contracts may include all the documents used in the estimating and bidding process, such as:

- Bidding documents;
- Surety bond forms;
- General conditions;
- Supplementary conditions;
- Drawings;
- Specifications;
- Supplements; and
- Addenda.

A. BIDDING DOCUMENTS

The Invitation to Bid describes the project and outlines the procedures for bidding and award of the contract. It states how contractors may obtain a copy of the contract documents and when, where, and in what manner bids will be accepted by the owner.

The Instructions to Bidders presents specific rules that the contractors must follow in assembling and submitting their bids. The primary purpose of the Instructions to Bidders is to standardize the bids so that they may be analyzed and evaluated consistently.

Note: While estimating documents are always included in the Agreement, bid documents are not always included. For example, some AIA forms do not include bidding documents as contract documents unless otherwise agreed.

B. CONTRACT SURETY BONDS AND INSURANCE

Surety bonds are guarantees backed by an insurance company. The primary bonds involved with the contract are the performance bond, payment bond, and lien bond. The performance bond is a guarantee that the contractor will satisfactorily complete the project according to the plans specified in the contract. The payment bond is a guarantee that the contractor will pay for all materials and labor. The lien bond guarantees that the property will not be encumbered by a lien from subcontractors. Contractors may also be required to provide proof of liability and employee insurance.

C. GENERAL CONDITIONS

The General Conditions to the Contract for Construction provides additional scope and detail, and specifies the rights, duties, and responsibilities of the owner, contractor, architect, and/or the construction manager. The General Conditions usually consists of forms with standard provisions that would apply to most projects. Standard forms of General Conditions are published by the federal and many state governments, the AGC, and the AIA.

D. Supplementary or Special Conditions

The purpose of the Supplementary or Special Conditions is to tailor the standardized provisions of the General Conditions in order to account for special conditions and circumstances that are unique to a particular project. There is usually a specific reason for each special or supplemental condition, and it is important to understand the intended effect of each condition before accepting it as part of the overall construction contract.

E. Drawings and Specifications

The actual physical description of the project to be constructed is contained in the drawings. Drawings and specifications are prepared by a qualified and licensed designer/architect/engineer. For most large and/or complex projects, separate sets of drawings are generally prepared for each of the major construction disciplines:

- Architectural;
- Civil;
- Electrical;
- Mechanical; and
- Structural.

The drawings explain the type, quantity, size, and location of each item that is to be incorporated into the construction of the project. The specifications describe how a project is to be built. The success of any project is largely dependent on the completeness and accuracy of the drawings.

F. Addenda

It is often necessary to make changes to the contract documents before the execution of the Standard Form of Agreement. Addenda are issued before the date bids are accepted and often contain information that may affect bid prices. Once issued, addenda become a part of the contract documents and, thus, a part of the Standard Form of Agreement for Construction.

G. Modifications

Once the Standard Form of Agreement is signed, any changes are usually known as modifications. There are several kinds of modifications, including written change orders, bulletins, clarifications, interpretations issued by the architect, and field memoranda.

Basic Contractual Responsibilities and Rights

Each participant in the construction process has particular roles and responsibilities. Those roles and responsibilities are defined in the contract and clearly establish the relationships between participants. Once established in the contract, those relationships and responsibilities become legally binding and form the basis for dispute resolution.

A. Basic Contractual Rights and Responsibilities of the Owner

The standard construction contract specifies both the owner's and the contractor's rights and responsibilities. For example, the owner must:

- Provide adequate plans and specifications;
- Provide a legally unencumbered property on which to build;
- Provide access to the job site (property easements); and
- Make timely contractor payments.

The owner also has several basic rights that are normally found in a standard construction contract, including the right to:

- Make modifications, additions, or deletions to the project;
- Offer other contracts related to the project;
- Inspect project work;
- Perform any work on which a contractor defaults;
- Utilize completed portions of the work;
- Require contract bonds from the contractor;
- Accelerate or extend completion times; and
- Withhold or deduct payments when work is not completed.

Owners are not allowed to interfere with the contractor's work, direction, methods, or control. A general contractor is considered to be "independent." Owners who do not allow a contractor to function independently take upon themselves the legal liabilities previously held by the contractor.

B. BASIC CONTRACTUAL RIGHTS AND RESPONSIBILITIES OF THE CONTRACTOR

The standard construction contract typically specifies many contractor responsibilities and fewer contractor rights. The contractor's primary contractual right focuses on being paid. The contract specifies when and how progress payments are made. The contract defines procedures for allowing and paying for added project costs. The contract sets parameters for start and completion dates, time extensions, and project accelerations. The contract establishes schedules for bonuses, for withholding pay because of incomplete or inadequate work, as well as establishing consequences for late work.

Contracts allow contractors to employ subcontractors, order materials, and implement whatever construction methods, processes, and schedules are deemed appropriate by the contractor. The contract may possess an escalation clause or the means by which the contractor is reimbursed for unexpected rises in the cost of labor, equipment, or materials.

The contractor has a number of basic responsibilities, including:

- Giving full-time attention to the project;
- Completing the project as specified;
- Following project designs, drawings, and specifications;
- Obeying all laws and regulations (employment, environmental, safety, etc.);
- Providing all relevant insurance coverage; and
- Informing owners of any delays, problems, or errors.

The contractor is also responsible for work performed by the subcontractors, and is obligated to provide adequate overall supervision. Inadequate supervision is the root of many contracting problems. On even moderate projects, a contractor may meet this responsibility by employing a project superintendent. While the contractor gives up no liability, a superintendent becomes the contractor's agent on the job site and has the full authority to represent the contractor.

The standard construction contract details how contractors and owners may seek recourse for breach of contract, how to terminate the contract, and how to appeal the decision of the other party. In the event of contractual dispute, the contract will also stipulate how the added cost of arbitration, legal counsel, and court costs will be paid. In most cases, the losing party is held responsible for administrative and legal costs.

SPECIAL CONTRACT RELATIONSHIPS

The most simple construction management approach is establishing a direct relationship between an owner and a single contractor. When special needs arise, additional contractual relationships are put into the contract. Deviations from the traditional process include the following.

A. Design/Build

The design/build option is defined as one person being responsible for the entire design and construction process. This person supervises the overall architectural, engineering, bidding, contracting, building, and inspection from the beginning to the end of the project. The advantage of having a single person in charge of all aspects of the project is that an owner does not have to step in to mediate disputes between architects, engineers, contractors, etc.

B. Turnkey Construction

A "turnkey" construction project is similar to the design/build process except that the contractor develops the entire project. In addition to building the project, the contractor obtains financing, acquires the land, procures the designs and plans, etc. The additional tasks add responsibility, liability, and increased income to the turnkey contractor.

C. Phased or Fast-Track Design and Construction

When time is the highest priority, an owner and contractor may agree to a phased (fast-track) project approach. The fast-track approach is the process of starting actual construction even though all of the plans and drawings are not complete. This allows for construction to begin without being delayed by the design and bidding process. In the phased approach, each phase is bid and contracted separately. Because the total project cost may not be known until the project is nearly complete, the initial contract may contain provisions pertaining to cost ranges and limits.

D. Multiple General Contractors

An owner may choose to contract with more than one general contractor. Owners may feel that a demanding or a diverse project may require too much expertise from a single contractor. The owner may choose to have one general contractor for challenging subsurface work (tunneling or drainage), one for a complex, weight-bearing structural design, and one for special finishing work. In such cases, the architect will offer separate bids for each project component. Each contract must specify procedures and consequences in the event one of the general contractors delays, damages, or otherwise interferes with the contracts of the other general contractors. Because the work is divided among contractors, the owner accepts additional responsibility to manage and coordinate the entire project. This added owner responsibility should also be defined in the contract.

E. Partnering

Partnering is an approach used to reduce conflict and litigation on the construction site. Under this arrangement, the owner, designer, contractor, and other interested parties agree in advance to a set of project goals and terms. They agree to bring the project to a successful completion and to work together in a cooperative fashion to solve problems and complete the project successfully.

Other Important Aspects of the Construction Contract

A. Indemnification

A contract will contain a provision pertaining to indemnification, or the notion that certain parties are not liable for personal injury or property damage in the construction process. A contract clause may be valid that requires the contractor to hold the owner harmless against injury or damage that results from mutual negligence. Indemnification issues are closely related to insurance issues. For this reason, contractors are well advised to consult their insurance company before accepting construction site liability.

B. Time is "Of the Essence"

Construction contracts will contain conditions relating to time, in particular the project starting date and the project completion date. Even if the project completion date is not precisely set, it is presumed that time is "of the essence" or that time itself has a high value.

If a project is started or completed late, either by missing a predetermined start or completion date, or by a contractor not performing as if time was of the essence, a breach of contract occurs. Contracts often stipulate rewards for early completion and impose damages for late completions. This compensation may be in whatever form mutually agreed upon, for example, a percentage of the project cost. These damages, called liquidated damages, involve a set dollar amount according to the number of days the project goes uncompleted beyond the completion date.

Liquidated damages differ from actual damages. Construction contracts usually fix liquidated damage amounts in advance such as $100 per day of delay in completion. The use of liquidated damages in a contract provides a way for owner and contractor to settle without need for legal action. If a contract specifies liquidated damages, an owner may not sue for actual damages.

A construction contract should define project completion. A project is considered to be complete when the activity for which it was built can be engaged in normally and fully, even though small tasks or items may not be totally finished. A contractor must anticipate any foreseeable hindrance to starting and completing any contract.

C. Time Extensions

Unavoidable conditions may arise that delay the construction project. Some delays are justifiable; others are not. A contract usually addresses justifiable conditions that merit a time extension. When these conditions lead to a delay, an extension to the completion date may be allowed. In such cases, the contractor does not breach the contract or face liquidated damages.

Examples of justifiable delays that may lead to time extensions are:
- Owner/architect project changes;
- Owner/architect start date changes;
- Owner/architect project design errors;
- Owner/architect project additions;
- Legal delays (not caused by the contractor);
- Public agency/utility delays (not caused by the contractor);
- Environmental delays;
- Extreme weather delays (earthquake, flood, fire, hurricane);
- Labor strike, civil uprising, or war; and
- Acts of God.

Contracts normally contain a provision that allows owner-caused delays to extend project time. Some contracts designate that expenses that result from owner-caused delays are incurred by the owner. Other contracts specify that owners are not liable for damages or expenses stemming from owner-caused delays.

Time extensions are usually not authorized for conditions that a reasonable contractor should have anticipated or for conditions that existed when the contractor signed the contracts. For example, in New Jersey an extension may be given because of unusually severe weather, such as a hurricane, but probably not be given because of excessive rain.

Whenever a contractor discovers a significant construction delay (typically 10 or more days), the contractor must notify the owner in writing regarding the exact nature of the delay. Failure to do so may result in a time extension not being allowed.

Of course, for every extendable delay, there are as many or more possible unextendable delays. A contractor must anticipate and plan for them all. Contractors are often able to circumvent delays even when a justifiable condition arises. The consistent ability to foresee, adjust, and remedy such conditions may lead the owner to flexibility when future delays occur. In such cases, an owner may grant a time extension as a gesture of appreciation for previous timely efforts. For this reason, a contractor will likely have more success with owners when time extensions are used judiciously.

D. TIME ACCELERATION

In the contract, an owner may stipulate the option to direct the contractor to complete the project before the established completion date. Any additional expenses incurred from accelerating the project must be covered by the owner.

One exception is when a project has been delayed by fault of the contractor. An owner may require the contractor to accelerate the project in order to meet the original completion date. In such cases, the contractor may be liable for any added acceleration expenses. Contractors are likely to be agreeable to covering the added expenses because they do not owe damages if the project is completed on time.

E. PROJECT CHANGES

Nearly all construction contracts allow owners to make both significant and minor building changes during construction. The owner normally may not make drastic changes without rewriting the contract. Change may stem from:

- Project additions;
- Project deletions;
- Design error corrections;
- Contractor suggestions;
- Material substitutions; and
- Changes in building methods.

The standard construction contract will usually have a change clause that outlines change procedures. Contracts also require that anticipated changes discovered by the contractor must be submitted in a detailed written notice to the owner.

F. CHANGE ORDERS

Contracts usually stipulate that a written change order must be issued prior to beginning the work. The written change order becomes a supplement to the original contract. The change order normally contains a description of the work to be performed, the amount of time it will add to the project completion date, and the added compensation. To be valid, the change order needs both the contractor's dated signature and the dated signature of the owner or owner's designated representative. The architect does not necessarily have the authority to represent the owner.

As is common in the profession, a change order may be instigated orally by the owner, though in the end, a written change order should be obtained. An oral directive of a significant change is referred to as a "constructive change." A minor change that is not expected to result in any appreciable extra cost or time may not require a change order; this type of informal change by the owner is called a "field order."

G. ARTISTIC CHANGES

While plans and specifications describe the project in objective detail, they may not necessarily communicate the architect's artistic intent for the project. The aesthetic intent clause in a contract allows the architect the right to make in-progress changes to ensure the actual construction reflects the intended construction (vision). This right to make changes for the sake of subjective artistry places all parties in a situation that may require negotiation and compromise. An additional clause may be wisely included in the contract that sets a limit on artistic changes.

H. BRAND X

A contractor may want to use materials or equipment that differ only slightly from those called for in the specifications. This may be advantageous to the owner, because it often results in using similar products that are less expensive or more readily available than the specified item. Such substitutions are allowed by the contract specification that permits the use of "Brand X or equal." The owner and/or the architect make any final decision on substituted material.

I. SITE CONDITIONS

A primary factor that often leads to construction delays involves the project site. The standard construction contract specifies what steps are to be taken to resolve any issues that arrive from unexpected or highly peculiar job-site conditions.

The standard construction contract will contain adjustment provisions in the event unforeseen site conditions impact costs or schedules. The contract typically stipulates that in order to receive special adjustment considerations, site conditions must:

- Significantly differ from those expected;
- Significantly impact project schedule, methods, or costs; and
- Not be differences that would have been foreseeable to a contractor with reasonable skill.

During the bidding process, the owner is obligated to fully disclose all available information pertaining to the site. At the same time, contractors are obligated to assess the information provided and compare it to the finding of the prebid site inspection. Contracts usually contain disclaimers to the effect that the owners and architect are not liable for variances in the subsurface data they supply, and that contractors must themselves investigate the actual conditions.

If project documents contain mistaken or misleading information about the site, the owner will be liable for added construction costs. Otherwise, a contractor has the privilege to collect additional costs due to peculiar site conditions only to the extent that those privileges are agreed to in the contract.

J. SITE ACCESS

Unless otherwise agreed to in the contract, the owner has an implied duty to provide the contractor with adequate and timely access to the job site. Likewise, the contractor's job-site interference with the owner's or other independent contractors' use should be minimal and reasonable.

K. CLEANUP

The construction contract will likely make clear that it is the duty of the contractor to keep the job site clean during construction. The contractor is also responsible to remove all construction debris at the end of the project. Some contracts designate the owner to clean the site and charge the contractor for final cleanup and removal costs.

L. PERMITS, FEES, AND LICENSES

Contracts stipulate who pays for and obtains any permits and fees. Generally, the owner must obtain any permits that are required before the contract is awarded. The contractor is responsible to obtain and pay for any necessary permits, fees, licenses, and inspections after the contract is signed.

M. Code Conformity

The contractor is usually not responsible to ensure that the plans, specifications, and other contract documents conform to building codes and zoning regulations. The plan's designer has that responsibility. However, the contractor must inform the owner of any contract provisions that do not conform to applicable laws and codes.

N. Value Engineering

Projects seldom go precisely as planned. Contractor and labor skill can vary tremendously. Largely depending on the contractor's ability, attention, and motivation, two similar projects with the same amount of resources and money can result in widely varying outcomes. In order to motivate contractors to complete a project in both a skillful and cost-efficient fashion, value engineering (VE) clauses are now being included in many contracts.

During the course of construction, if a contractor proposes changes that would accomplish the project's functional requirements at a lower labor, time, or material cost, the contractor is practicing VE. The VE clause normally provides that when an owner agrees to a contractor's cost-saving suggestions, the net savings of each proposal is shared with the contractor at a stated reasonable rate.

O. Warranties

The construction contract will contain provisions that give the owner the right to require the contractor to correct inferior or flawed work. Provisions in the warranty should define all items to be covered and the duration of the warranty coverage. The contract may also stipulate that items covered by longer manufacturer's warranties commit the contractor to cover the labor for those extended times. In some states, faulty workmanship must be corrected at the expense of the contractor even though the contract warranty period has lapsed.

P. Certificate of Substantial Completion

When the building, or a portion thereof, is complete to the degree that the owner can use the building for its intended purpose, a certificate of substantial completion is issued by the architect.

Q. Certificate of Occupancy

A certificate of occupancy is a document issued by the building inspector certifying that the structure conforms to all relevant code sections and is, therefore, safe for use. An owner must obtain a certificate of occupancy before a building can be used. In some instances, a partial certificate of occupancy will be issued for portions of the building to be occupied.

Payment for Completed Work

A. Progress Payments

Construction projects can take months or years to complete. Most contractors receive partial payments, or progress payments, while the project is in process. Progress payments may be based on time (monthly is common) or on the completion of certain tasks (when excavation is complete, when foundation work is complete, when walls are up, etc.). The construction contract must explain these conditions. If the contractor stipulates that progress payments are made monthly, then the invoice is calculated by dividing the total project cost by the estimated number of months of the project.

A sample progress payment schedule follows.

First Invoice

Total project cost	$250,000.00
Estimated months of project	10
$250,000/10	$25,000.00
Less 10% retainage	($2,500.00)
Payments received	0
Progress payment	$22,500.00

Second Invoice

Total project cost	$250,000.00
Estimated months of project	10
$250,000/20	$50,000.00
Less 10% retainage	($5,000.00)
Payments received	$22,500.00
Progress payment	$22,500.00

Third Invoice

Total project cost	$250,000.00
Estimated months of project	10
$250,000/30	$75,000.00
Less 10% retainage	($7,500.00)
Payments received	$45,000.00
Progress payment	$22,500.00

If the contract stipulates that progress payments are made at every 10% of project completion, the same project's invoice would be calculated as follows:

$250,000 x 10%	$25,000.00
Less 10% retainage	($2,500.00)
Progress payment due	$22,500.00

B. RETAINAGE

In a construction contract, retainage is money earned by a contractor but not paid to the contractor until the completion of construction or some other agreed-upon date. The amount is held back as assurance for the quality of the work. Retainage is used to provide funding of paid work not completed, paid work that must be repaired, and to pay labor and material suppliers who have not been fully paid.

Typically, retainage is withheld as a percentage of each payment made beginning with the very first payment. While the percentage of retainage may vary from one contract to the other, 10% is a typical retainage amount. The release of retainage monies is most often the final payment after a Certificate of Occupancy has been issued. Contractors operating construction businesses should be prepared for this delay in the release of the final payment and retainage when calculating operating expenses and cash flow.

Where a subcontractor has provided the contractor evidence of a bond or other acceptable collateral, the retention amount withheld by the contractor from his/her subcontractors or material suppliers should be the same percentage of retainage as between the owner and the contractor.

C. FINAL PAYMENT

When the project is complete, the entire unpaid balance is turned over to the contractor. There are two types of final payment depending on whether or not there was retainage. When there is no retainage, the last progress payment is the final payment. Usually, however, the final payment is the release of retainage held by the owner.

In both instances, the release of the final payment is dependent upon all inspections and approvals having been made, all paperwork being completed, and agreement by all parties that all work on the project is satisfactorily finished.

Documents usually required at the conclusion of a project and that might affect the release of the final payment are:

- Documentation from the architect that all work is completed and is acceptable as specified within the contract;
- Labor and material warranties;
- Equipment operating instructions;
- Maintenance bonds;
- As-built drawings;
- Affidavits that labor, material, equipment, and subcontractor's costs have been paid;
- Releases or waiver of any liens by the contractor, subcontractor, or suppliers; and
- Written descriptions of any unresolved disputes or claims.

Contractors must always be aware of the potential for delay of final payment while all required approvals and paperwork are being processed. The need to repair or finish work against the punch list may cause the final progress payment to be held as well and may cause problems for contractors not financially able to withstand the delay.

Whether the final payment is the release of the last progress payment or the release of retainage, the process can be time consuming and a financial strain on contractors. Failure to maintain an adequate paperwork system can cause severe problems in attaining the final payment.

TYPES OF CONSTRUCTION CONTRACTS

An owner may choose from a variety of construction contract types. Differing construction contracts have been developed to suit the nature of how the project is negotiated. The fundamental difference between contracts focuses on the aspect of financial risk. Some contracts place more financial risk on the owner; others put greater risk on the contractor.

A. DETAILED SURVEY (LUMP SUM) CONTRACT

A detailed survey (lump sum) contract is normally used in situations that call for a detailed survey estimate. The contractor agrees to perform a project for a predetermined lump sum payment amount. The detailed survey (lump sum) contract stipulates that the contractor is obliged to satisfactorily complete the project regardless of whether the contractor makes a profit or suffers a financial loss.

If inclement weather, peculiar job-site conditions, or rising equipment, labor, or material costs add unforeseen expenses, the contractor is nonetheless responsible to pay for them. A contractor may not recoup these additional expenses from the owner.

On the other hand, if good weather, smooth job-site conditions, and lower equipment, labor, or material costs lead to a project being completed at rates that are lower than the bid amount, the contractor can keep the amount saved as added profit. An owner is not allowed to pay less than the agreed upon lump sum.

For these reasons, the detailed survey (lump sum) contract is advantageous to owners who do not want to be faced with extra charges for unforeseen costs. This type of contract appeals to contractors who are able to accurately estimate project costs. When contractors are able to deliver a completed project at or below cost, on or before the completion date, both owner and contractor benefit.

Because contractors stand to make greater profit, they are given greater risk with the detailed survey (lump sum) contract – namely the risk of losing money on cost overruns.

It should be noted that few contracts are so absolute that they place the entire financial risk on the contractor. As previously stated in this chapter, most contracts contain provisions to allow added costs for unforeseen conditions to be paid by the owner or shared between owner and contractor based on a predetermined proportion or scale.

B. UNIT PRICE CONTRACT

A unit-price contract is used when a project is estimated by the unit-price method. Unit-price estimating, as discussed in Chapter 3, is a format that consists of assigning costs to each unit of construction work. Because the total number of units is usually not known, the total sum to be paid to the contractor is not finalized until the project is completed. The unit-price contract guarantees prices for each unit, but leaves the final total project cost relatively open.

The unit-price contract focuses on the contractor's obligation to complete the project even though the finished project may have resulted in fewer or more units than originally estimated. The owner is contractually obligated to pay for all those units, even though the number of units may have differed from the projected number. As with the detailed survey contract, provisions can be included to unit-price contracts that provide for unforeseen additional unit costs.

C. COST-PLUS-FEE AND COST-PLUS-PERCENTAGE CONTRACT

A cost-plus contract is an agreement that the owner will pay for all construction costs (labor, material, equipment, etc.) plus an added amount to the contractor. The added amount paid to the contractor may be set in a number of ways. The amount may be a set fee, a fixed percentage, or a sliding percentage of the total costs.

Additional provisions can specify a fee limit, a fee minimum, bonuses for early or exceptional work, or penalties for late, expensive, or below-standard work. Some cost-plus contracts set a maximum cost ceiling. In this case, a contractor is liable for any costs that go beyond this maximum.

The cost-plus contract usually includes an estimate of the total project target cost. When a cost-plus-fee method is used, the fee is set in the contract. When the more open-ended cost-plus-percentage method is used, the contract must clearly establish what items are included in the total cost. For example, it should be clarified if the contractor is paid a percentage of general overhead and project overhead costs. In any case, the contract usually contains a clear list of items paid by the owner.

The cost-plus-fee contract is often used when costs can be reasonably well defined. The cost-plus-percentage contract is useful in situations when an accurate construction estimate is not possible, such as in an emergency or after an earthquake, flood, or storm.

CONTRACTOR CLAIMS AND CONTRACT DISPUTES

A claim is an additional amount that the contractor says is owed by the owner, but is disputed by the owner. A claim is not to be confused with a request for payment of moneys agreed to by all parties. Any additional work performed on a project should be documented with a change order and approved to ensure that the claim process is not necessary. However, there are instances when work must be accomplished that was not noted in the contract documents (for example: mandatory code compliance that was not in effect at the time the contract was signed). Who should pay for additional costs can become a source of dispute. A contractor should take all necessary steps during the course of construction to prevent the need to use the claim process. Claims stem from added costs from owner-caused delays, accelerations, extensions, or interference.

If an owner refuses to pay a claim, the contractor cannot simply stop the project work. One exception is a dispute over safety. When disputes arise where safety is an issue, the disputed activity must cease until an appropriate solution is reached. Also, the provision to continue work does not apply if the work in question is beyond the scope of the contract. Sometimes, particularly when the dispute involves project changes, it is difficult to determine what is and what is not within the scope of the contract.

If any unreasonable dispute between the owner and contractor arises, the construction contract usually requires one party to inform the other of the dispute in writing and within a specified period of time. In most cases, the contractor is expected to continue the work involved in the dispute. Project schedules are still followed, and contractor diligence is still required. One of the primary purposes of the contract is to provide for settlement of disputes without jeopardizing or delaying the project.

A construction contract may or may not stipulate the sequence of the dispute process. Typically, when a work item dispute arises, the contractor and owner will first sit down to work out an amenable solution. If the matter cannot be settled by mutual agreement, it is then put to the architect. If the architect's decision is not satisfactory to either party, the matter is then open to arbitration or legal action.

Because arbitration is usually speedier and less expensive than litigation, arbitration is the usual next step in construction disputes. Arbitration is the process of presenting the dispute to one or more impartial persons. The arbitrator's decision may or may not be subject to appeal, depending on the terms in the construction contract. General contractors commonly include arbitration clauses in their contracts.

Such clauses provide that disputes between the owner and general contractor that cannot be resolved by mutual agreement must be referred to arbitration before litigation.

CONTRACT ASSIGNMENT

Most contracts forbid the owner or contractor from assigning their obligations without the consent of the other party. An owner awards a construction contract in part due to the contractor's skill and reputation. Owners cannot be forced to rely on another party whose abilities and reliability may not be known.

CONTRACT TERMINATION

Construction contracts allow either a contractor or an owner to terminate the contract under highly prescribed conditions. The legal basis for terminating a contract is breach of contract, in other words, one party has violated the terms of the contract to the extent that the contract is no longer salvageable or valid.

Such conditions would include financial insolvency or failure to make payments by an owner, and shabby work or insufficient progress by a contractor. Legal counsel is highly advisable before either party attempts to terminate the contract. An owner or contractor who terminates a contract without substantial evidence that the contract was materially breached may be subject to litigation and up to triple damages.

SUBCONTRACTS

A subcontract is an agreement between the general contractor and a subcontractor. In this relationship, the general contractor takes a contractual position similar to an owner, while the subcontractor takes a position similar to a contractor. The subcontractor agrees to do; the general contractor agrees to pay.

The subcontract is a contract between only the contractor and the subcontractor. The subcontract creates no contractual relationship between the subcontractor and the owner, though the general construction contract may stipulate that the owner or architect approve all subcontractors. Furthermore, most contracts specify that subcontractors must abide by all conditions of the general contract and the project documents.

The general industry practice is that subcontractors on small projects often work without a written subcontract. This should be an area of concern to any professional contractor. Simply because a written contract does not exist does not mean there is no contract. Oral agreements are also contracts. However, it is very difficult to remember what was agreed to in an oral contract, and it is nearly impossible to prove or disprove particulars of an oral agreement. Generally, oral contracts are legal and valid, but they are difficult to enforce. A detailed written subcontract will help avoid many potential disputes and lead to higher quality, timely, subcontract work.

Subcontracts contain nearly all of the items and content found in a general construction contract, including the:

- Contractor's name and address;
- Subcontractor's name and address;
- Nature, general description, and scope of the project;
- Exact description of the work to be subcontracted;
- Address and general description of the property;
- Starting and completion dates of the subcontracted work;
- Identification of relevant drawings and specifications;
- Subcontract amount and payment arrangements; and
- Plainly worded offer.

The written acceptance must include a specific reference to the offer, a clear and unconditional acceptance of that offer, the date of acceptance, and the signature of the contractor and the subcontractor. In some cases, the approval of the owner is also required.

As with the general project, subcontractor payments may be based on a detailed survey (lump sum), unit price, or on a cost-plus arrangement. The subcontractor contract also has varying provisions in the event that an owner does not pay the general contractor. Virtually all subcontracts mandate that the general contractor must pay subcontractors promptly following owner payments to the general contractor. As with general contracts, subcontracts often contain clauses related to progress payments, retainage, and bonding.

SUMMARY

It is important that contractors have a working knowledge of contract law, particularly construction contracts. The nature of construction leaves too much room for misunderstanding. Misunderstanding may escalate to unforeseen claims that, in turn, may escalate to disputes and litigation. The more clear and comprehensive the construction contract and its attached documents are worded, read, and understood, the less likely misunderstanding will arise. However, as disagreements are inevitable, the construction contract also provides a number of reasonable remedies for claims and disputes. Executed properly, the construction contract will provide a high degree of confidence, cooperation, and comfort for both the owner and the contractor.

5
PROJECT MANAGEMENT

OVERVIEW

Project management has been described as the wise or careful allocation and efficient use of resources for timely completion of a project within the estimated construction budget. The project management practices introduced in this chapter are common among successful construction firms. They do not replace a company's need for professional advice; instead, they serve as general guidelines for planning, organizing, and managing a successful project. Effective project management requires both individual expertise and organizational coordination.

Every project is unique. Effective management skills can save projects from failing and provide the company with reliable cash flow and profitable performance. They create satisfied customers who bring other projects and refer potential customers. Important phases of project management include:

- Estimating;
- Planning and Scheduling;
- Supervising;
- Monitoring; and
- Project Closeout.

Each of these aspects is essential to the success of the construction project. Estimating was discussed in Chapter 3. This chapter will address each of the other topics and outline some of the procedures necessary to ensure that they contribute to the desired end product.

PLANNING AND SCHEDULING

Even though planning and scheduling are related, they should not be seen as a single activity.

Project planning involves analyzing each of the tasks that must be performed in order to complete a project and determining the most effective means of performing that task. Planning not only considers the sequence of events that **must** be followed (foundations must be formed before they can be poured), but also considers the sequence that **should** be followed to prevent different activities from interfering with each other. For example, it is conceivable to have painters and floor finishers working in the same room at the same time, but productivity would probably suffer.

To start the planning process, the contractor looks at the basic start and complete dates. The next step is to divide the project into fundamental operations. Each of these operations is then analyzed to determine:

- Sequence of work, called "job logic" (concrete forming, concrete pouring, concrete finishing);
- Duration of tasks (including curing times);
- Relative independence of tasks (roofing, landscaping); and
- Location of tasks (upstairs drywalling, downstairs kitchen cabinetry).

At this point, the contractor can plan when materials and equipment are going to be needed and can move on to the scheduling process.

Project scheduling is the process of assigning each activity to a time slot so that the requirements of the plan can be met. During the scheduling process, time slots are adjusted to avoid conflicts such as the same crane being needed in two places at the same time. Nearly every task is related to other tasks and each must be performed in its proper sequence. Each of these tasks will likely involve the coordination of materials, labor, and equipment. The schedule must be neither so general as to preclude effective use of time or so detailed that flexibility is lost.

Scheduling is a dynamic process that continues throughout the job. Many factors can cause project activities to change. The schedule will be continually adjusted to reflect actual conditions and used to control the project efficiently. In the end, a number of schedules will be created: a general time schedule for the owner and contractor, a more specific schedule for the project manager and superintendent, and highly specific schedules for foremen, expediters, and subcontractors.

Together, planning and scheduling determine when materials, labor, and equipment will be used. On large projects, planning and scheduling can be the difference between completing the project with a profit and completing the project at a loss. Even on small projects, good planning and scheduling help in controlling costs. The benefits of good planning and scheduling include:

- Minimizing peaks and valleys in resource usage;
- Increasing worker and management awareness of time required for various tasks;
- Promoting better project cash flow;
- Providing increased control over materials;
- Reducing overtime and idle time; and
- Reducing total job time.

To provide effective time management on a project, a contractor must take into consideration the factors that may affect the project.

A. DURATION OF TASKS

A schedule should be created to show the time needed to complete each task. This can be expressed in hours or shifts, but is most often expressed in working days. Once a time unit is designated, it should be used for all tasks and calculations.

The precision of the schedule will rely on the accuracy of estimating the duration of the project tasks. There are some general guides that exist to assist in the initial estimate of the duration of tasks. The contractor may:

- **Base the estimate on typical labor and equipment resources**. After making the initial duration estimate, time is added or subtracted based on known increases or reductions in labor and equipment.
- **Estimate each task duration independently from all other tasks**. After making the initial duration, time is added or subtracted based on the task's relationship to other tasks.
- **Base the estimate on typical workdays and workweeks**. Weekends and holidays are not normally considered workdays. The average month has 21 workdays. After making the initial duration, time is added or subtracted based on known overtime needs.
- **Base the time estimates independently from time allocated for project completion**. After making the initial estimates, they can be compared to the allowed project completion time. If the total duration schedule would exceed the allowed completion time, the durations should not arbitrarily be changed. In such cases, the project must either be given more resources or a longer completion time frame. Either instance may require added expense and consultation between the owner and contractor. Producing an accurate schedule and takeoff during the estimating phase will reduce the likelihood that such changes will be needed.

Accuracy of time estimates may also be enhanced by dividing the tasks into small units. With special knowledge of the project, experienced foremen and subcontractors can enhance the time estimates.

B. CONTINGENCY TIME

After the project tasks are divided and subdivided and task duration times are established, the next step is to schedule in contingency times. Ideally, a project progresses without problems. The reality of construction is that delays are virtually inevitable. Materials may arrive late; equipment may break down; unforeseen job-site difficulties may arise; inclement weather may affect the work progress.

Contingency time is a buffer, reducing the negative impact unexpected delays have on the remaining schedule. The amount of contingency time added to each task depends on how likely a delay is to occur. For example, more contingency time would be allocated for work done out-of-doors than work done indoors. More contingency time would be allocated for specialized work than for standard work. More contingency time would be allocated for work done high above ground than work done on ground level. Experience can be invaluable in offering added scheduling insight.

C. EARLIEST AND LATEST TASK TIME RANGES

Once the schedule sequence, task duration, and contingency times are calculated, task starting and finishing date ranges can be determined. Each task is assigned an "earliest start" date and a "latest start" date. The earliest start date is the earliest time the task may begin if every necessary preceding task is completed on time. The latest start date is the last date the task must begin in order not to delay subsequent tasks.

After the earliest and latest start times are estimated for a task, the task duration is figured, resulting in an "earliest finish" date and "latest finish" date. The earliest finish date is the earliest date the task could be completed assuming every step of the task proceeds as planned and all the preceding tasks were on time. The latest finish date is the date by which the task must be completed in order not to delay subsequent tasks.

Calculating earliest and latest time ranges provides the project manager a guide to how far ahead or behind schedule a task or the entire project may be. It also allows subcontractors a planning window.

D. FLOAT TIME

Float time is any amount of time left over after a task is complete. If every task goes smoothly, float time will always exist. Every task would begin at the earliest start date and end at or before the earliest finish date. The free time between the early completion of a task and the earliest start time of the next task is called free float. When delays occur, float time is used to finish the task on time. If delays do not occur, float time may be used for preparation, repairs, time off, or, in some cases, project acceleration.

SCHEDULING PROGRAMS

Several computerized programs are available that are very effective for planning and scheduling construction projects. Most of these programs use an adaptation of the critical path method (CPM) of project analysis. This method of analysis produces a diagram depicting the longest continuous sequence of activities in a project (the critical path). The critical path determines the overall amount of time required to complete the project. Subcontractors must review and sign off on the CPM schedule.

In **Figure 5-1**, CPM Legend, each project activity is represented by a network symbol (a letter or set of letters). A key, or legend, indicates what construction activity each symbol represents.

Figure 5-1. CPM Legend

ACTIVITY	NETWORK SYMBOL
AWARD OF CONTRACT PROCEDURES	A
ASPHALTIC CONCRETE SURFACE	B
BLOCK MASONRY	C
CEILING INSTALLATION	D
CLEAN-UP	E
CONCRETE - CURB AND WALKS	F
CONCRETE - FLOOR SLABS	G
CONCRETE - FOUNDATION SYSTEM, ELEV. PITS	H
CONCRETE - PRECAST PANEL INSTALLATION	I
EARTHWORK - BACKFILL	J
EARTHWORK - EXCAVATION	K
ELECTRICAL - FINISH	L
ELECTRICAL - ROUGH-IN	M
FINAL INSPECTION	N
FINISH FLOORING AND MOLDING	O
HARDWARE AND FIXTURES	P
HEATING, VENTILATION, AND AIR CONDITIONING INSTALLATION	Q
INSULATION	R
LANDSCAPING	S
MATERIALS - ORDERED AND DELIVERED	T
MECHANICAL - ELEVATOR	U
PAINTING	V
PARTITION AND DRYWALL INSTALLATION	W
PAVING, SUBGRADE, AND BASE COURSE	X
PERMIT (APPLICATION TIME)	Y
PILE DRIVING	Z
PLANTER CONSTRUCTION	AA
PLUMBING - FINISH	BB
PLUMBING - ROUGH-IN	CC
ROOFING	DD
SITE CLEARING AND GRUBBING	EE
SITE SURVEY - BUILDING LAYOUT	FF
SITE SURVEY - EXTERIOR IMPROVEMENTS	GG
STAIRWAY INSTALLATION	HH
STRUCTURAL STEEL AND STEEL BAR JOISTS	II
TRIM	JJ
UTILITIES (SITE)	KK
WINDOWS AND DOORS	LL

Figure 5-2 is a Sample of a Critical Path. The critical path is the sequence of events that take the longest period of time to complete. The legend symbol is written over an arrow. Below each symbol on the diagram is the number of days needed to perform that activity. A series of nodes, or circles with numbers in them, represent dates in the construction schedule. The arrows (activities) on the diagram connect the nodes. All activities leading up to a node must be completed before those activities that follow the node can be started. Activities on parallel arrows can take place simultaneously. The project cannot be completed any sooner than the number of days indicated on the critical path.

In Figure 5-2, the critical path is: 1 - 2 - 3 - 4 - 5 - 6 - 7 - 8 - 9 - 13 - 18 - 19 - 22 - 23 - 26 - 27 - 28.

Figure 5-2. Sample Critical Path

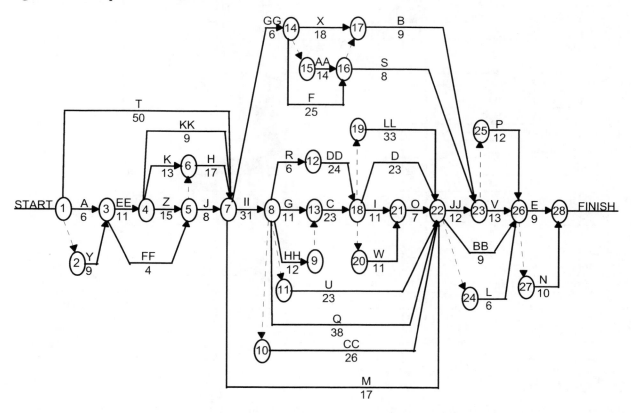

Other activities to be performed within the same time frame as those on the critical path require less time to complete than those on the critical path. This creates float time that is available for the noncritical activities. If they are started late or take slightly longer than planned, they will not affect the start of the next critical task and will not delay the project.

For example, examine the critical path area 4 - 5 - 6 - 7.

- Activity Z must be completed before Activity H can begin.
- Both Activity H and Activity KK must be completed before the next activity can begin (Activity II).
- Activity KK must be performed during the same time period as activities Z and H.
- Activity KK will take only 9 days to complete compared to 32 days required for activities Z and H.
- There are 23 float days (32 minus 9) available for Activity KK.

The start of noncritical Activity KK could be delayed by as many as 23 days without affecting the scheduled completion date of the project. If a critical path activity were delayed even one day, completion of the entire project would then also be delayed by one day.

Once the CPM chart is constructed and dates are computed for the nodes, a bar chart or Gantt chart can be created. **Figure 5-3**, Bar Chart Schedule for a Home, is an example of a bar chart or Gantt chart. The chart simply shows a timetable for each task. It does not show the overall project relationship, but gives the subcontractor critical information about when the tasks must take place and the time needed to complete them. On large projects, separate charts are sometimes created that list only the tasks for each specific trade or subcontractor.

Figure 5-3. Bar Chart Schedule for a Home

WORK DESCRIPTION	JANUARY	FEBRUARY	MARCH	APRIL
1. Excavate foundation	■			
2. Pour footings	■			
3. Pour foundation	■			
4. Frame	■	■		
5. Construct chimney	■			
6. Install drains, rough plumbing		■		
7. Pour basement floor		■		
8. Install rough wiring		■		
9. Install water lines		■		
10. Install heating ducts		■		
11. Sheet rock walls		■	■	
12. Finish flooring			■	
13. Install kitchen equipment			■	
14. Install bath plumbing			■	
15. Perform cabinet work			■	
16. Lay roofing		■		
17. Install downspouts, gutters		■		
18. Paint walls and trims				■
19. Sand and varnish floors				■
20. Install electrical fixtures				■
21. Finish grade lot				■
22. Landscape				■

SUPERVISION

All construction projects have field managers. Larger projects may employ a variety of management personnel, such as the project manager, project coordinator, superintendent, foreman, and expediter. On small projects, the contractor may carry out many management functions. These managers work solely for the contractor, though they often coordinate with other parties. In order to adhere to the contractor/owner agreement and ensure specifications are followed exactly, the project management organization should be precisely defined.

Supervisor training is offered through construction organizations, unions, consultants, and technical schools. The Associated Builders and Contractors, Inc. (www.abc.org); the Associated General Contractors of America (www.agc.org); and other national organizations may also offer training programs. Such programs provide instruction in work planning, laws and rules, cost-effectiveness, interpersonal communication, leadership, and problem solving.

A. Project Manager

A skilled project manager needs to carefully organize, schedule, and control all phases of project operations. The project manager is responsible to complete the project on time and on budget, including maintaining schedules, budgets, records, and change orders. If the project manager is someone other than the contractor, the project manager can speak for and act with the broad authority of the contractor.

The project manager coordinates with all project parties including:
- Architects;
- Subcontractors;
- Suppliers;
- Equipment dealers;
- Home and/or on-site office;
- Government agencies; and
- Unions.

B. Project Superintendent

A project superintendent is responsible for day-to-day, on-site operations and reports to the project manager. The superintendent is the contractor's representative responsible for continuous field supervision, coordination, and completion of the work. Project superintendent tasks include, but are not limited to:
- Organizing, coordinating, and supervising the work of employees on the construction job site;
- Keeping cost records on work performed and materials;
- Controlling costs in materials and wages;
- Inspecting construction work to enforce conformity to specifications; and
- Exercising control over rate of construction progress in order to complete the construction project within time limits.

C. Foremen

In support of the project superintendent, a number of project foremen are used to manage the project area of their expertise. A project may have a concrete foreman, a carpenter foreman, an electric foreman, a plumbing foreman, a roofing foreman, etc. On smaller projects, the foreman may work as well as manage. In any case, foremen provide feedback to superintendents, maintain quality control in their areas of expertise, and directly lead workers.

D. Expediter

Availability and delivery of materials is vitally important to construction projects. Delays of materials can throw an entire project off schedule. To ensure that ordered materials are delivered on schedule, an expediter may be hired. This is especially critical on unique or high-demand items or items whose delay could significantly interfere with the construction schedule months in advance.

The expediting process may involve tracking material order dates and availability dates, issuing purchase orders, coordinating shop drawings between suppliers and the project manager, and tracking material deliveries for both the contractor and the subcontractors.

When a shipment of materials is due to be delivered on a job site, the expediter gives notice to the project superintendent since pre-delivery preparation is usually needed. Permits, on-site storage space, truck routing, and escorts may be necessary in some cases.

Before the material is accepted, its condition must be checked to ensure that it meets the quality, quantity, and style specified. Any deviation or damage must be noted on the delivery bill and signed by the delivery person. The delivery bill should then be sent to the contractor's office with the damages or shortages clearly noted.

The expediter will periodically provide the contractor and project manager with a material status report, including warnings of any anticipated material delays. On large projects, the expediter may work on the project site. On small projects, the expediter may work on a number of projects from the company office.

E. OWNER'S REPRESENTATIVE AND ARCHITECT

While the construction contract is between the owner and the contractor, the owner may authorize a representative to act on his or her behalf both on and off the project site. In addition to funneling information to and from the owner, the owner's representative may provide informal quality control and oversight of any aspect of the project. Often the owner's representative has the right, specified in the contract agreement, to inspect production records, examine materials, and generally have unrestrained access to the project.

The owner may also employ inspectors to inspect and test components of the project. The architect or engineer may observe construction and be available to assist in interpreting plans or solving problems encountered during construction.

Because the workers, managers, and subcontractors are responsible only to the contractor, the owner's representative and architect have no direct authority over them. If the owner's representative or architect has a concern, the concern is communicated to the project manager or contractor. Neither the owner nor the architect accept, by virtue of their informal inspections, the responsibility for any work or lack of work done by persons under the contractor's control.

MONITORING

After project planning, scheduling, and staffing have been accomplished, the actual project work can begin on a solid preparatory foundation. Still, it is expected that some problems will arise. It is now that management skills are put to work. Planning and scheduling cannot guarantee good weather, accident-free work, breakdown-proof equipment, or timely material delivery. Supervisory personnel are expected to use their skills to overcome any obstacle to the project.

From the first day of work through the final day of project completion, constant monitoring of progress is needed. In addition to identifying work bottlenecks, the schedule will serve as an invaluable measure of progress. When the project is behind schedule, the field managers will apply their energies to the problem to catch up. Managers should be able to adapt the schedule to meet any project changes.

A. QUALITY CONTROL

A quality control program includes approval of materials, inspections, and testing or review of workmanship. If these requirements are in the contract, the contractor must ensure that they are scheduled and carried out. Quality control programs can vary greatly depending on the type, size, location, and special conditions of a project.

The owner may require the contractor to actively inspect the work process and give quality control reports on a daily or weekly basis about project progress, problems, and remedies taken. A designated quality control inspector or representative has no authority to change work, manage, or relieve the contractor from any obligations. The inspector can simply observe that work does or does not conform to contract requirements.

B. WORK RECORDS

The contractor and other parties need to stay abreast of the status of the project. Constant and timely feedback about project progress can help prevent small problems from escalating into expensive ones. In addition to the original contract documents and the time schedule, daily records are implemented to collect information on even small tasks. These work records become part of the permanent project record. Such records include:

- Periodic progress reports;
- Cost reports;
- Change orders;
- Accident reports;
- Contractor correspondence;
- Subcontractor correspondence;
- Purchase orders;
- Field surveys;
- Test reports;
- Progress photographs;
- Shop drawings; and
- Daily log.

1. SHOP DRAWINGS

The architect's plans and specifications are not adequate for many construction tasks. In order to be useful to the workers, the specifications need to be clarified. The contractor must approve and the architect must review all shop drawings. Shop drawings may include but are not limited to:

- Fabrication drawings;
- Controls and wiring diagrams;
- Erection drawings;
- Manufacturer's standard drawings; and
- Performance and test data.

Shop drawings may be produced by the material supplier or in special cases, by the contractor. In either case, the shop drawings must be closely compared with the specifications and project plans. The contractor must furnish exact copies of shop drawings to all interested parties. If the work performed complies with the shop drawings, the contractor and subcontractors have lived up to their contractual obligations.

2. DAILY LOG

Regardless of the size of a project, completing a daily job report (or job log), is a good management practice. The daily log should be sturdy, completed in ink, without erasures, without skipped workdays, and signed daily. There are a variety of report forms or journals that can be used. Most important is that it be written in and signed daily. The log includes descriptions of:

- Work performed;
- Equipment used;
- Deliveries;
- Weather conditions;
- Type and amount of work on site;
- Subcontractors on site;
- A list of any visitors, including the owner, inspectors, union, utility, and government agents;
- Any problems or accidents and how they were resolved; and
- Photographs or videotapes.

The log should include any deviation from the norm. For example, entries regarding material deliveries should contain any scheduled deliveries that failed to arrive, any damages or shortages, any unloading problems, etc.

The daily log, including any visual images, establishes facts and work performed to support a contractor when resolving disagreements. The log does not constitute legal proof or evidence in itself, however, it is supportive in nature and is meant to reduce misunderstanding.

C. ADJUSTING THE SCHEDULE

If problems arise, schedule changes may be required to adjust start and finish dates, float time, and critical tasks. Sometimes accelerations and extensions may require adjusting the project completion date. Small changes may be handled with very limited schedule adjustment. Large changes may require a complete overhaul of the schedule. Trying to fit too many changes into an unmodified schedule will negate the advantage of planning and scheduling. When the accumulated changes start to render the network and its schedule ineffective, it is time to revise it.

An advantage of using the Critical Path Method is the relative ease of making in-progress schedule changes. Such changes will require the approval of the owner, as well as coordination with material and equipment suppliers, subcontractors, and inspectors.

D. COST CONTROL

Job cost control begins the moment the contract is signed. An owner has the right to expect the contractor to exert total control of costs and find all possible cost savings in every aspect of construction. Controlling project costs is a key responsibility of the contractor. When done appropriately, cost control management is not an expense, but a profit-making endeavor.

Constant monitoring of costs:

- Improves control over cash flow;
- Enhances job-site performance;
- Gives a comparison for future estimates;
- Provides a way to evaluate profit margins between different types of work;
- Assists the contractor in calculating amounts due for in-progress payments; and
- Supplies individual project profit and loss performance data.

A successful contractor constantly compares actual costs, both labor and materials, with those of the budget (based on the estimate) to produce cost information that is reliable, detailed, and timely. Gathering cost information will justify project expenses and serve as a basis for future estimates. Unreliable, overly general, or delayed information will significantly diminish cost-control decisions.

A common cost-gathering procedure is to establish cost codes for each work area. Several organizations have standardized such codes, including the American Home Builders Association, the Associated General Contractors of America, and, perhaps most predominantly, the Construction Specifications Institute (CSI). Separate codes may be assigned to one piece of equipment or worker/crew that works on more than one work item.

With a system for collecting and assigning cost data, it is possible to monitor in-progress costs. Costs are often analyzed both on an item-by-item report and on a summary cost report. While item-by-item reports provide a detailed cost analysis, a summary cost report allows a contractor to consider the whole cost picture. For example, higher-than-budgeted labor costs may result in lower overall concrete costs. Perhaps the initial budget was too low on labor and too high on material. Perhaps the additional labor will speed the overall project completion. In either case, when the summary report shows cost savings, the contractor is well advised to accept an item overrun for an overall project cost savings.

Job-cost reports generally focus more on labor and equipment costs than on material, subcontractor, and company overhead costs, because the latter are usually more fixed and therefore, more certain. While general cost reports may be produced monthly, specific labor and equipment reports are often produced weekly, daily, or even hourly depending on the scope of the project, the interest of the contractor, and the requirements of the project contract.

Generally, labor receives hourly wages. Each employee uses a time card showing hours worked and allocates those hours to a given project and task item. The project manager reports daily the amount of work performed by workers. Work amounts can be measured in a variety of ways (number of bricks laid, square footage of bricks laid, linear feet of bricks laid). The method of measurement is usually consistent with what was used in the estimated method.

Weekly time cards and weekly production reports can be used to determine the production rate of each worker. For example, if a crew of 10 masons worked 40 hours a week and cost $20 per labor hour, they would work a total of 400 hours ($8,000) in one week, and average 500 blocks per day (2,500 blocks). The productivity and unit cost would be 6.25 blocks per labor hour or $3.20 per block. If this labor cost is higher than estimated, the contractor may explore ways to reduce or justify it.

If information collected is not accurate, it may lead a contractor to take action when none is required, or to not take action when something should be done to lower costs. If information is not provided in a timely manner, it may be too late to make a cost-control correction.

E. INVENTORY CONTROL

The proper size of inventory depends on several factors, such as type of work, volume of work, and distance from suppliers. Excess materials tie up work space and working capital. Good inventory control in contracting is to purchase material for individual jobs and have it shipped directly to the job site. Utilizing a purchase order system with a limited number of authorized users is another element of good inventory control.

By carefully controlling inventory, several benefits are realized, including:

- Increased net working capital;
- Simplified job costing;
- Reduced exposure to theft or loss; and
- Reduced time and expenses in handling materials.

PROJECT CLOSEOUT

Project closeout occurs when the project, or a specified part of it, is complete enough that the owner can use it for its intended purpose. All parties working on the project, including architects, subcontractors, material vendors, and manufacturers' representatives should be involved in the project closeout. It is always wise to plan for closeout during the estimate and construction phases so costs and responsibilities are fully covered in the budget and project plan. Project closeout is an important part of the construction process as it initiates the transfer of responsibility and risk from the contractor to the owner for the completed project.

Depending on the scope of work, the project closeout process may include the following:

- The contractor submits formal notification to the architect and the owner that the construction project is substantially complete.
- Based on the contractor's observations and discussions with the contractor, the architect documents substantial completion with the owner and contractor. Substantial completion may activate certain warranties, depending on provisions of the contract.

- During phased projects, the architect and the owner may recognize some but not all the building systems as being substantially complete. This should be clearly documented since start dates for warranty and guarantee periods for various building systems may vary.
- The architect and owner make an on-site walk-through punch list noting needed corrections. The contractor corrects all work noted on the punch list. The architect and owner may then make a final observation of the corrected work. When the owner accepts the work, the architect issues a certificate of completion to the contractor with a copy to the owner. The certificate documents that the contractor has completed the work specified in the contract documents.
- The contractor documents and delivers to the owner a complete keying schedule, with master, submaster, room, and specialty keys.
- The contractor submits all record drawings, as-built drawings or plans, testing and balancing reports, and other documents required by the contract.
- The contractor submits all guarantees, warranties, certificates, and bonds required by the contract documents or technical specifications.
- All required operating manuals and maintenance instructions are forwarded to the owner.
- The contractor submits the final consolidated payment request, including approved and signed change orders, as final accounting of the project.
- In the final accounting documents, the contractor submits final lien waivers and any affidavits, as required by the contract. Generally, the contractor needs to show the owner that all invoices, including those from any subcontractors or suppliers, have been paid with the exception of amounts due on the final payment request. The contractor submits these documents with the final payment request.
- The architect sends a final certificate of payment to the owner with a copy to the contractor.
- The contractor provides any required certificate of occupancy, indicating that the building authorities who have jurisdiction over the project approve occupancy of the space for the intended use.
- The owner makes final payment to the contractor and notifies the architect.

SUMMARY

Effective project management requires equal parts of preparing, monitoring, and administering. Preparing focuses on planning, scheduling, and coordinating materials, labor, and equipment – as early as the estimating phase. Monitoring requires developing and implementing an information gathering system. Daily logs, progress reports, shop drawings, and inspections are common tools used to monitor the progress of the project.

Effective project management also requires supervision by project managers, superintendents, and foremen. These managers must make certain that all work complies with the specifications of the project. They must also keep the contractor informed of all progress, problems, and resources.

Since the contractor is ultimately responsible for the quality and correctness of the project, he or she needs to understand and be adept at both construction processes and basic management principles. Because virtually all construction projects face challenges, contractors must be able to anticipate and remedy any obstacles.

6

RISK MANAGEMENT

Risk management may be defined as a comprehensive approach to protecting against damages due to any possible cause. A construction contracting business is constantly subject to uncertainty and risk. Natural disasters, fire, theft, and accidents can harm or even destroy a business. A contractor must understand how to avoid or minimize the effects of disaster.

ASSESSING RISK

In applying the principles of risk management to a contracting business, a contractor should:

- Take time to think about the job and its possible risks. Be familiar enough with the project so that any risks involved in the planned construction can be recognized and measured. The contract should then be analyzed and the nature of the work outlined to anticipate any special risks that might arise.
- Try to pinpoint the possible severity and frequency of the losses that could occur from each identified risk.
- Determine the best way to protect the business against the identified risks. The contractor might ask, "Can risk be eliminated or reduced by different contractual arrangements? What insurance or bonding plan will best protect this project? Can losses be reduced by an employee safety program or similar program of loss control?"

Typically, contractors rely on two primary sources to reduce financial risk: insurance and bonding.

INSURANCE

Insurance is the financial safety net for most contractors. Without adequate insurance, a profitable business can be wiped out overnight by a single natural disaster or major accident. Typically, the standard construction contract places total liability on the contractor in a number of important areas. The contractor is responsible for damages caused from contractor-caused project delay, for substandard work, for contractor-caused added costs, for project accidents, etc. In order to lessen the degree of financial risk, contractors employ insurance companies to insure those risks will be covered.

Even from seemingly clearly written contracts, expert attorneys and courts are kept busy trying to establish who may be liable and to what extent. It would not be wise for contractors to assume that a signed contract is a guarantee against litigation or the final word as to who is liable for what. For this reason, contractors assign this risk to insurance companies. Because construction insurance is complex, contractors should consult with an experienced insurance agent who is familiar with the construction industry to determine the best coverage for each project.

An insurance policy is an agreement (policy) between the insurance company (insurer) and the contractor (insuree) that for a premium (a payment in advance) the insurance company will accept a contractor's financial liability (coverage) for specified losses and damages.

The policy will clearly define the extent of the coverage. It will list many items or circumstances that are either expressly included or excluded from coverage. For example, intentional losses or losses due to malice are usually not covered. When a covered loss occurs, the insurer must make it right. This is usually done in the form of monetary pay. The insurer is obligated to provide legal defense in the event a legal action is taken against the insuree.

The cost of insurance is set by experts (called actuaries) who predict risk based on considering many factors. Actuarial records track each insuree. It is presumed that contractors with a history of losses are at greater risk for future losses. By the same reasoning, contractors with a history of lower losses are at lower risk for future losses. Taken together, the tracked histories provide the basis for each contractor to be given a risk rating. The risk rating determines the cost the contractor will pay for insurance coverage.

A. REQUIRED COVERAGE

Construction contracts usually require specified insurance coverage be paid by the contractor, such as builder's risk insurance, general liability insurance, property insurance, equipment insurance, and employer liability insurance. Some insurance may also be required by law, such as unemployment insurance, workers' compensation insurance, Social Security insurance, and vehicle insurance.

Special insurance may be required of the contractor to cover any unusual risks, such as working underground, high above ground, or in areas with additional safety risks (demolition, mountains, water bodies, congested areas, etc.). Special coverage may be included in provisions within a policy, attached as an insurance rider, or issued in a separate policy. Insurance companies may require the contractor to submit a copy of the contract for their review.

Even if the construction contract does not specify it, contractors are considered legally responsible for damages caused by their own intentional or unintentional acts, and for actions that reasonably should have been taken to prevent a loss. Contractors also assume liability for the actions of their subcontractors.

B. DETERMINING EXTENT OF COVERAGE

It is not financially realistic for a contractor to maintain every type of insurance at all times; the cost would be prohibitive. Though insurance brokers can find or create coverage for nearly any risk, coverage for events such as acts of God or war is usually not available. The contractor, often with the help of a reliable insurance agent, must assess the risks of the project, limit them as much as possible, and select sensible insurance. Working together, the contractor and insurance agent can customize the coverage to match both foreseeable and reasonably possible risks while at the same time keeping coverage costs as low as possible.

The contractor will be expected by the insurer to expertly plan and implement construction procedures that minimize the risk of loss. Insurance companies must keep losses lower than premiums otherwise the insurer could not stay in business long. Federal and state agencies regulate insurance company effectiveness to maintain strong financial standing and the reputation of the insurance industry. For the same reason, private research firms give strength ratings to insurance companies.

Once project risks are assessed, choosing the extent of coverage (for example, whether to purchase $10,000 or $25,000 of coverage) is largely a process of assuming risk. A contractor assumes more risk by choosing less coverage. Conversely, more coverage means less risk to the contractor. Whichever party assumes the most risk stands to make the most profit or suffer the greatest losses. In essence, insurance premiums amount to contractors sharing a portion of the anticipated profits with the insurers. Contractors must balance the need for profit with the need to reduce risk. The resulting decision should lead to coverage amounts that are both adequate and affordable.

C. PROPERTY INSURANCE ON A PROJECT

Generally, the contractor is responsible for the project and its property from the first day of work until its completion and acceptance. Property insurance on the project includes builder's risk insurance. Risk insurance policies are very flexible and can include protective provisions other than merely covering the expenses of physical loss or damage. For example, a builder's risk policy can be written to include coverage for lost rents or other business losses resulting when a structure is not finished on schedule because of fire or other disaster.

Builder's risk insurance covers project buildings and structures against loss from fire, wind, water, explosion, freezing, and collapse. The standard American Institute of Architects (AIA) agreement specifies that the owner will purchase and maintain builder's risk insurance. Contractors often prefer to provide the insurance themselves because they feel they are more acquainted with this insurance than owners might be, and they feel more confident that a contractor-tailored policy will better suit their needs.

Because of the varied scope and character of construction projects, builder's risk insurance varies greatly both in coverage and in cost. Standard policies can be customized appropriate to the likely risks. A common policy provision is that the contractor is not liable for damage from unforeseeable causes, causes beyond the contractor's control, or causes not the fault of the contractor, such as extreme weather, civil riot, or war. A policy may or may not include flood or earthquake damage.

Builder's risk insurance usually has a number of stipulations and exclusions. For example, buildings and structures must not be occupied during construction. Examples of other clauses are that faulty workmanship, faulty design, and faulty materials – and the consequences thereof – are not covered. Damage or loss of drawings, plans, on-site funds, etc., are usually not covered.

Contractors may purchase a blanket (multiproject) policy or a single project policy. Accepting higher deductible levels can significantly lower premium amounts. Premiums are either paid in a lump sum advance payment or in monthly payments as agreed upon. Damages are usually calculated at replacement cost rather than at cash value. In addition to replacement of damages, a policy may include coverage for damages due to interruption of work, loss of income, and increased costs. Generally, insurance policies can be canceled at any time at the request of the policyholder.

Normally, two types of Builder's Risk Insurance are used on a construction project: All-Risk Builder's Risk Insurance and Named-Peril Builder's Risk Insurance. Both policies usually require that the structure not be occupied during construction.

All-Risk Builder's Risk Insurance covers virtually every loss (or peril) for which a contractor is liable unless specifically excluded on the insurance policy. It covers buildings, temporary structures, tools, equipment, supplies, and materials in transit, at delivery, and in storage. Listed exclusions commonly include damage due to freezing, glass breakage, rain, snow, earthquakes, and floods. All-risk is the most common type of insurance protecting construction project property.

Named-Peril Builder's Risk Insurance covers losses (or perils) that occur that are specifically listed on the insurance policy. Commonly covered perils could be wind, hail, fire, and/or lightning. It is less commonly used than all-risk insurance. However, this type of policy may offer a variety of endorsements that cover losses due to specific causes including vandalism, smoke, windstorm, hail, explosion, or civil commotion and riot. Many other special endorsements are also available, including losses caused by water damage, floods, and earthquakes.

D. INSURANCE ON A CONTRACTOR'S PROPERTY

Property Insurance covers the contractor's company office, buildings, storage facilities, grounds, and personal property. It also generally covers property in the care or control of the contractor. Property insurance protects against loss by theft, vandalism, fire, smoke, water, freezing, etc. Policies can also include protection against flood, earthquake, and other special threats. In most cases, coverage must be sufficient to insure the full value of all property. Additional coverage can be purchased to pay losses that result in business interruption, added costs, or interim rental costs.

Fire Insurance on Contractor's Buildings provides coverage for offices, sheds, warehouses, and stored contents. Endorsements are available for extended coverage and for vandalism.

An **Equipment Floater Policy** protects the contractor's equipment from loss or damage. Banks require mortgaged equipment to be adequately protected. Equipment floater policies are flexible and can be made to protect equipment that is loaned, rented, or leased. The floater policy insures against external damage to equipment on-site, in transit, or in storage. The insurer will require the contractor to provide a list and value of all equipment. Usually, equipment is covered at 100% of current cash value. Policies usually provide for rental equipment until settlement or replacement is made. Like project insurance, an equipment floater policy can be either all-risk or named-peril.

Transportation Floater Insurance provides coverage against damage to property that belongs to the contractor while it is being transported. **Motor Truck Cargo Insurance** covers equipment carried on a contractor's truck from the supplier to a warehouse or building site.

E. AUTOMOBILE INSURANCE

Automobile Liability Insurance covers financial risk against property damage or bodily injury stemming from the use of covered vehicles, including cars, trucks, trailers, and other self-propelled or towed vehicles designed for public highway travel. Automobile coverage may cover damage to persons or other property only (liability coverage), or damage to the owned or leased vehicle as well (collision and comprehensive coverage). Automobile liability usually does not cover damage to hauled equipment or material, nor does it cover employee injuries.

Amounts of coverage and deductibles vary significantly. High deductibles and low total coverage may be relatively inexpensive but may not adequately reduce contractor financial risk. On the other hand, high total coverage with low deductibles may provide excellent coverage, but premiums may be too expensive for the contractor. Policies can be tailored to the needs of the contractor. For example, an older vehicle may have only liability insurance. A new vehicle may have full liability, collision, and comprehensive coverage. Deductibles can also be varied for each vehicle.

An umbrella policy can be purchased to raise the liability limit for one or a fleet of vehicles. Various additional coverages (endorsements) can provide further protection, such as the use of rented vehicles or the use of an employee's vehicle for business.

F. INSURANCE AGAINST CRIME

Contractors usually purchase and tailor an insurance package to protect against criminal acts, such as burglary, vandalism, theft, and destruction. **Burglary Insurance** protects the contractor against loss due to burglary, theft, or robbery.

Employee dishonesty is typically covered by a fidelity bond, sometimes referred to as employee dishonesty insurance. The bond protects contractors against damage due to theft, embezzlement, larceny, forgery, or illegal actions of their bonded employees. A fidelity bond may be purchased to cover individually named employees, or specified positions (accountant, estimator), or in a blanket policy that covers all employees.

With blanket coverage, it is not necessary to prove which employee caused the loss, but only show that the loss was employee caused and fraudulent. With the named-person policy, the contractor must prove that the covered employee caused the fraudulent loss. Additionally, a named-person policy requires changing the policy whenever names change. For these reasons, blanket coverage is more common in the construction industry.

G. LIABILITY INSURANCE

Contractors protect against claims by third parties by purchasing **Liability Insurance**. Liability insurance does not cover damage or loss of the contractor's property. Liability insurance covers legal expenses and judgments that stem from civil actions against the contractor. The insurance company has the right to settle claims without going to court.

Liability insurance covers the contractor for damages to either employee or non-employee persons. Liability coverage also extends to all areas that contractors agree to or assume in a construction contract, purchase order, etc. **Contractual Insurance** protects contractors against third-party claims for damages pertaining to their contract obligations. **Contingent Liability** is indirect or secondary contractor responsibility for the actions of subcontractors or other persons in contractor control. **Post Completion Liability** is contractor responsibility that may exist after the project is completed and accepted by the owner.

Personal Injury Liability may stem from bodily injury, unlawful detention (perhaps by a security guard), slander, libel, wrongful eviction, wrongful entry, etc. **Vehicle Operator Liability** covers injuries or damages due to the contractor or employee driving either on or off the project site, though street vehicles themselves are covered under automobile insurance.

Contractor's Public Liability and Property Damage Insurance is used to protect the contractor against claims brought by third parties who are not his or her employees. It does not protect the contractor against loss or damage to his or her own property. A contractor may be directly responsible for injury or damage to a third person on his or her property by an act of commission or omission.

Contractors should be aware of a special legal concept known as "attractive nuisance." Because job sites are often considered by the courts to be attractive and inviting to children, a contractor has a special legal obligation to protect children who trespass on a building site. The courts require contractors with hazardous premises to protect the public by installing fences or providing security guards or other protective measures.

Contractor's Protective Public and Property Damage Liability Insurance provides insurance when a contractor is liable for the acts of others, such as subcontractors, for whom he or she has responsibility.

Contractual Liability Insurance provides coverage when the contractor is liable, by the terms of the contract, for the owner, architect, or other parties. Liability may arise from a project after the work has been completed, or as a result of the operation of the contractor's vehicles.

Completed Operations Liability Insurance protects contractors from liability to third parties arising out of projects that have been completed or abandoned. For the most part, a contractor is not liable for injuries or property damage on a project once it is completed and accepted by the owner. However, there are many exceptions to this rule. Courts may shift more liability to the individual contractor, even in the absence of negligence, thus making this type of liability insurance necessary.

Comprehensive General Liability Insurance is commonly available to contractors since they all require the same types of liability insurance. In general, a comprehensive liability policy will cover a contractor for liability arising out of his own operations, from the actions of his or her subcontractors, and from their completed projects. Despite its name, a comprehensive general liability policy will not cover damage to the contractor's vehicles, or his or her own employees. An umbrella policy is designed to increase the dollar limits of underlying insurance. If the underlying insurance is not properly in place, the umbrella policy offers no coverage.

Professional Liability protects a contractor from liability arising out of errors or negligent acts in performing design or architectural duties. Contractors are expected to perform their duties at a professional level. Contractors' mistakes and negligence may lead to damages for which they may be found financially liable. Professional liability insurance provides financial protection for damages resulting from contractor error. It can be written to also cover contractor contingent liability to protect against professional negligence of subcontractors, architects, or other related professionals. This type of insurance is especially important when the contractor provides professional services as well as construction services to the owner, such as a design/construct project.

H. LIABILITY INSURANCE ON EMPLOYEES

Employer's Liability Insurance is customarily written in combination with workers' compensation insurance. It provides coverage over and above workers' compensation in case of injury or death of an employee.

I. SUBROGATION

A builder's risk insurance policy will contain a subrogation clause. Subrogation is the right granted by the contractor to the insurance company to cover negligent damages caused by other parties. Subrogation may result in the insurance company taking legal action, in the name of the insured, to sue the offending party for negligence damages. If the owner provided the builder's risk insurance, the contractor may be sued for negligent actions that lead to a loss. Subcontractors are similarly vulnerable. For this reason, including the owner, contractor, and all subcontractors as co-insurees of the policy is increasingly common. Another way to avoid the effect of subrogation is for owners, contractors, and subcontractors to waive all rights to sue each other for damages. However, this may deter insurance companies from offering coverage.

J. REQUIRING SUBCONTRACTORS TO INSURE

Contractors usually require subcontractors to provide their own insurance coverage for themselves and their employees. The nature and extent of coverage is determined in the subcontractor's contract, and usually is similar to the insurance carried by the contractor. The contractor can be held liable for damages not covered by the subcontractor's insurance. In the event that a subcontractor does not maintain adequate insurance, the contractor may either obtain the needed coverage and charge the costs to the subcontractor, or stop the subcontract on a breach of contract claim.

K. WRAP-UP LIABILITY INSURANCE

On large construction projects, the owner may choose to carry insurance for the entire project. This **Wrap-Up Liability Insurance** covers, in one policy, the owner(s), architects, contractors, project managers, superintendents, foremen, and all subcontractors from liability damages. In such cases, a single insurance company provides all of the project-related insurance, including general liability, builder's risk, workers' compensation, employer's liability, and umbrella insurance for the duration of the project. It does not cover non-work-related health, disability, or life insurances. Contractors may be required by the owner to accept wrap-up coverages. The owner pays for all the premiums and the contractor does not include insurance costs in the project estimate.

L. LABOR-RELATED INSURANCE

If contractors have employees, they are required to pay for several types of labor-related insurances: Social Security (discussed further in Chapter 10) and workers' compensation and unemployment (discussed further in Chapter 8). Contractors may also provide health and disability insurance.

1. SOCIAL SECURITY INSURANCE

Social Security is an insurance fund managed by the federal government. It provides retirement benefits, survivor benefits, and long-term disability benefits. Benefits are accrued through nonvoluntary employee and employer contributions.

2. WORKERS' COMPENSATION INSURANCE

Workers' compensation is a private insurance that must meet government regulations. Workers' compensation covers on-the-job injury (including occupation-related diseases) to employees. It can account for as much as one-half or more of a contractor's insurance costs. While contractors may vary coverage to meet the circumstances of their company or project, they must be careful to select coverage that meets workers' compensation statutes and laws.

Workers' compensation rules vary according to the type of work and the relationship of the worker to the business. Coverage for most employees is mandated, with risk of criminal penalties and possible civil action by workers for noncompliance.

Premium rates for workers' compensation vary widely. Premiums are initially determined by occupational risk and company business dollar volume. Later, premiums may be raised or lowered depending on a contractor's history of claims. The contractor pays the entire premium; no amount of the premium may be paid by employees.

When an employee injury occurs that lingers beyond a short waiting period, the injured employee may file a claim with the appropriate state commission. When a claim is approved (workers' compensation will not cover off-the-job or intentionally caused self-injuries), the insurance company guarantees treatment and benefits in accordance with state guidelines.

The insurance policy pays for a variety of expenses, including medical treatment, rehabilitation, and a set percentage of the employee's wages until the employee is able to return to work. In the event that an injury results in death, a lump-sum payment may be made to the estate of the deceased. Permanent disabilities may also result in a lump sum or monthly payment based on the nature of the disability. Payment amounts and limits vary by state. If the injured employee is not satisfied with the judgment of the commission, the employee can appeal.

Employer's Liability Insurance is customarily written in combination with workers' compensation insurance. It provides coverage over and above workers' compensation in case of injury or death of an employee.

3. UNEMPLOYMENT INSURANCE

Unemployment insurance provides workers benefits when they are laid off. Benefits are not paid to workers who quit, cause their own termination, or will not or cannot work. Each state sets its own qualifications and benefits. Benefits are paid by employers through a nonvoluntary tax based on a percentage of company payroll. The percentage is based on a company's unemployment history. Contractors who seldom lay off employees often will pay significantly less than employers who do so frequently.

4. NON-WORK-RELATED HEALTH, DISABILITY, AND LIFE INSURANCE

Many contractors subsidize non-work-related health and disability insurance. Health insurance is typically handled through private insurance companies or health maintenance organizations. Health insurance commonly covers expenses for medical treatment, hospitalization, prescription drugs, preventive medicine, etc. Health insurance programs vary widely as to coverage, cost, deductibles, and exclusion.

As with life insurance, health insurance is usually seen as a voluntary benefit subsidized partially or totally by the employer. Because of the relationship to workers' compensation, some states regulate and manage disability insurance programs. Depending on state law, disability premiums may be paid entirely by the employer, or shared by employer and employee.

BONDS

The fundamental responsibility of a contractor to an owner is to complete the construction project. The primary means by which contractors guarantee owners that the project will be completed is by bonding. A contract surety bond is a three-party agreement under which a surety company assumes liability for the performance of a contractor's contractual obligations. Should the contractor default, the surety bond guarantees that work will be completed. Bonds are similar to insurance in that they offer financial reparation for specified damages. However, surety bonds differ from insurance in that the bond does not protect the contractor. Instead, the contractor remains responsible to pay back any money spent by the surety bond company to complete a project.

In the event a contractor defaults on a contract, the surety company has the following options:
- Finance the contractor until obligations are met;
- Employ another contractor to finish the project;
- Allow the owner to finish the project and reimburse the owner for additional costs incurred; or
- Pay any outstanding debts covered by the bond.

The contractor may obtain a bond through a surety company that underwrites the contractor's account. A construction bond guarantees the owner (obligee) that the project will be successfully completed. If the contractor breaches or defaults on the construction contract, the surety must pay all costs incurred in completing the project – up to the amount of the bond.

A. STATUTORY AND COMMON-LAW BONDS

Private projects are covered by common-law bonds that address only the provisions written into the bond. Public projects are covered by statutory bonds that contain coverage designed to meet the statutes (laws) of governmental acts. A claim under a statutory bond need not be specifically outlined in the statutory bond; such claims are covered under the statute. Claims of private projects, on the other hand, must be specifically covered in the written language in the common-law bond.

For this reason, common-law bonds have been standardized to insure that all relevant issues are covered. One commonly used standard form for private projects is published by The American Institute of Architects (AIA). Likewise, most public projects utilize standardized statutory bond forms that comply with the applicable statutes of the municipality or state. The federal government uses a standard statutory bond based on the statutes under the *Miller Act*.

B. THE MILLER ACT

The *Miller Act* is a federal statute passed in 1935 that requires contract surety bonds on federal construction projects. The *Miller Act* provides that, before a contract that exceeds $100,000 in amount for the construction, alteration, or repair of any building or public work of the United States is awarded to any person, that person shall furnish the federal government with the following:

1. A performance bond in an amount that the contracting officer regards as adequate for the protection of the federal government.

2. A separate payment bond for the protection of suppliers of labor and materials. The amount of the payment bond shall be equal to the total amount payable by the terms of the contract unless the contracting officer awarding the contract makes a written determination supported by specific findings that a payment bond in that amount is impractical, in which case the amount of the payment bond shall be set by the contracting officer. The amount of the payment bond shall not be less than the amount of the performance bond.

The *Miller Act* payment bond covers subcontractors and material suppliers who have direct contracts with the general contractor. These are called first-tier claimants. Subcontractors and material suppliers who have contracts with a subcontractor, but not those who have contracts with a supplier, are covered as second-tier claimants. Anyone further down the contract chain is considered too remote and cannot assert a claim against a *Miller Act* payment bond posted by the contractor.

The final step in perfecting a claim on a payment bond is filing a lawsuit. For both first- and second-tier claimants, suit must be filed no sooner than 90 days after the last labor and material were furnished and no later than one year after that date. A contractor should always seek legal counsel before starting any lien action and should consult with an attorney well in advance of any filing deadlines.

Many states have adapted the *Miller Act* for use at the state level. These state statutes may be referred to as "*Little Miller Acts*." State courts interpreting their own laws will often look to federal case law for guidance.

C. BONDING RATING AND CAPACITY

Surety companies are very careful when providing bonds for contracting firms. For this reason, contract surety bonds are not granted easily to a contractor. Before a surety company will provide a bond, a contractor is thoroughly investigated, including experience, reputation, equipment, and financial status. Personal habits of the firm's owners and key personnel are carefully examined. The company's past financial statements and current bank credit are investigated. Information about the company's bookkeeping methods and cost management techniques must be provided.

Following a thorough investigation, a contractor is given a rating (A-1, A, B, or Miscellaneous) that establishes the degree of risk the contractor presents to completing a project. The bonding rating establishes the bond costs (premiums). In addition to a risk rating, the investigation provides information to determine a maximum bonding level, referred to as bonding capacity or bonding line, for each contractor. The bonding capacity establishes a financial limit beyond which the bonding company is not responsible for claims. The bonding capacity will, in effect, limit the contractor to only those projects that fit the contractor's resources and capacities. It further limits the contractor from accepting additional projects until previous projects are completed.

D. Contract Surety Companies

Because the worth of a bond is no greater than the financial soundness of the surety company, surety companies are subject to public regulation in the same way as insurance companies. They operate under state charters and file their insurance rate schedules with designated public authorities.

Best's Key Rating Guide provides financial ratings for insurance and surety companies. Another source of information about surety companies is provided by the U.S. Department of the Treasury, which must approve all surety companies used on federal projects.

Contract bonds may be required by the owner, developer, or government agency involved in the contract. Public works must be bonded in every state.

E. Bid Bonds

A bid bond guarantees that the contractor who is declared to be the successful bidder will sign a contract with the owner for the amount of the bid submitted. Bid bonds are most often used on government projects.

There are two types of bid bonds commonly in use: the liquidated damages bond and the difference-in-price bond. Under the liquidated damages bond, the surety company agrees to pay the owner the entire bond amount as damages for default. The difference-in-price bond requires the surety company to pay the owner the difference between the defaulted low bid and the next responsible bid, up to the bond face amount.

F. Performance Bonds

A performance bond is a guarantee to the owner that the project will be completed according to the plans and terms specified in the contract. If the contractor defaults on the contract, the surety company is responsible for completing the project. All performance bonds have a face value that limits the financial responsibility of the surety company. If the contractor defaults on the project, the burden to fulfill the contract falls on the surety company. A performance bond also extends to cover any warranties for which the contractor is responsible.

G. Payment Bonds

A payment bond guarantees payment for labor and materials used or supplied in the performance of the contract. The payment bond protects the owner, developer, and contractor against liens filed by unpaid parties to the work.

In private projects, payment bonds guarantee payment for work, materials, equipment, and overhead costs that are directly related to the project, and to subcontractors who have a direct contract with the general contractor. Because liens cannot be made against public property, public project costs are addressed in accordance to state or federal law and are usually covered by a statutory payment bond.

The concept of "double payment" liability is that a contractor may, according to state law, be liable to pay the defaulted bills of subcontractors – even if a subcontractor was paid in full.

H. Lien Bonds

A lien bond is an instrument used to "bond around" a lien. A typical form of lien bond assures an owner, lender, or title company that a claim of lien filed by a subcontractor will not impair the title to property. It allows construction loan draws, progress payments, or even the sale of property to continue unobstructed. The surety in effect guarantees that a subcontractor will be paid on a project at some point in time, provided that the debt can be proven. The form of lien bond varies greatly from state to state based on the unique circumstances involved and the filing requirements of the lien law.

I. MISCELLANEOUS BONDS

A number of miscellaneous bonds may be obtained by contractors depending on the circumstances of the project, the nature of the contractor's business, and the demands of the owner.

A **Subcontractor Bond** is obtained by subcontractors to cover any claims under their direct control. Because the general contractor is responsible for any unpaid subcontractor bills, subcontractors are often required to obtain subcontractor performance and payment bonds.

A **Maintenance Bond** protects an owner against unpaid costs stemming from faulty workmanship or materials. Coverage periods vary from several years (for concrete and paving) to 20 or more years (for roofing). If the contractor does not repair or resolve problems in warranted workmanship or materials, the bonding company will either direct the repairs or pay the owner to do so.

An **Indemnity Against Liens Bond** protects the owner from liens and claims. Owners may require a contractor to provide a bond in advance that protects the owner against any damage caused by liens or claims. If a lien or claim is already filed, a **Bond to Discharge Liens or Claims** may be necessary. A bond to discharge liens and claims will allow a judge to release any frozen property, assets, and/or finances needed to complete the project. The bond serves as a guarantee to lien holders and the owner that the liens and claims will be paid and resolved.

A **Rented Equipment and Property Bond** is a guarantee that contractors will pay rental charges, fees, and maintenance costs of rented or leased equipment, vehicles, storage facilities, and parking areas. As previously stated in this chapter, a **Fidelity Bond** protects employers from the damages caused by dishonest and illegal employee acts such as theft, fraud, etc. A **Judicial (Court) Bond** guarantees payment of court costs and judgments in the event that a contractor is a plaintiff in a legal action.

A **License (Permit) Bond** is sometimes required by state or local law to receive a contractor's license. A license bond guarantees that the contractor will comply with all laws related to the license. A **Union Wage Bond** is a guarantee that the contractor will pay union wages and fringe benefits. A **Bond to Release Retainage** allows the owner to release full retainage payments. The contractor usually must provide a surety bond for the amount of the advanced retainage. A **Subdivision Bond** is provided by a subdivision developer. It guarantees completion of all promised or required improvements and utilities.

A **Bank Bond, or Letter of Credit** is not a bond, per se, but an agreement between the bank, the contractor, and the owner to hold contractor funds in trust to be used to pay unpaid claims against the contractor. The bank may also offer the contractor an additional line of credit for this purpose. This practice is an alternative to bonding through surety companies and is relied upon by contractors who have not been able to obtain a surety bond. In the event of contractor default, the owner may present claims to the bank. The bank is obligated to pay the claims and seek remuneration from the contractor. The bank must pay even if the contractor disputes the claim. The contractor can reclaim the funds through civil action.

J. CLAIM PAYMENT PROCESS

When a party has not received payment after exercising reasonable means to be paid by the contractor or subcontractor, a claim is filed with the bonding company. On private projects, the filing process is outlined in the bonding instrument (document). The filing process for public projects is determined by government statute. In practice, the filing process will require the assistance of an attorney, though attorneys' fees are not usually covered on public projects.

Filing requirements vary depending on whether the claimant has a direct contract with the contractor or a subcontractor. In any event, the filing process may require the claimant to provide written notice of the claim to the contractor, owner, or surety company within a specified time period. If a claim is disputed, payment is not made until after the dispute is resolved.

K. PROJECT CHANGES

Project changes are agreements between the owner and the contractor. The bonding company is only liable for the conditions specified in the original contract. The bonding company is not liable for any debts incurred as a result of project changes, unless it agrees. The owner and contractor should obtain written coverage from the bonding company before they agree to any substantial project changes.

L. PROJECT DEFAULT

If a contractor defaults on a project, the bonding company will either pay the owner to complete the project through contracting with another contractor or directly assume charge of the project. If the owner completes the project, the bonding company will pay the costs up to the limit of the bond. If the bonding company takes control of the project, the bonding company will pay all the costs – even if the costs exceed the limit of the bond.

In the hands of the bonding company, a new contractor may be brought in on a cost-plus-fee or even by competitive bidding. As defaults may be brought about by several factors beyond the control of the contractor, the bonding company often chooses to use the original contractor to complete the project. Providing financial support to the original contractor serves both to complete the project and to keep the contractor in business.

If the owner defaults, the bonding company will pay any directly related project claims and seek retribution from the owner.

SUMMARY

Liability is incurred whenever a contractor makes a contract, hires employees, orders materials, or performs work. The financial risks pertaining to this liability can be covered through appropriate insurance and bonding.

Insurance expenses are normally included in project estimates and budgets as a normal cost of doing business. The construction contract should stipulate what insurances are necessary and who (owner or contractor) should obtain, maintain, and pay for them.

Some insurance policies are legally mandated (Social Security, workers' compensation, unemployment) for employers; others are optional (non-work related disability, life, and health). Premiums for both insurance and surety bonds can vary substantially and often depend on the strength and history of the contractor's company.

Bonding is the means by which owners, contractors, subcontractors, and suppliers are guaranteed payment for their work and materials. Bonding differs from insurance in that bonding companies will seek reimbursement from the defaulting party. Bonding is not easily obtained. Contractors' capabilities, financial standing, and reputation are subject to extensive investigation. The resulting contractor rating and bonding capacity effectually limit the number and scope of projects that a contractor may procure.

Contractors must balance the costs of insurance and bonding against the risk of liability. Such decisions will require the coordinated expertise of insurance agents, accountants, and legal counsel.

7

SAFETY

FEDERAL OSHA

The *Federal Occupational Safety and Health Act* (OSHA) became a part of national law in 1971. Employers must comply with OSHA standards to ensure a safe working environment. The Act consists of several volumes. Specific parts of the Act that contain minimum safety standards for the construction industry are *29 CFR 1904, Recording and Reporting Occupational Injuries and Illnesses; 29 CFR 1910, Occupational Safety and Health Standards;* and *29 CFR 1926, Safety and Health Regulations for Construction.* These documents are available online at www.osha.gov; from the district or state Office of Occupational Safety and Health; or from the Superintendent of Documents, U.S. Government Printing Office, Washington, D.C. 20402.

A. RECORDING AND REPORTING OCCUPATIONAL INJURIES AND ILLNESSES

OSHA **recordkeeping requirements** apply to most private sector employers. If a company had 10 or fewer employees during all of the preceding calendar year, it is exempt from most recordkeeping requirements. However, all companies, no matter how many employees they have, must still comply with the reporting requirements noted below.

OSHA requires all employers, regardless of size or industry, to report the work-related death of any employee or hospitalizations of three or more employees. OSHA generally requires construction employers to keep records of workplace injuries and illnesses. Even if a construction company has fewer than 10 employees, it must maintain a log of occupational injuries and illnesses and make reports if it is notified in writing by the Bureau of Labor Statistics that it has been chosen to participate in a statistical survey. Each employer with 11 or more employees must maintain records of all occupational injuries and illnesses, regardless of severity.

Employers must differentiate between employees and independent contractors. This is especially important in the construction field. A person is considered an employee if the employer:

- Hires the employee;
- Supervises the employee;
- Pays the employee;
- Withholds taxes, Social Security, and Medicare from the employees wages; and
- Has the authority to terminate the employee.

If a business is organized as a sole proprietorship or partnership, the owner or partners are not considered employees for recordkeeping purposes. Self-employed individuals are not covered by the *OSH Act* or this regulation.

All covered employers **must post** the OSHA Job Safety and Health Poster (or state plan equivalent) in a prominent location in the workplace. Where employers are engaged in activities that are physically dispersed, such as construction, the OSHA Poster must be posted at the location to which employees report each day. The OSHA Poster is available online at **www.osha.gov**.

The Occupational Safety and Health Act prohibits employers from discriminating against employees for reporting a work-related fatality, injury, or illness. It is also unlawful to discriminate against employees who file a safety and health complaint, ask for access to the Part 1904 records, or otherwise exercises any rights afforded by the *OSH Act*.

1. RECORDABLE ILLNESSES AND INJURIES

Record those work-related injuries and illnesses (defined in 29 CFR 1904 and reprinted at the end of this chapter) that result in:

- Death;
- Loss of consciousness;
- Days away from work;
- Restricted work or transfer to another job; or
- Medical treatment beyond first aid.

Any significant work-related injury or illness that is diagnosed by a physician or other licensed health care professional must be recorded. Any work-related case involving cancer, chronic irreversible disease, a fractured or cracked bone, or a punctured eardrum must also be recorded. (See 29 CFR 1904.7).

The decision tree in **Figure 7-1** shows the steps involved in making the determination of whether a work-related injury or illness should be recorded.

Figure 7-1.   Decision Tree for Recording Injury or Illness under the *OSH Act*

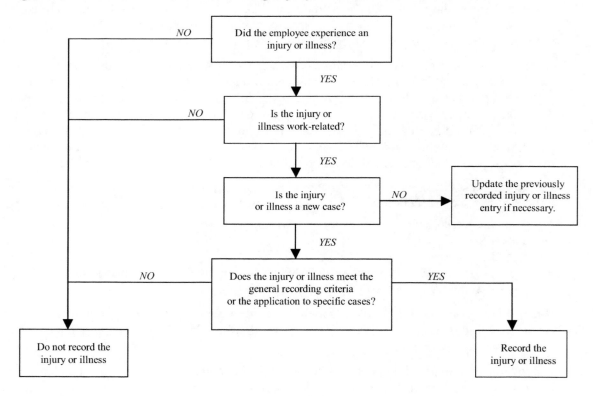

a. MEDICAL TREATMENT

Medical treatment includes managing and caring for a patient for the purpose of combating disease or disorder. The following are not considered medical treatments and are **not** recordable:

- Visits to a physician or other licensed health care professional solely for observation or counseling;
- Diagnostic procedures, such as x-rays and blood tests, including the administration of prescription medications used solely for diagnostic purposes; and
- Any procedure that can be labeled first aid. (See next section.)

b. FIRST AID

The following are generally considered first aid treatment (one-time treatment and subsequent observation of minor injuries). Do **not** record the case if it involves only:

- Using a nonprescription medication at nonprescription strength;
- Administering tetanus immunizations;
- Cleaning, flushing or soaking wounds on the surface of the skin;
- Using wound coverings such as bandages, Band-Aids™, gauze pads, etc.; or using butterfly bandages or Steri-Strips™;
- Using hot or cold therapy;
- Using any non-rigid means of support, such as elastic bandages, wraps, non-rigid back belts, etc.;
- Using temporary immobilization devices while transporting an accident victim (splints, slings, neck collars, or back boards, etc.);
- Drilling of a fingernail or toenail to relieve pressure, or draining fluid from a blister;
- Using eye patches;
- Removing foreign bodies from the eye using only irrigation or a cotton swab;
- Removing splinters or foreign material from areas other than the eye by irrigation, tweezers, cotton swabs or other simple means;
- Using finger guards;
- Using massages;
- Drinking fluids for relief of heat stress.

2. RECORDING FORMS

There are three primary OSHA forms that are used to record work-related injuries and illnesses. These include: OSHA Form 300 Log of Work-Related Injuries and Illnesses; OSHA Form 300A Summary of Work-Related Injuries and Illnesses; and OSHA Form 301 Injury and Illness Incident Report. These forms can be obtained from www.osha.gov/recordkeeping/RKforms.html. According to Public Law 91-596 and 29 CFR 1904, a business must keep these forms on file for five years following the year to which they pertain.

Within eight hours after the death of any employee from a work-related accident or the in-patient hospitalization of three or more employees as a result of a work-related accident, an employer must orally report the fatality/multiple hospitalization by telephone or in person to the Area Office of the Occupational Safety and Health Administration (OSHA), U.S. Department of Labor, that is nearest to the site of the incident. Employers may also use OSHA's toll-free telephone number, 800.321.OSHA (800.321.6742). Employers, who do not learn of a reportable incident until after it occurs, must make the report within eight hours of the time the incident was reported to them.

a. OSHA's Form 300

The *Log of Work-Related Injuries and Illnesses* (**Form 300**) is used to classify work-related injuries and illnesses and to note the extent and severity of each case. When an incident occurs, use the *Log* to record specific details about what happened and how it happened. Employers also must record the recordable injuries and illnesses that occur to employees who are not on their payroll if the employer supervises these employees on a day-to-day basis. Employers should coordinate efforts with any temporary help service, employee leasing service, personnel supply service, or contractor to make sure that each injury and illness is recorded only once by whichever company provides day-to-day supervision of the employee.

Every work-related injury or illness that involves loss of consciousness, restricted work activity or job transfer, days away from work, or medical treatment beyond first aid should be recorded, as well as any significant work-related injuries and illnesses that are diagnosed by a physician or licensed health care professional.

If a business has more than one establishment (not job site), a separate *Log* and *Summary* must be kept for each physical office that is expected to be in operation for one year or longer.

Cases listed on the *Log of Work-Related Injuries and Illnesses* are not necessarily eligible for workers' compensation or other insurance benefits. Listing a case on the *Log* does not mean that the employer or worker was at fault or that an OSHA standard was violated.

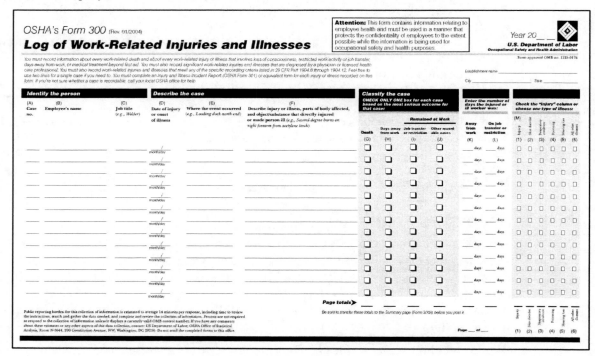

b. OSHA's Form 300A

The ***Summary of Work-Related Injuries and Illnesses*** (**Form 300A**) shows the work-related injury and illness totals for the year in each category. At the end of the year, count the number of incidents in each category and transfer the totals from the *Log* to the *Summary*. Unless specifically asked to do so, the completed forms do not have to be sent to OSHA. The *Summary* must be posted by February 1 of the year following the year covered by the form and kept posted until April 30 of that year.

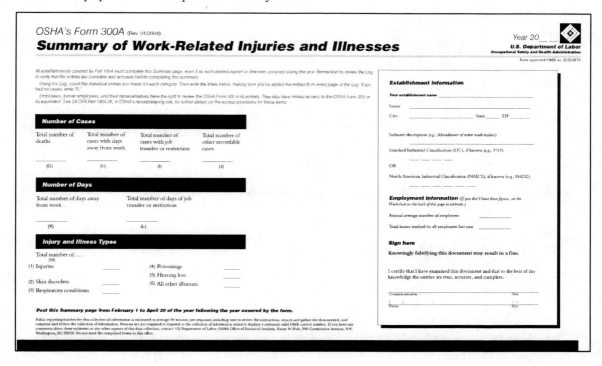

c. OSHA's Form 301

Within seven calendar days after an employer receives information that a recordable work-related injury or illness has occurred, the ***Injury and Illness Incident Report*** (**Form 301**) must be filled out. Some state workers' compensation, insurance, or other reports may be acceptable substitutes to Form 301. To be considered an equivalent form, any substitute must contain all the information asked for on this form. This form goes into specific details about each individual case.

OSHA's Form 301
Injury and Illness Incident Report

Attention: This form contains information relating to employee health and must be used in a manner that protects the confidentiality of employees to the extent possible while the information is being used for occupational safety and health purposes.

U.S. Department of Labor
Occupational Safety and Health Administration

Form approved OMB no. 1218-0176

This *Injury and Illness Incident Report* is one of the first forms you must fill out when a recordable work-related injury or illness has occurred. Together with the *Log of Work-Related Injuries and Illnesses* and the accompanying *Summary*, these forms help the employer and OSHA develop a picture of the extent and severity of work-related incidents.

Within 7 calendar days after you receive information that a recordable work-related injury or illness has occurred, you must fill out this form or an equivalent. Some state workers' compensation, insurance, or other reports may be acceptable substitutes. To be considered an equivalent form, any substitute must contain all the information asked for on this form.

According to Public Law 91-596 and 29 CFR 1904, OSHA's recordkeeping rule, you must keep this form on file for 5 years following the year to which it pertains.

If you need additional copies of this form, you may photocopy and use as many as you need.

Completed by _____

Title _____

Phone (____) ____ - ____   Date ___ / ___ / ___

Information about the employee

1) Full name _____

2) Street _____
   City _____ State ____ ZIP _____

3) Date of birth ___ / ___ / ___
4) Date hired ___ / ___ / ___
5) ☐ Male
   ☐ Female

Information about the physician or other health care professional

6) Name of physician or other health care professional _____

7) If treatment was given away from the worksite, where was it given?
   Facility _____
   Street _____
   City _____ State ____ ZIP _____

8) Was employee treated in an emergency room?
   ☐ Yes
   ☐ No

9) Was employee hospitalized overnight as an in-patient?
   ☐ Yes
   ☐ No

Information about the case

10) Case number from the Log _____ (Transfer the case number from the Log after you record the case.)
11) Date of injury or illness ___ / ___ / ___
12) Time employee began work _____ AM / PM
13) Time of event _____ AM / PM ☐ Check if time cannot be determined

14) **What was the employee doing just before the incident occurred?** Describe the activity, as well as the tools, equipment, or material the employee was using. Be specific. *Examples:* "climbing a ladder while carrying roofing materials"; "spraying chlorine from hand sprayer"; "daily computer key-entry."

15) **What happened?** Tell us how the injury occurred. *Examples:* "When ladder slipped on wet floor, worker fell 20 feet"; "Worker was sprayed with chlorine when gasket broke during replacement"; "Worker developed soreness in wrist over time."

16) **What was the injury or illness?** Tell us the part of the body that was affected and how it was affected; be more specific than "hurt," "pain," or "sore." *Examples:* "strained back"; "chemical burn, hand"; "carpal tunnel syndrome."

17) **What object or substance directly harmed the employee?** *Examples:* "concrete floor"; "chlorine"; "radial arm saw." *If this question does not apply to the incident, leave it blank.*

18) **If the employee died, when did death occur?** Date of death ___ / ___ / ___

Public reporting burden for this collection of information is estimated to average 22 minutes per response, including time for reviewing instructions, searching existing data sources, gathering and maintaining the data needed, and completing and reviewing the collection of information. Persons are not required to respond to the collection of information unless it displays a current valid OMB control number. If you have any comments about this estimate or any other aspects of this data collection, including suggestions for reducing this burden, contact: US Department of Labor, OSHA Office of Statistical Analysis, Room N-3644, 200 Constitution Avenue, NW, Washington, DC 20210. Do not send the completed forms to this office.

B. HAZARDOUS MATERIALS

OSHA regulations govern the storage and use of a variety of hazardous chemicals and other materials used in the construction industry. Many of the materials regulated by OSHA are suspected of causing cancer if used improperly or if exposure to them exceeds permissible limits. Among these substances are asbestos and materials derived from coal tar pitch volatile, nitrobenzenes or derivatives, benzidine, vinyl chloride, inorganic arsenic, coke oven emissions, and cotton dust. The OSHA *Safety and Health Standard for the Construction Industry* contains a complete listing of all materials considered hazardous and should be referred to when questions arise concerning the safety of any material used in the construction process. It can be found online at www.osha.gov/doc/index.html.

Strict procedures govern the use and storage of hazardous substances. All hazardous substances must be stored in "closed systems" provided with continuous local exhaust ventilation so that air movement is always from ordinary work areas to the operation. No hazardous material may be transported in open vessels or containers. Access to hazardous materials storage and work areas must be closely regulated.

All employees having access to hazardous material areas must be provided with protective clothing and possibly some form of cartridge-type or supplied-air respirators. All protective clothing and equipment must be placed in impervious containers within the closed system for disposal or decontamination. Drinking fountains, the storage or consumption of food, chewing gum, and tobacco products are all prohibited in closed systems.

All hazardous material storage and work areas must be posted with appropriate signs at entrances and exits informing employees of the procedures that must be followed in entering and leaving a regulated area. Material Safety Data Sheets (MSDS) or acceptable, alternative methods must be used to identify contents of all containers in these areas.

Each employee having access to a regulated area must receive adequate training and information concerning proper procedures for handling the hazardous material in question.

C. PENALTIES

OSHA penalties range from $0 to $70,000, depending upon how likely the violation is to result in serious harm to workers. Other-than-serious violations often carry no penalties but may result in penalties of up to $7,000. Serious violations may have penalties up to $7,000. Repeat and willful violations may have penalties as high as $70,000. Penalties may be discounted if an employer has a small number of employees, has demonstrated good faith, or has few or no previous violations. For more information on OSHA penalties, see Section 17 of the *OSH Act* or information online at www.osha.gov.

D. SAFETY STANDARDS

Federal OSHA safety standards contained in Title 29, Part 1926 (Construction) are regulations that contractors must be aware of and follow. Each contractor is responsible for determining standards of safety for each project. If specific safety clothing or equipment is required, the employer is responsible for providing it.

NEW JERSEY OSHA

New Jersey has adopted federal occupational safety and health standards for all private sector employees. Public employees are covered by safety standards contained in the Public Employees Occupational Safety and Health Act (PEOSH).

Employers may contact one of the four, federal area OSHA offices in New Jersey to obtain more information about federal OSHA laws. Office locations and phone numbers can be found online at **www.osha.gov/oshdir/nj.html**. A reprint of OSHA *Part 1904* is reprinted in this chapter.

The New Jersey Department of Labor and Workforce Development, Division of Public Safety and Occupational Safety and Health, enforces laws and regulations that provide for safe and healthful working conditions throughout New Jersey's public and private sector. The Division's Occupational Safety and Health Training Unit provides occupational safety and health training for both public and private sector employers and employees.

Most of the training courses are based on OSHA Standards; others were developed from national consensus standards such as ANSI and NIOSH. The training is delivered by experienced consultants who will customize courses for employers when needed. All training is provided at no cost to the employer and is provided at the employer's facility. Employers can request training by calling 609.633.2587. More information is available on the Division's Web site at **http://lwd.dol.state.nj.us/labor/lsse/safetyhealth_index.html**.

The New Jersey Department of Health and Senior Services' Workplace Health and Safety unit is focused on reducing occupational injuries and illnesses experienced by workers in New Jersey. The unit can provide educational materials and presentations, and technical consultations regarding occupational health to employers. More information is available on the Department's Web site at **www.state.nj.us/health/**.

PART 1904 – RECORDING AND REPORTING OCCUPATIONAL INJURIES AND ILLNESSES

Subpart A – Purpose

1904.0 Purpose.
The purpose of this rule (Part 1904) is to require employers to record and report work-related fatalities, injuries and illnesses.

Note to § 1904.0: Recording or reporting a work-related injury, illness, or fatality does not mean that the employer or employee was at fault, that an OSHA rule has been violated, or that the employee is eligible for workers' compensation or other benefits.

Note to Subpart B: All employers covered by the Occupational Safety and Health Act (OSH Act) are covered by these Part 1904 regulations. However, most employers do not have to keep OSHA injury and illness records unless OSHA or the Bureau of Labor Statistics (BLS) informs them in writing that they must keep records. For example, employers with 10 or fewer employees and business establishments in certain industry classifications are partially exempt from keeping OSHA injury and illness records.

1904.1 Partial exemption for employers with 10 or fewer employees.
(a) Basic requirement.

(a)(1) If your company had ten (10) or fewer employees at all times during the last calendar year, you do not need to keep OSHA injury and illness records unless OSHA or the BLS informs you in writing that you must keep records under § 1904.41 or § 1904.42. However, as required by § 1904.39, all employers covered by the OSH Act must report to OSHA any workplace incident that results in a fatality or the hospitalization of three or more employees.

(a)(2) If your company had more than ten (10) employees at any time during the last calendar year, you must keep OSHA injury and illness records unless your establishment is classified as a partially exempt industry under § 1904.2.

(b) Implementation.

(b)(1) Is the partial exemption for size based on the size of my entire company or on the size of an individual business establishment? The partial exemption for size is based on the number of employees in the entire company.

(b)(2) How do I determine the size of my company to find out if I qualify for the partial exemption for size? To determine if you are exempt because of size, you need to determine your company's peak employment during the last calendar year. If you had no more than 10 employees at any time in the last calendar year, your company qualifies for the partial exemption for size.

1904.2 Partial exemption for establishments in certain industries.

(a) Basic requirement.

(a)(1) If your business establishment is classified in a specific low hazard retail, service, finance, insurance or real estate industry listed in Appendix A to this Subpart B, you do not need to keep OSHA injury and illness records unless the government asks you to keep the records under § 1904.41 or § 1904.42. However, all employers must report to OSHA any workplace incident that results in a fatality or the hospitalization of three or more employees (see § 1904.39).

(a)(2) If one or more of your company's establishments are classified in a non-exempt industry, you must keep OSHA injury and illness records for all of such establishments unless your company is partially exempted because of size under § 1904.1.

(b) Implementation.

(b)(1) Does the partial industry classification exemption apply only to business establishments in the retail, services, finance, insurance or real estate industries (SICs 52-89)? Yes, business establishments classified in agriculture; mining; construction; manufacturing; transportation; communication, electric, gas and sanitary services; or wholesale trade is not eligible for the partial industry classification exemption.

(b)(2) Is the partial industry classification exemption based on the industry classification of my entire company or on the classification of individual business establishments operated by my company? The partial industry classification exemption applies to individual business establishments. If a company has several business establishments engaged in different classes of business activities, some of the company's establishments may be required to keep records, while others may be exempt.

(b)(3) How do I determine the Standard Industrial Classification code for my company or for individual establishments? You determine your Standard Industrial Classification (SIC) code by using the Standard Industrial Classification Manual, Executive Office of the President, Office of Management and Budget. You may contact your nearest OSHA office or State agency for help in determining your SIC.

1904.3 Keeping records for more than one agency.

If you create records to comply with another government agency's injury and illness recordkeeping requirements, OSHA will consider those records as meeting OSHA's Part 1904 recordkeeping requirements if OSHA accepts the other agency's records under a memorandum of understanding with that agency, or if the other agency's records contain the same information as this Part 1904 requires you to record. You may contact your nearest OSHA office or State agency for help in determining whether your records meet OSHA's requirements.

1904 Subpart B App A Non-Mandatory Appendix A to Subpart B – Partially Exempt Industries.

Employers are not required to keep OSHA injury and illness records for any establishment classified in the following Standard Industrial Classification (SIC) codes, unless they are asked in writing to do so by OSHA, the Bureau of Labor Statistics (BLS), or a state agency operating under the authority of OSHA or the BLS. All employers, including those partially exempted by reason of company size or industry classification, must report to OSHA any workplace incident that results in a fatality or the hospitalization of three or more employees (see § 1904.39).

SIC code	Industry description
525	Hardware Stores
542	Meat and Fish Markets
544	Candy, Nut, and Confectionery Stores
545	Dairy Products Stores
546	Retail Bakeries
549	Miscellaneous Food Stores
551	New and Used Car Dealers
552	Used Car Dealers
554	Gasoline Service Stations
557	Motorcycle Dealers
56	Apparel and Accessory Stores
573	Radio, Television, & Computer Stores
58	Eating and Drinking Places
591	Drug Stores and Proprietary Stores
592	Liquor Stores
594	Miscellaneous Shopping Goods Stores
599	Retail Stores, Not Elsewhere Classified
60	Depository Institutions (banks & savings institutions)
61	Nondepository
62	Security and Commodity Brokers
63	Insurance Carriers
64	Insurance Agents, Brokers & Services
653	Real Estate Agents and Managers
654	Title Abstract Offices
67	Holding and Other Investment Offices
722	Photographic Studios, Portrait
723	Beauty Shops
724	Barber Shops
725	Shoe Repair and Shoeshine Parlors
726	Funeral Service and Crematories
729	Miscellaneous Personal Services
731	Advertising Services
732	Credit Reporting and Collection Services
733	Mailing, Reproduction, & Stenographic Services
737	Computer and Data Processing Services
738	Miscellaneous Business Services
764	Reupholster and Furniture Repair
78	Motion Picture
791	Dance Studios, Schools, and Halls
792	Producers, Orchestras, Entertainers
793	Bowling Centers
801	Offices & Clinics Of Medical Doctors
802	Offices and Clinics Of Dentists
803	Offices Of Osteopathic
804	Offices Of Other Health Practitioners
807	Medical and Dental Laboratories
809	Health and Allied Services, Not Elsewhere Classified

81	Legal Services
82	Educational Services (schools, colleges, universities and libraries)
832	Individual and Family Services
835	Child Day Care Services
839	Social Services, Not Elsewhere Classified
841	Museums and Art Galleries
86	Membership Organizations
87	Engineering, Accounting, Research, Management, and Related Services
899	Services, not elsewhere classified

1904.4 Recording criteria.

Note to Subpart C: This Subpart describes the work-related injuries and illnesses that an employer must enter into the OSHA records and explains the OSHA forms that employers must use to record work-related fatalities, injuries, and illnesses.

(a) Basic requirement. Each employer required by this Part to keep records of fatalities, injuries, and illnesses must record each fatality, injury and illness that:

(a)(1) Is work-related; and

(a)(2) Is a new case; and

(a)(3) Meets one or more of the general recording criteria of § 1904.7 or the application to specific cases of § 1904.8 through § 1904.12.

(b) Implementation.

(b)(1) What sections of this rule describe recording criteria for recording work-related injuries and illnesses? The table below indicates which sections of the rule address each topic.

(b)(1)(i) Determination of work-relatedness. See § 1904.5.

(b)(1)(ii) Determination of a new case. See § 1904.6.

(b)(1)(iii) General recording criteria. See § 1904.7.

(b)(1)(iv) Additional criteria. (Needlestick and sharps injury cases, tuberculosis cases, hearing loss cases, medical removal cases, and musculoskeletal disorder cases). See § 1904.8 through § 1904.12.

(b)(2) How do I decide whether a particular injury or illness is recordable? The decision tree for recording work-related injuries and illnesses below shows the steps involved in making this determination.

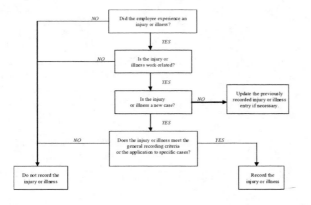

1904.5 Determination of work-relatedness.

(a) Basic requirement. You must consider an injury or illness to be work-related if an event or exposure in the work environment either caused or contributed to the resulting condition or significantly aggravated a pre-existing injury or illness. Work-relatedness is presumed for injuries and illnesses resulting from events or exposures occurring in the work environment, unless an exception in § 1904.5(b)(2) specifically applies.

(b) Implementation.

(b)(1) What is the "work environment"? OSHA defines the work environment as "the establishment and other locations where one or more employees are working or are present as a condition of their employment. The work environment includes not only physical locations, but also the equipment or materials used by the employee during the course of his or her work."

(b)(2) Are there situations where an injury or illness occurs in the work environment and is not considered work-related? Yes, an injury or illness occurring in the work environment that falls under one of the following exceptions is not work-related, and therefore is not recordable.

1904.5(b)(2)	You are not required to record injuries and illnesses if . . .
(i)	At the time of the injury or illness, the employee was present in the work environment as a member of the general public rather than as an employee.
(ii)	The injury or illness involves signs or symptoms that surface at work but result solely from a non-work-related event or exposure that occurs outside the work environment.
(iii)	The injury or illness results solely from voluntary participation in a wellness program or in a medical, fitness, or recreational activity such as blood donation, physical examination, flu shot, exercise class, racquetball, or baseball.
(iv)	The injury or illness is solely the result of an employee eating, drinking, or preparing food or drink for personal consumption (whether bought on the employer's premises or brought in). For example, if the employee is injured by choking on a sandwich while in the employer's establishment, the case would not be considered work-related. **Note:** If the employee is made ill by ingesting food contaminated by workplace contaminants (such as lead), or gets food poisoning from food supplied by the employer, the case would be considered work-related.
(v)	The injury or illness is solely the result of an employee doing personal tasks (unrelated to their employment) at the establishment outside of the employee's assigned working hours.
(vi)	The injury or illness is solely the result of personal grooming, self-medication for a non-work-related condition, or is intentionally self-inflicted.
(vii)	The injury or illness is caused by a motor vehicle accident and occurs on a company parking lot or company access road while the

	employee is commuting to or from work.
(viii)	The illness is the common cold or flu (Note: contagious diseases such as tuberculosis, brucellosis, hepatitis A, or plague are considered work-related if the employee is infected at work).
(ix)	The illness is a mental illness. Mental illness will not be considered work-related unless the employee voluntarily provides the employer with an opinion from a physician or other licensed health care professional with appropriate training and experience (psychiatrist, psychologist, psychiatric nurse practitioner, etc.) stating that the employee has a mental illness that is work-related.

(b)(3) How do I handle a case if it is not obvious whether the precipitating event or exposure occurred in the work environment or occurred away from work? In these situations, you must evaluate the employee's work duties and environment to decide whether or not one or more events or exposures in the work environment either caused or contributed to the resulting condition or significantly aggravated a pre-existing condition.

(b)(4) How do I know if an event or exposure in the work environment "significantly aggravated" a preexisting injury or illness? A preexisting injury or illness has been significantly aggravated, for purposes of OSHA injury and illness recordkeeping, when an event or exposure in the work environment results in any of the following:

(b)(4)(i) Death, provided that the preexisting injury or illness would likely not have resulted in death but for the occupational event or exposure.

(b)(4)(ii) Loss of consciousness, provided that the preexisting injury or illness would likely not have resulted in loss of consciousness but for the occupational event or exposure.

(b)(4)(iii) One or more days away from work, or days of restricted work, or days of job transfer that otherwise would not have occurred but for the occupational event or exposure.

(b)(4)(iv) Medical treatment in a case where no medical treatment was needed for the injury or illness before the workplace event or exposure, or a change in medical treatment was necessitated by the workplace event or exposure.

(b)(5) Which injuries and illnesses are considered pre-existing conditions? An injury or illness is a preexisting condition if it resulted solely from a non-work-related event or exposure that occurred outside the work environment.

(b)(6) How do I decide whether an injury or illness is work-related if the employee is on travel status at the time the injury or illness occurs? Injuries and illnesses that occur while an employee is on travel status are work-related if, at the time of the injury or illness, the employee was engaged in work activities "in the interest of the employer." Examples of such activities include travel to and from customer contacts, conducting job tasks, and entertaining or being entertained to transact, discuss, or promote business (work-related entertainment includes only entertainment activities being engaged in at the direction of the employer).

Injuries or illnesses that occur when the employee is on travel status do not have to be recorded if they meet one of the exceptions listed below.

1904.5(b)(6)	If the employee has . . .	You may use the following to determine if an injury or illness is work-related
(i)	checked into a hotel or motel for one or more days.	When a traveling employee checks into a hotel, motel, or into a other temporary residence, he or she establishes a "home away from home." You must evaluate the employee's activities after he or she checks into the hotel, motel, or other temporary residence for their work-relatedness in the same manner as you evaluate the activities of a non-traveling employee. When the employee checks into the temporary residence, he or she is considered to have left the work environment. When the employee begins work each day, he or she re-enters the work environment. If the employee has established a "home away from home" and is reporting to a fixed worksite each day, you also do not consider injuries or illnesses work-related if they occur while the employee is commuting between the temporary residence and the job location.
(ii)	taken a detour for personal reasons.	Injuries or illnesses are not considered work-related if they occur while the employee is on a personal detour from a reasonably direct route of travel (e.g., has taken a side trip for personal reasons).

(b)(7) How do I decide if a case is work-related when the employee is working at home? Injuries and illnesses that occur while an employee is working at home, including work in a home office, will be considered work-related if the injury or illness occurs while the employee is performing work for pay or compensation in the home, and the injury or illness is directly related to the performance of work rather than to the general home environment or setting. For example, if an employee drops a box of work documents and injures his or her foot, the case is considered work-related. If an employee's fingernail is punctured by a needle from a sewing machine used to perform garment work at home, becomes infected and requires medical treatment, the injury is considered work-related. If an employee is injured because he or she trips on the family dog while rushing to answer a work phone call, the case is not considered work-related. If an employee working at home is electrocuted because of faulty home wiring, the injury is not considered work-related.

1904.6 Determination of new cases.

(a) Basic requirement. You must consider an injury or illness to be a "new case" if:

(a)(1) The employee has not previously experienced a recorded injury or illness of the same type that affects the same part of the body, or

(a)(2) The employee previously experienced a recorded injury or illness of the same type that affected the same part of the body but had recovered completely (all signs and symptoms had disappeared) from the previous injury or illness and an event or exposure in the work environment caused the signs or symptoms to reappear.

(b) Implementation.

(b)(1) When an employee experiences the signs or symptoms of a chronic work-related illness, do I need to consider each recurrence of signs or symptoms to be a new case? No, for occupational illnesses where the signs or symptoms may recur or continue in the absence of an exposure in the workplace, the case must only be recorded once. Examples may include occupational cancer, asbestosis, byssinosis and silicosis.

(b)(2) When an employee experiences the signs or symptoms of an injury or illness as a result of an event or exposure in the workplace, such as an episode of occupational asthma, must I treat the episode as a new case? Yes, because the episode or recurrence was caused by an event or exposure in the workplace, the incident must be treated as a new case.

(b)(3) May I rely on a physician or other licensed health care professional to determine whether a case is a new case or a recurrence of an old case? You are not required to seek the advice of a physician or other licensed health care professional. However, if you do seek such advice, you must follow the physician or other licensed health care professional's recommendation about whether the case is a new case or a recurrence. If you receive recommendations from two or more physicians or other licensed health care professionals, you must make a decision as to which recommendation is the most authoritative (best documented, best reasoned, or most authoritative), and record the case based upon that recommendation.

1904.7 General recording criteria.

(a) Basic requirement. You must consider an injury or illness to meet the general recording criteria, and therefore to be recordable, if it results in any of the following: death, days away from work, restricted work or transfer to another job, medical treatment beyond first aid, or loss of consciousness. You must also consider a case to meet the general recording criteria if it involves a significant injury or illness diagnosed by a physician or other licensed health care professional, even if it does not result in death, days away from work, restricted work or job transfer, medical treatment beyond first aid, or loss of consciousness.

(b) Implementation.

(b)(1) How do I decide if a case meets one or more of the general recording criteria? A work-related injury or illness must be recorded if it results in one or more of the following:

(b)(1)(i) Death. See § 1904.7(b)(2).

(b)(1)(ii) Days away from work. See § 1904.7(b)(3).

(b)(1)(iii) Restricted work or transfer to another job. See § 1904.7(b)(4).

(b)(1)(iv) Medical treatment beyond first aid. See § 1904.7(b)(5).

(b)(1)(v) Loss of consciousness. See § 1904.7(b)(6).

(b)(1)(vi) A significant injury or illness diagnosed by a physician or other licensed health care professional. See § 1904.7(b)(7).

(b)(2) How do I record a work-related injury or illness that results in the employee's death? You must record an injury or illness that results in death by entering a check mark on the OSHA 300 Log in the space for cases resulting in death. You must also report any work-related fatality to OSHA within eight (8) hours, as required by § 1904.39.

(b)(3) How do I record a work-related injury or illness that results in days away from work? When an injury or illness involves one or more days away from work, you must record the injury or illness on the OSHA 300 Log with a check mark in the space for cases involving days away and an entry of the number of calendar days away from work in the number of days column. If the employee is out for an extended period of time, you must enter an estimate of the days that the employee will be away, and update the day count when the actual number of days is known.

(b)(3)(i) Do I count the day on which the injury occurred or the illness began? No, you begin counting days away on the day after the injury occurred or the illness began.

(b)(3)(ii) How do I record an injury or illness when a physician or other licensed health care professional recommends that the worker stay at home but the employee comes to work anyway? You must record these injuries and illnesses on the OSHA 300 Log using the check box for cases with days away from work and enter the number of calendar days away recommended by the physician or other licensed health care professional. If a physician or other licensed health care professional recommends days away, you should encourage your employee to follow that recommendation. However, the days away must be recorded whether the injured or ill employee follows the physician or licensed health care professional's recommendation or not. If you receive recommendations from two or more physicians or other licensed health care professionals, you may make a decision as to which recommendation is the most authoritative, and record the case based upon that recommendation.

(b)(3)(iii) How do I handle a case when a physician or other licensed health care professional recommends that the worker return to work but the employee stays at home anyway? In this situation, you must end the count of days away from work on the date the physician or other licensed health care professional recommends that the employee return to work.

(b)(3)(iv) How do I count weekends, holidays, or other days the employee would not have worked anyway? You must count the number of calendar days the employee was unable to work as a result of the injury or illness, regardless of whether or not the employee was scheduled to work on those day(s). Weekend days, holidays, vacation days or other days off are included in the total number of days recorded if the employee would not have been able to work on those days because of a work-related injury or illness.

(b)(3)(v) How do I record a case in which a worker is injured or becomes ill on a Friday and reports to work on a Monday, and was not scheduled to work on the weekend? You need to record this case only if you receive information from a physician or other licensed health care professional indicating that the employee should not have worked, or should have performed only restricted work, during the weekend. If so, you must record the injury or illness as a case with days away from work or restricted work, and enter the day counts, as appropriate.

(b)(3)(vi) How do I record a case in which a worker is injured or becomes ill on the day before scheduled time off such as a holiday, a planned vacation, or a temporary plant closing? You need to record a case of this type only if you receive information from a physician or other licensed health care professional indicating that the employee should not have worked, or should have performed only restricted work, during the scheduled time off. If so, you must record the injury or illness as a case with days away from work or restricted work, and enter the day counts, as appropriate.

(b)(3)(vii) Is there a limit to the number of days away from work I must count? Yes, you may "cap" the total days away at 180 calendar days. You are not required to keep track of the number of calendar days away from work if the injury or illness resulted in more than 180 calendar days away from work and/or days of job transfer or restriction. In such a case, entering 180 in the total day's away column will be considered adequate.

(b)(3)(viii) May I stop counting days if an employee who is away from work because of an injury or illness retires or leaves my company? Yes, if the employee leaves your company for some reason unrelated to the injury or illness, such as retirement, a plant closing, or to take another job, you may stop counting days away from work or days of restriction/job transfer. If the employee leaves your company because of the injury or illness, you must estimate the total number of days away or days of restriction/job transfer and enter the day count on the 300 Log.

(b)(3)(ix) If a case occurs in one year but results in days away during the next calendar year, do I record the case in both years? No, you only record the injury or illness once. You must enter the number of calendar days away for the injury or illness on the OSHA 300 Log for the year in which the injury or illness occurred. If the employee is still away from work because of the injury or illness when you prepare the annual summary, estimate the total number of calendar days you expect the employee to be away from work, use this number to calculate the total for the annual summary, and then update the initial log entry later when the day count is known or reaches the 180-day cap.

(b)(4) How do I record a work-related injury or illness that results in restricted work or job transfer? When an injury or illness involves restricted work or job transfer but does not involve death or days away from work, you must record the

injury or illness on the OSHA 300 Log by placing a check mark in the space for job transfer or restriction and an entry of the number of restricted or transferred days in the restricted workdays column.

(b)(4)(i) How do I decide if the injury or illness resulted in restricted work? Restricted work occurs when, as the result of a work-related injury or illness:

(b)(4)(i)(A) You keep the employee from performing one or more of the routine functions of his or her job, or from working the full workday that he or she would otherwise have been scheduled to work; or

(b)(4)(i)(B) A physician or other licensed health care professional recommends that the employee not perform one or more of the routine functions of his or her job, or not work the full workday that he or she would otherwise have been scheduled to work.

(b)(4)(ii) What is meant by "routine functions"? For recordkeeping purposes, an employee's routine functions are those work activities the employee regularly performs at least once per week.

(b)(4)(iii) Do I have to record restricted work or job transfer if it applies only to the day on which the injury occurred or the illness began? No, you do not have to record restricted work or job transfers if you, or the physician or other licensed health care professional, impose the restriction or transfer only for the day on which the injury occurred or the illness began.

(b)(4)(iv) If you or a physician or other licensed health care professional recommends a work restriction, is the injury or illness automatically recordable as a "restricted work" case? No, a recommended work restriction is recordable only if it affects one or more of the employee's routine job functions. To determine whether this is the case, you must evaluate the restriction in light of the routine functions of the injured or ill employee's job. If the restriction from you or the physician or other licensed health care professional keeps the employee from performing one or more of his or her routine job functions, or from working the full workday the injured or ill employee would otherwise have worked, the employee's work has been restricted and you must record the case.

(b)(4)(v) How do I record a case where the worker works only for a partial work shift because of a work-related injury or illness? A partial day of work is recorded as a day of job transfer or restriction for recordkeeping purposes, except for the day on which the injury occurred or the illness began.

(b)(4)(vi) If the injured or ill worker produces fewer goods or services than he or she would have produced prior to the injury or illness but otherwise performs all of the routine functions of his or her work, is the case considered a restricted work case? No, the case is considered restricted work only if the worker does not perform all of the routine functions of his or her job or does not work the full shift that he or she would otherwise have worked.

(b)(4)(vii) How do I handle vague restrictions from a physician or other licensed health care professional, such as that the employee engage only in "light duty" or "take it easy for a week"? If you are not clear about the physician or other licensed health care professional's recommendation, you may ask that person whether the employee can do all of his or her routine job functions and work all of his or her normally assigned work shift. If the answer to both of these questions is "Yes," then the case does not involve a work restriction and does not have to be recorded as such. If the answer to one or both of these questions is "No," the case involves restricted work and must be recorded as a restricted work case. If you are unable to obtain this additional information from the physician or other licensed health care professional that recommended the restriction, record the injury or illness as a case involving restricted work.

(b)(4)(viii) What do I do if a physician or other licensed health care professional recommends a job restriction meeting OSHA's definition, but the employee does all of his or her routine job functions anyway? You must record the injury or illness on the OSHA 300 Log as a restricted work case. If a physician or other licensed health care professional recommends a job restriction, you should ensure that the employee complies with that restriction. If you receive recommendations from two or more physicians or other licensed health care professionals, you may make a decision as to which recommendation is the most authoritative, and record the case based upon that recommendation.

(b)(4)(ix) How do I decide if an injury or illness involved a transfer to another job? If you assign an injured or ill employee to a job other than his or her regular job for part of the day, the case involves transfer to another job. Note: This does not include the day on which the injury or illness occurred.

(b)(4)(x) Are transfers to another job recorded in the same way as restricted work cases? Yes, both job transfer and restricted work cases are recorded in the same box on the OSHA 300 Log. For example, if you assign, or a physician or other licensed health care professional recommends that you assign, an injured or ill worker to his or her routine job duties for part of the day and to another job for the rest of the day, the injury or illness involves a job transfer. You must record an injury or illness that involves a job transfer by placing a check in the box for job transfer.

(b)(4)(xi) How do I count days of job transfer or restriction? You count days of job transfer or restriction in the same way you count days away from work, using § 1904.7(b)(3)(i) to (viii), above. The only difference is that, if you permanently assign the injured or ill employee to a job that has been modified or permanently changed in a manner that eliminates the routine functions the employee was restricted from performing, you may stop the day count when the modification or change is made permanent. You must count at least one day of restricted work or job transfer for such cases.

(b)(5) How do I record an injury or illness that involves medical treatment beyond first aid? If a work-related injury or illness results in medical treatment beyond first aid, you must record it on the OSHA 300 Log. If the injury or illness did not involve death, one or more days away from work, one or more days of restricted work, or one or more days of job transfer, you enter a check mark in the box for

cases where the employee received medical treatment but remained at work and was not transferred or restricted.

(b)(5)(i) What is the definition of medical treatment? "Medical treatment" means the management and care of a patient to combat disease or disorder. For the purposes of Part 1904, medical treatment does not include:

(b)(5)(i)(A) Visits to a physician or other licensed health care professional solely for observation or counseling;

(b)(5)(i)(B) The conduct of diagnostic procedures, such as x-rays and blood tests, including the administration of prescription medications used solely for diagnostic purposes (e.g., eye drops to dilate pupils); or

(b)(5)(i)(C) "First aid" as defined in paragraph (b)(5)(ii) of this section.

(b)(5)(ii) What is "first aid"? For the purposes of Part 1904, "first aid" means the following:

(b)(5)(ii)(A) Using a non-prescription medication at nonprescription strength (for medications available in both prescription and non-prescription form, a recommendation by a physician or other licensed health care professional to use a non-prescription medication at prescription strength is considered medical treatment for recordkeeping purposes);

(b)(5)(ii)(B) Administering tetanus immunizations (other immunizations, such as Hepatitis B vaccine or rabies vaccine, are considered medical treatment);

(b)(5)(ii)(C) Cleaning, flushing or soaking wounds on the surface of the skin;

(b)(5)(ii)(D) Using wound coverings such as bandages, Band-Aids™, gauze pads, etc.; or using butterfly bandages or Steri-Strips™ (other wound closing devices such as sutures, staples, etc., are considered medical treatment);

(b)(5)(ii)(E) Using hot or cold therapy;

(b)(5)(ii)(F) Using any non-rigid means of support, such as elastic bandages, wraps, non-rigid back belts, etc. (devices with rigid stays or other systems designed to immobilize parts of the body are considered medical treatment for recordkeeping purposes);

(b)(5)(ii)(G) Using temporary immobilization devices while transporting an accident victim (e.g., splints, slings, neck collars, backboards, etc.).

(b)(5)(ii)(H) Drilling of a fingernail or toenail to relieve pressure, or draining fluid from a blister;

(b)(5)(ii)(I) Using eye patches;

(b)(5)(ii)(J) Removing foreign bodies from the eye using only irrigation or a cotton swab;

(b)(5)(ii)(K) Removing splinters or foreign material from areas other than the eye by irrigation, tweezers, cotton swabs or other simple means;

(b)(5)(ii)(L) Using finger guards;

(b)(5)(ii)(M) Using massages (physical therapy or chiropractic treatment are considered medical treatment for recordkeeping purposes); or

(b)(5)(ii)(N) Drinking fluids for relief of heat stress.

(b)(5)(iii) Are any other procedures included in first aid? No, this is a complete list of all treatments considered first aid for Part 1904 purposes.

(b)(5)(iv) Does the professional status of the person providing the treatment have any effect on what is considered first aid or medical treatment? No, OSHA considers the treatments listed in § 1904.7(b)(5)(ii) of this Part to be first aid regardless of the professional status of the person providing the treatment. Even when these treatments are provided by a physician or other licensed health care professional, they are considered first aid for the purposes of Part 1904. Similarly, OSHA considers treatment beyond first aid to be medical treatment even when it is provided by someone other than a physician or other licensed health care professional.

(b)(5)(v) What if a physician or other licensed health care professional recommends medical treatment but the employee does not follow the recommendation? If a physician or other licensed health care professional recommends medical treatment, you should encourage the injured or ill employee to follow that recommendation. However, you must record the case even if the injured or ill employee does not follow the physician or other licensed health care professional's recommendation.

(b)(6) Is every work-related injury or illness case involving a loss of consciousness recordable? Yes, you must record a work-related injury or illness if the worker becomes unconscious, regardless of the length of time the employee remains unconscious.

(b)(7) What is a "significant" diagnosed injury or illness that is recordable under the general criteria even if it does not result in death, days away from work, restricted work or job transfer, medical treatment beyond first aid, or loss of consciousness? Work-related cases involving cancer, chronic irreversible disease, a fractured or cracked bone, or a punctured eardrum must always be recorded under the general criteria at the time of diagnosis by a physician or other licensed health care professional.

Note to § 1904.7: OSHA believes that most significant injuries and illnesses will result in one of the criteria listed in § 1904.7(a): death, days away from work, restricted work or job transfer, medical treatment beyond first aid, or loss of consciousness. However, there are some significant injuries, such as a punctured eardrum or a fractured toe or rib, for which neither medical treatment nor work restrictions may be recommended. In addition, there are some significant progressive diseases, such as byssinosis, silicosis, and some types of cancer, for which medical treatment or work restrictions may not be recommended at the time of diagnosis but are likely to be recommended as the disease progresses. OSHA believes that cancer, chronic irreversible diseases, fractured or cracked bones, and punctured eardrums are generally considered significant injuries and illnesses, and must be recorded at the initial diagnosis even if medical treatment or work restrictions are not recommended, or are postponed, in a particular case.

1904.8 Recording criteria for needlestick and sharps injuries.

(a) Basic requirement. You must record all work-related needlestick injuries and cuts from sharp objects that are contaminated with another person's blood or other potentially infectious material (as defined by 29 CFR 1910.1030). You must enter the case on the OSHA 300 Log as an injury. To protect the employee's privacy, you may not enter the employee's name on the SHA 300 Log (see the requirements for privacy cases in paragraphs 1904.29(b)(6) through 1904.29(b)(9)).

(b) Implementation.

(b)(1) What does "other potentially infectious material" mean? The term "other potentially infectious materials" is defined in the OSHA Bloodborne Pathogens standard at § 1910.1030(b). These materials include:

(b)(1)(i) Human bodily fluids, tissues and organs, and

(b)(1)(ii) Other materials infected with the HIV or hepatitis B (HBV) virus such as laboratory cultures or tissues from experimental animals.

(b)(2) Does this mean that I must record all cuts, lacerations, punctures, and scratches? No, you need to record cuts, lacerations, punctures, and scratches only if they are work-related and involve contamination with another person's blood or other potentially infectious material. If the cut, laceration, or scratch involves a clean object, or a contaminant other than blood or other potentially infectious material, you need to record the case only if it meets one or more of the recording criteria in § 1904.7.

(b)(3) If I record an injury and the employee is later diagnosed with an infectious bloodborne disease, do I need to update the OSHA 300 Log? Yes, you must update the classification of the case on the OSHA 300 Log if the case results in death, days away from work, restricted work, or job transfer. You must also update the description to identify the infectious disease and change the classification of the case from an injury to an illness.

(b)(4) What if one of my employees is splashed or exposed to blood or other potentially infectious material without being cut or scratched? Do I need to record this incident? You need to record such an incident on the OSHA 300 Log as an illness if:

(b)(4)(i) It results in the diagnosis of a bloodborne illness, such as HIV, hepatitis B, or hepatitis C; or

(b)(4)(ii) It meets one or more of the recording criteria in § 1904.7.

1904.9 Recording criteria for cases involving medical removal under OSHA standards.

(a) Basic requirement. If an employee is medically removed under the medical surveillance requirements of an OSHA standard, you must record the case on the OSHA 300 Log.

(b) Implementation.

(b)(1) How do I classify medical removal cases on the OSHA 300 Log? You must enter each medical removal case on the OSHA 300 Log as either a case involving days away from work or a case involving restricted work activity, depending on how you decide to comply with the medical removal requirement. If the medical removal is the result of a chemical exposure, you must enter the case on the OSHA 300 Log by checking the "poisoning" column.

(b)(2) Do all of OSHA's standards have medical removal provisions? No, some OSHA standards, such as the standards covering bloodborne pathogens and noise, do not have medical removal provisions. Many OSHA standards that cover specific chemical substances have medical removal provisions. These standards include, but are not limited to, lead, cadmium, methylene chloride, formaldehyde, and benzene.

(b)(3) Do I have to record a case where I voluntarily removed the employee from exposure before the medical removal criteria in an OSHA standard are met? No, if the case involves voluntary medical removal before the medical removal levels required by an OSHA standard, you do not need to record the case on the OSHA 300 Log.

1904.10 Recording criteria for cases involving occupational hearing loss.
(a) Basic requirement. If an employee's hearing test (audiogram) reveals that the employee has experienced a work-related Standard Threshold Shift (STS) in hearing in one or both ears, and the employee's total hearing level is 25 decibels (dB) or more above audiometric zero (averaged at 2000, 3000, and 4000 Hz) in the same ear(s) as the STS, you must record the case on the OSHA 300 Log.

(b) Implementation.

(b)(1) What is a Standard Threshold Shift? A Standard Threshold Shift, or STS, is defined in the occupational noise exposure standard at 29 CFR 1910.95(c)(10)(i) as a change in hearing threshold, relative to the baseline audiogram for that employee, of an average of 10 decibels (dB) or more at 2000, 3000, and 4000 hertz (Hz) in one or both ears.

(b)(2) How do I evaluate the current audiogram to determine whether an employee has an STS and a 25-dB hearing level?

(b)(2)(i) *STS.* If the employee has never previously experienced a recordable hearing loss, you must compare the employee's current audiogram with that employee's baseline audiogram. If the employee has previously experienced a recordable hearing loss, you must compare the employee's current audiogram with the employee's revised baseline audiogram (the audiogram reflecting the employee's previous recordable hearing loss case).

(b)(2)(ii) *25-dB loss.* Audiometric test results reflect the employee's overall hearing ability in comparison to audiometric zero. Therefore, using the employee's current audiogram, you must use the average hearing level at 2000, 3000, and 4000 Hz to determine whether or not the employee's total hearing level is 25 dB or more.

(b)(3) May I adjust the current audiogram to reflect the effects of aging on hearing? Yes. When you are determining whether an STS has occurred, you may age adjust the employee's current audiogram results by using Tables F-1 or F-2, as appropriate, in Appendix F of 29 CFR

1910.95. You may not use an age adjustment when determining whether the employee's total hearing level is 25 dB or more above audiometric zero.

(b)(4) Do I have to record the hearing loss if I am going to retest the employee's hearing? No, if you retest the employee's hearing within 30 days of the first test, and the retest does not confirm the recordable STS, you are not required to record the hearing loss case on the OSHA 300 Log. If the retest confirms the recordable STS, you must record the hearing loss illness within seven (7) calendar days of the retest. If subsequent audiometric testing performed under the testing requirements of the § 1910.95 noise standard indicates that an STS is not persistent, you may erase or line-out the recorded entry.

(b)(5) Are there any special rules for determining whether a hearing loss case is work-related? No. You must use the rules in § 1904.5 to determine if the hearing loss is work-related. If an event or exposure in the work environment either caused or contributed to the hearing loss, or significantly aggravated a pre-existing hearing loss, you must consider the case to be work related.

(b)(6) If a physician or other licensed health care professional determines the hearing loss is not work-related, do I still need to record the case? If a physician or other licensed health care professional determines that the hearing loss is not work-related or has not been significantly aggravated by occupational noise exposure, you are not required to consider the case work-related or to record the case on the OSHA 300 Log.

(b)(7) How do I complete the 300 Log for a hearing loss case? When you enter a recordable hearing loss case on the OSHA 300 Log, you must check the 300 Log column for hearing loss. (Note: § 1904.10(b)(7) is effective beginning January 1, 2004.)

1904.11 Recording criteria for work-related tuberculosis cases.
(a) Basic requirement. If any of your employees has been occupationally exposed to anyone with a known case of active tuberculosis (TB), and that employee subsequently develops a tuberculosis infection, as evidenced by a positive skin test or diagnosis by a physician or other licensed health care professional, you must record the case on the OSHA 300 Log by checking the "respiratory condition" column.

(b) Implementation.

(b)(1) Do I have to record, on the Log, a positive TB skin test result obtained at a pre-employment physical? No, you do not have to record it because the employee was not occupationally exposed to a known case of active tuberculosis in your workplace.

(b)(2) (May I lineout or erase a recorded TB case if I obtain evidence that the case was not caused by occupational exposure?) Yes, you may lineout or erase the case from the Log under the following circumstances:

(b)(2)(i) The worker is living in a household with a person who has been diagnosed with active TB;

(b)(2)(ii) The Public Health Department has identified the worker as a contact of an individual with a case of active TB unrelated to the workplace; or

(b)(2)(iii) A medical investigation shows that the employee's infection was caused by exposure to TB away from work, or proves that the case was not related to the workplace TB exposure.

1904.12 [Removed] As of June 30, 2003, this standard has been archived and no longer represents OSHA policy.

1904.29 Forms.

(a) Basic requirement. You must use OSHA 300, 300-A, and 301 forms, or equivalent forms, for recordable injuries and illnesses. The OSHA 300 form is called the Log of Work-Related Injuries and Illnesses, the 300-A is the Summary of Work-Related Injuries and Illnesses, and the OSHA 301 form is called the Injury and Illness Incident Report.

(b) Implementation.

(b)(1) What do I need to do to complete the OSHA 300 Log? You must enter information about your business at the top of the OSHA 300 Log, enter a one or two line description for each recordable injury or illness, and summarize this information on the OSHA 300-A at the end of the year.

(b)(2) What do I need to do to complete the OSHA 301 Incident Report? You must complete an OSHA 301 Incident Report form, or an equivalent form, for each recordable injury or illness entered on the OSHA 300 Log.

(b)(3) How quickly must each injury or illness be recorded? You must enter each recordable injury or illness on the OSHA 300 Log and 301 Incident Report within seven (7) calendar days of receiving information that a recordable injury or illness has occurred.

(b)(4) What is an equivalent form? An equivalent form is one that has the same information, is as readable and understandable, and is completed using the same instructions as the OSHA form it replaces. Many employers use an insurance form instead of the OSHA 301 Incident Report, or supplement an insurance form by adding any additional information required by OSHA.

(b)(5) May I keep my records on a computer? Yes, if the computer can produce equivalent forms when they are needed, as described under §§ 1904.35 and 1904.40, you may keep your records using the computer system.

(b)(6) Are there situations where I do not put the employee's name on the forms for privacy reasons? Yes, if you have a "privacy concern case," you may not enter the employee's name on the OSHA 300 Log. Instead, enter "privacy case" in the space normally used for the employee's name. This will protect the privacy of the injured or ill employee when another employee, a former employee, or an authorized employee representative is provided access to the OSHA 300 Log under § 1904.35(b)(2). You must keep a separate, confidential list of the case numbers and employee names for your privacy concern cases so you can update the cases and provide the information to the government if asked to do so.

(b)(7) How do I determine if an injury or illness is a privacy concern case? You must consider the following injuries or illnesses to be privacy concern cases:

(b)(7)(i) An injury or illness to an intimate body part or the reproductive system;

(b)(7)(ii) An injury or illness resulting from a sexual assault;

(b)(7)(iii) Mental illnesses;

(b)(7)(iv) HIV infection, hepatitis, or tuberculosis;

(b)(7)(v) Needlestick injuries and cuts from sharp objects that are contaminated with another person's blood or other potentially infectious material (see § 1904.8 for definitions); and;

(b)(7)(vi) Other illnesses, if the employee voluntarily requests that his or her name not be entered on the log.

(b)(8) May I classify any other types of injuries and illnesses as privacy concern cases? No, this is a complete list of all injuries and illnesses considered privacy concern cases for Part 1904 purposes.

(b)(9) If I have removed the employee's name, but still believe that the employee may be identified from the information on the forms, is there anything else that I can do to further protect the employee's privacy? Yes, if you have a reasonable basis to believe that information describing the privacy concern case may be personally identifiable even though the employee's name has been omitted, you may use discretion in describing the injury or illness on both the OSHA 300 and 301 forms. You must enter enough information to identify the cause of the incident and the general severity of the injury or illness, but you do not need to include details of an intimate or private nature. For example, a sexual assault case could be described as "injury from assault," or an injury to a reproductive organ could be described as lower abdominal injury."

(b)(10) What must I do to protect employee privacy if I wish to provide access to the OSHA Forms 300 and 301 to persons other than government representatives, employees, former employees or authorized representatives? If you decide to voluntarily disclose the Forms to persons other than government representatives, employees, former employees or authorized representatives (as required by §§ 1904.35 and 1904.40), you must remove or hide the employees' names and other personally identifying information, except for the following cases. You may disclose the Forms with personally identifying information only:

(b)(10)(i) to an auditor or consultant hired by the employer to evaluate the safety and health program;

(b)(10)(ii) to the extent necessary for processing a claim for workers' compensation or other insurance benefits; or

(b)(10)(iii) to a public health authority or law enforcement agency for uses and disclosures for which consent, an authorization, or opportunity to agree or object is not required under Department of Health and Human Services Standards for Privacy of Individually Identifiable Health Information, 45 CFR 164.512.

1904.30 Multiple business establishments.

(a) Basic requirement. You must keep a separate OSHA 300 Log for each establishment that is expected to be in operation for one year or longer.

(b) Implementation.

(b)(1) Do I need to do to keep OSHA injury and illness records for short-term establishments (i.e., establishments that will exist for less than a year)? Yes, however, you do not have to keep a separate OSHA 300 Log for each such establishment. You may keep one OSHA 300 Log that covers all of your short-term establishments. You may also include the short-term establishments' recordable injuries and illnesses on an OSHA 300 Log that covers short-term establishments for individual company divisions or geographic regions.

(b)(2) May I keep the records for all of my establishments at my headquarters location or at some other central location? Yes, you may keep the records for an establishment at your headquarters or other central location if you can:

(b)(2)(i) Transmit information about the injuries and illnesses from the establishment to the central location within seven (7) calendar days of receiving information that a recordable injury or illness has occurred; and

(b)(2)(ii) Produce and send the records from the central location to the establishment within the time frames required by § 1904.35 and § 1904.40 when you are required to provide records to a government representative, employees, former employees or employee representatives.

(b)(3) Some of my employees work at several different locations or do not work at any of my establishments at all. How do I record cases for these employees? You must link each of your employees with one of your establishments, for recordkeeping purposes. You must record the injury and illness on the OSHA 300 Log of the injured or ill employee's establishment, or on an OSHA 300 Log that covers that employee's short-term establishment.

(b)(4) How do I record an injury or illness when an employee of one of my establishments is injured or becomes ill while visiting or working at another of my establishments, or while working away from any of my establishments? If the injury or illness occurs at one of your establishments, you must record the injury or illness on the OSHA 300 Log of the establishment at which the injury or illness occurred. If the employee is injured or becomes ill and is not at one of your establishments, you must record the case on the OSHA 300 Log at the establishment at which the employee normally works.

1904.31 Covered employees.

(a) Basic requirement. You must record on the OSHA 300 Log the recordable injuries and illnesses of all employees on your payroll, whether they are labor, executive, hourly, salary, part-time, seasonal, or migrant workers. You also must record the recordable injuries and illnesses that occur to employees who are not on your payroll if you supervise these employees on a day-to-day basis. If your business is organized as a sole proprietorship or partnership, the owner or partners are not considered employees for recordkeeping purposes.

(b) Implementation.

(b)(1) If a self-employed person is injured or becomes ill while doing work at my business, do I need to record the injury or illness? No, self-employed individuals are not covered by the OSH Act or this regulation.

(b)(2) If I obtain employees from a temporary help service, employee leasing service, or personnel supply service, do I have to record an injury or illness occurring to one of those employees? You must record these injuries and illnesses if you supervise these employees on a day-to-day basis.

(b)(3) If an employee in my establishment is a contractor's employee, must I record an injury or illness occurring to that employee? If the contractor's employee is under the day-to-day supervision of the contractor, the contractor is responsible for recording the injury or illness. If you supervise the contractor employee's work on a day-to-day basis, you must record the injury or illness.

(b)(4) Must the personnel supply service, temporary help service, employee leasing service, or contractor also record the injuries or illnesses occurring to temporary, leased or contract employees that I supervise on a day-to-day basis? No, you and the temporary help service, employee leasing service, personnel supply service, or contractor should coordinate your efforts to make sure that each injury and illness is recorded only once: either on your OSHA 300 Log (if you provide day-to-day supervision) or on the other employer's OSHA 300 Log (if that company provides day-to-day supervision).

1904.32 Annual summary.

(a) Basic requirement. At the end of each year you must:

(a)(1) Review the OSHA 300 Log to verify that the entries are complete and accurate, and correct any deficiencies identified;

(a)(2) Create an annual summary of injuries and illnesses recorded on the OSHA 300 Log;

(a)(3) Certify the summary; and

(a)(4) Post the annual summary.

(b) Implementation.

(b)(1) How extensively do I have to review the OSHA 300 Log entries at the end of the year? You must review the entries as extensively as necessary to make sure that they are complete and correct.

(b)(2) How do I complete the annual summary? You must:

(b)(2)(i) Total the columns on the OSHA 300 Log (if you had no recordable cases, enter zeros for each column total); and.

(b)(2)(ii) Enter the calendar year covered, the company's name, establishment name, establishment address, annual average number of employees covered by the OSHA 300 Log, and the total hours worked by all employees covered by the OSHA 300 Log.

(b)(2)(iii) If you are using an equivalent form other than the OSHA 300-A summary form, as permitted under § 1904.6(b)(4), the summary you use must also include the employee access and employer penalty statements found on the OSHA 300-A Summary form.

(b)(3) How do I certify the annual summary? A company executive must certify that he or she has examined the OSHA 300 Log and that he or she reasonably believes, based on his or her knowledge of the process by which the information was recorded, that the annual summary is correct and complete.

(b)(4) Who is considered a company executive? The company executive who certifies the log must be one of the following persons:

(b)(4)(i) An owner of the company (only if the company is a sole proprietorship or partnership);

(b)(4)(ii) An officer of the corporation;

(b)(4)(iii) The highest ranking company official working at the establishment; or

(b)(4)(iv) The immediate supervisor of the highest ranking company official working at the establishment.

(b)(5) How do I post the annual summary? You must post a copy of the annual summary in each establishment in a conspicuous place or places where notices to employees are customarily posted. You must ensure that the posted annual summary is not altered, defaced or covered by other material.

(b)(6) When do I have to post the annual summary? You must post the summary no later than February 1 of the year following the year covered by the records and keep the posting in place until April 30.

1904.33 Retention and updating.
(a) Basic requirement. You must save the OSHA 300 Log, the privacy case list (if one exists), the annual summary, and the OSHA 301 Incident Report forms for five (5) years following the end of the calendar year that these records cover.

(b) Implementation.

(b)(1) Do I have to update the OSHA 300 Log during the five-year storage period? Yes, during the storage period, you must update your stored OSHA 300 Logs to include newly discovered recordable injuries or illnesses and to show any changes that have occurred in the classification of previously recorded injuries and illnesses. If the description or outcome of a case changes, you must remove or line out the original entry and enter the new information.

(b)(2) Do I have to update the annual summary? No, you are not required to update the annual summary, but you may do so if you wish.

(b)(3) Do I have to update the OSHA 301 Incident Reports? No, you are not required to update the OSHA 301 Incident Reports, but you may do so if you wish.

1904.34 Change in business ownership.
If your business changes ownership, you are responsible for recording and reporting work-related injuries and illnesses only for that period of the year during which you owned the establishment. You must transfer the Part 1904 records to the new owner. The new owner must save all records of the establishment kept by the prior owner, as required by § 1904.33 of this Part, but need not update or correct the records of the prior owner.

1904.35 Employee involvement.
(a) Basic requirement. Your employees and their representatives must be involved in the recordkeeping system in several ways.

(a)(1) You must inform each employee of how he or she is to report an injury or illness to you.

(a)(2) You must provide limited access to your injury and illness records for your employees and their representatives.

(b) Implementation.

(b)(1) What must I do to make sure that employees report work-related injuries and illnesses to me?

(b)(1)(i) You must set up a way for employees to report work-related injuries and illnesses promptly; and

(b)(1)(ii) You must tell each employee how to report work-related injuries and illnesses to you.

(b)(2) Do I have to give my employees and their representatives access to the OSHA injury and illness records? Yes, your employees, former employees, their personal representatives, and their authorized employee representatives have the right to access the OSHA injury and illness records, with some limitations, as discussed below.

(b)(2)(i) Who is an authorized employee representative? An authorized employee representative is an authorized collective bargaining agent of employees.

(b)(2)(ii) Who is a "personal representative" of an employee or former employee? A personal representative is:

(b)(2)(ii)(A) Any person that the employee or former employee designates as such, in writing; or

(b)(2)(ii)(B) The legal representative of a deceased or legally incapacitated employee or former employee.

(b)(2)(iii) If an employee or representative asks for access to the OSHA 300 Log, when do I have to provide it? When an employee, former employee, personal representative, or authorized employee representative asks for copies of your current or stored OSHA 300 Log(s) for an establishment the employee or former employee has worked in, you must give the requester a copy of the relevant OSHA 300 Log(s) by the end of the next business day.

(b)(2)(iv) May I remove the names of the employees or any other information from the OSHA 300 Log before I give copies to an employee, former employee, or employee representative? No, you must leave the names on the 300 Log. However, to protect the privacy of injured and ill employees, you may not record the employee's name on the OSHA 300 Log for certain "privacy concern cases," as specified in paragraphs 1904.29(b)(6) through 1904.29(b)(9).

(b)(2)(v) If an employee or representative asks for access to the OSHA 301 Incident Report, when do I have to provide it?

(b)(2)(v)(A) When an employee, former employee, or personal representative asks for a copy of the OSHA 301 Incident Report describing an injury or illness to that employee or former employee, you must give the requester a copy of the OSHA 301 Incident Report containing that information by the end of the next business day.

(b)(2)(v)(B) When an authorized employee representative asks for a copies of the OSHA 301 Incident Reports for an establishment where the agent represents employees under a collective bargaining agreement, you must give copies of those forms to the authorized employee representative within 7 calendar days. You are only required to give the authorized employee representative information from the OSHA 301 Incident Report section titled "Tell us about the case." You must remove all other information from the copy of the OSHA 301 Incident Report or the equivalent substitute form that you give to the authorized employee representative.

(b)(2)(vi) May I charge for the copies? No, you may not charge for these copies the first time they are provided. However, if one of the designated persons asks for additional copies, you may assess a reasonable charge for retrieving and copying the records.

1904.36 Prohibition against discrimination.
Section 11(c) of the Act prohibits you from discriminating against an employee for reporting a work-related fatality, injury or illness. That provision of the Act also protects the employee who files a safety and health complaint, asks for access to the Part 1904 records, or otherwise exercises any rights afforded by the OSH Act.

1904.37 State recordkeeping regulations.
(a) Basic requirement. Some States operate their own OSHA programs, under the authority of a State Plan approved by OSHA. States operating OSHA-approved State Plans must have occupational injury and illness recording and reporting requirements that are substantially identical to the requirements in this Part (see 29 CFR 1902.3(k), 29 CFR 1952.4 and 29 CFR 1956.10(i)).

(b) Implementation.

(b)(1) State-Plan States must have the same requirements as Federal OSHA for determining which injuries and illnesses are recordable and how they are recorded.

(b)(2) For other Part 1904 provisions (for example, industry exemptions, reporting of fatalities and hospitalizations, record retention, or employee involvement), State-Plan State requirements may be more stringent than or supplemental to the Federal requirements, but because of the unique nature of the national recordkeeping program, States must consult with and obtain approval of any such requirements.

(b)(3) Although State and local government employees are not covered Federally, all State-Plan States must provide coverage, and must develop injury and illness statistics, for these workers. State Plan recording and reporting requirements for State and local government entities may differ from those for the private sector but must meet the requirements of paragraphs 1904.37(b)(1) and (b)(2).

(b)(4) A State-Plan State may not issue a variance to a private sector employer and must recognize all variances issued by Federal OSHA.

(b)(5) A State Plan State may only grant an injury and illness recording and reporting variance to a State or local government employer within the State after obtaining approval to grant the variance from Federal OSHA.

1904.38 Variances from the recordkeeping rule.
(a) Basic requirement. If you wish to keep records in a different manner from the manner prescribed by the Part 1904 regulations, you may submit a variance petition to the Assistant Secretary of Labor for Occupational Safety and Health, U.S. Department of Labor, Washington, DC 20210. You can obtain a variance only if you can show that your alternative recordkeeping system:

(a)(1) Collects the same information as this Part requires;

(a)(2) Meets the purposes of the Act; and

(a)(3) Does not interfere with the administration of the Act.

(b) Implementation.

(b)(1) What do I need to include in my variance petition? You must include the following items in your petition:

(b)(1)(i) Your name and address;

(b)(1)(ii) A list of the State(s) where the variance would be used;

(b)(1)(iii) The address(es) of the business establishment(s) involved;

(b)(1)(iv) A description of why you are seeking a variance;

(b)(1)(v) A description of the different recordkeeping procedures you propose to use;

(b)(1)(vi) A description of how your proposed procedures will collect the same information as would be collected by this Part and achieve the purpose of the Act; and

(b)(1)(vii) A statement that you have informed your employees of the petition by giving them or their authorized representative a copy of the petition and by posting a statement summarizing the petition in the same way as notices are posted under § 1903.2(a).

(b)(2) How will the Assistant Secretary handle my variance petition? The Assistant Secretary will take the following steps to process your variance petition.

(b)(2)(i) The Assistant Secretary will offer your employees and their authorized representatives an opportunity to submit written data, views, and arguments about your variance petition.

(b)(2)(ii) The Assistant Secretary may allow the public to comment on your variance petition by publishing the petition in the **Federal Register**. If the petition is published, the notice will establish a public comment period and may include a schedule for a public meeting on the petition.

(b)(2)(iii) After reviewing your variance petition and any comments from your employees and the public, the Assistant Secretary will decide whether or not your proposed recordkeeping procedures will meet the purposes of the Act, will not otherwise interfere with the Act, and will provide the same information as the Part 1904 regulations provide. If your procedures meet these criteria, the Assistant Secretary may grant the variance subject to such conditions as he or she finds appropriate.

(b)(2)(iv) If the Assistant Secretary grants your variance petition, OSHA will publish a notice in the **Federal Register** to announce the variance. The notice will include the practices the variance allows you to use, any conditions that apply, and the reasons for allowing the variance.

(b)(3) If I apply for a variance, may I use my proposed recordkeeping procedures while the Assistant Secretary is processing the variance petition? No, alternative recordkeeping practices are only allowed after the variance is approved. You must comply with the Part 1904 regulations while the Assistant Secretary is reviewing your variance petition.

(b)(4) If I have already been cited by OSHA for not following the Part 1904 regulations, will my variance petition have any effect on the citation and penalty? No, in addition, the Assistant Secretary may elect not to review your variance petition if it includes an element for which you have been cited and the citation is still under review by a court, an Administrative Law Judge (ALJ), or the OSH Review Commission.

(b)(5) If I receive a variance, may the Assistant Secretary revoke the variance at a later date? Yes, the Assistant Secretary may revoke your variance if he or she has good cause. The procedures revoking a variance will follow the same process as OSHA uses for reviewing variance petitions, as outlined in paragraph 1904.38(b)(2). Except in cases of willfulness or where necessary for public safety, the Assistant Secretary will:

(b)(5)(i) Notify you in writing of the facts or conduct that may warrant revocation of your variance; and

(b)(5)(ii) Provide you, your employees, and authorized employee representatives with an opportunity to participate in the revocation procedures.

1904.39 Reporting fatalities and multiple hospitalization incidents to OSHA.

(a) Basic requirement. Within eight (8) hours after the death of any employee from a work-related incident or the in-patient hospitalization of three or more employees as a result of a work-related incident, you must orally report the fatality/multiple hospitalization by telephone or in person to the Area Office of the Occupational Safety and Health Administration (OSHA), U.S. Department of Labor, that is nearest to the site of the incident. You may also use the OSHA toll-free central telephone number, 1-800-321-OSHA (1-800-321-6742).

(b) Implementation.

(b)(1) If the Area Office is closed, may I report the incident by leaving a message on OSHA's answering machine, faxing the area office, or sending an e-mail? No, if you can't talk to a person at the Area Office, you must report the fatality or multiple hospitalization incident using the 800 number.

(b)(2) What information do I need to give to OSHA about the incident? You must give OSHA the following information for each fatality or multiple hospitalization incident:

(b)(2)(i) The establishment name;

(b)(2)(ii) The location of the incident;

(b)(2)(iii) The time of the incident;

(b)(2)(iv) The number of fatalities or hospitalized employees;

(b)(2)(v) The names of any injured employees;

(b)(2)(vi) Your contact person and his or her phone number; and

(b)(2)(vii) A brief description of the incident.

(b)(3) Do I have to report every fatality or multiple hospitalization incident resulting from a motor vehicle accident? No, you do not have to report all of these incidents. If the motor vehicle accident occurs on a public street or highway, and does not occur in a construction work zone, you do not have to report the incident to OSHA. However, these injuries must be recorded on your OSHA injury and illness records, if you are required to keep such records.

(b)(4) Do I have to report a fatality or multiple hospitalization incident that occurs on a commercial or public transportation system? No, you do not have to call OSHA to report a fatality or multiple hospitalization incident if it involves a commercial airplane, train, subway or bus accident. However, these injuries must be recorded on your OSHA injury and illness records, if you are required to keep such records.

(b)(5) Do I have to report a fatality caused by a heart attack at work? Yes, your local OSHA Area Office director will decide whether to investigate the incident, depending on the circumstances of the heart attack.

(b)(6) Do I have to report a fatality or hospitalization that occurs long after the incident? No, you must only report each fatality or multiple hospitalization incident that occurs within thirty (30) days of an incident.

(b)(7) What if I don't learn about an incident right away? If you do not learn of a reportable incident at the time it occurs and the incident would otherwise be reportable under paragraphs (a) and (b) of this section, you must make the report within eight (8) hours of the time the incident is reported to you or to any of your agent(s) or employee(s).

1904.40 Providing records to government representatives.

(a) Basic requirement. When an authorized government representative asks for the records you keep under Part 1904, you must provide copies of the records within four (4) business hours.

(b) Implementation.

(b)(1) What government representatives have the right to get copies of my Part 1904 records? The government representatives authorized to receive the records are:

(b)(1)(i) A representative of the Secretary of Labor conducting an inspection or investigation under the Act;

(b)(1)(ii) A representative of the Secretary of Health and Human Services (including the National Institute for Occupational Safety and Health -- NIOSH) conducting an investigation under section 20(b) of the Act, or

(b)(1)(iii) A representative of a State agency responsible for administering a State plan approved under section 18 of the Act.

(b)(2) Do I have to produce the records within four (4) hours if my records are kept at a location in a different time zone? OSHA will consider your response to be timely if you give the records to the government representative within four (4) business hours of the request. If you maintain the records at a location in a different time zone, you may use the business hours of the establishment at which the records are located when calculating the deadline.

1904.41 Annual OSHA injury and illness survey of ten or more employers.

(a) Basic requirement. If you receive OSHA's annual survey form, you must fill it out and send it to OSHA or OSHA's designee, as stated on the survey form. You must report the following information for the year described on the form:

(a)(1) the number of workers you employed;

(a)(2) the number of hours worked by your employees; and

(a)(3) the requested information from the records that you keep under Part 1904.

(b) Implementation.

(b)(1) Does every employer have to send data to OSHA? No, each year, OSHA sends injury and illness survey forms to employers in certain industries. In any year, some employers will receive an OSHA survey form and others will not. You do not have to send injury and illness data to OSHA unless you receive a survey form.

(b)(2) How quickly do I need to respond to an OSHA survey form? You must send the survey reports to OSHA, or OSHA's designee, by mail or other means described in the survey form, within 30 calendar days, or by the date stated in the survey form, whichever is later.

(b)(3) Do I have to respond to an OSHA survey form if I am normally exempt from keeping OSHA injury and illness records? Yes, even if you are exempt from keeping injury and illness records under § 1904.1 to § 1904.3, OSHA may inform you in writing that it will be collecting injury and illness information from you in the following year. If you receive such a letter, you must keep the injury and illness records required by § 1904.5 to § 1904.15 and make a survey report for the year covered by the survey.

(b)(4) Do I have to answer the OSHA survey form if I am located in a State-Plan State? Yes, all employers who receive survey forms must respond to the survey, even those in State-Plan States.

(b)(5) Does this section affect OSHA's authority to inspect my workplace? No, nothing in this section affects OSHA's statutory authority to investigate conditions related to occupational safety and health.

1904.42 Requests from the Bureau of Labor Statistics for data.

(a) Basic requirement. If you receive a Survey of Occupational Injuries and Illnesses Form from the Bureau of Labor Statistics (BLS), or a BLS designee, you must promptly complete the form and return it following the instructions contained on the survey form.

(b) Implementation.

(b)(1) Does every employer have to send data to the BLS? No, each year, the BLS sends injury and illness survey forms to randomly selected employers and uses the information to create the Nation's occupational injury and illness statistics. In any year, some employers will receive a BLS survey form and others will not. You do not have to send injury and illness data to the BLS unless you receive a survey form.

(b)(2) If I get a survey form from the BLS, what do I have to do? If you receive a Survey of Occupational Injuries and Illnesses Form from the Bureau of Labor Statistics (BLS), or a BLS designee, you must promptly complete the form and return it, following the instructions contained on the survey form.

(b)(3) Do I have to respond to a BLS survey form if I am normally exempt from keeping OSHA injury and illness records? Yes, even if you are exempt from keeping injury and illness records under § 1904.1 to § 1904.3, the BLS may inform you in writing that it will be collecting injury and illness information from you in the coming year. If you receive such a letter, you must keep the injury and illness records required by § 1904.5 to § 1904.15 and make a survey report for the year covered by the survey.

(b)(4) Do I have to answer the BLS survey form if I am located in a State-Plan State? Yes, all employers who receive a survey form must respond to the survey, even those in State-Plan States.

1904.43 Summary and posting of 2001 data.

(a) Basic requirement. If you were required to keep OSHA 200 Logs in 2001, you must post a 2000 annual summary from the OSHA 200 Log of occupational injuries and illnesses for each establishment.

(b) Implementation.

(b)(1) What do I have to include in the summary?

(b)(1)(i) You must include a copy of the totals from the 2001 OSHA 200 Log and the following information from that form:

(b)(1)(i)(A) The calendar year covered;

(b)(1)(i)(B) Your company name;

(b)(1)(i)(C) The name and address of the establishment; and

(b)(1)(i)(D) The certification signature, title and date.

(b)(1)(ii) If no injuries or illnesses occurred at your establishment in 2001, you must enter zeros on the totals line and post the 2001 summary.

(b)(2) When am I required to summarize and post the 2001 information?

(b)(2)(i) You must complete the summary by February 1, 2002; and

(b)(2)(ii) You must post a copy of the summary in each establishment in a conspicuous place or places where notices to employees are customarily posted. You must ensure that the summary is not altered, defaced or covered by other material.

(b)(3) You must post the 2001 summary from February 1, 2002 to March 1, 2002.

1904.44 Retention and updating of old forms.

You must save your copies of the OSHA 200 and 101 forms for five years following the year to which they relate and continue to provide access to the data as though these forms were the OSHA 300 and 301 forms. You are not required to update your old 200 and 101 forms.

1904.45 OMB control numbers under the Paperwork Reduction Act.

The following sections each contain a collection of information requirement which has been approved by the Office of Management and Budget under the control number listed.

29 CFR citation	OMB Control No.
04.4-35	18-0176
04.39-41	18-0176
04.42	20-0045
04.43-44	18-0176

1904.46 Definitions.

The Act. The Act means the Occupational Safety and Health Act of 1970 (29 U.S.C. 651 **et seq.**). The definitions contained in section 3 of the Act (29 U.S.C. 652) and related interpretations apply to such terms when used in this Part 1904.

Establishment. An establishment is a single physical location where business is conducted or where services or industrial operations are performed. For activities where employees do not work at a single physical location, such as construction; transportation; communications, electric, gas and sanitary services; and similar operations, the establishment is represented by main or branch offices, terminals, stations, etc. that either supervise such activities or are the base from which personnel carry out these activities.

(1) Can one business location include two or more establishments? Normally, one business location has only one establishment. Under limited conditions, the employer may consider two or more separate businesses that share a single location to be separate establishments. An employer may divide one location into two or more establishments only when:

(1)(i) Each of the establishments represents a distinctly separate business;

(1)(ii) Each business is engaged in a different economic activity;

(1)(iii) No one industry description in the Standard Industrial Classification Manual (1987) applies to the joint activities of the establishments; and

(1)(iv) Separate reports are routinely prepared for each establishment on the number of employees, their wages and salaries, sales or receipts, and other business information. For example, if an employer operates a construction company at the same location as a lumber yard, the employer may consider each business to be a separate establishment.

(2) Can an establishment include more than one physical location? Yes, but only under certain conditions. An employer may combine two or more physical locations into a single establishment only when:

(2)(i) The employer operates the locations as a single business operation under common management;

(2)(ii) The locations are all located in close proximity to each other; and

(2)(iii) The employer keeps one set of business records for the locations, such as records on the number of employees, their wages and salaries, sales or receipts, and other kinds of business information. For example, one manufacturing establishment might include the main plant, a warehouse a few blocks away, and an administrative services building across the street.

(3) If an employee telecommutes from home, is his or her home considered a separate establishment? No, for employees who telecommute from home, the employee's home is not a business establishment and a separate 300 Log is not required. Employees who telecommute must be linked to one of your establishments under § 1904.30(b)(3).

Injury or illness. An injury or illness is an abnormal condition or disorder. Injuries include cases such as, but not limited to, a cut, fracture, sprain, or amputation. Illnesses include both acute and chronic illnesses, such as, but not limited to, a skin disease, respiratory disorder, or poisoning. (Note: Injuries and illnesses are recordable only if they are new, work-related cases that meet one or more of the Part 1904 recording criteria.)

Physician or Other Licensed Health Care Professional. A physician or other licensed health care professional is an individual whose legally permitted scope of practice (i.e., license, registration, or certification) allows him or her to independently perform, or be delegated the responsibility to perform, the activities described by this regulation.

You. "You" means an employer as defined in Section 3 of the Occupational Safety and Health Act of 1970 (29 U.S.C. 652).

8

LABOR LAWS

All companies, large and small, must deal with personnel issues. Hiring, setting salaries, motivating, supervising, and firing are critical and sensitive functions. In carrying out these processes, a company must make sure that it follows all employee-related rules and regulations. All employers must conform to regulations governing wage and hour requirements, the employment of minors, workers' compensation, and federal and state tax laws.

WAGE AND HOUR REGULATIONS

The U.S. Department of Labor, Wage and Hour Division, administers federal wage and hour laws and regulations, including recordkeeping requirements. Contractors also must comply with regulations that pertain to discrimination based on an employee's age, sex, or race.

A. FEDERAL WAGE REQUIREMENTS

The federal *Fair Labor Standards Act* (FLSA) establishes minimum wage compensation, overtime pay, recordkeeping, and child labor standards affecting U.S. workers. The federal minimum wage is $7.25 per hour effective July 24, 2009. Many states also have minimum wage laws. In cases where an employee is subject to both state and federal minimum wage laws, the employee is entitled to the higher minimum wage.

A business in the construction industry must have two or more employees and have an annual gross sales volume of $500,000 or more to be subject to the FLSA. Employers who are covered under the FLSA must pay employees the federal minimum wage, establish a workweek, and must pay overtime of at least one-and-one-half times an employee's regular rate of pay when hours worked exceed 40 in the workweek. The practice of paying overtime only after 80 hours in a biweekly pay period is illegal since each workweek must stand alone.

The following terms and phrases used in the FLSA are defined below:

Workweek: A workweek is a period of 168 hours during seven consecutive 24-hour periods. It may begin on any day of the week and at any hour of the day established by the employer.

Hours Worked: Generally, "hours worked" includes all time an employee must be on duty, or on the employer's premises, or at a prescribed workplace from the beginning of the first principal activity of the work day to the end of the last principal activity of the workday.

The Wage and Hour Division also enforces provisions of the following acts that may affect contractors who work on federally financed projects:

- **Davis-Bacon Act** – Requires payment of prevailing wage rates and fringe benefits on federally financed or assisted construction.
- **Walsh-Healey Public Contracts Act** – Requires payment of minimum wage rates and daily or weekly overtime pay on contracts to provide goods to the federal government.
- **Service Contract Act** – Requires payment of prevailing wage rates and fringe benefits on contracts to provide services to the federal government.

- **Contract Work Hours and Safety Standards Act** – Sets overtime standards for federal service and construction contracts.
- **Wage Garnishment Law** – Limits the amount of an individual's income that may be legally garnished and prohibits the firing of an employee whose pay is garnished for payment of a single debt.

B. State Wage and Hour Laws

The New Jersey Department of Labor and Workforce Development, Division of Wage and Hour Compliance administers and enforces New Jersey State Labor Laws by enforcing a minimum wage, methods of wage payment, and by enforcing the laws concerning the employment of children.

Effective July 24, 2009, the minimum wage rate in New Jersey is $7.25 per hour.

The New Jersey State Wage and Hour Law requires the payment of time-and-one-half per hour for actual hours worked in excess of 40 hours, with certain exemptions for certain salaried employees who meet the definition of an executive, administrative, or professional.

Wage laws provide regulations regarding how and when wages must be paid. New Jersey law states that all employers must pay wages to all employees in full at least twice during each calendar month on regular paydays that have been designated in advance. Employees shall receive pay no more than 10 days after the end of a pay period.

Wages are defined as all payment paid for personal services, including commissions, bonuses, and the cash value of all payments in any medium other than cash. The name by which payment for services is designated is immaterial. Tips, payments on a piecework basis, and payments on a profit-sharing basis are also wages. In general, wages include all pay to regular employees, full-time employees, part-time employees, temporary employees, and short-time employees. It makes no difference whether payment is on an hourly basis, a daily basis, or is a fixed weekly, monthly, or annual salary. The payment may be in cash or some other medium. Therefore, house rent, meals, room and board, utilities, merchandise, and other types of payment are wages if furnished as payment for services. The reasonable cash value of these payments in kind must be included in wage reports to the government entity.

The Construction Industry Independent Contractor Act concerns the improper classification of employees as independent contractors in the construction industry. Individuals who perform services in the making of improvements to real property for remuneration paid by an employer shall be deemed to be an employee unless and until it is shown to the satisfaction of the Department of Labor and Workforce Development that:

- The individual has been and will continue to be free from control or direction over the performance of that service;
- The service performed by the individual is either outside the usual course of the business for the employer, or the service is performed outside of all the places of business of the employer; and
- The individual is customarily engaged in an independently established trade, occupation, profession, or business.

The failure to withhold federal or state income taxes or to pay unemployment compensation contributions or workers' compensation premiums with respect to an individual's wages shall not be considered in making a determination as to employee status.

C. Federal Child Labor Provisions

The Department of Labor is the sole federal agency that monitors child labor and enforces child labor laws under the FLSA. FLSA child labor provisions are designed to protect the educational opportunities of youth and prohibit their employment in jobs and under conditions detrimental to their health or safety, including work involving excavation, driving, mining, manufacturing explosives, and the operation of many types of power-driven equipment.

As a general rule, the FLSA sets 14 years of age as the minimum age for employment, and limits the number of hours worked by minors under the age of 16. Once an employee is 18 years of age, there are no federal child labor rules.

Child labor laws vary from state to state. When federal and state standards are different, the rules that provide the most protection to young workers will apply.

D. State Child Labor Laws

The *New Jersey Child Labor Laws and Regulations* are much more detailed than the FLSA. New Jersey laws specify the hours of work for minors, the type of occupations minors are permitted to be performed, and the issuance of proper employment certificates for all minors under 18 years of age. Excerpts of these regulations are reprinted at the end of this chapter.

E. Keeping Records

The FLSA requires employers to keep records on employee personal information, workweek hours, hours worked, pay rates, accumulated overtime, deductions from wages, total wages, and the date of payment.

Employers must also keep records of employee withholdings (income tax, social security, and unemployment tax). The records must contain: (a) employer identification number; (b) copies of returns filed; and (c) dates and amounts of deposits made.

Every employer of employees subject to the FLSA's minimum wage provisions must post, and keep posted, a notice explaining the Act in a place in all of their establishments where employees are able to readily read it. The poster is provided at no charge to employers. It can be obtained from the employer's local Wage and Hour Division office or downloaded from www.dol.gov/whd/regs/compliance/posters/flsa.htm.

Americans With Disabilities Act

Since 1994, the Americans with Disabilities Act (ADA) has prohibited employers with 15 or more employees from discriminating against qualified individuals with disabilities. The ADA guarantees equal opportunity for people with disabilities in the areas of employment, public accommodations, transportation, government services, and telecommunications. The ADA applies to discrimination during employment-related activities like job application procedures, hiring or firing, promotions, compensation, fringe benefits, training, or conditions of employment.

Under both state and federal law, a "person with a disability" is:

- An individual who has a physical or mental impairment that substantially limits one or more major life activities, such as hearing, seeing, speaking, breathing, performing manual tasks, walking, caring for oneself, learning, or working;
- A person who has a record of such an impairment; or
- A person who is regarded as having such an impairment.

An employer must not only refrain from discriminating against individuals with disabilities, but also must reasonably accommodate the disabilities of qualified applicants or employees unless an undue hardship would result. Reasonable accommodation is a modification or adjustment that enables a person with a disability to apply for a job (holding a job interview in an accessible location), to perform the essential functions of a position (purchasing an amplifier to allow a hearing-impaired person to talk on the telephone), or to enjoy the same benefits and privileges of employment as other employees (holding a business function in a location accessible to all employees).

An overview titled "The ADA: Your Responsibilities as an Employer," is located at the end of this chapter. For more specific information about ADA requirements affecting employment, visit the Equal Employment Opportunity Commission Web site at www.eeoc.gov/.

VERIFYING EMPLOYEE ELIGIBILITY

U.S. Citizenship and Immigration Services (USCIS) is the government agency that oversees lawful immigration to the United States. Under the USCIS, the Department of Homeland Security (DHS) is responsible for the administration of the *Immigration Reform and Control Act* (IRCA). The *Act* seeks to control illegal immigration by eliminating employment opportunity as an incentive for unauthorized persons to come to the United States by prohibiting the hiring of aliens who are unauthorized to work in the United States. To comply with the law, employers must verify the employment eligibility and identity of all individuals hired by completing an Employment Eligibility Verification form (Form I-9) for all employees, including U.S. citizens. A copy of Form I-9 appears at the end of this chapter.

A. FORM I-9 REQUIREMENTS

To comply with Form I-9 requirements, employers must:

- Complete the I-9 form and keep it on file for at least three years from the date of employment or for one year after the employee leaves the job, whichever is later.
- Verify on the I-9 form that they have seen documents establishing identity and work authorization. This must be done for both U.S. citizens and noncitizens.
- Accept any valid documents listed on the last page of the I-9 form. Employers may not ask for more documents than those required, and may not demand to see specific documents.
- Be aware that work authorization documents must be renewed on or before their expiration date. I-9 forms must be updated at the same time.

It is in an employer's best interest to develop training on I-9 procedures, implement a compliance program, and develop a tickler file as a reminder of when I-9 forms need to be reverified or when they can be destroyed.

The DHS may impose penalties if an investigation reveals that an employer has knowingly hired or knowingly continued to employ an unauthorized alien, or has failed to comply with the employment eligibility verification requirements. More information about the employment verification process is available online at www.uscis.gov/portal/site/uscis.

B. AVOIDING DISCRIMINATION

In practice, employers should treat employees equally when recruiting, hiring, and verifying employment authorization and identity during the Form I-9 process. Discriminatory practices related to verifying employment authorization during the Form I-9 process is called document abuse. This happens when employers: 1) improperly request that employees produce more documents than are required by Form I-9; 2) request that employees present a particular document; 3) improperly reject documents that reasonably appear to be genuine and belong to the employee presenting them; and 4) improperly treat groups of applicants differently, such as requiring employees who sound "foreign" to produce particular documents the employer does not ask other employees to produce.

To avoid document abuse, an employer should:

- Let the employee choose which documents he or she will produce from the "List of Acceptable Documents" on the Form I-9;
- Accept documents that appear to be valid;
- Treat all people equally when announcing the job, taking applications, interviewing, offering the job, verifying employment eligibility, hiring, and firing;
- Give out the same job information over the phone and use the same form for all job applicants;
- Avoid "citizens only" hiring policies; and
- Base all decisions about hiring and firing on job performance and on-the-job behavior rather than on appearance, accent, name, or citizenship status of employees.

WORKERS' COMPENSATION

When an employee is injured or has a work-related illness, the employer is liable for the employee's medical treatment, wage replacement, and permanent disability compensation. Workers' compensation insurance coverage provides a limitation on that liability where an approved claim exists. Excerpts from "An Employer's Guide to Workers' Compensation in New Jersey" appear at the end of this chapter.

In New Jersey, the Division of Workers' Compensation, located within the Department of Labor and Workforce Development, is responsible for the administration of the New Jersey Workers' Compensation Law. The law requires that all New Jersey employers, not covered by federal programs, have workers' compensation coverage or be approved for self-insurance. Workers' compensation insurance coverage may be obtained in one of two ways.

1. A **Workers' Compensation Insurance Policy** is written by a mutual or stock carrier authorized to write insurance in New Jersey. Premiums for such insurance are generally based upon the classification(s) of the work being performed by employees, the claims experience of the employer, and the payroll of the employer.

2. **Self Insurance** is obtained through an application to and approval by the Commissioner of the Department of Banking and Insurance. Approval for self-insurance is based upon financial ability of the employer to meet its obligations under the law and the permanence of the business. The posting of security for such obligations may be required.

Employers may **not** deduct the cost of workers' compensation from the wages of their employees. Employers also may **not** discharge any employee who has claimed workers' compensation benefits or testified in a workers' compensation case.

Willful failure to provide workers' compensation insurance coverage if required is considered a fourth-degree crime subject to monetary penalties.

Posting Notice. New Jersey law requires every employer to post and maintain, in a conspicuous place or places in and about the worksite, a form stating that the employer has secured workers' compensation insurance coverage or has qualified with the Department of Banking and Insurance as a self-insured employer. The notice must include the name of the insurance carrier and other items as required by the Department. To obtain copies of this notice, employers should contact their insurer.

Reporting Work Accidents and Occupational Exposures. When an employer receives notice about a work-related accident or occupational exposure, he or she should immediately notify the insurance carrier or third party administrator so that a First Report of Injury form can be filed with the state of New Jersey. Within 26 weeks after the worker has reached maximum medical improvement or has returned to work, a second report, called a Subsequent Report of Injury, must be filed with the state.

For questions about New Jersey's workers' compensation program, contact:

New Jersey Department of Labor and Workforce Development
Division of Workers' Compensation
P.O. Box 381
Trenton, NJ 08625-0381
609.292.2515
http://lwd.state.nj.us/labor/wc/wc_index.html

For questions about workers' compensation insurance rates or obtaining coverage, contact:

New Jersey Compensation Rating and Inspection Bureau
60 Park Place
Newark, NJ 07102
973.622.6014
www.njcrib.com

UNEMPLOYMENT COMPENSATION

Unemployment compensation laws establish a form of insurance to protect workers who lose their jobs through no fault of their own, and are able and available for work. This insurance is paid for wholly by a payroll tax on employers. There are **no** deductions from the employees' wages. The amount of unemployment benefits payable to an unemployed person is set by statute and is based on his or her earnings while employed.

In New Jersey, if a business has at least one employee, the business is required to register with the Division of Employer Accounts, located within the New Jersey Department of Labor and Workforce Development. Registration for unemployment compensation is included in the new business registration process.

The *Employer Handbook for Unemployment and Disability Insurance Programs* provides a detailed explanation of the responsibilities and rights of employers subject to the New Jersey Unemployment Compensation and Temporary Disability Laws. The *Handbook* can be found online at http://lwd.dol.state.nj.us/labor/employer/ea/ea_index.html, then clicking on the Employer Handbook link on the right-hand side of the page. It covers the most significant aspects of the laws, including employer record-keeping, wage reporting, tax payments, and the benefit process as it applies to both claimants and employers.

For questions about New Jersey's workers' compensation program, contact:

New Jersey Department of Labor and Workforce Development
Division of Employer Accounts
P.O. Box 913
Trenton, NJ 08625-0913
609.633.6400
http://lwd.dol.state.nj.us/labor/employer/ea/ea_index.html

Handy Reference Guide
to the *Fair Labor Standards Act* (FLSA)

U.S. Department of Labor
Wage and Hour Division
WH Publication 1282, Revised September 2010

The Fair Labor Standards Act (FLSA) establishes minimum wage, overtime pay, recordkeeping, and child labor standards affecting full-time and part-time workers in the private sector and in Federal, State, and local governments.

The Wage and Hour Division (WHD) of the U.S. Department of Labor (DOL) administers and enforces the FLSA with respect to private employment, State and local government employment, and Federal employees of the Library of Congress, U.S. Postal Service, Postal Rate Commission, and the Tennessee Valley Authority. The FLSA is enforced by the U.S. Office of Personnel Management for employees of other Executive Branch agencies, and by the U.S. Congress for covered employees of the Legislative Branch.

Special rules apply to State and local government employment involving fire protection and law enforcement activities, volunteer services, and compensatory time off instead of cash overtime pay.

Basic Wage Standards

Covered nonexempt workers are entitled to a minimum wage of $7.25 per hour effective July 24, 2009. Nonexempt workers must be paid overtime pay at a rate of not less than one and one-half times their regular rates of pay after 40 hours of work in a workweek.

Wages required by FLSA are due on the regular payday for the pay period covered. Deductions made from wages for such items as cash or merchandise shortages, employer-required uniforms, and tools of the trade, are not legal to the extent that they reduce the wages of employees below the minimum rate required by FLSA or reduce the amount of overtime pay due under FLSA.

The FLSA contains some exemptions from these basic standards. Some apply to specific types of businesses; others apply to specific kinds of work.

While FLSA does set basic minimum wage and overtime pay standards and regulates the employment of minors, there are a number of employment practices, which FLSA does not regulate.

For example, FLSA does not require:

(1) vacation, holiday, severance, or sick pay;

(2) meal or rest periods, holidays off, or vacations;

(3) premium pay for weekend or holiday work;

(4) pay raises or fringe benefits; or

(5) a discharge notice, reason for discharge, or immediate payment of final wages to terminated employees.

The FLSA does not provide wage payment or collection procedures for an employee's usual or promised wages or commissions in excess of those required by the FLSA. However, some States do have laws under which such claims (sometimes including fringe benefits) may be filed.

Also, FLSA does not limit the number of hours in a day or days in a week an employee may be required or scheduled to work, including overtime hours, if the employee is at least 16 years old.

The above matters are for agreement between the employer and the employees or their authorized representatives.

Who is Covered?

All employees of certain enterprises having workers engaged in interstate commerce, producing goods for interstate commerce, or handling, selling, or otherwise working on goods or materials that have been moved in or produced for such commerce by any person, are covered by FLSA.

A covered enterprise is the related activities performed through unified operation or common control by any person or persons for a common business purpose and --

(1) whose annual gross volume of sales made or business done is not less than $500,000 (exclusive of excise taxes at the retail level that are separately stated); or

(2) is engaged in the operation of a hospital, an institution primarily engaged in the care of the sick, the aged, or the mentally ill who reside on the premises; a school for mentally or physically disabled or gifted children; a preschool, an elementary or secondary school, or an institution of higher education (whether operated for profit or not for profit); or

(3) is an activity of a public agency.

Any enterprise that was covered by FLSA on March 31, 1990, and that ceased to be covered because of the revised $500,000 test, continues to be subject to the overtime pay, child labor and recordkeeping provisions of FLSA.

Employees of firms which are not covered enterprises under FLSA still may be subject to its minimum wage, overtime pay, recordkeeping, and child labor provisions if they are individually engaged in interstate commerce or in the production of goods for interstate commerce, or in any closely-related process or occupation directly essential to such production. Such employees include those who: work in communications or transportation; regularly use the mails, telephones, or telegraph for interstate communication, or keep records of interstate transactions; handle, ship, or receive goods moving in interstate commerce; regularly cross State lines in the course of employment; or work for independent employers who contract to do clerical, custodial, maintenance, or other work for firms engaged in interstate commerce or in the production of goods for interstate commerce.

Domestic service workers such as day workers, housekeepers, chauffeurs, cooks, or full-time babysitters are covered if:

(1) their cash wages from one employer in calendar year 2010 are at least $1,700 (this calendar year threshold is adjusted by the Social Security Administration each year); or

(2) they work a total of more than 8 hours a week for one or more employers.

Tipped Employees

Tipped employees are individuals engaged in occupations in which they customarily and regularly receive more than $30 a month in tips. The employer may consider tips as part of

wages, but the employer must pay at least $2.13 an hour in direct wages.

The employer who elects to use the tip credit provision must inform the employee in advance and must be able to show that the employee receives at least the applicable minimum wage (see above) when direct wages and the tip credit allowance are combined. If an employee's tips combined with the employer's direct wages of at least $2.13 an hour do not equal the minimum hourly wage, the employer must make up the difference. Also, employees must retain all of their tips, except to the extent that they participate in a valid tip pooling or sharing arrangement.

Employer-Furnished Facilities

The reasonable cost or fair value of board, lodging, or other facilities customarily furnished by the employer for the employee's benefit may be considered part of wages.

Industrial Homework

The performance of certain types of work in an employee's home is prohibited under the law unless the employer has obtained prior certification from the Department of Labor. Restrictions apply in the manufacture of knitted outerwear, gloves and mittens, buttons and buckles, handkerchiefs, embroideries, and jewelry (where safety and health hazards are not involved). The manufacture of women's apparel (and jewelry under hazardous conditions) is generally prohibited. If you have questions on whether a certain type of work is restricted, or who is eligible for a homework certificate, or how to obtain a certificate, you may contact the local WHD office.

Subminimum Wage Provisions

The FLSA provides for the employment of certain individuals at wage rates below the statutory minimum. Such individuals include student-learners (vocational education students), as well as full-time students in retail or service establishments, agriculture, or institutions of higher education. Also included are individuals whose earning or productive capacity is impaired by a physical or mental disability, including those related to age or injury, for the work to be performed. Employment at less than the minimum wage is authorized to prevent curtailment of opportunities for employment. Such employment is permitted only under certificates issued by WHD.

Youth Minimum Wage

A minimum wage of not less than $4.25 an hour is permitted for employees under 20 years of age during their first 90 consecutive calendar days of employment with an employer. Employers are prohibited from taking any action to displace employees in order to hire employees at the youth minimum wage. Also prohibited are partial displacements such as reducing employees' hours, wages, or employment benefits.

Exemptions

Some employees are exempt from the overtime pay provisions or both the minimum wage and overtime pay provisions.

Because exemptions are generally narrowly defined under FLSA, an employer should carefully check the exact terms and conditions for each. Detailed information is available from local WHD offices.

Following are examples of exemptions which are illustrative, but not all-inclusive. These examples do not define the conditions for each exemption.

Exemptions from Both Minimum Wage and Overtime Pay

(1) Executive, administrative, and professional employees (including teachers and academic administrative personnel in elementary and secondary schools), outside sales employees, and employees in certain computer-related occupations (as defined in Department of Labor regulations);

(2) Employees of certain seasonal amusement or recreational establishments, employees of certain small newspapers, seamen employed on foreign vessels, employees engaged in fishing operations, and employees engaged in newspaper delivery;

(3) Farmworkers employed by anyone who used no more than 500 "man-days" of farm labor in any calendar quarter of the preceding calendar year;

(4) Casual babysitters and persons employed as companions to the elderly or infirm.

Exemptions from Overtime Pay Only

(1) Certain commissioned employees of retail or service establishments; auto, truck, trailer, farm implement, boat, or aircraft sales-workers, or parts-clerks and mechanics servicing autos, trucks, or farm implements, who are employed by nonmanufacturing establishments primarily engaged in selling these items to ultimate purchasers;

(2) Employees of railroads and air carriers, taxi drivers, certain employees of motor carriers, seamen on American vessels, and local delivery employees paid on approved trip rate plans;

(3) Announcers, news editors, and chief engineers of certain nonmetropolitan broadcasting stations;

(4) Domestic service workers living in the employer's residence;

(5) Employees of motion picture theaters; and

(6) Farmworkers.

Partial Exemptions from Overtime Pay

(1) Partial overtime pay exemptions apply to employees engaged in certain operations on agricultural commodities and to employees of certain bulk petroleum distributors.

(2) Hospitals and residential care establishments may adopt, by agreement with their employees, a 14-day work period instead of the usual 7-day workweek, if the employees are paid at least time and one-half their regular rates for hours worked over 8 in a day or 80 in a 14-day work period, whichever is the greater number of overtime hours.

(3) Employees who lack a high school diploma, or who have not attained the educational level of the 8th grade, can be required to spend up to 10 hours in a workweek engaged in remedial reading or training in other basic skills without receiving time and one-half overtime pay for these hours. However, the employees must receive their normal wages for hours spent in such training and the training must not be job specific.

(4) Public agency fire departments and police departments may establish a work period ranging from 7 to 28 days in which overtime need only be paid after a specified number of hours in each work period.

Child Labor Provisions

The FLSA child labor provisions are designed to protect the educational opportunities of minors and prohibit their employment in jobs and under conditions detrimental to their health or well-being. The provisions include restrictions on hours of work for minors under 16 and lists of hazardous occupations orders for both farm and non-farm jobs declared by the Secretary of Labor to be too dangerous for minors to perform. Further information on prohibited occupations is available from http://www.youthrules.dol.gov.

Nonagricultural Jobs (Child Labor)

Regulations governing child labor in non-farm jobs differ somewhat from those pertaining to agricultural employment. In non-farm work, the permissible jobs and hours of work, by age, are as follows:

(1) Youths 18 years or older may perform any job, whether hazardous or not, for unlimited hours;

(2) Minors 16 and 17 years old may perform any nonhazardous job, for unlimited hours; and

(3) Minors 14 and 15 years old may work outside school hours in various nonmanufacturing, nonmining, nonhazardous jobs under the following conditions: no more than 3 hours on a school day, 18 hours in a school week, 8 hours on a nonschool day, or 40 hours in a nonschool week. Also, work may not begin before 7 a.m., nor end after 7 p.m., except from June 1 through Labor Day, when evening hours are extended to 9 p.m. Under a special provision, youths 14 and 15 years old enrolled in an approved Work Experience and Career Exploration Program (WECEP) may be employed for up to 23 hours in school weeks and 3 hours on school days (including during school hours). In addition, academically oriented youths enrolled in an approved Work-Study Program (WSP) may be employed during school hours.

Fourteen is the minimum age for most nonfarm work. However, at any age, minors may deliver newspapers; perform in radio, television, movie, or theatrical productions; work for parents in their solely-owned nonfarm business (except in mining, manufacturing or on hazardous jobs); or gather evergreens and make evergreen wreaths.

Farm Jobs (Child Labor)

In farm work, permissible jobs and hours of work, by age, are as follows:

(1) Minors 16 years and older may perform any job, whether hazardous or not, for unlimited hours;

(2) Minors 14 and 15 years old may perform any nonhazardous farm job outside of school hours;

(3) Minors 12 and 13 years old may work outside of school hours in nonhazardous jobs, either with a parent's written consent or on the same farm as the parent(s);

(4) Minors under 12 years old may perform jobs on farms owned or operated by parent(s), or with a parent's written consent, outside of school hours in nonhazardous jobs on farms not covered by minimum wage requirements.

Minors of any age may be employed by their parents at any time in any occupation on a farm owned or operated by their parents.

Recordkeeping

The FLSA requires employers to keep records on wages, hours, and other items, as specified in DOL recordkeeping regulations. Most of the information is of the kind generally maintained by employers in ordinary business practice and in compliance with other laws and regulations. The records do not have to be kept in any particular form and time clocks need not be used. With respect to an employee subject to the minimum wage provisions or both the minimum wage and overtime pay provisions, the following records must be kept:

(1) personal information, including employee's name, home address, occupation, sex, and birth date if under 19 years of age;

(2) hour and day when workweek begins;

(3) total hours worked each workday and each workweek;

(4) total daily or weekly straight-time earnings;

(5) regular hourly pay rate for any week when overtime is worked;

(6) total overtime pay for the workweek;

(7) deductions from or additions to wages;

(8) total wages paid each pay period; and

(9) date of payment and pay period covered.

Records required for exempt employees differ from those for nonexempt workers. Special information is required for homeworkers, for employees working under uncommon pay arrangements, for employees to whom lodging or other facilities are furnished, and for employees receiving remedial education.

Nursing Mothers

The Patient Protection and Affordable Care Act ("PPACA"), signed into law on March 23, 2010 (P.L. 111-148), amended Section 7 of the FLSA, to provide a break time requirement for nursing mothers.

Employers are required to provide reasonable break time for an employee to express breast milk for her nursing child for one year after the child's birth each time such employee has need to express the milk. Employers are also required to provide a place, other than a bathroom, that is shielded from view and free from intrusion from coworkers and the public, which may be used by an employee to express breast milk.

The FLSA requirement of break time for nursing mothers to express breast milk does not preempt State laws that provide greater protections to employees (for example, providing compensated break time, providing break time for exempt employees, or providing break time beyond 1 year after the child's birth).

Employers are required to provide a reasonable amount of break time to express milk as frequently as needed by the nursing mother. The frequency of breaks needed to express milk as well as the duration of each break will likely vary.

A bathroom, even if private, is not a permissible location under the Act. The location provided must be functional as a space for expressing breast milk. If the space is not dedicated to the nursing mother's use, it must be available when needed in order to meet the statutory requirement. A space temporarily created or converted into a space for expressing milk or made available when needed by the nursing mother is sufficient provided that the space is shielded from view, and free from any intrusion from co-workers and the public.

Only employees who are not exempt from the FLSA's overtime pay requirements are entitled to breaks to express milk. While employers are not required under the FLSA to provide breaks to nursing mothers who are exempt from the overtime pay requirements of Section 7, they may be obligated to provide such breaks under State laws.

Employers with fewer than 50 employees are not subject to the FLSA break time requirement if compliance with the provision would impose an undue hardship. Whether compliance would be an undue hardship is determined by looking at the difficulty or expense of compliance for a specific employer in comparison to the size, financial resources, nature, and structure of the employer's business. All employees who work for the covered employer, regardless of work site, are counted when determining whether this exemption may apply.

Employers are not required under the FLSA to compensate nursing mothers for breaks taken for the purpose of expressing milk. However, where employers already provide compensated breaks, an employee who uses that break time to express milk must be compensated in the same way that other employees are compensated for break time. In addition, the FLSA's general requirement that the employee must be completely relieved from duty or else the time must be compensated as work time applies.

Terms Used in FLSA

Workweek -- A workweek is a period of 168 hours during 7 consecutive 24-hour periods. It may begin on any day of the week and at any hour of the day established by the employer. Generally, for purposes of minimum wage and overtime payment each workweek stands alone; there can be no averaging of two or more workweeks. Employee coverage, compliance with wage payment requirements, and the application of most exemptions are determined on a workweek basis.

Hours Worked -- Covered employees must be paid for all hours worked in a workweek. In general, "hours worked" includes all time an employee must be on duty, or on the employer's premises or at any other prescribed place of work from the beginning of the first principal activity of the work day to the end of the last principal work activity of the workday. Also included is any additional time the employee is allowed (i.e., suffered or permitted) to work.

Computing Overtime Pay

Overtime must be paid at a rate of at least one and one-half times the employee's regular rate of pay for each hour worked in a workweek in excess of the maximum allowable in a given type of employment. Generally, the regular rate includes all payments made by the employer to or on behalf of the employee (except for certain statutory exclusions). The following examples are based on a maximum 40-hour workweek applicable to most covered nonexempt employees.

(1) **Hourly rate** (regular pay rate for an employee paid by the hour) -- If more than

40 hours are worked, at least one and one-half times the regular rate for each hour over 40 is due.

Example: An employee paid $8.00 an hour works 44 hours in a workweek. The employee is entitled to at least one and one-half times $8.00, or $12.00, for each hour over 40. Pay for the week would be $320 for the first 40 hours, plus $48.00 for the four hours of overtime - a total of $368.00.

(2) **Piece rate** -- The regular rate of pay for an employee paid on a piecework basis is obtained by dividing the total weekly earnings by the total number of hours worked in that week. The employee is entitled to an additional one-half times this regular rate for each hour over 40, plus the full piecework earnings.

Example: An employee paid on a piecework basis works 45 hours in a week and earns $405. The regular rate of pay for that week is $405 divided by 45, or $9.00 an hour. In addition to the straight-time pay, the employee is also entitled to $4.50 (half the regular rate) for each hour over 40 - an additional $22.50 for the five overtime hours - for a total of $427.50.

Another way to compensate pieceworkers for overtime, if agreed to before the work is performed, is to pay one and one-half times the piece rate for each piece produced during the overtime hours. The piece rate must be the one actually paid during nonovertime hours and must be enough to yield at least the minimum wage per hour.

(3) **Salary** -- The regular rate for an employee paid a salary for a regular or specified number of hours a week is obtained by dividing the salary by the number of hours for which the salary is intended to compensate. The employee is entitled to an additional one-half times this regular rate for each hour over 40, plus the salary.

If, under the employment agreement, a salary sufficient to meet the minimum wage requirement in every workweek is paid as straight time for whatever number of hours are worked in a workweek, the regular rate is obtained by dividing the salary by the number of hours worked each week. To illustrate, suppose an employee's hours of work vary each week and the agreement with the employer is that the employee will be paid $480 a week for whatever number of hours of work are required. Under this

agreement, the regular rate will vary in overtime weeks. If the employee works 50 hours, the regular rate is $9.60 ($480 divided by 50 hours). In addition to the salary, half the regular rate, or $4.80, is due for each of the 10 overtime hours, for a total of $528 for the week. If the employee works 60 hours, the regular rate is $8.00 ($480 divided by 60 hours). In that case, an additional $4.00 is due for each of the 20 overtime hours, for a total of $560 for the week.

In no case may the regular rate be less than the minimum wage required by FLSA.

If a salary is paid on other than a weekly basis, the weekly pay must be determined in order to compute the regular rate and overtime pay. If the salary is for a half month, it must be multiplied by 24 and the product divided by 52 weeks to get the weekly equivalent. A monthly salary should be multiplied by 12 and the product divided by 52.

Enforcement

WHD's enforcement of FLSA is carried out by investigators stationed across the U.S, regardless of immigration status. As WHD's authorized representatives, they conduct investigations and gather data on wages, hours, and other employment conditions or practices, in order to determine compliance with the law. Where violations are found, they also may recommend changes in employment practices to bring an employer into compliance.

It is a violation to fire or in any other manner discriminate against an employee for filing a complaint or for participating in a legal proceeding under FLSA.

Willful violations may be prosecuted criminally and the violator fined up to $10,000. A second conviction may result in imprisonment.

Employers who violate the child labor provisions of FLSA are subject to a civil money penalty of up to $11,000 for each employee who was the subject of a violation. These penalties may be increased up to $50,000 for each violation that caused the death or serious injury of any employee who is a minor, and may be doubled, up to $100,000, when the violation was determined to be willful or repeated.

Employers who willfully or repeatedly violate the minimum wage or overtime pay requirements are subject to a civil money penalty of up to $1,100 for each such violation.

The FLSA prohibits the shipment of goods in interstate commerce which were produced in violation of the minimum wage, overtime pay, child labor, or special minimum wage provisions.

Recovery of Back Wages

Listed below are methods which FLSA provides for recovering unpaid minimum and/or overtime wages.

(1) WHD may supervise payment of back wages.

(2) The Secretary of Labor may bring suit for back wages and an equal amount as liquidated damages.

(3) An employee may file a private suit for back pay and an equal amount as liquidated damages, plus attorney's fees and court costs.

(4) The Secretary of Labor may obtain an injunction to restrain any person from violating FLSA, including the unlawful withholding of proper minimum wage and overtime pay.

An employee may not bring suit if he or she has been paid back wages under the supervision of WHD or if the Secretary of Labor has already filed suit to recover the wages.

A 2-year statute of limitations applies to the recovery of back pay, except in the case of willful violation, in which case a 3-year statute applies.

Other Labor Laws

In addition to FLSA, WHD enforces and administers a number of other labor laws. Among these are:

(1) the **Davis-Bacon and Related Acts**, which require payment of prevailing wage rates and fringe benefits on federally-financed or assisted construction;

(2) the **Walsh-Healey Public Contracts Act**, which requires payment of minimum wage rates and overtime pay on contracts to provide goods to the Federal Government;

(3) the **Service Contract Act**, which requires payment of prevailing wage rates and fringe benefits on contracts to provide services to the Federal Government;

(4) the **Contract Work Hours and Safety Standards Act**, which sets overtime standards for service and construction contracts;

(5) the **Migrant and Seasonal Agricultural Worker Protection Act**, which protects farm workers by imposing certain requirements on agricultural employers and associations and requires the registration of crewleaders who must also provide the same worker protections;

(6) the **Wage Garnishment Law**, which limits the amount of an individual's income that may be legally garnished and prohibits firing an employee whose pay is garnished for payment of a single debt;

(7) the **Employee Polygraph Protection Act**, which prohibits most private employers from using any type of lie detector test either for pre-employment screening of job applicants or for testing current employees during the course of employment;

(8) the **Family and Medical Leave Act**, which entitles eligible employees of covered employers to take up to 12 weeks of unpaid job-protected leave each year, with maintenance of group health insurance, for the birth and care of a child, for the placement of a child for adoption or foster care, for the care of a child, spouse, or parent with a serious health condition, or for the employee's serious health condition; and

(9) the **Immigration and Nationality Act**, as amended, which:

- under the H-2A provisions, provides for the enforcement of contractual obligations of job offers which have been certified to by employers of temporary alien nonimmigrant agricultural workers;

- under the H-2B provisions, provides for the enforcement of employment conditions in the application for alien non-immigrants in temporary, non-agricultural jobs.

- under the H-1C provisions, provides for the enforcement of employment conditions attested to by employers in disadvantaged areas employing H-1C temporary alien nonimmigrant registered nurses;

- under the D-1 provisions, provides for the enforcement of employment conditions attested to by employers seeking to employ alien crewmembers to perform specified longshore activity at U.S. ports; and

- under the H-1B provisions, provides for the enforcement of labor condition applications filed by employers wishing to employ aliens in specialty occupations and as fashion models of distinguished merit and ability.

More detailed information on FLSA and other laws administered by WHD is available by calling our toll-free help line 1-866-4US-WAGE (1-866-487-9243). For those who have access to the Internet, further information may also be obtained on WHD's Internet Home Page which can be located at the following address: www.wagehour.dol.gov.

Small Business Regulatory Enforcement Fairness Act of 1996 (SBREFA)

In accordance with the provisions of the SBREFA, the Small Business Administration has established a National Small Business and Agriculture Regulatory Ombudsman and 10 Regional Fairness Boards to receive comments from small entities about federal agency enforcement actions. The Ombudsman annually evaluates enforcement activities and rates each agency's responsiveness to small entities. Small entities wishing to comment on Wage and Hour Division enforcement activities may call 1-888-REG-FAIR (1-888-734-3247), or write to the Office of the National Ombudsman, U.S. Small Business Administration, 409 3rd Street, SW, MC2120, Washington, DC 20416-0005, or visit the Ombudsman's internet website, www.sba.gov/ombudsman/.

The right to file a comment with the Ombudsman is in addition to any other rights a small entity may have, including the right to contest the assessment of a civil money penalty. Filing a comment with the Ombudsman neither extends the maximum time period for contesting the assessment of a penalty, nor takes the place of filing the response required to secure an administrative hearing on a penalty. WHD does not consider filing of a comment with the Ombudsman as a factor in determining how to resolve issues raised during a compliance action.

Equal Pay Provisions

The equal pay provisions of FLSA prohibit sex-based wage differentials between men and women employed in the same establishment who perform jobs that require equal skill, effort, and responsibility and which are performed under similar working conditions. These provisions, as well as other statutes prohibiting discrimination in employment, are enforced by the Equal Employment Opportunity Commission. More detailed information is available by calling 1-800-669-4000 or visiting www.eeoc.gov.

The ADA: Your Responsibilities as an Employer

Notice Concerning the Americans with Disabilities Act Amendments Act of 2008

The Americans with Disabilities Act (ADA) Amendment Act of 2008 was signed into law on September 25, 2008 and becomes effective January 1, 2009. Because this law makes several significant changes, including changes to the definition of the term "disability," the EEOC will be evaluating the impact of these changes on this document and other publications. See the list of specific changes to the ADA made by the ADA Amendments Act.

ADDENDUM

Since **The Americans with Disabilities Act: Your Responsibilities as an Employer** was published, the Supreme Court has ruled that the determination of whether a person has an ADA "disability" must take into consideration whether the person is substantially limited in performing a major life activity **when using a mitigating measure.** This means that if a person has little or no difficulty performing any major life activity because s/he uses a mitigating measure, then that person will not meet the ADA's first definition of "disability." The Supreme Court's rulings were in <u>Sutton v. United Airlines, Inc.</u>, 527 U.S. ____ (1999), and <u>Murphy v. United Parcel Service, Inc.</u>, 527 U.S. ____ (1999).

As a result of the Supreme Court's ruling, this document's guidance on mitigating measures, found in the section **"Additional Questions and Answers on the Americans with Disabilities Act,"** is **superseded.** Following the Supreme Court's ruling, whether a person has an ADA "disability" is determined by taking into account the positive and negative effects of mitigating measures used by the individual. The Supreme Court's ruling does not change anything else in this document.

For more information on the Supreme Court rulings and their impact on determining whether specific individuals meet the definition of "disability," consult the *Instructions for Field Offices: Analyzing ADA Charges After Supreme Court Decisions Addressing "Disability" and "Qualified,"* which can be found on EEOC's website at www.eeoc.gov.

The *Americans with Disabilities Act of 1990* (ADA) makes it unlawful to discriminate in employment against a qualified individual with a disability. The ADA also outlaws discrimination against individuals with disabilities in State and local government services, public accommodations, transportation and telecommunications. This booklet explains the part of the ADA that prohibits job discrimination. This part of the law is enforced by the U.S. Equal Employment Opportunity Commission and State and local civil rights enforcement agencies that work with the Commission.

Are You Covered?

Job discrimination against people with disabilities is illegal if practiced by:

- private employers;
- state and local governments;
- employment agencies;
- labor organizations; and
- labor-management committees.

The part of the ADA enforced by the EEOC outlaws job discrimination by:

- all employers, including state and local government employers, with 25 or more employees after July 26, 1992; and
- all employers, including state and local government employers, with 15 or more employees after July 26, 1994.

Another part of the ADA, enforced by the U.S. Department of Justice (DOJ), prohibits discrimination in state and local government programs and activities, including discrimination by all state and local governments, regardless of the number of employees, after January 26, 1992.

Because the ADA establishes overlapping responsibilities in both EEOC and DOJ for employment by state and local governments, the federal enforcement effort will be coordinated by EEOC and DOJ to avoid duplication in investigative and enforcement activities. In addition, since some private and governmental employers are already covered by nondiscrimination and affirmative action requirements under the Rehabilitation Act of 1973, EEOC, DOJ, and the Department of Labor will similarly coordinate the enforcement effort under the ADA and the Rehabilitation Act.

What Employment Practices are Covered?

The ADA makes it unlawful to discriminate in all employment practices such as:

- recruitment
- pay
- hiring
- firing
- promotion
- job assignments
- training
- leave
- lay-off
- benefits
- all other employment related activities.

The ADA prohibits an employer from retaliating against an applicant or employee for asserting his rights under the ADA. The Act also makes it unlawful to discriminate against an applicant or employee, whether disabled or not, because of the individual's family, business, social or other relationship or association with an individual with a disability.

Who Is Protected?

Title I of the ADA protects qualified individuals with disabilities from employment discrimination. Under the ADA, a person has a disability if he has a physical or mental impairment that substantially limits a major life activity. The ADA also protects individuals who have a record of a substantially limiting impairment, and people who are regarded as having a substantially limiting impairment.

To be protected under the ADA, an individual must have, have a record of, or be regarded as having a substantial, as opposed to a minor, impairment. A substantial impairment is one that significantly limits or restricts a major life activity such as hearing, seeing, speaking, breathing, performing manual tasks, walking, caring for oneself, learning, or working.

An individual with a disability must also be qualified to perform the essential functions of the job with or without reasonable accommodation, in order to be protected by the ADA. This means that the applicant or employee must:

- satisfy your job requirements for educational background, employment experience, skills, licenses, and any other qualification standards that are job related; and
- be able to perform those tasks that are essential to the job, with or without reasonable accommodation.

The ADA does not interfere with your right to hire the best qualified applicant. Nor does the ADA impose any affirmative action obligations. The ADA simply prohibits you from discriminating against a qualified applicant or employee because of her disability.

How Are Essential Functions Determined?

Essential functions are the basic job duties that an employee must be able to perform, with or without reasonable accommodation. You should carefully examine each job to determine which functions or tasks are essential to performance. (This is particularly important before taking an employment action such as recruiting, advertising, hiring, promoting or firing.)

Factors to consider in determining if a function is essential include:

- whether the reason the position exists is to perform that function;
- the number of other employees available to perform the function or among whom the performance of the function can be distributed; and
- the degree of expertise or skill required to perform the function.

Your judgment as to which functions are essential, and a written job description prepared before advertising or interviewing for a job will be considered by EEOC as evidence of essential functions. Other kinds of evidence that EEOC will consider include the:

- actual work experience of present or past employees in the job;
- time spent performing a function;
- consequences of not requiring that an employee perform a function; and
- terms of a collective bargaining agreement.

What Are My Obligations to Provide Reasonable Accommodations?

Reasonable accommodation is any change or adjustment to a job or work environment that permits a qualified applicant or employee with a disability to participate in the job application process, to perform the essential functions of a job, or to enjoy benefits and privileges of employment equal to those enjoyed by employees without disabilities. For example, reasonable accommodation may include:

- acquiring or modifying equipment or devices;
- job restructuring;
- part-time or modified work schedules;
- reassignment to a vacant position;
- adjusting or modifying examinations, training materials or policies;
- providing readers and interpreters; and
- making the workplace readily accessible to and usable by people with disabilities.

Reasonable accommodation also must be made to enable an individual with a disability to participate in the application process, and to enjoy benefits and privileges of employment equal to those available to other employees.

It is a violation of the ADA to fail to provide reasonable accommodation to the known physical or mental limitations of a qualified individual with a disability, unless to do so would impose an undue hardship on the operation of your business. Undue hardship means that the accommodation would require significant difficulty or expense.

What Is The Best Way To Identify A Reasonable Accommodation?

Frequently, when a qualified individual with a disability requests a reasonable accommodation, the appropriate accommodation is obvious. The individual may suggest a reasonable accommodation based upon her own life or work experience. However, when the appropriate accommodation is not readily apparent, you must make a reasonable effort to identify one. The best way to do this is to consult informally with the applicant or employee about potential accommodations that would enable the individual to participate in the application process or perform the essential functions of the job. If this consultation does not identify an appropriate accommodation, you may contact the EEOC, state or local vocational rehabilitation agencies, or state or local organizations representing or providing services to individuals with disabilities. Another resource is the Job Accommodation Network (JAN). JAN is a free consultant service that helps employers make individualized accommodations. The telephone number is 1-800-526-7234.

When Does A Reasonable Accommodation Become An Undue Hardship?

It is not necessary to provide a reasonable accommodation if doing so would cause an undue hardship. Undue hardship means that an accommodation would be unduly costly, extensive, substantial or disruptive, or would fundamentally alter the nature or operation of the business. Among the factors to be considered in determining whether an accommodation is an undue hardship are the cost of the accommodation, the employer's size, financial resources and the nature and structure of its operation.

If a particular accommodation would be an undue hardship, you must try to identify another accommodation that will not pose such a hardship. If cost causes the undue hardship, you must also consider whether funding for an accommodation is available from an outside source, such as a vocational rehabilitation agency, and if the cost of providing the accommodation can be offset by state or federal tax credits or deductions. You must also give the applicant or employee with a disability the opportunity to provide the accommodation or pay for the portion of the accommodation that constitutes an undue hardship.

Can I Require Medical Examinations Or Ask Questions About An Individual's Disability?

It is unlawful to:

- ask an applicant whether she is disabled or about the nature or severity of a disability; or
- require the applicant to take a medical examination before making a job offer.

You can ask an applicant questions about ability to perform job-related functions, as long as the questions are not phrased in terms of a disability. You can also ask an applicant to describe or to demonstrate how, with or without reasonable accommodation, the applicant will perform job-related functions.

After a job offer is made and prior to the commencement of employment duties, you may require that an applicant take a medical examination if everyone who will be working in the job category must also take the examination. You may condition the job offer on the results of the medical examination. However, if an individual is not hired because a medical examination reveals the existence of a disability, you must be able to show that the reasons for exclusion are job related and necessary for conduct of your business. You also must be able to show that there was no reasonable accommodation that would have made it possible for the individual to perform the essential job functions.

Once you have hired an applicant, you cannot require a medical examination or ask an employee questions about disability unless you can show that these requirements are job related and necessary for the conduct of your business. You may conduct voluntary medical examinations that are part of an employee health program.

The results of all medical examinations or information from inquiries about a disability must be kept confidential, and maintained in separate medical files. You may provide medical information required by state workers' compensation laws to the agencies that administer such laws.

Do Individuals Who Use Drugs Illegally Have Rights Under the ADA?

Anyone who is currently using drugs illegally is not protected by the ADA and may be denied employment or fired on the basis of such use. The ADA does not prevent employers from testing applicants or employees for current illegal drug use, or from making employment decisions based on verifiable results. A test for the illegal use of drugs is not considered a medical examination under the ADA; therefore, it is not a prohibited pre-employment medical examination and you will not have to show that the administration of the test is job related and consistent with business necessity. The ADA does not encourage, authorize or prohibit drug tests.

How Will The ADA Be Enforced and What Are The Available Remedies?

The provisions of the ADA which prohibit job discrimination will be enforced by the U.S. Equal Employment Opportunity Commission. After July 26, 1992, individuals who believe they have been discriminated against on the basis of their disability can file a charge with the Commission at any of its offices located throughout the United States. A charge of discrimination must be filed within 180 days of the discrimination, unless there is a state or local law that also provides relief for the discrimination on the basis of disability. In those cases, the complainant has 300 days to file a charge.

The Commission will investigate and initially attempt to resolve the charge through conciliation, following the same procedures used to handle charges of discrimination filed under Title VII of the *Civil Rights Act* of 1964. The ADA also incorporates the remedies contained in Title VII. These remedies include hiring, promotion, reinstatement, back pay and attorney's fees. Reasonable accommodation is also available as a remedy under the ADA.

How Will EEOC Help Employers Who Want to Comply With The ADA?

The Commission believes that employers want to comply with the ADA, and that if they are given sufficient information on how to comply, they will do so voluntarily.

Accordingly, the Commission conducts an active technical assistance program to promote voluntary compliance with the ADA. This program will be designed to help employers understand their responsibilities and assist people with disabilities to understand their rights and the law.

In January 1992, EEOC published a Technical Assistance Manual, providing practical application of legal requirements to specific employment activities, with a directory of resources to aid compliance. EEOC publishes other educational materials, provides training on the law for employers and for people with disabilities, and participates in meetings and training programs of other organizations. EEOC staff also will respond to individual requests for information and assistance. The Commission's technical assistance program is separate and distinct from its enforcement responsibilities. Employers who seek information or assistance from the Commission will not be subject to any enforcement action because of such inquiries.

The Commission also recognizes that differences and disputes about the ADA requirements may arise between employers and people with disabilities as a result of misunderstandings. Such disputes frequently can be resolved more effectively through informal negotiation or mediation procedures, rather than through the formal enforcement process of the ADA. Accordingly, EEOC will encourage efforts to settle such differences through alternative dispute resolution, providing that such efforts do not deprive any individual of legal rights provided by the statute.

Additional Questions and Answers on the Americans with Disabilities Act?

Q. **What is the relationship between the ADA and the Rehabilitation Act of 1973?**

A. The Rehabilitation Act of 1973 prohibits discrimination on the basis of handicap by the federal government, federal contractors and by recipients of federal financial assistance. If you were covered by the Rehabilitation Act prior to the passage of the ADA, the ADA will not affect that coverage. Many of the provisions contained in the ADA are based on Section 504 of the Rehabilitation Act and its implementing regulations. If you are receiving federal financial assistance and are in compliance with Section 504, you are probably in compliance with the ADA requirements affecting employment except in those areas where the ADA contains additional requirements. Your nondiscrimination requirements as a federal contractor under Section 503 of the Rehabilitation Act will be essentially the same as those under the ADA; however, you will continue to have additional affirmative action requirements under Section 503 that do not exist under the ADA.

Q. **If I have several qualified applicants for a job, does the ADA require that I hire the applicant with a disability?**

A. No. You may hire the most qualified applicant. The ADA only makes it unlawful for you to discriminate against a qualified individual with a disability on the basis of disability.

Q. **One of my employees is a diabetic, but takes insulin daily to control his diabetes. As a result, the diabetes has no significant impact on his employment. Is he protected by the ADA?**

A. Yes. The determination as to whether a person has a disability under the ADA is made without regard to mitigating measures, such as medications, auxiliary aids and reasonable accommodations. If an individual has an impairment that substantially limits a major life activity, she is protected under the ADA, regardless of the fact that the disease or condition or its effects may be corrected or controlled.

Q. **One of my employees has a broken arm that will heal but is temporarily unable to perform the essential functions of his job as a mechanic. Is this employee protected by the ADA?**

A. No. Although this employee does have an impairment, it does not substantially limit a major life activity if it is of limited duration and will have no long term effect.

Q. **Am I obligated to provide a reasonable accommodation for an individual if I am unaware of her physical or mental impairment?**

A. No. An employer's obligation to provide reasonable accommodation applies only to known physical or mental limitations. However, this does not mean that an applicant or employee must always inform you of a disability. If a disability is obvious, e.g., the applicant uses a wheelchair, the employer "knows" of the disability even if the applicant never mentions it.

Q. **How do I determine whether a reasonable accommodation is appropriate and the type of accommodation that should be made available?**

A. The requirement generally will be triggered by a request from an individual with a disability, who frequently can suggest an appropriate accommodation. Accommodations must be made on a case-by-case basis, because the nature and extent of a disabling condition and the requirements of the job will vary. The principal test in selecting a particular type of accommodation is that of effectiveness, i.e., whether the accommodation will enable the person with a disability to perform the essential functions of the job. It need not be the best accommodation, or the accommodation the individual with a disability would prefer, although primary consideration should be given to the preference of the individual involved. However, as the employer, you have the discretion to choose between effective accommodations, and you may select one that is least expensive or easier to provide.

Q. **When must I consider reassigning an employee with a disability to another job as a reasonable accommodation?**

A. When an employee with a disability is unable to perform her present job even with the provision of a reasonable accommodation, you must consider reassigning the employee to an existing position that she can perform with or without a reasonable accommodation. The requirement to consider reassignment applies only to employees and not to applicants. You are not required to create a position or to bump another employee in order to create a vacancy. Nor are you required to promote an employee with a disability to a higher level position.

Q. **What if an applicant or employee refuses to accept an accommodation that I offer?**

A. The ADA provides that an employer cannot require a qualified individual with a disability to accept an accommodation that is neither requested nor needed by the individual. However, if a necessary reasonable accommodation is refused, the individual may be considered not qualified.

Q. **If our business has a health spa in the building, must it be accessible to employees with disabilities?**

A. Yes. Under the ADA, workers with disabilities must have equal access to all benefits and privileges of employment that are available to similarly situated employees without disabilities. The duty to provide reasonable accommodation applies to all non-work facilities provided or maintained by you for your employees. This includes cafeterias, lounges, auditoriums, company-provided transportation and counseling services. If making an existing facility accessible would be an undue hardship, you must provide a comparable facility that will enable a person with a disability to enjoy benefits and privileges of employment similar to those enjoyed by other employees, unless this would be an undue hardship.

Q. **If I contract for a consulting firm to develop a training course for my employees, and the firm arranges for the course to be held at a hotel that is inaccessible to one of my employees, am I liable under the ADA?**

A. Yes. An employer may not do through a contractual or other relationship what it is prohibited from doing directly. You would be required to provide a location that is readily accessible to, and usable by your employee with a disability unless to do so would create an undue hardship.

Q. **What are my responsibilities as an employer for making my facilities accessible?**

A. As an employer, you are responsible under Title I of the ADA for making facilities accessible to qualified applicants and employees with disabilities as a reasonable accommodation, unless this would cause undue hardship. Accessibility must be provided to enable a qualified applicant to participate in the application process, to enable a qualified individual to perform essential job functions and to enable an employee with a disability to enjoy benefits and privileges available to other employees. However, if your business is a place of public accommodation (such as a restaurant, retail store or bank) you have different obligations to provide accessibility to the general public, under Title III of the ADA. Title III also will require places of public accommodation and commercial facilities (such as office buildings, factories and warehouses) to provide accessibility in new construction or when making alterations to existing structures. Further information on these requirements may be obtained from the U.S. Department of Justice, which enforces Title III.

Q. **Under the ADA, can an employer refuse to hire an individual or fire a current employee who uses drugs illegally?**

A. Yes. Individuals who currently use drugs illegally are specifically excluded from the ADA's protections. However, the ADA does not exclude:

- persons who have successfully completed or are currently in a rehabilitation program and are no longer illegally using drugs; and
- persons erroneously regarded as engaging in the illegal use of drugs.

Q. **Does the ADA cover people with AIDS?**

A. Yes. The legislative history indicates that Congress intended the ADA to protect persons with AIDS and HIV disease from discrimination.

Q. **Can I consider health and safety in deciding whether to hire an applicant or retain an employee with a disability?**

A. The ADA permits an employer to require that an individual not pose a direct threat to the health and safety of the individual or others in the work-place. A direct threat means a significant risk of substantial harm. You cannot refuse to hire or fire an individual because of a slightly increased risk of harm to himself or others. Nor can you do so based on a speculative or remote risk. The determination that an individual poses a direct threat must be based on objective, factual evidence regarding the individual's present ability to perform essential job functions. If an applicant or employee with a disability poses a direct threat to the health or safety of himself or others, you must consider whether the risk can be eliminated or reduced to an acceptable level with a reasonable accommodation.

Q. **Am I required to provide additional insurance for employees with disabilities?**

A. No. The ADA only requires that you provide an employee with a disability equal access to whatever health insurance coverage you provide to other employees. For example, if your health insurance coverage for certain treatments is limited to a specified number per year, and an employee, because of a disability, needs more than the specified number, the ADA does not require that you provide additional coverage to meet that employee's health insurance needs. The ADA also does not require changes in insurance plans that exclude or limit coverage for pre-existing conditions.

Q. **Does the ADA require that I post a notice explaining its requirements?**

A. The ADA requires that you post a notice in an accessible format to applicants, employees and members of labor organizations, describing the provisions of the Act. EEOC will provide employers with a poster summarizing these and other federal legal requirements for nondiscrimination. EEOC will also provide guidance on making this information available in accessible formats for people with disabilities.

For more specific information about ADA requirements affecting *employment* contact:

Equal Employment Opportunity Commission
1801 L Street, NW
Washington, DC 20507
800-669-4000 (Voice), 800-669-6820 (TDD)
(202) 663-4900 (Voice for 202 Area Code)
(202) 663-4494 (TDD for 202 Area Code)

For more specific information about ADA requirements affecting public accommodations and state and local government services contact:

Department of Justice
Office on the Americans with Disabilities Act Civil Rights Division
P.O. Box 66118
Washington, DC 20035-6118
(202) 514-0301 (Voice)
(202) 514-0381 (TDD)
(202) 514-0383 (TDD)

For more specific information about requirements for *accessible design in new construction and alterations* contact:

Architectural and Transportation Barriers Compliance Board
1111 18th Street, NW, Suite 501
Washington, DC 20036
800 USA-ABLE
800 USA-ABLE (TDD)

For more specific information about ADA requirements affecting *transportation* contact:

Department of Transportation
400 Seventh Street, SW
Washington, DC 20590
(202) 366-9305
(202) 755-7687 (TDD)

For more specific information about ADA requirements for *telecommunications* contact:

Federal Communications Commission
1919 M Street, NW
Washington, DC 20554
(202) 634-1837
(202) 632-1836 (TDD)

For more specific information about federal disability-related *tax credits and deductions for business* contact:

Internal Revenue Service
Department of the Treasury
1111 Constitution Avenue, NW
Washington, DC 20044
(202) 566-2000

This booklet is available in Braille, large print, audiotape and electronic file on computer disk. To obtain accessible formats call the Office of Equal Employment Opportunity on (202) 663-4395 (voice) or (202) 663-4399 (TDD), or write to this office at 1801 L Street, N.W., Washington, D.C. 20507.

This page was last modified on August 1, 2008.

This information can also be found on the Web at: http://www.eeoc.gov/facts/ada17.html

OMB No. 1615-0047; Expires 08/31/12

Department of Homeland Security

U.S. Citizenship and Immigration Services

FORM I-9, Employment

Eligibility Verification

Instructions

Please read all instructions carefully before completing this form.

Anti-Discrimination Notice. It is illegal to discriminate against any individual (other than an alien not authorized to work in the U.S.) in hiring, discharging, or recruiting or referring for a fee because of that individual's national origin or citizenship status. It is illegal to discriminate against work-authorized individuals. Employers CANNOT specify which document(s) they will accept from an employee. The refusal to hire an individual because the documents presented have a future expiration date may also constitute illegal discrimination. For more information, call the Office of Special Counsel for Immigration Related Unfair Employment Practices at 1-800-255-8155.

What is the Purpose of This Form?

The purpose of this form is to document that each new employee (both citizen and non-citizen) hired after November 6, 1986 is authorized to work in the United States.

When Should Form I-9 Be Used?

All employees (citizens and noncitizens) hired after November 6, 1986 and working in the United States must complete Form I-9.

Filling Out Form I-9

Section 1, Employee

This part of the form must be completed no later than the time of hire, which is the actual beginning of employment. Providing the Social Security number is voluntary, except for employees hired by employers participating in the USCIS Electronic Employment Eligibility Verification Program (E-Verify). **The employer is responsible for ensuring that Section 1 is timely and properly completed**.

Noncitizen nationals of the United States are persons born in American Samoa, certain former citizens of the former Trust Territory of the Pacific islands, and certain children of noncitizen nationals born abroad.

Employers should note the work authorization expiration date (if any) shown in **Section 1**. For

employees who indicate an employment authorization expiration date in **Section 1**, employers are required to reverify employment authorization for employment on or before the date shown. Note that some employees may leave the expiration date blank if they are aliens whose work authorization does not expire (e.g., asylees, refugees, certain citizens of the Federated States of Microneisa or the Republic of the Marshall Islands). For such employees, reverification does not apply unless they choose to present in Section 2 evidence of employment authorization that contains an expiration date (e.g., Employment Authorization Document (Form I-766))..

Preparer/Translator Certification. The Preparer/ Translator Certification must be completed if **Section 1** is prepared by a person other than the employee. A preparer/translator may be used only when the employee is unable to complete **Section 1** on his/her own. However, the employee must still sign **Section 1** personally.

Section 2, Employer

For the purpose of completing this form, the term "employer" means all employers including those recruiters and referrers for a fee who are agricultural associations, agricultural employers, or farm labor contractors. Employers must complete **Section 2** by examining evidence of identity and employment eligibility within three business days of the date employment begins. However, if an employer hires an individual for less than three business days, **Section 2** must be completed at the time employment begins. Employers cannot specify which document(s) listed on the last page of Form I-9 employees present to establish identity and employment authorization. Employees may present any List A document **OR** a combination of a List B and a List C document.

If an employee is unable to present a required document (or documents), the employee must present an acceptable receipt in lieu of a document listed on the last page of this form. Receipts showing that a person has applied for an initial grant of employment authorization, or for renewal of employment authorization, are not acceptable. Employees must present receipts within three business days of the date employment begins and must present valid replacement documents within 90 days or other specified time.

Employers must record in Section 2:

1. Document title;
2. Issuing authority;
3. Document number;
4. Expiration date, if any; and
5. The date employment begins.

Employers must sign and date the certification in **Section 2**. Employees must present original documents. Employers may, but are not required to, photocopy the document(s) presented. If photocopies are made, they must be made for all new hires. Photocopies may only be used for the verification process and must be retained with Form I-9. **Employers are still responsible for completing and retaining Form I-9.**

For more detailed information, you may refer to the *USCIS Handbook for Employers* (Form M-274). You may obtain the handbook using the contract information found under the header "USCIS Forms and Information.".

Section 3, Updating and Reverification

Employers must complete **Section 3** when updating and/or reverifying Form I-9. Employers must reverify employment eligibility of their employees on or before the expiration date recorded in **Section 1**(if any). Employers **CANNOT** specify which document(s) they will accept from an employee.

A. If an employee's name has changed at the time this form is being updated/reverified, complete Block A.

B. If an employee is rehired within three years of the date this form was originally completed and the employee is still authorized to be employed on the same basis as previously indicated on this form (updating), complete Block B and the signature block.

C. If an employee is rehired within three years of the date this form was originally completed and the employee's work authorization has expired **or** if a current employee's work authorization is about to expire (reverification), complete Block B and:

1. Examine any document that reflects the employee is authorized to work in the U.S. (see List A **or** C);
2. Record the document title, document number and expiration date (if any) in Block C; and

3. Complete the signature block.

Note that for reverification purposes, employers have the option of completing a new Form I-9 instead of completing **Section 3**.

What is the Filing Fee?

There is no associated filing fee for completing Form I-9. This form is not filed with USCIS or any government agency. Form I-9 must be retained by the employer and made available for inspection by U.S. Government officials as specified in the Privacy Act Notice below.

USCIS Forms and Information

To order USCIS forms, you can download them from our website at www.uscis.gov/forms or call our toll-free number at 1-800-870- 3676. You can obtain information about Form I-9 from our website at www.uscis.gov or by calling 1-888-464-4218.

Information about E-Verify, a free and voluntary program that allows participating employers to electronically verify the employment eligibility of their newly hired employees, can be obtained from our website at www.uscis.gov/e-verify or by calling 1-888-464-4218.

General information on immigration laws, regulations, and procedures can be obtained by telephoning our National Customer Service Center at 1-800-375-5283 or visiting our website at www.uscis.gov.

Photocopying and Retaining Form I-9

A blank Form I-9 may be reproduced, provided both sides are copied. The Instructions must be available to all employees completing this form. Employers must retain completed Forms I-9 for three years after the date of hire or one year after the date employment ends, whichever is later.

Form I-9 may be signed and retained electronically, as authorized in Department of Homeland Security regulations at 8 CFR 274a.2.

Privacy Act Notice

The authority for collecting this information is the Immigration Reform and Control Act of 1986, Pub. L. 99-603 (8 USC 1324a).

This information is for employers to verify the eligibility of individuals for employment to preclude the unlawful hiring, or recruiting or referring for a fee, of aliens who are not authorized to work in the United States.

This information will be used by employers as a record of their basis for determining eligibility of an employee to work in the United States. The form will be kept by the employer and made available for inspection by authorized officials of the Department of Homeland Security, Department of Labor, and Office of Special Counsel for Immigration-Related Unfair Employment Practices.

Submission of the information required in this form is voluntary. However, an individual may not begin employment unless this form is completed, since employers are subject to civil or criminal penalties if they do not comply with the Immigration Reform and Control Act of 1986.

Paperwork Reduction Act

An agency may not conduct or sponsor an information collection and a person is not required to respond to a collection of information unless it displays a currently valid OMB control number. The public reporting burden for this collection of information is estimated at 12 minutes per response, including the time for reviewing instructions and completing and submitting the form. Send comments regarding this burden estimate or any other aspect of this collection of information, including suggestions for reducing this burden, to: U.S. Citizenship and Immigration Services, Regulatory Management Division, 111 Massachusetts Avenue, N.W., 3rd Floor, Suite 3008, Washington, DC 20529. OMB No. 1615-0047. **Do not mail your completed Form I-9 to this address**.

OMB No. 1615-0047; Expires 08/31/12

Department of Homeland Security

U.S. Citizenship and Immigration Services

FORM I-9, Employment

Eligibility Verification

Read instructions carefully before completing this form. The instructions must be available during completion of this form.

ANTI-DISCRIMINATION NOTICE: It is illegal to discriminate against work-authorized individuals. Employers CANNOT specify which document(s) they will accept from an employee. The refusal to hire an individual because the documents have a future expiration date may also constitute illegal discrimination.

Section 1. Employee Information and Verification *(To be completed and signed by employee at the time employment begins.)*

Print Name:	Last	First	Middle Initial	Maiden Name

Address *(Street Name and Number)*		Apt. #	Date of Birth *(month/day/year)*

City		State	ZIP Code	Social Security #

I am aware that federal law provides for imprisonment and/or fines for false statements or use of false documents in connection with the completion of this form.

I attest, under penalty of perjury, that I am (check on of the following):

☐ A citizen of the United States

☐ A noncitizen national of the United States (see instructions)

☐ A lawful permanent resident (Alien #) _____

☐ An alien authorized to work (Alien # or Admission #) _____ until (expiration date, if applicable – month/day/year)

Employee's Signature	Date *(month/day/year)*

Preparer and/or Translator Certification *(To be completed and signed if Section 1 is prepared by a person other than the employee.)* I attest, under penalty of perjury, that I have assisted in the completion of this form and that to the best of my knowledge the information is true and correct.

Preparer's/Translator's Signature	Print Name

Address (Street Name and Number, City, State, Zip Code)	Date *(month/day/year)*

Section 2. Employer Review and Verification *(To be completed and signed by employer. Examine one document from List A OR examine one document from List B and one from List C, as listed on the reverse side of this form, and record the title, number, and expiration date, if any, of the document(s).)*

	LIST A	**OR**	**LIST B**	**AND**	**LIST C**
Document title:					
Issuing authority:					
Document #:					
Expiration Date *(if any)*:					
Document #:					
Expiration Date *(if any)*:					

CERTIFICATION: I attest, under penalty of perjury, that I have examined the document(s) presented by the above-named employee, that the above-listed document(s) appear to be genuine and to relate to the employee named, that the employee began employment on *(month/day/year)* _____ **and that to the best of my knowledge the employee is authorized to work in the United States. (State employment agencies may omit the date the employee began employment.)**

Signature of Employer or Authorized Representative	Print name	Title

Business or Organization Name and Address *(Street Name and Number, City, State, Zip Code)*	Date *(month/day/year)*

Section 3. Updating and Reverification *(To be completed and signed by employer.)*

A. New Name *(if applicable)*	B. Date of Rehire *(month/day/year)* *(if applicable)*

C. If employee's previous grant of work authorization has expired, provide the information below for the document that establishes current employment authorization.

Document Title: _____ Document #: _____ Expiration Date *(if any)*: _____

I attest, under penalty of perjury, that to the best of my knowledge, this employee is authorized to work in the United States, and if the employee presented document(s) I have examined appear to be genuine and to relate to the individual.

Signature of Employer or Authorized Representative	Date *(month/day/year)*

LISTS OF ACCEPTABLE DOCUMENTS

All documents must be unexpired

LIST A	LIST B	LIST C
Documents that Establish Both Identity and Employment Authorization	**Documents that Establish Identity**	**Documents that Establish Employment Authorization**

OR ... **AND**

LIST A	LIST B	LIST C
1. U.S. Passport or U.S. Passport Card	1. Driver's license or ID card issued by a State or outlying possession of the United States provided it contains a photograph or information such as name, date of birth, gender, height, eye color, and address	1. Social Security Account Number card other than one that specifies on the face that the issuance of the card does not authorize employment in the United States
2. Permanent Resident Card or Alien Registration Receipt Card (Form I-551)		
3. Foreign passport that contains a temporary I-551 stamp or temporary I-551 printed notation on a machine-readable immigrant visa	2. ID card issued by federal, state or local government agencies or entities, provided it contains a photograph or information such as name, date of birth, gender, height, eye color and address	2. Certification of Birth Abroad issued by the Department of State (Form FS-545)
4. Employment Authorization Document that contains a photograph (Form I-766)	3. School ID card with a photograph	3. Certification of Report of Birth issued by the Department of State (Form DS-1350)
	4. Voter's registration card	
5. In the case of a nonimmigrant alien authorized to work for a specific employer incident to state, a foreign passport with Form I-94 or Form I-94A bearing the same name as the passport and containing an endorsement of the alien's nonimmigrant status, as long as the period of endorsement has not yet expired and the proposed employment is not in conflict with any restrictions or limitations identified on the form	5. U.S. Military card or draft record	4. Original or certified copy of birth certificate issued by a State, county, municipal authority, or territory of the United States bearing an official seal
	6. Military dependent's ID card	5. Native American Tribal Document
	7. U.S. Coast Guard Merchant Mariner Card	6. U.S. Citizen ID Card (Form I-197)
	8. Native American Tribal Document	
	9. Driver's license issued by a Canadian government authority	7. Identification Card for Use of Resident Citizen in the United States (Form I-179)
	For persons under age 18 who are unable to present a document listed above:	
6. Passport from the Federated States of Micronesia (FSM) or the Republic of the Marshall Islands (RMI) with Form I-94 or I-94A indicating nonimmigrant admission under the Compact of Free Association Between the United States and the FSM or RMI	10. School record or report card	8. Employment authorization document issued by the Department of Homeland Security
	11. Clinic, hospital or doctor record	
	12. Day-care or nursery school record	

Illustrations of many of these documents appear in Part 8 of the Handbook for Employers (M-274)

Form I-9 (Rev. 08/07/09) Y

NEW JERSEY ADMINISTRATIVE CODE

TITLE 12, CHAPTER 56: WAGE AND HOUR REGULATIONS

SUBCHAPTER 3. MINIMUM WAGE RATES

12:56-3.1 Statutory minimum wage rates for specific years
Except as provided in N.J.A.C. 12:56-3.2, employees shall be paid not less than the minimum hourly wage rate set by section 6(a)(1) of the Federal "Fair Labor Standards Act of 1938" (29U.S.C.206(a)(1)) or the rate provided under N.J.S.A. 34:11-56a4, whichever is greater.

12:56-3.2 Exemptions from the statutory minimum wage rates
(a) Employees in the following occupations shall be exempt from the statutory minimum wage rates:

1. Full-time students employed by the college or university at which they are enrolled at not less than 85 percent of the effective minimum wage rate, effective March 1, 1979;

2. Outside sales person;

3. Sales person of motor vehicles;

4. Part time employees primarily engaged in the care and tending of children in the home of the employer;

5. Minors under 18 years of age except as provided in N.J.A.C. 12:56-11, 12:56-13 and 12:56-14 and N.J.A.C. 12:57, Wage Orders for Minors; and

6. At summer camps, conferences and retreats operated by any nonprofit or religious corporation or association during the months of June, July, August and September.

SUBCHAPTER 4. RECORDS

12:56-4.1 Contents
Every employer shall keep records which contain the name and address of each employee, the birth date if under the age of 18, the hours worked each day and each workweek, earnings, including the regular hourly wage, gross to net amounts with itemized deductions, and the basis on which wages are paid.

12:56-4.2 Time keeping system
The employer may use any system of time keeping containing the items specified in N.J.A.C. 12:56-4.1, provided it is a complete, true and accurate record.

12:56-4.3 Fixed working schedule
(a) Many employees, particularly in offices, are on a fixed working schedule from which they seldom vary. In these instances, the employer may keep a record showing the exact schedule of daily and weekly work hours that the employee is expected to follow and merely indicate each workweek that the schedule was followed.

(b) When the employee works longer or shorter hours than the schedule indicates, the employer shall record the hours the employee actually worked.

12:56-4.4 Retention period
Records containing the information required by this subchapter shall be kept for six years.

12:56-4.5 Location; inspection
(a) Records shall be kept at the place of employment or in a central office in New Jersey, except as provided in (b) below.

(b) In unusual circumstances where it is not feasible to keep records in New Jersey, exception from this provision may be obtained from the Commissioner.

(c) All records shall be open to inspection by the Commissioner at any reasonable time.

12:56-4.6 Employer gratuity records
Supplementary to the provisions of any section of this chapter pertaining to the records to be kept with respect to employee, every employer of employees who receive gratuities shall also maintain and preserve payroll or other records containing the total gratuities received by each employee during the payroll week.

12:56-4.7 Employee gratuity reports

(a) Employees receiving gratuities shall report them either daily or weekly as required by the employer. The information in the report shall include:

1. The employee's name, address and social security number;

2. The name and address of the employer;

3. The calendar day or week covered by the report; and

4. The total amount of gratuities received.

12:56-4.8 Acceptable gratuity report form

The United States Treasury Department, Internal Revenue Service, "Employee's Report on Tips" shall be acceptable in those instances where the report is made on a weekly basis or less.

12:56-4.9 Food or lodging records

(a) Supplementary to the provisions of any section of this chapter pertaining to the records to be kept with respect to employees, every employer, who claims credit for food or lodging as a cash substitute for employees who receive food or lodgings supplied by the employer, shall maintain and preserve records substantiating the cost of furnishing such food or lodgings.

(b) Such records shall include the nature and amount of any expenditures entering into the computation of the fair value of the food or lodging and shall contain the date required to compute the amount of the depreciated investment in any assets allocable to the furnishing of the lodgings, including the date of acquisition or construction, the original cost, the rate of depreciation and the total amount of accumulated depreciation on such assets. No particular degree of itemization is prescribed. The amount of detail shall be sufficient to enable the Commissioner, assistant director or his or her authorized representative to verify the nature of the expenditure and amount by reference to the basic records which shall be preserved pursuant to this chapter.

12:56-4.10 Additions to wages

If additions to wages paid so affect the total cash wages due in any workweek as to result in the employee receiving less in cash than the minimum hourly wage provided in the act or in any applicable wage order or if the employee works in excess of 40 hours a week the employer shall maintain records showing those additions to wages by reason of gratuities or food, or lodgings paid on a workweek basis.

SUBCHAPTER 5. HOURS WORKED

12:56-5.1 Payment

Employees entitled to the benefits of the act shall be paid for all hours worked.

12:56-5.2 Computation

(a) All the time the employee is required to be at his or her place of work or on duty shall be counted as hours worked.

(b) Nothing in this chapter requires an employer to pay an employee for hours the employee is not required to be at his or her place of work because of holidays, vacation, lunch hours, illness and similar reasons.

12:56-5.3 Accounting for irregular hours of resident employees

Employees who reside on the employer's premises and whose hours worked are irregular and intermittent to the extent that it is not feasible to account for the hours actually on duty may be compensated for not less than eight hours for each day on duty in lieu of any other applicable provisions.

12:56-5.4 Workweek construed

(a) A workweek shall be a regularly recurring period of 168 hours in the form of seven consecutive 24-hour periods.

(b) The workweek need not be the same as the calendar week and may begin any day of the week and any hour of the day.

(c) The workweek shall be designated to the employee in advance.

(d) Once the beginning time of an employee's workweek is established, it remains fixed regardless of the schedule of the hours worked.

(e) The beginning of the workweek may be changed if the change is intended to be permanent and is not intended to evade the overtime requirements of the act.

12:56-5.5 Reporting for work

(a) An employee who by request of the employer reports for duty on any day shall be paid for at least one hour at the applicable wage rate, except as provided in (b) below.

(b) The provisions of (a) above shall not apply to an employer when he or she has made available to the employee the minimum number of hours of work agreed upon by the employer and the employed prior to the commencement of work on the day involved.

12:56-5.6 On-call time

(a) When employees are not required to remain on the employer's premises and are free to engage in their own pursuits, subject only to the understanding that they leave word at their home or with the employer where they may be reached, the hours shall not be considered hours worked. When an employee does go out on an on-call assignment, only the time actually spent in making the call shall be counted as hours worked.

(b) If calls are so frequent or the "on-call" conditions so restrictive that the employees are not really free to use the intervening periods effectively for their own benefit, they may be considered as "engaged to wait" rather than "waiting to be engaged". In that event, the waiting time shall be counted as hours worked.

12:56-5.7 On-call employees required to remain at home

"On-call" employees may be required by their employer to remain at their homes to receive telephone calls from customers when the company office is closed. If "on-call" employees have long periods of uninterrupted leisure during which they can engage in the normal activities of living, any reasonable agreement of the parties for determining the number of hours worked shall be accepted. The agreement shall take into account not only the actual time spent in answering the calls but also some allowance for the restriction on the employee's freedom to engage in personal activities resulting from the duty of answering the telephone.

12:56-5.8 Use of time clocks

(a) Differences between clock records and actual hours worked. Time clocks are not required. In those cases where time clocks are used, employees who voluntarily come in before their regular starting time or remain after their closing time, do not have to be paid for such periods provided, of course, that they do not engage in any work. Their early or late clock punching may be disregarded. Minor differences between the clock records and actual hours worked cannot ordinarily be avoided, but major discrepancies should be discouraged since they raise a doubt as to the accuracy of the records of the hours actually worked.

(b) "Rounding" practices. It has been found that in some industries, particularly where time clocks are used, there has been the practice for many years of recording the employees' starting time and stopping time to the nearest 5 minutes, or to the nearest 1/10 or quarter of an hour. Presumably, this arrangement averages out, so that the employees are fully compensated for all the time they actually work. For enforcement purposes this practice of computing working time will be accepted, provided that it is used in such a manner that it will not result, over a period of time, in failure to compensate the employees properly for all the time they have actually worked.

SUBCHAPTER 6. OVERTIME

12:56-6.1 Rate of overtime payment

For each hour of working time in excess of 40 hours in any week, except as provided in N.J.A.C. 12:56-7.6, every employer shall pay to each of his or her employees, wages at a rate of not less than 1-1/2 times such employee's regular hourly wage.

12:56-6.2 Computation

(a) Overtime and minimum wage pay shall be computed on the basis of each workweek standing alone.

(b) Hours shall not be averaged over two or more workweeks.

12:56-6.3 Actual wage basis

Covered employees shall be entitled to overtime pay based upon their actual wages and not the specified minimum wages.

12:56-6.4 Workweek hours

(a) Covered employees shall be paid 1-1/2 times the regular hourly wage for each hour of working time in excess of 40 hours in any workweek.

(b) There is no requirement that an employee be paid premium overtime compensation for hours in excess of eight hours per day, nor for work on Saturdays, Sundays, holidays or regular days of rest, other than the required overtime for over 40 hours per week; provided, however, nothing shall relieve an employer of any obligation he or she may have assumed by contract or of any obligation imposed by other State or Federal law limiting overtime hours of work or to pay premium rates for work which are in excess of the minimum required by this chapter.

12:56-6.5 "Regular hourly wage" payment basis

(a) The "regular hourly wage" is a rate per hour.

(b) The act does not require employers to compensate employees on an hourly rate basis. Their earnings may be determined on a piece-rate, salary, bonus, commission or other basis, but the overtime compensation due to employees shall be paid on the basis of the hourly rate derived therefrom. Therefore, the regular hourly wage of an employee is determined by dividing his or her total remuneration for employment, exclusive of overtime premium pay, in any workweek, by the total number of hours worked in that workweek for which such compensation was paid.

(c) If an employee is remunerated solely on the basis of a single hourly rate, the hourly rate shall be his or her "regular hourly wage."

12:56-6.6 Items excluded from "regular hourly wage"

(a) The "regular hourly wage" shall not be deemed to include:

1. Payments in the nature of gifts made on holidays or on other special occasions or as a reward for service, the amounts of which are not measured by or dependent on hours worked, production or efficiency;

2. Payments made for occasional periods when no work is performed due to vacation, holiday or other similar cause;

3. Reasonable payments for traveling or other expenses incurred by an employee in the furtherance of his or her employer's interests and properly reimbursable by the employer which are not made as compensation for employment;

4. Sums paid in recognition of services performed during a given period if either:

   i. Both the fact that payment is to be made and the amount of payment are determined at the sole discretion of the employer at or near the end of the period and not pursuant to any prior contract, agreement or promise causing the employee to expect such payments regularly; or

   ii. The payments are made pursuant to a bona fide profit-sharing plan or trust, or thrift or savings plan to the extent to which the amounts paid to the employee are determined without regard to hours of work, production or efficiency; or

5. Contributions irrevocably made by an employer to a trustee or third person pursuant to a bona fide plan providing for old age, retirement, life, accident, or health insurance or similar benefits for employees; or

6. Additional premium compensation for hours worked in excess of eight hours per day, or for work on Saturdays, Sundays, holidays, or regular days of rest; or

7. Overtime premiums.

12:56 6.7 Offsets; cash payments

(a) Overtime premium payments shall not be offset by allowances for the value of food, lodging or gratuities since such allowances are already considered in determining the straight time wages paid. Overtime premium payments shall be cash payments by the employer.

(b) Where the employee's pay includes the value of gratuities, food or lodging and it is not feasible to determine the exact regular hourly wage during a particular week, the employer shall be deemed to have fulfilled the overtime requirements of this chapter if the premium payment for the overtime hours is paid in cash on the basis of the agreed hourly wage, but in no event shall the premium payment be at a rate less than the applicable minimum rate.

SUBCHAPTER 7. EXEMPTIONS FROM OVERTIME

12:56-7.1 Definition of executive

(a) "Executive" means any employee:

1. Whose primary duty consists of the management of the enterprise in which he or she is employed or of a customarily recognized department or subdivision thereof; and

2. Who customarily and regularly directs the work of two or more other employees therein; and

3. Who has the authority to hire or fire other employees or whose suggestions and recommendations as to the hiring and firing and as to the advancement and promotion of any other change of status of other employees will be given particular weight; and

4. Who customarily and regularly exercises discretionary powers; and

5. Who devotes less than 20 percent of his or her workweek to non-exempt work or less than 40 percent if employed by a retail or service establishment, provided that in either case he or she retains his or her role as manager and supervises two or more full time employees; and

6. Who is compensated for his or her services on a salary basis exclusive of gratuities, board, lodging or other facilities, at a rate of not less than $300.00 per week effective November 5, 1990, $350.00 per week effective April 1, 1991, and $400.00 per week effective April 1, 1992.

(b) "Executive" shall also include employees owning a bona fide equity in the enterprise of 20 percent or more.

(c) "Executive" shall not include employees training to become executives and not actually performing the duties of an executive.

12:56-7.2 Definition of administrative

(a) "Administrative" means any employee:

1. Whose primary duty consists of the performance of office or non-manual work directly related to management policies or general internal business operations; and

2. Who customarily and regularly exercises discretion and independent judgment; and

3. Who regularly and directly assists a proprietor, or an employee employed in a bona fide executive or administrative capacity; or who performs under only general supervision work along specialized or technical lines requiring special training, experience, or knowledge; or who executes under only general supervision special assignments and tasks; and

4. Who devotes less than 20 percent of his or her work to nonexempt work or less than 40 percent if employed by a retail or service establishment; and

5. Who is compensated for his or her services on a salary or fee basis, exclusive of gratuities, board, lodging or other facilities at a rate of not less than $300.00 per week effective November 5, 1990, $350.00 per week effective April 1, 1991 and $400.00 per week effective April 1, 1992.

(b) "Administrative" shall also include an employee whose primary duty consists of sales activity and who receives at least 50 percent of his or her total compensation from commissions and a total compensation of not less than $300.00 per week effective November 5, 1990, $350.00 per week effective April 1, 1991 and $400.00 per week effective April 1, 1992.

12:56-7.3 Definition of professional

(a) "Professional" means any employee:

1. Whose primary duty consists of the performance of work:

    i. Requiring knowledge of an advanced type in a field of science or learning customarily acquired by a prolonged course of specialized intellectual instruction and study, as distinguished from a general academic education and from an apprenticeship, and from training in the performance of routine mental, manual, or physical processes; or

    ii. Which is original and creative in character in a recognized field of artistic endeavor (as opposed to work which can be produced by a person endowed with general manual or intellectual ability and training), and the result of which depends primarily on the invention, imagination or talent of the employee; or

iii. Which requires theoretical and practical application of highly-specialized knowledge in computer systems analysis, programming, and software engineering, and who is employed and engaged in these activities as a computer systems analyst, computer programmer, software engineer, or other similarly skilled worker in the computer software field, as provided in 29 C.F.R. 541.303; and

2. Whose work requires the consistent exercise of discretion and judgment in its performance; and

3. Whose work is predominantly intellectual and varied in character (as opposed to routine mental, manual, mechanical or physical work) and is of such a character that the output produced or the result accomplished cannot be standardized to a given period of time; and

4. Who devotes less than 20 percent of his or her workweek to nonexempt work; and

5. Who is compensated for his or her services on a salary or fee basis, exclusive of gratuities, board, lodging or other facilities at a rate of not less than $300.00 per week effective November 5, 1990, $350.00 per week effective April 1, 1991 and $400.00 per week effective April 1, 1992.

12:56-7.4 Definition of outside sales person

(a) "Outside sales person" means any employee:

1. Who is employed for the purpose of and who is customarily and regularly engaged away from his or her employer's place or places of business in:

i. Making sales; or

ii. Obtaining orders or contracts for services or for the use of facilities for which a consideration will be paid by the client or customer; and

2. Whose hours of work of a nature other than that described in (a)1 above do not exceed 20 percent of hours worked in the workweek; provided, that work performed incidental to and in conjunction with the outside sales person's own personal sales or solicitations, including incidental deliveries and collection, shall be regarded as exempt work. Employees who basically drive vehicles and who only incidentally or occasionally make sales shall not qualify for this exemption.

12:56-7.5 Outside service employees

Employees who are dispatched to perform a service and solicit performance of an additional service shall not qualify for this exemption.

12:56-7.6 Employees exempt from overtime

(a) Employees in a bonafide executive, administrative or professional capacity and outside sales persons shall be exempt from the overtime requirements of N.J.A.C. 12:56-6.1, with the exception of (b) below.

(b) Those employees who qualify as professionals under N.J.A.C. 12:56-7.3(a)1iii, who are also compensated on an hourly basis, must be compensated at a rate of not less than $27.63 an hour in order to be exempt from the overtime requirements of N.J.A.C. 12:56-6.1.

NEW JERSEY STATUTES ANNOTATED
TITLE 34: LABOR AND WORKMEN'S COMPENSATION
ARTICLE 2: CHILD LABOR

34:2-21. 1 Definitions

(a) "Employment certificate" means a certificate granted by the issuing officer authorizing the employment of a child as permitted under this act.

(b) "Age certificate" means a certificate issued for a person between the ages of 18 and 21 years.

(c) "Issuing officer" means any superintendent of schools, supervising principal, or teacher in a school district who is designated by the board of education in the district to issue certificates or permits in accordance with the provisions of this act.

(d) "School district" means any geographical area having authority over the public schools within that area.

(e) "Agriculture" includes farming in all its branches and among other things includes the cultivation and tillage of the soil, dairying, the production, cultivation, growing, and harvesting of any agricultural or horticultural commodities (including commodities defined as agricultural commodities in subsection (g) of section 15 of the Agricultural Marketing Act, 12 U.S.C.A. s. 141 et seq. as amended) the planting, transplanting and care of trees and shrubs and plants, the raising of livestock, bees, fur-bearing animals or poultry, and any practices (including any forestry or lumbering operations) performed by a farmer or on a farm as an incident to or in conjunction with such farming operations, including preparation for market, delivery to storage or to market or to carriers for transportation to market, provided that such practices shall be performed in connection with the handling of agricultural or horticultural commodities the major portion of which have been produced upon the premises of an owning or leasing employer.

(f) "Newspaper carrier" means any minor between 12 and 18 years of age who engages in the occupation of delivering, soliciting, selling and collecting for, newspapers outside of school hours on residential routes.

(g) "Restaurant" means any establishment or business primarily engaged in the preparation and servicing of meals or refreshments, both food and drink, and shall include but not be limited to the following: dining establishments, catering establishments, industrial caterers, and drive-in restaurants.

(h) "Theatrical production" means and includes stage, motion picture and television performances and rehearsals therefor.

(i) "Seasonal amusement" means any exclusively recreational or amusement establishment or business which does not operate more than seven months in any calendar year or which has received during any consecutive six months of the preceding calendar year average receipts equal to or less than 331/3 percent of its average receipts for the other six months of that year. "Seasonal amusement" includes but is not limited to amusement rides and amusement device ticket sales, and operations of games. However, "seasonal amusement" does not include retail, eating or drinking concessions, camps, beach and swimming facilities, movie theaters, theatrical productions, athletic events, professional entertainment, pool and billiard parlors, circuses and outdoor shows, sports activities or centers, country club athletic facilities, bowling alleys, race tracks and like facilities which are not part of a diversified amusement enterprise.

34:2-21.2 Minors under 16 not to be employed; exceptions; nonresidents

No minor under 16 years of age shall be employed, permitted, or suffered to work in, about, or in connection with any gainful occupation at any time; provided, that minors between 14 and 16 years of age may be employed, permitted or suffered to work outside school hours and during school vacations but not in or for a factory or in any occupation otherwise prohibited by law or by order or regulation made in pursuance of law; and provided, further, that minors under 16 years of age may engage in professional employment in theatrical productions upon the obtaining of a permit therefor and may engage outside school hours and during school vacations in agricultural pursuits or in street trades and as newspaperboys as defined in this act, in accordance with the provisions of N.J.S.A. 34:2-21.15. Minors may also engage in employment in domestic services performed outside of school hours or during school vacation with the permission of the minor's parent or legal guardian, in a residence other than the minor's own home. Nothing in this act shall be construed to apply to the work of a minor engaged in domestic service or agricultural pursuits performed outside of school hours or during school vacation in connection with the minor's own home and directly for his parent or legal guardian.

Except as to the employment of a minor for whom a theatrical employment permit has been issued, no minor under 16 years of age not a resident of this State shall be employed, permitted or suffered to work in any occupation or service whatsoever at any time during which the law of the State of his residence required his attendance at school, or at any time during the hours when the public schools in the district in which employment in such occupation or services may be available are in session.

34:2-21.3 Limitations on minors' working hours

Except as provided in N.J.S.A. 34:2-21.15 and except for domestic service or messengers employed by communications companies subject to the supervision and control of the Federal Communications Commission, no minor under 18 years of age shall be employed, permitted, or suffered to work in, about, or in connection with any gainful occupation more than six consecutive days in any one week, or more than 40 hours in any one week, or more than eight hours in any one day, nor shall any minor under 16 years of age be so employed, permitted, or suffered to work before 7 a.m. or after 7 p.m. of any day, except a minor who is 14 or 15 years of age may work in a restaurant, supermarket or other retail establishment, or in any occupation not prohibited by the provisions of this act, P.L. 1940, c.153 (C.34:2 21.1 et seq.), or by regulations promulgated by the commissioner pursuant to this act, P.L. 1940, c.153 (C.34:2-21.1 et seq.), during the period beginning on the last day of a minor's school year and ending on Labor Day of each year until 9 p.m. of any day with written permission from a parent or legal guardian, and except a minor who is 14 or 15 years of age may be employed as a little league umpire for little leagues chartered by Little League Baseball, Incorporated, until 9 p.m. of any day with written permission from a parent or legal guardian; nor shall any minor between 16 and 18 years of age be so employed, permitted or suffered to work before 6 a.m. or after 11 p.m. of any day; provided, that minors between 16 and 18 years of age may be employed after 11 p.m. during any regular vacation season, and on days which do not precede a regularly scheduled school day, with a special written permit from their parents or legal guardian stating the hours they are permitted to work; provided that minors between 16 and 18 years of age may be employed in a seasonal amusement or restaurant occupation after 11 p.m. and following 12:01 a.m. of the next day if that employment is a continuation of a work day which began before 11 p.m. either during any regular school vacation season, or on work days which do not begin on a day which precedes a regularly scheduled school day, with a special written permit from their parents or legal guardian stating the hours they are permitted to work, except that in no case shall minors between 16 and 18 years of age be employed after 3 a.m. or before 6 a.m. on a day which precedes a regularly scheduled school day; provided, further, that minors may be employed in a concert or a theatrical performance up to 11:30 p.m.; and provided, further that minors not less than 16 years of age and who are attending school may be employed as pinsetters, lane attendants, or busboys in public bowling alleys up to 11:30 p.m., but may not be so employed during the school term without a special written permit from the superintendent of schools or the supervising principal as the case may be, which permit shall state that the minor has undergone a complete physical examination by the medical inspector, and, in the opinion of the superintendent or supervising principal may be so employed, without injury to health or interference with progress in school, such special permits to be good for a period of three months only and are revocable in the discretion of the superintendent or supervising principal. Such permit may not be renewed until satisfactory evidence has been submitted to the superintendent or supervising principal showing that the minor has had a physical examination and the minor's health is not being injured by said work; and provided, further, that minors between 16 and 18 years of age may not be employed after 10 p.m. during the regular school vacation seasons in or for a factory or in any occupation otherwise prohibited by law or by order or regulation made in pursuance of law. The hours of work of minors under 16 employed outside school hours shall not exceed three hours in any one day when school is in session and shall not exceed in any one week when school is in session the maximum number of hours permitted for that period under the federal "Fair Labor Standards Act of 1938," 29 U.S.C. § 201 et seq., and regulations promulgated pursuant to that federal act.

This section is not applicable to the employment of a minor between 16 and 18 years of age during the months of June, July, August or September by a summer resident camp, conference or retreat operated by a nonprofit or religious corporation or association, unless the employment is primarily general maintenance work or food service activities.

34:2-21.4 Lunch period for minors under 18

No minor under eighteen years of age shall be employed or permitted to work for more than five hours continuously without an interval of at least thirty minutes for a lunch period, and no period of less than thirty minutes shall be deemed to interrupt a continuous period of work.

34:2-21.5 Posting of law, list of prohibited occupations and schedule of hours of labor; permitting minors to begin later or stop earlier than time stated in schedule

Every employer shall post and keep conspicuously posted in the establishment wherein any minor under 18 is employed, permitted, or suffered to work a printed abstract of this act and a list of the occupations prohibited to such minors, to be furnished by the Department of Labor, and a schedule of hours of labor which shall contain the name of each minor under 18 the maximum number of hours he shall be required or permitted to work during each day of the week, the total hours per week, the time of commencing and stopping work each day, and the time for the beginning and ending of the daily meal period. An employer may permit such minor to begin work after the time for beginning, and stop before the time for ending work stated in the schedule; but he shall not otherwise employ or permit him to work except as stated in the schedule. This schedule shall be on a form provided by the Department of Labor and shall remain the property of that department. Nothing in this section shall apply to the employment of minors in agricultural pursuits or in domestic service in private homes, or as newspaperboys as provided in this act.

34:2-21.6 Record of employment of minors under 19

Every employer shall keep a record, in a form approved by the Department of Labor, which shall state the name, date of birth and address of each person under 19 years of age employed, the number of hours worked by said person each day of the week, the hours of beginning and ending such work, the hours of beginning and ending meal periods, the amount of wages paid, and such other information as the department shall by regulation require. Such record shall be kept on file for at least 1 year after the entry of the record and shall be open to the inspection of the Department of Labor, of attendance officers and of police officers. Nothing in this section shall apply to the employment of minors in agricultural pursuits, or in domestic service in private homes, or as newspaperboys as provided in this act.

34:2-21.7 Employment certificates for minors

(a) Except as permitted under N.J.S.A. 34:2-21.15, no minor under 18 years of age shall be employed, permitted, or suffered to work in, about, or in connection with any gainful occupation, unless and until the person employing such minor shall procure and keep on file an employment certificate or special permit for such minor, issued by the issuing officer of the school district in which the child resides, or of the district in which the child has obtained a promise of employment if the child is a nonresident of the State; provided, that:

(1) No certificate or special permit shall be required for any child 16 years of age or over employed in agricultural pursuits;

(2) No certificate or special permit shall be required for any child 14 years of age or over employed at such times as the schools of his district are not in session, at any agricultural fair, horse, dog, or farm show the duration of which does not exceed 10 days; and

(3) No vacation certificate shall be required in the first 14 days of employment for any minor 15 years of age or over employed in seasonal amusement, food service, restaurant or retail occupations, at such times as the schools of his district are not in session, provided that no minor under 16 years of age shall be permitted to operate, or service, or to work in, about, or in connection with power-driven machinery.

(b) The employment covered under this section shall not require or involve work in, about, or in connection with employments prohibited by N.J.S.A. 34:2-21.15 and 34:2-21.17, of the child labor laws.

(c) Such certificate or special permit shall be issued in triplicate in such form and in accordance with such instructions as may be prescribed by the Commissioner of Education. The Commissioner of Education shall supply to the issuing officers all blank forms to be used in connection with the issuance of such certificates, and special permits as provided for in N.J.S.A. 34:2-21.15.

(d) Employment certificates shall be of two kinds, regular certificates permitting employment during school hours, and vacation certificates permitting employment during the school vacation and during the school term at such times as the public schools are not in session.

(e) The original copy of the employment certificate shall be mailed by the issuing officer to the prospective employer of the minor for whom it is issued; a duplicate copy shall be mailed to the Department of Labor and Industry in Trenton as provided in N.J.S.A. 34:2-21.12, and a triplicate copy shall be kept in the files of the issuing officer. The issuing officer may refuse to grant a certificate, if in his judgment, the best interests of the minor would be served by such refusal and he shall keep a record of such refusals, and the reason therefor.

34:2-21.8 Issuance of certificates; prerequisites

The issuing officer shall issue such certificates only upon the application in person of the minor desiring employment, and after having approved and filed the following papers:

(1) A promise of employment signed by the prospective employer or by someone duly authorized by him, setting forth the specific nature of the occupation in which he intends to employ such minor, the wage to be paid such minor, and the number of hours per day and days per week which said minor shall be employed.

(2) Evidence of age showing that the minor is of the age required by this act, which evidence shall consist of one of the following proofs of age and shall be required in the order herein designated, as follows:

(a) A birth certificate or certified transcript thereof or a signed statement of the recorded date and place of birth issued by a registrar of vital statistics or other officer charged with the duty of recording births, or

(b) A baptismal certificate or attested transcript thereof showing the date and place of birth, and date and place of baptism of the minor, or

(c) Other documentary evidence of age satisfactory to the issuing officer, such as a bona fide contemporary record of the date and place of the minor's birth kept in the Bible in which the records of the births in the family of the minor are preserved, or a passport, showing the age of the minor, or a certificate of arrival in the United States, issued by the Office of Immigration and Naturalization Services, showing the age of the minor, or a life insurance policy, provided that such other documentary evidence has been in existence at least one year prior to the time it is offered as evidence, and provided further that a school record of age or an affidavit of a parent or guardian or other written statement of age shall not be accepted, except as specified in paragraph (d) of this section.

(d) In the case none of the aforesaid proofs of age shall be obtainable and only in such case, the issuing officer may accept the school record or the school-census record of the age of the minor together with the sworn statement of a parent or guardian as to the age of the minor and also with a certificate signed by the physician or advanced practice nurse authorized to sign the statements of physical fitness required by this section, specifying what in his opinion is the physical age of the minor. Such certificates shall show the height and weight of the minor and other facts concerning his physical development which were revealed by such examination and upon which the opinion of the physician or advanced practice nurse is based as to the physical age of the minor. If the school or school-census record of age is not obtainable, the sworn statement of the minor's parent or guardian, certifying to the name, date and place of birth of the minor, together with a physician's or advanced practice nurse's certificate of age as hereinbefore specified, may be accepted as evidence of age. The issuing officer shall administer said sworn statement.

The issuing officer shall, in issuing a certificate for a minor, require the evidence of age specified in paragraph (a) of this section in preference to that specified in paragraphs (b), (c) and (d) of this section and shall not accept the evidence of age permitted by any subsequent paragraph unless he shall receive and file evidence that the evidence of age required by the preceding paragraph or paragraphs cannot be obtained.

(3) A statement of physical fitness, signed by a medical inspector employed by the applicable board of education, or any other physician licensed to practice medicine and surgery, or advanced practice nurse, setting forth that such minor has been thoroughly examined by such medical inspector, or such other physician licensed to practice medicine and surgery, or advanced practice nurse, that he either is physically fit for employment in occupations permitted for persons under 18 years of age, or is physically fit to be employed under certain limitations, specified in the statement. If the statement of physical fitness is limited, the employment certificate issued thereon shall state clearly the limitations upon its use, and shall be valid only when used under the limitations so stated. The method of making such examinations shall be prescribed jointly by the Commissioner of Education and the State Department of Health and Senior Services; provided, however, no minor shall be required to submit to a physical examination, whose parent or guardian objects thereto in writing on the grounds such examination is contrary to his religious beliefs and practices.

(4) A school record signed by the principal of the school which the minor has last attended or by someone duly authorized by him, giving the full name, date of birth, grade last completed, and residence of the minor, provided, that in the case of a vacation certificate issued for work before or after school hours, such record shall also state that the child is a regular attendant at school, and in the opinion of the principal may perform such work without impairment of his progress in school, but such principal's statement shall not be required for the issuance of a vacation certificate for work during regular school vacations.

34:2-21.9 Age certificates to persons between 18 and 21; contents; retention by employer during employment
Upon request, it shall be the duty of the issuing officer to issue to any young person between the ages of eighteen and twenty-one years residing in his district and applying in person, who expresses a desire to enter employment, an age certificate upon presentation of the same proof of age as is required for the issuance of employment certificates under this act. A young person between the said ages nonresident of the State may apply to the issuing authority of any district where such person states he intends to seek employment. The age certificate shall state the color, name, sex, date and place of birth, residence, color of hair and eyes, height, and distinguishing facial marks, if any, and the kind of proof of age submitted. All copies thereof shall be signed in person by the applicant in the presence of the said issuing officer in whose name it is issued.

Any employer before employing a minor may require him to produce an age certificate and sign his name for comparison with the signature on the certificate. If in his judgment the signature and characteristics of the child correspond with the signature and description in the certificate, the employer, on employing the child, may require and retain the certificate during the minor's employment and shall return it to the minor upon the termination of his employment.

34:2-21.10 Employment certificate; contents
An employment certificate shall state the name, sex, color, date and place of birth, residence, color of hair and eyes, height, weight, any distinguishing facial marks of the child--the employer's name, address and type of business, the occupation of the child, the kind of proof of age submitted, the grade completed, physician's approval and the name and address of parent. Every such certificate shall be signed in the presence of the issuing officer by the child in whose name it is issued.

34:2-21.11 Certificate or permit as conclusive evidence of age
An employment or age certificate or special permit issued in accordance with this act shall be conclusive evidence of the age of the minor for whom issued in any proceeding involving the employment of a minor under the child-labor or workmen's compensation law or any other labor law of the State, as to any act occurring subsequent to its issuance.

34:2-21.12 Filing of duplicate certificates or permits; cancellation; return of original papers; destruction of certificates and permits when minors become 21
Every issuing officer issuing an employment or an age certificate or special permit, shall send immediately to the Department of Labor at Trenton, a duplicate of the certificate or permit and the original papers upon which the certificate or special permit was granted. The department shall examine and promptly return to the issuing officer the said original papers and shall keep on file the duplicate of said certificate or permit. Whenever there is reason to believe that an employment or an age certificate or special permit was improperly issued, the Commissioner of Labor shall notify the Commissioner of Education and the board of education of the school district in which the certificate was issued. The board of education of the school district may cancel any employment or any age certificate or special permit issued by it, and shall cancel the same when directed so to do by the Commissioner of Education. Whenever any employment certificate has been cancelled, the board of education cancelling the same shall immediately notify the Commissioner of Education, the Commissioner of Labor and the person by whom the child is employed, of its action, and such employer shall immediately upon receiving notice forward the certificate to the board of education.

All birth certificates, baptismal certificates, passports, insurance policies or other original papers submitted in proof of age shall be returned to the minor upon request after they have been returned to the issuing officer by the Department of Labor and after the issuing officer has transcribed for his files information pertinent to the issuance of the certificates. The Commissioner of Labor and the issuing officer may destroy all employment and age certificates and special permits or copies thereof when the birth dates set forth in such certificates and special permits are more than twenty-one years before the date of destruction.

34:2-21.13 Employment of children who are nonresidents of school district; duplicate of certificate
If a child within the ages for compulsory school attendance is employed in a school district other than that in which he lives, the issuing officer of the district in which the child lives shall immediately send a duplicate of the certificate, properly filled out and the address of the employer to the superintendent of schools of the county in which the child resides who shall thereupon send said duplicate to the superintendent of schools of the county in which the child is employed.

34:2-21.14 Return of certificate after employment terminates; new certificates; certificate valid only for one employer and one occupation; employer to keep certificate accessible; prima facie evidence
Every employer receiving an employment certificate shall within two days after termination of the employment return said certificate to the person issuing it. A new employment certificate shall not be issued for any minor except upon the presentation of a new promise of employment. An employment certificate shall be valid only for the employer for whom issued and for the occupation designated in the promise of employment. Said employer shall, during the period of the minor's employment, keep such certificate on file at the place of employment and accessible to any issuing officer and to any attendance officer, inspector, or other person authorized to enforce this act. The failure of any employer to produce for inspection such employment certificate, or the presence of any minor under eighteen years of age in his place of work at any time other than that specified in the posted schedule of hours required by this act, shall be prima facie evidence of the unlawful employment of the minor. The presence of any minor under eighteen years of age in any place of employment shall be prima facie evidence of the employment of such minor, except that the presence on any farm or place of agricultural pursuit of any such minor shall not constitute such prima facie evidence.

34:2-21.15 Street trade; agricultural pursuits; ages when permitted; special permits; newspaper carriers
Except as hereinafter provided as to newspaper carriers, no minor under 14 years of age may engage in any street trade, which term, for the purpose of this section shall include the selling, offering for sale, soliciting for, collecting for, displaying, or distributing any articles, goods, merchandise, commercial service, posters, circulars, newspapers or magazines or in blacking shoes on any street or other public place or from house to house. No minor under 12 years of age may be employed in agricultural pursuits.

Whenever a minor has graduated from vocational school, approved by the Commissioner of Education and is 17 years of age, the minor's diploma or certified copy thereof and an employment certificate mailed to the employer by the issuing officer shall be deemed a special permit to engage in those pursuits in which the minor majored in said vocational school during those hours permitted for persons 18 years of age and over.

Except as hereinafter provided as to newspaper carriers, whenever a minor under 16 years of age desires to work during such times as the schools of the district in which the minor resides are not in session in any street trade or in agricultural pursuits, the parent, guardian or other person having the custody and control of the minor may file with the issuing officer in the school district in which the minor resides an application for a special permit authorizing such work. Such application shall show the exact character of the work the minor is to do, and the hours and wages and special conditions under which said work is to be performed.

If upon investigation it is found that the facts set forth in the application are true and that the work will not interfere with the minor's health or standing in school, the issuing officer shall, upon presentation to the issuing officer of the same proof of age as is required for the issuance of an employment certificate, issue a special permit, allowing the minor to work at such times as the public schools in the district are not in session, but such work except in agricultural pursuits, and as newspaper carriers, to be otherwise subject to the maximum hours of labor provisions set for minors under 16 years of age in section 3 of this act; provided, that nothing in this act shall prevent newspaper carriers as defined in this act, between 11 and 14 years of age, from delivering, soliciting, selling and collecting for newspapers on routes in residential neighborhoods between the hours of 6:00 o'clock in the morning and 7:00 o'clock in the evening of any day; and newspaper carriers 14 years of age and older from delivering, soliciting, selling and collecting for newspapers on routes in residential neighborhoods between the hours of 5:30 o'clock in the morning and 8:00 o'clock in the evening of any day; and provided further that no newspaper carrier under the age of 18 years shall be permitted to engage in such occupation beyond the period of time wherein the combined hours devoted to said occupation as a newspaper carrier and the hours in school shall exceed a total of 40 hours per week and not more than 8 hours in any 1 day; and provided, further, that minors engaged in agricultural pursuits may be employed no more than 10 hours per day.

Such special permit shall show the name, address, and date of birth of the minor for whom it is issued, the kind of proof of age submitted, the nature of the occupation in which the minor is to engage, and such other information as the commissioner of Education may require.

Any such special permit for work in agriculture shall be issued for a period not to exceed 6 months and shall show its date of expiration. Any person employing a minor under 16 years of age in agriculture shall obtain such a certificate from the minor and keep it on file during the period of the minor's employment and shall return it to the minor to whom it is issued upon termination of the minor's employment.

Upon application by the parent, guardian or other person having custody and control of a newspaper carrier as defined in this act, between the ages of 11 and 18 years of age, to the publisher of any newspaper in this State and upon receiving satisfactory proof of age and a signed statement of physical fitness, such publisher may issue to such newspaper carrier a special permit on a form prescribed and approved by the Commissioner of Education, whereby the newspaper carrier shall be permitted to deliver, solicit, sell and collect for newspapers outside of the newspaper carrier's school hours on residential routes, and on Sundays and during school vacations and no other employment certificate shall be required.

Such special permit shall show the name, address and date of birth of the newspaper carrier for whom it is issued, and such other information as the Commissioner of Education may require.

The publisher shall forthwith mail 3 copies of such special permit to the issuing officer as defined in section 1 of this act, one of which copies shall be forwarded to the Commissioner of Education and one copy to the Commissioner of Labor and Industry in such manner as may be provided by regulation of said commissioners. A copy of such special permit shall also be furnished by the publisher to the parent, guardian or other person having custody and control of the newspaper carrier and the publisher shall retain at all times a file copy thereof.

The special permit shall remain in full force and effect unless and until the publisher has knowledge of or is notified by the issuing officer or the Commissioner of Labor and Industry that the newspaper carrier is not physically fit or that in the opinion of the issuing officer or the Commissioner of Labor and Industry, engaging in the occupation as a newspaper carrier will be harmful to the newspaper carrier's education. In such case, the said special permit shall be suspended unless and until the issuing officer shall revoke said notification. In the event of such notification and suspension, however, if either the parent, guardian or other person having custody and control of the newspaper carrier or the publisher shall deem such decision to be erroneous, an appeal may be made to the Commissioner of Education who shall have authority to affirm, reverse or modify such decision of the issuing officer or the Commissioner of Labor and Industry.

The publisher shall keep a record of the name, address and birth date of each newspaper carrier to whom such special permit is issued; the date said newspaper carrier commenced and ceased delivering newspapers published by said publisher together with a record of the number of newspapers sold to each newspaper carrier and a general description of the area of the route served by each newspaper carrier. Such records shall be kept on file by said publisher for a period of 2 years after the newspaper carrier has ceased delivering newspapers published by said publisher.

The special permit shall remain in full force and effect unless and until the publisher is notified by the issuing officer or the Commissioner of Labor and Industry that the newspaper carrier is not physically fit or that the newspaper carrier's school record is such that engaging in the occupation of a newspaper carrier will be harmful to the newspaper carrier's education. In such case, however, if either the parent, guardian or other person having custody and control of the newspaper carrier or the publisher shall deem such decision to be erroneous, an appeal may be made to the Commissioner of Education who shall have authority to reverse or modify such decision of the issuing officer or the Commissioner of Labor and Industry.

34:2-21.16 Fees or expenses not to be paid by child, parent or guardian
No fees or expenses incurred in obtaining any certificates under this act shall be charged to or paid by any child, parent, guardian or other person having custody or control of such a child for any service had under this act.

34:2-21.17 Prohibited employments for minors under 16 and under 18; exceptions
No minor under 16 years of age shall be employed, permitted or suffered to work in, about, or in connection with power-driven machinery.

No minor under 18 years of age shall be employed, permitted or suffered to work in, about, or in connection with the following:
- the manufacture or packing of paints, colors, white lead, or red lead;
- the handling of dangerous or poisonous acids or dyes; injurious quantities of toxic or noxious dust, gases, vapors or fumes;
- work involving exposure to benzol or any benzol compound which is volatile or which can penetrate the skin;
- the manufacture, transportation or use of explosives or highly inflammable substances;
- oiling, wiping, or cleaning machinery in motion or assisting therein;

- operation or helping in the operation of power-driven woodworking machinery; provided, that apprentices operating under conditions of bona fide apprenticeship may operate such machines under competent instruction and supervision;
- grinding, abrasive, polishing or buffing machines, provided that apprentices operating under conditions of bona fide apprenticeship may grind their own tools;
- punch presses or stamping machines if the clearance between the ram and the die or the stripper exceeds 1/4 inch;
- cutting machines having a guillotine action;
- corrugating, crimping or embossing machines;
- paper lace machines;
- dough brakes or mixing machines in bakeries or cracker machinery;
- calendar rolls or mixing rolls in rubber manufacturing;
- centrifugal extractors; or mangles in laundries or dry cleaning establishments;
- ore reduction works, smelters, hot rolling mills, furnaces, foundries, forging shops, or any other place in which the heating, melting, or heat treatment of metals is carried on;
- mines or quarries;
- steam boilers carrying a pressure in excess of 15 pounds;
- construction work of any kind, except in the construction of affordable housing as a volunteer for a nonprofit organization as provided in section 1 of P.L.1994, c.82 (C.34:2-21.17d);
- fabrication or assembly of ships;
- operation or repair of elevators or other hoisting apparatus;
- the transportation of payrolls other than within the premises of the employer.

No minor under 18 years of age shall be employed, permitted, or suffered to work in, about, or in connection with any establishment where alcoholic liquors are distilled, rectified, compounded, brewed, manufactured, bottled, or are sold for consumption on the premises, or in a pool or billiard room; provided, however, this paragraph shall not apply to minors 16 years of age or over, employed as pinsetters, lane attendants, or busboys in public bowling alleys as provided in section 3 of P.L.1940, c.153 (C.34:2-21.3) or to minors employed in theatrical productions where alcoholic beverages are sold on the premises.

Minors 14 years of age or over may be employed as golf course caddies and pool attendants.

No minor under 18 years of age shall be employed, permitted, or suffered to work in any place of employment, or at any occupation hazardous or injurious to the life, health, safety, or welfare of such minor, as such occupation shall, from time to time, be determined and declared by the Commissioner of Labor to be hazardous or injurious to the life, health, safety, or welfare of such minor, after a public hearing thereon and after such notice as the commissioner may by regulation prescribe.

None of the provisions of this section regarding employment in connection with alcoholic liquors shall be construed to prevent the employment of minors 16 years of age or more in a restaurant as defined in section 1 of P.L.1940, c.153 (C.34:2-21.1) and as provided for in section 3 of P.L.1940, c.153 (C.34:2-21.3), in a public bowling alley as provided in this section, or in the executive offices, maintenance departments, or pool or beach areas of a hotel, motel or guesthouse; provided, however, that no minor shall engage in the preparation, sale or serving of alcoholic beverages, nor in the preparation of photographs, nor in any dancing or theatrical exhibition or performance which is not part of a theatrical production where alcoholic beverages are sold on the premises, while so employed; and provided, further, that any minor so employed shall be closely supervised while engaged in the clearing of alcoholic beverages.

Nothing in this section shall be deemed to apply to the work done by pupils in public or private schools of New Jersey, under the supervision and instruction of officers or teachers of such organizations or schools, or to a minor who is 17 years of age employed in the type of work in which such minor majored under the conditions of the special vocational school graduate permit provided in section 15 of P.L.1940, c.153 (C.34:2-21.15).

Nothing in this section shall be construed to prevent minors 16 years of age or older who are members of a Junior Firemen's Auxiliary, created pursuant to N.J.S.40A:14-95, from engaging in any activities authorized by N.J.S.40A:14-98.

Notwithstanding any provision of this section to the contrary, a minor who is 15 years of age or older may work as a cashier or bagger on or near a supermarket or retail establishment cash register conveyor belt.

34:2-21.17a Inapplicability of s. 34:2-21.17 to participants in junior achievement program
Section 17 to P.L. 1940, c. 153 (C. 34:2-21.17) shall not apply to minors under the age of 18 years who participate or work in any junior achievement program. As used in this act "junior achievement program" means any program under which minors under the age of 18 engage in business enterprises or activities pursuant to an economics education program conducted under the guidance of adult sponsors from private business and industry.

34:2-21.17b. Provisions for minors as volunteers at recycling centers
Concurrent with all other provisions of P.L. 1940, c. 153 (C. 34:2-21.1 et seq.), minors who are 12 through 17 years of age shall be permitted to work as volunteers at community operated noncommercial recycling centers operated by a municipality or a community service organization authorized by a municipality to operate a recycling center subject to the following provisions:

a.   That these recycling centers handle only those waste products normally included in the municipal waste stream such as newspapers and glass and metal beverage containers;

b.   That under no circumstances shall a minor be permitted to work in a community recycling center that is in any way associated with a profit making commercial enterprise other than to sell the recyclable products referred to in subsection a.;

c.   That no minor shall operate, perform maintenance, clean, inspect or work in, about, or in connection with any power-driven machinery involved in the recycling process;

d.   That no minor shall work in a community recycling center without the safety equipment required by law;

e.   That no minor shall be permitted to work as a volunteer at a recycling center except under the direct supervision of an adult;

f.   That no minor shall handle or be exposed to hazardous waste products or other hazardous substances; and

g.   That the municipality which operates the center or authorizes the operation of the center by a community service organization has secured adequate liability insurance to provide compensation for all injuries sustained by minors working voluntarily at the center.

For the purposes of this section, "community operated noncommercial recycling center" means any recycling center that is sponsored by a municipality and is engaged in the recycling activity as a community service.

34:2-21.17c. Not considered employee
A minor working voluntarily at a recycling center shall not be deemed an employee under R.S. 34:15-36. A municipality or community service organization which uses the services of a minor under this act shall not be subject to R.S. 34:15-10, provided that the municipality or organization has fully complied with P.L. 1940, c. 153 (C. 34:2-21.1 et seq.) and the provisions of this act.

34:2-21.17d. Employment of minors as volunteers in certain nonprofit organizations
Concurrent with all other provisions of P.L.1940, c.153 (C.34:2-21.1 et seq.), minors who are 14 through 17 years of age shall be permitted to work as volunteers for nonprofit organizations engaged in the construction of affordable housing as determined by the Commissioner of Labor subject to the following provisions:

a.   That under no circumstances shall a minor be permitted to work in a project involving the construction of affordable housing that is in any way associated with a profit-making commercial enterprise;

b.   That no minor shall operate, perform maintenance, clean, inspect or work in, about, or in connection with any power-driven machinery involved in the construction of affordable housing;

c.   That no minor shall engage in the construction of affordable housing without the safety equipment required by law;

d.   That no minor shall be permitted to work as a volunteer in the construction of affordable housing except under the direct supervision of an adult;

e.   That no minor shall be exposed to hazardous waste products or other hazardous substances;

f.   That no minor shall be permitted to work on any excavation, scaffolding or roofing;

g.   That no minor shall be permitted to work:

(1) during school hours;

(2) before 7 a.m.;

(3) after 7 p.m.; except that minors may work until 9 p.m. between Memorial Day and Labor Day;

(4). for more than five consecutive hours without a half-hour break; and

(5) for more than 18 hours per week when school is in session; and

h. That the nonprofit organization engaged in the construction of affordable housing has secured liability insurance to provide compensation for all injuries, including, but not limited to, occupational illness, sustained by minors working voluntarily in the construction of affordable housing. The insurance required by this section shall have coverage limits of at least $2,500,000 per occurrence, at least $2,500,000 aggregate per year and $250,000 for property damage, or such higher amounts as the Commissioner of Insurance may promulgate from time to time to adjust for inflation.

34:2-21.17e. Minor working voluntarily not deemed employee

A minor working voluntarily in the construction of affordable housing pursuant to section 1 of this act shall not be deemed an employee under R.S.34:15-36. A nonprofit organization which uses the services of a minor under this act shall not be subject to R.S.34:15-10, provided that the nonprofit organization has fully complied with P.L.1940, c.153 (C.34:2-21.1 et seq.) and the provisions of this act.

34:2-21.17f Inapplicability of C.34:2-21.17 under certain circumstances; "educational program in science" defined

Section 17 of P.L.1940, c.153 (C.34:2-21.17) shall not apply to minors under the age of 18 who have successfully reached the ninth or higher grade level and who have the approval of a parent or guardian to participate or work in any educational program in science. A school student shall not participate or work in the program more than 20 hours per week during the school year.

As used in this act "educational program in science" means a program in which any minor under the age of 18 who has successfully reached the ninth or higher grade level participates in a scientific project or activity located in a research facility pursuant to an educational program under the supervision of the minor's school and adult sponsors from private business and industry, provided that no supervision by a school shall be required if the minor is a high school graduate.

34:2-21.17g Rules, regulations

The Commissioner of Labor, in consultation with the Commissioner of Education, shall, pursuant to the "Administrative Procedure Act," P.L.1968, c.410 (C.52:14B-1 et seq.), adopt rules and regulations necessary to implement the provisions of this act.

34:2-21.18 Enforcement of act; inspection of places and certificates

It shall be the duty of the Department of Labor and its inspectors and agents, acting under the Commissioner of Labor, to enforce the provisions of this act, to make complaints against persons violating its provisions, and to prosecute violations of the same. The Commissioner of Labor and any inspector or other authorized person acting under him, attendance officers and other persons employed by law to compel the attendance of children at school, and officers and agents of any duly incorporated society for the protection of children from cruelty and neglect, shall have authority to enter and inspect at any time any place or establishment covered by this act, and to have access to employment or age certificates or special permits kept on file by the employers and such other records as may aid in the enforcement of this act.

34 2-21.19 Penalty, Child Labor Enforcement Trust Fund, Advisory Board; annual report

a. Whoever employs or permits or suffers any minor to be employed or to work in violation of this act, or of any order or ruling issued under the provisions of this act, or obstructs the Department of Labor and Workforce Development, its officers or agents, or any other person authorized to inspect places of employment under this act, and whoever, having under his control or custody any minor, permits or suffers him to be employed or to work in violation of this act, shall be guilty of an offense. If a defendant acts knowingly, an offense under this section shall be a crime of the fourth degree. Otherwise it shall be a disorderly persons offense and the defendant shall, upon conviction for a violation, be punished by a fine of not less than $100 nor more than $2,000 for an initial violation and not less than $200 nor more than $4,000 for each subsequent violation. Each day during which any violation of this act continues shall constitute a separate and distinct offense, and the employment of any minor in violation of the act shall with respect to each minor so employed, constitute a separate and distinct offense.

b. As an alternative to or in addition to any other sanctions provided by law for violations of P.L.1940, c.153 (C.34:2-21.1 et seq.), when the Commissioner of Labor and Workforce Development finds that an individual has violated that act, the commissioner is authorized to assess and collect administrative penalties of not more than $500 for a first violation, not more than $1,000 for a second violation, and not more than $2,500 for each subsequent violation, specified in a schedule of penalties to be promulgated as a rule or regulation by the commissioner in accordance with the "Administrative Procedure Act," P.L.1968, c.410 (C.52:14B-1 et seq.). When determining the amount of the penalty imposed because of a violation, the commissioner shall consider factors which include the history of previous violations by the employer, the seriousness of the violation, the good faith of the employer, and the size of the employer's business. No administrative penalty shall be levied pursuant to this section unless the Commissioner of Labor and Workforce Development provides the alleged violator with notification of the violation and of the amount of the penalty by certified mail and an opportunity to request a hearing before the commissioner or his designee within 15 days following the receipt of the notice. If a hearing is requested, the commissioner shall issue a final order upon such hearing and a finding that a violation has occurred. If no hearing is requested, the notice shall become a final order upon expiration of the 15-day period. Payment of the penalty is due when a final order is issued or when the notice becomes a final order. Any penalty imposed pursuant to this section may be recovered with costs in a summary proceeding commenced by the commissioner pursuant to the "Penalty Enforcement Law of 1999," P.L.1999, c. 274 (C.2A:58-10 et seq.). Any sum collected as a fine or penalty pursuant to this section shall be deposited in the Child Labor Law Enforcement Trust Fund established pursuant to subsection c. of this section.

c.   There is established in the Department of Labor and Workforce Development the Child Labor Law Enforcement Trust Fund. All moneys in the fund shall be applied by the department toward the enforcement of the provisions of P.L.1940, c.153 (C.34:2-21.1 et seq.) and to disseminate information and publicity regarding those provisions to employers, employer organizations, employees, unions, and teachers, counselors, social workers and other professionals engaged in work involving the welfare of children.

d.   There is established a Child Labor Law Enforcement Advisory Board to advise the Commissioner of Labor and Workforce Development, and issue an annual report, regarding the use of moneys from the Child Labor Law Enforcement Trust Fund and other issues the board deems appropriate concerning child labor, including the impact of excessive or hazardous work on the educational success, health and general well-being of children. The board shall consist of the commissioner or his designee, who shall serve as the chair, and seven members appointed by the commissioner as follows: two members representing organizations of employers in industries with significant numbers of employees who are minors, two members representing labor unions in industries with significant numbers of employees who are minors, one member representing an organization of school administrators, one member representing an organization of school employees, and one member who is an individual with expertise on the impact of excessive or hazardous work on the educational success, health, and general well-being of children. Members appointed by the commissioner shall be appointed for two-year terms and may be appointed for any number of terms. Members shall serve without compensation, but shall be reimbursed for necessary expenses incurred in the performance of their duties. Action may be taken by the board by an affirmative vote of a majority of its members. The first annual report shall be issued not later than 12 months after the effective date of this act. Each annual report may include recommendations to enhance the enforcement and publicizing of the provisions of P.L.1940, c.153 (C.34:2-21.1 et seq.). The advisory board shall have access to reports, data and other information regarding child labor in the possession of the department and assistance from department personnel as required to perform its duties.

34 2-21.20 Partial invalidity

If any provisions of this act or the application thereof to any person or circumstances is held invalid, the remainder of the act and the application of such provisions to other persons or circumstances shall not be affected thereby.

An Employer's Guide
to Workers' Compensation in New Jersey

New Jersey Department of Labor and Workforce Development

I. WHAT IS WORKERS' COMPENSATION?

Workers' compensation is a "no fault" insurance program that provides medical treatment, wage replacement, and permanent disability compensation to employees who suffer job-related injuries or illnesses. It also provides death benefits to dependents of workers who have died as a result of their employment. An injured employee will receive benefits regardless of who was at fault. In exchange for these guaranteed benefits, the worker does not have the right to bring a civil action against the employer for pain and suffering or other damages, except in cases of intentional acts.

The Division of Workers' Compensation is responsible for the administration of the New Jersey Workers' Compensation Act (N.J.S.A. 34:15-1 et seq.). This is accomplished by:

- ensuring that workers receive fair and timely workers' compensation benefits for work-related injuries from their employers and/or insurance carriers;

- enforcing the law that requires employers to secure workers' compensation insurance coverage from commercial insurance carriers or self-insurance programs;

- providing certain benefit payments to injured workers who are totally and permanently disabled as a result of their last work-related injury combined with the worker's pre-existing disabilities. These benefits commence at the conclusion of the payment of benefits from the worker's employer.

The Division of Workers' Compensation does not have jurisdiction over insurance premium rate setting. That responsibility falls under the jurisdiction of the Compensation Rating and Inspection Bureau of the Department of Banking and Insurance.

II. WORKERS' COMPENSATION BENEFITS

Medical Benefits: Necessary and reasonable medical treatment, prescriptions, and hospital services related to the work injury are paid by the employer's insurance carrier or directly by the employer if self-insured. The employer and/or its insurance carrier have the right to designate medical providers for all work-related injuries.

Temporary Total Benefits: If an injured worker is disabled for a period of more than seven days, he or she will be eligible to receive temporary total benefit, retroactive to the first day of lost time. The benefit will be paid at a rate of 70% of the worker's average weekly wage, not to exceed the statutory maximum rate or fall below the statutory minimum rate established annually by the Commissioner of Labor and Workforce Development. These benefits are provided until the worker has returned to work, has reached maximum medical improvement, or has reached the statutory 400-week maximum.

Permanent Partial Benefits: When a job-related injury or illness results in a permanent bodily impairment, benefits are based on the individual's functional loss. These benefits are paid weekly and are due after the date temporary disability ends.

Permanent Total Benefits: When a work injury or illness prevents a worker from returning to any type of gainful employment, he or she may be entitled to receive permanent total disability benefits. These weekly benefits are provided initially for a period of 450 weeks. Benefits continue beyond the initial 450 weeks provided that the injured worker is able to show that he or she remains totally disabled. The benefits are paid weekly and are based upon 70% of the average weekly wage, not to exceed the statutory maximum or fall below the statutory minimum.

Death Benefits: Dependents of a worker who dies as a result of a work-related injury or illness may be eligible to receive death benefits and funeral expenses up to $3,500. The weekly benefits are 70% of the wage of the deceased worker, not to exceed the statutory maximum.

III. INSURANCE REQUIREMENTS

- **TYPES OF COVERAGE**

New Jersey law requires that all New Jersey employers not covered by federal programs have workers' compensation coverage or be approved for self-insurance. Even out-of-state employers may need workers' compensation coverage if a contract of employment is entered into in New Jersey or if work is performed in New Jersey. Coverage may be obtained in one of two ways:

Workers' Compensation Insurance Policy written by a mutual or stock carrier authorized to write insurance in New Jersey.

Premiums for such insurance are based on the classification(s) of the work being performed by employees, the claims experience of the employer, and the payroll of the employer.

Self-Insurance through application to and approval by the Commissioner of the Department of Banking and Insurance. Approval for self-insurance is based upon the financial ability of the employer to meet its obligations under the law and the permanence of the business. The posting of security for such obligations may be required.

A self-insured employer has the option of administering its own workers' compensation claims or contracting with a third-party administrator (TPA) to provide these services. For more information about self-insurance, please refer to N.J.S.A. 34:15-77 of the New Jersey Workers' Compensation statute or contact the Department of Banking and Insurance at (609) 292-5350, ext. 50099.

Note: Governmental agencies are required to provide workers' compensation benefits to their employees but are not required to purchase insurance or receive approval as a self-insurer. They generally either 1) obtain an insurance policy, 2) participate in an insurance pool, or 3) maintain a separate appropriation for workers' compensation.

The following employing entities must have workers' compensation insurance in effect:

Corporations – All corporations operating in New Jersey must maintain workers' compensation insurance or be approved for self-insurance so long as any one or more individuals, including corporate officers, perform services for the corporation for prior, current or anticipated financial consideration.*

Partnerships/LLCs – All partnerships and limited liability companies (LLCs) operating in New Jersey must maintain workers' compensation insurance or be approved for self-insurance so long as any one or more individuals, excluding partners or members of the LLC, perform services for the partnership or LLC for prior, current or anticipated financial consideration.*

Sole Proprietorship – All sole proprietorships operating in New Jersey must maintain workers' compensation insurance or be approved for self-insurance so long as any one or more individuals, excluding the principal owner, performs services for the business for prior, current or anticipated financial consideration.*

*Financial consideration means any remuneration for services and includes cash or other remuneration in lieu of cash such as products, services, shares of or options to buy corporate stock, meals or lodging, etc.

- **DEFINITION OF "EMPLOYEE"**

The New Jersey Workers' Compensation Act is liberally interpreted with respect to the definition of "employee" and is broader than the Internal Revenue Code and Unemployment Compensation statute. A variety of working relationships have been determined to be that of an employer-employee, including some that would not appear to be a typical employment situation. Further, a contract or other agreement as to whether an individual is an employee is not binding in determining whether an employee–employer situation is present.

New Jersey courts, in deciding this issue, have developed two tests: the "control test" and the "relative nature of the work test."

Under the "control test," the relationship between a business and the individual is reviewed. There is employment if the business retains the right to supervise the individual and control what is done as well as how it shall be done.

Under the "relative nature of the work test," there is employment if an individual relies on income from the business and the work performed by the individual is an integral part of the activities of the business.

If any or both of these tests are met, an employee–employer relationship is established.

- ## OBTAINING WORKERS' COMPENSATION COVERAGE

The New Jersey Compensation Rating and Inspection Bureau (NJCRIB), an agency in the New Jersey Department of Banking and Insurance, is responsible for establishing and maintaining regulations and premium rates for workers' compensation and employers' liability insurance.

Workers' compensation insurance coverage can be obtained from any of the more than 400 private licensed insurance companies authorized to sell workers' compensation policies in New Jersey. A policy can be purchased directly from an insurance carrier, an insurance agent, or an insurance broker. For assistance with obtaining coverage, please contact:

New Jersey Compensation Rating and Inspection Bureau
60 Park Place
Newark, NJ 07102
www.njcrib.com
(973) 622-6014

- ## INSURANCE PREMIUM RATES

The primary device used to determine workers' compensation insurance premiums is the classification system, which groups New Jersey businesses into various classifications. The purpose of this system is to bring together, within each classification, employers engaged in the same type of business. Accompanying each classification is a rate that represents the average work-injury experience for that classification. This rate is adjusted annually according to the latest available work-injury experience data.

It is also recognized that no two employers, although they may be in the same business, have exactly the same operations or identical conditions of employment. Within any given classification, there are employers with better-than-average work injury experience and those with worse-than-average work injury experience. To account for such differences, an additional refinement to the classification system is offered through another program known as the Experience Rating Plan. In this plan, an employer's own work injury experience is used to modify its premium, higher or lower, by comparing it to the average work-injury experience of all employers in the classification to which the employer is assigned.

For more information on how rates are established, you may wish to read the WC Reference Guide available on NJCRIB's Web site (www.njcrib.com/ReferenceGuide/cribcnst.asp).

- ## WHAT A WORKERS' COMPENSATION POLICY COVERS

A workers' compensation policy covers the following:

For injured employees:

- Reasonable medical services necessary to treat the job injury or illness
- Temporary disability benefits to help replace lost wages up to statutory maximum
- Permanent disability benefits to compensate for the continued effects of the injury
- Burial and death benefits for dependents in cases of fatal injury

For employers:

- Coverage of financial liabilities for work-related injuries and illnesses
- Legal representation

- ## PENALTIES FOR FAILURE TO INSURE

The consequences for failure to provide workers' compensation coverage can be very significant, even without a work-related injury. Specifically, the law provides that failing to insure is a disorderly persons offense and, if determined to be knowing, a crime of the fourth degree. Moreover, penalties for such failure can be assessed up to $5,000 for the first 10 days with additional assessments of $5,000 for each 10-day period of failure to insure thereafter. In the case of a corporation, liability for failure to insure can extend to the corporate officers individually. Penalties assessed for failure to insure are not dischargeable in bankruptcy.

Where a work-related injury or death has occurred, the employer, including individual corporate officers, partners or members of an LLC, is directly liable for medical expenses, temporary disability, and permanent disability or dependency benefits. In addition to awards for medical expenses and other benefits, New Jersey law also provides for civil penalties against the employer and its officers where failure to insure is determined. Awards and penalties arising from these claims can become liens against the uninsured employer and its officers, which are generally enforceable in the New Jersey Superior Court against any assets belonging to the uninsured employer and its officers.

HOW UNINSURED EMPLOYERS ARE IDENTIFIED

State employer records are compared, or "cross-matched," with the database at the Department of Banking and Insurance's Compensation Rating and Inspection Bureau (NJCRIB) on a regular basis to identify uninsured employers.

When an employer is identified through this cross-match as a possibly uninsured employer, a letter and a cross-match response form is issued. Mandatory insurance should be immediately obtained if an employer is uninsured and verification of insurance must be provided. Penalties may still be assessed for failure to have insurance at the time of the cross-match.

If you are an employer that has insurance and has received this form, you should provide the information requested about your workers' compensation coverage as soon as possible to ensure that penalties are not improperly assessed against you.

Also, if you are aware of an uninsured employer, you may provide this information to the Division of Workers' Compensation by e-mail (oscf@dol.state.nj.us), by calling (609) 292-0165 or by completing and submitting a "Report of Non-Compliance" form, available on the Web site of the Division of Workers' Compensation. You need not identify yourself but you should be prepared to provide the name and exact address of the employer and, if possible, the names of the principle operators of the business.

IV. BEFORE AN INJURY OCCURS

- **POSTING NOTICE**

New Jersey law requires every employer to post and maintain, in a conspicuous place or places in and about the worksite, a form prescribed by the Commissioner of the Department of Banking and Insurance, stating that the employer has secured workers' compensation insurance coverage or has qualified with the Department of Banking and Insurance as a self-insured employer.

For insured employers, the notice must include the name of the insurance carrier and other items as required by the Department of Banking and Insurance. To obtain copies of this notice, employers should contact their insurer.

- **ESTABLISH CLEAR PROCEDURES FOR EMPLOYEES AND MANAGERS**

At the time of hire and periodically thereafter, employees should be provided the following information:

- An explanation of their workers' compensation coverage and benefits
- How, when, and to whom to report an injury
- Where to go for medical treatment if injured while working

The Division of Workers' Compensation has a general brochure on workers' compensation available for injured workers, called "A Worker's Guide to Workers' Compensation." The brochure, which can be downloaded for distribution to employees from the division's Web site (*www.nj.gov/labor/wc/wcindex.html*), is available in English and Spanish.

V. REPORTING WORK ACCIDENTS AND OCCUPATIONAL EXPOSURES

Every work accident or occupational exposure should be recorded on an accident report form. Such documentation should prompt an immediate investigation, which not only assists in determining the cause of the accident or exposure, but is also important in the prevention of future accidents.

When an employer receives notice about a work-related accident or occupational exposure, it should notify its insurance carrier or third-party administrator (TPA) immediately so that a First Report of Injury form can be filed by the carrier or TPA with the state of New Jersey. This form, which is filed electronically, gives the Division of Workers' Compensation initial information about the work accident or exposure and any resulting injuries. A copy of this report is sent by the carrier or TPA to the employer for verification of the information submitted.

Within 26 weeks after the worker has reached maximum medical improvement or has returned to work, the insurance carrier or TPA must electronically file a second report, called a Subsequent Report of Injury, with the state. Information from this report, including an explanation of any benefits paid on the claim, is also sent to the injured worker.

Note: If you are a self-administered self-insurer or governmental entity, you will be required to file these two reports directly with the state. For more information on how to file, please visit the Division of Workers' Compensation's Electronic Data Interchange (EDI) Web page at *www.nj.gov/labor/wc/wcedi.html.*

VI. HOW TO REDUCE WORKERS' COMPENSATION COSTS

- ### ESTABLISH A SAFETY PROGRAM

The best way for an employer to lower workers' compensation costs is to prevent injuries from happening in the first place. Involve your employees in identifying hazardous work practices and potentially harmful situations, areas, or equipment. Safety teams and company incentives play a role in reducing costs. Most importantly, management must be willing to listen and put into practice appropriate recommendations.

Many insurance companies offer free advice to policyholders about how to establish and maintain safe workplaces. You can also use the New Jersey Department of Labor and Workforce Development's free On-Site Consultation Service to find out about potential hazards at your worksites and improve your occupational safety and health management systems. Information on this service can be obtained by contacting:

New Jersey Department of Labor and Workforce Development
Division of Public Safety and Occupational Safety and Health
P.O. Box 953
Trenton, NJ 08625www.nj.gov/labor/lsse/lsonsite.html
(609) 984-0785

- ### ESTABLISH RETURN-TO-WORK PROGRAMS

Creating return-to-work programs that include appropriate light-duty or modified jobs can encourage workers to return to employment sooner and lower business costs.

In addition, employers can partner with medical professionals and managed care specialists to design jobs that will not aggravate or re-injure workers who have recovered enough to return to work, but need additional time before resuming regular duties. The employer should provide an injured worker's job description to his or her medical care provider. Such information may facilitate early release of the worker to some type of modified duty.

Researchers have found that in companies offering return-to-work programs, workers felt more satisfied with the care they received.

- **ESTABLISH AND MAINTAIN GOOD COMMUNICATION WITH INJURED EMPLOYEES**

Pre-Injury:

Frequently communicate workers' compensation-related information to employees in plain, straightforward language. Publicize company procedures for job-related injuries or illnesses and encourage early reporting of such injuries. Let workers know which doctors they must see for work-related claims. When workers receive prior communication about what to do when a work-related injury or illness occurs, they are more likely to follow the employer's established procedures. When the same information is received after an injury has already occurred, employee reaction and response may be less positive.

Post-Injury:

Employers should actively become involved in every workers' compensation case. Communicate on a regular basis with your employees who are disabled with work related injuries. The communication, whether it is by telephone or in person, should be positive and upbeat.

If your company conducts an accident investigation, keep in mind that an important purpose of such an investigation should be to determine how the accident occurred so that such occurrences can be prevented in the future.

Studies have shown that prior communication and post-injury demonstrations of concern by the employer can result in higher levels of worker satisfaction and reduced time lost from work — factors that contribute to lower program costs.

- **ENSURE PROMPT TREATMENT FROM THE RIGHT MEDICAL PROVIDERS**

Helping the injured worker get immediate medical attention pays off for both worker and employer on several levels. Typically, the sooner injured workers receive proper treatment, the sooner they may return to work.

Under the New Jersey workers' compensation law, the employer and/or its insurance carrier select the medical providers to treat injured workers for work-related injuries. Such control of medical treatment is an important employer right and obligation.

When a workplace accident or occupational exposure occurs, the injured worker should be offered prompt medical treatment. Employers should keep in mind that providing medical coverage is not considered an admission of liability (N.J.S.A. 34:15-15).

VII. CLAIM PETITIONS IN WORKERS' COMPENSATION

Employees who are injured on the job may file a workers' compensation claim petition with the New Jersey Division of Workers' Compensation. Issues may include compensability of the claim (whether the injury/illness is considered work related), the type and extent of medical treatment, and/or the payment of temporary disability benefits. Further, a claim petition may seek permanent disability benefits and, in cases of alleged job-related death, dependency benefits. Workers are generally represented by an attorney but they may file a claim petition on their own (pro se). An insurance carrier will usually provide a legal defense on behalf of a covered employer. If you are a self-insured corporation, it is required that you or your third-party administrator obtain legal representation to defend your interests.

The vast majority of claim petitions are settled by mutual agreement as to the amount of benefits due and extent of disability. In cases where an agreement is not reached, a workers' compensation judge will resolve the disputed issues.

An insurance carrier, drawing on their extensive knowledge of the law and taking into consideration all the pertinent facts of the case, can make a decision to accept or deny a claim. Stay aware of whether claims are investigated timely, whether benefits are being paid on time, and whether claims are being disputed or accepted. The employer plays a key role in working with the carrier and the injured worker to ensure that the system works smoothly and fairly.

VIII. WHAT ELSE DOES AN EMPLOYER NEED TO KNOW?

- ### DISCRIMINATION COMPLAINTS

It is unlawful for any employer to discharge or otherwise discriminate against an employee because the employee claimed or attempted to claim workers' compensation benefits or because the employee testified or is about to testify in a workers' compensation matter. The Division of Workers' Compensation is responsible for investigating such claims.

- ### SECOND INJURY FUND

The Second Injury Fund (SIF), which is administered by the Division of Workers' Compensation, makes benefit payments to injured workers who are totally and permanently disabled as a result of work-related injuries combined with pre-existing disabilities.

The Second Injury Fund was established to encourage employers to hire disabled workers. The employer only pays for the work-related aspect of the total disability award.

- ### DIVISION OF WORKERS' COMPENSATION WEB SITE

The Division of Workers' Compensation maintains an Internet Web site that contains the latest information on New Jersey workers' compensation, including legal and administrative procedures, forms and brochures, statistical data, and program details.

The Web address is *http://nj.gov/labor/wc/*

- ### CONTACTS FOR QUESTIONS

If you have questions about New Jersey's workers' compensation program, please contact:

New Jersey Department of Labor and Workforce Development
Division of Workers' Compensation
P.O. Box 381
Trenton, NJ 08625-0381
(609) 292-2515
Fax: (609) 984-2515
e-mail: dwc@dol.state.nj.us

If you have questions about workers' compensation insurance rates or obtaining coverage, please contact:

New Jersey Compensation Rating and Inspection Bureau
60 Park Place
Newark, NJ 07102
www.njcrib.com
(973) 622-6014

WC-373 (10/09)

9

FINANCIAL MANAGEMENT

FINANCIAL MANAGEMENT

Business owners must manage the financial health of their business just as they manage the work performed by their employees at the job site. Business failures are more often due to time and financial problems than construction problems. Problems can be avoided and a business can be successful by following good finance and business management principles.

Starting a construction business can be expensive. How much will it cost to get the business up and running? What will happen if payment for a job comes in later than expected? When will the bills be paid? Will there be cash "flat spots" between jobs? What effect could this have on the business? What is the break-even point of the business – the right combination of gross profit on jobs, volume of work, and fixed overhead costs to show an overall net profit in the end?

This chapter introduces basic financial management principles associated with forming a business. Because this is a complicated subject, with many more issues than can be discussed here, individuals starting a business are encouraged to seek out other resources should they have more in-depth questions.

Information in this chapter gives a brief overview that will help the contractor begin to:

- Become familiar with basic accounting terms;
- Understand financial recordkeeping and accounting systems;
- Identify essential financial reports;
- Recognize what financial reports and ratios tell about a business; and
- Manage construction equipment costs.

BASIC ACCOUNTING TERMS

Accounting: The system of recording and summarizing business and financial transactions and analyzing, verifying, and reporting the results, primarily to be used in making economic decisions.

Accumulated Depreciation: The amount of a long-term asset's cost that has been allocated to Depreciation Expense since the time the asset was acquired.

Asset: Items that are resources owned by a company and which have future economic value that can be measured and expressed in dollars. Examples include cash, investments, accounts receivable, inventory, supplies, land, buildings, equipment, and vehicles. Assets are divided into current assets and fixed assets.

Budgeting: A process of developing periodic forecasts of future income and expenses for a fixed period of time. Actual income is periodically compared to the budget so management is given adequate feedback on the budget's effectiveness.

Cash Budget: An organized method of comparing expected receipts against planned expenses to ensure that there are sufficient funds to meet payroll, accounts payable, and other short-term obligations.

Cash Discount: A reduction in the selling price of merchandise or a percentage off the invoice price in exchange for payment under agreed upon terms.

Current Asset: An asset that can be converted into cash within one year or one operating cycle. Examples are cash, accounts receivable, inventory, loans owed to the business, notes receivable, and prepaid expenses. Current assets are presented in the order of liquidity, i.e., cash, temporary investments, accounts receivable, inventory, supplies, prepaid insurance.

Current Liability: Obligations due within one year or one operating cycle of the balance sheet date. Examples are notes payable, accounts payable, unpaid wages, and taxes due.

Depreciation: The process of allocating the cost of a tangible fixed asset over that asset's useful life. For instance, if a $7,000 piece of equipment has a useful life of seven years, its value on the balance sheet can be reduced by $1,000 each year. The $1,000 is entered in the accounts as an expense for each of the seven years. Land may not be depreciated.

Fixed Asset: A term used when referring to property, buildings, equipment, furniture and fixtures. It includes tangible property used in the operation of a business that does not fall into the category of current assets. Fixed assets other than land are depreciated.

Liability: Obligations of a company. Amounts owed to lenders and suppliers. Liabilities often have the word "payable" in the account title. Liabilities also include amounts received in advance for a future service to be performed.

Net Working Capital: Current assets minus current liabilities. For example, if a business has Current Assets of $30,000, and Current Liabilities of $20,000, then the Net Working Capital is $10,000.

Operating Cycle: The time required to purchase or manufacture a company's inventory, sell the product (goods or services), and collect the revenue from the sale of the product.

Owners' Equity: The book value of a company equal to the recorded amounts of assets minus the recorded amounts of liabilities. For example, if a business has Total Assets of $50,000 and Total Liabilities of $30,000, then its Net Worth is $20,000. Sometimes it is called Net Worth, or Stockholders' Equity or Partners' Equity.

Source Document: The foundation of accounting work. Includes check stubs, invoices received, invoices sent, cash receipt records, time cards, or other documents that are the basis for accounting journals or entries.

RECORDKEEPING SYSTEMS

A recordkeeping system is an important step in the accounting process. Recordkeeping organizes information that supports financial statements, tax returns, bid estimates, customer invoices, and analysis of business operations. In general, well-maintained financial records help to increase a business' success.

When recording transactions, remember to observe the following business practices:
- Always keep business and personal finances separate.
- Identify source of receipts. When cash is received, record the source.
- Record all deposits and expenses as they occur.
- Do not write checks payable to "Cash." Why the check was written is easily forgotten and difficult to substantiate. There is also no proof of how the money was spent. If a check must be written to "cash," follow up with a receipt showing the paid expense.
- When making a personal draw out of the business, the owner should make the check payable to him or herself, not payable to "cash." The draw should then be deposited into the owner's personal bank account.
- Record business expenses when they occur. To account for expenses, write a check when paying them. When writing checks, be sure to record in the checkbook register the amount, date, purpose, and to whom each check was written.

- Substantiate items on income tax returns. This allows the business to verify the items reported if the IRS examines the business' income tax return. A business must be able to support income and expense items on the return by sales slips, invoices, receipts, bank deposit slips, canceled checks, and other documents. These documents are necessary for adequate and complete records.

Good recordkeeping practices provide adequate records or sufficient proof of deductions. Receipts, canceled checks, or a petty cash log will provide such proof.

ACCOUNTING SYSTEMS

An accounting system is a set of procedures to collect, record, and summarize business transactions. There are different accounting methods that may be used to recognize business revenue, but any method used should include a system of controls to safeguard the information and provide accurate financial statements the business needs to use to make sound financial management decisions.

A. METHODS OF ACCOUNTING

An accounting method is a set of rules that dictates when to record business income and expenses. There are two basic methods: the cash method and the accrual method.

The Cash Method: This method records income when cash is received and records expenses when paid. In this system, a sale on credit is not recorded until the payment is received, and invoices from suppliers are not recorded until the bills are paid. Although the cash method is simple to use, it generally does not give an accurate picture of the business' real financial position as noncash transactions are not included. In addition, this method is not always acceptable for tax reporting purposes.

The Accrual Method: This method records income at the time the income is earned, even though payment may not be received until later. Expenses are recorded at the time incurred, even though payment may not be made until later. A disadvantage of using the accrual method is the additional required recordkeeping. An advantage is that financial statements show more thorough and useful information. The accrual method is the generally accepted method of accounting for the construction industry.

A framework of accounting practices has evolved over time for the construction industry. There are even accounting software programs designed specifically for the construction industry. Each project, and its related costs and incomes, can be easily tracked and managed. As costs and incomes occur, they are accounted directly or indirectly to the applicable project.

B. REVENUE RECOGNITION

A business owner must choose how he or she is going to "recognize" or "measure" the amount of revenue and profit or loss. Revenue comes from providing services and materials to customers. This revenue results in a profit or loss after expenses are deducted. In order to measure the revenues in a given accounting period, the owner needs to select the method of accounting that most accurately reflects his or her business activity.

Construction contracts often extend over long periods of time, making it difficult to correctly account for revenues and expenses. For construction contractors where contracts extend over a year or overlap the company's year end, revenue can be recognized using two methods:

Percentage-of-Completion Method (PCM). Under the PCM method, revenue, costs, and profits or losses are recognized in each accounting period as construction progresses to completion. This method typically is used for high-dollar and long-term contracts. The contractor's accounting system must provide reasonable estimates for completion rates and reliable recordkeeping for job cost control during progress of work. This system will support the contractor's progress billings.

Completed-Contract Method (CCM). Under this method, revenue, costs, and profits or losses are deferred until the project is complete. It is most often used for smaller or short-term contracts. The primary disadvantage to the completed contract method is that, when taxes are due, it does not represent the contractor's current financial status.

C. ACCOUNTING SYSTEM MECHANICS

Accounting systems range from simple checkbook registers to comprehensive computer programs. The best system for each business depends on the business' complexity, need for information, and ability to use the information generated. Either a single-entry or double-entry system may be used.

Single Entry. The single-entry system is a simple listing of transactions, like keeping a checkbook register. The single-entry system is the easiest to keep. A number of "write-it-once" single-entry systems are available at office supply stores.

Double Entry. A double-entry system records each transaction separately using credits and debits that must "balance" or equal each other. The double-entry system has built-in checks and balances that provide accuracy and control. It can be complicated to learn, although computerized accounting systems perform the double entries automatically and simplify the process significantly.

Journals and ledgers are used as components of an accounting system. Transactions are entered in the appropriate journal, usually on a daily basis. At the end of the month, the journal entries are added up and posted to a general ledger, which is summarized and used to prepare the financial statements. Journals are found in both handwritten and computerized accounting systems. Typical journals include:

- The *payroll journal,* which contains employee wage information. This system is set up to gather and monitor labor cost data broken down by specific job types. The data may be used for future contract estimates.
- The *cash disbursements journal*, in which all checks written are recorded, including the amount paid and the purpose of the payment.
- The *cash receipts journal*, showing all cash received and the source of the receipts.
- The *general journal*, which is used to record transactions that are not captured in the other journals or to make corrections.

D. INTERNAL CONTROLS

Internal controls are systems established to safeguard a business' assets, minimize errors, and assure information received about the business is reliable. The following are examples of internal control procedures.

Accounts Payable. All bills should be paid from the business bank account. No check should be signed by the owner or authorized officer without first reviewing and reconciling related documents such as the vendor invoice and packing slip. The invoice should be marked "paid" to reduce the potential for double payment.

Accounts Receivable. All receipts from customers should be compared to the original invoice sent to verify the payment amount. Receipts should be deposited in the business bank account as soon as possible.

Compare to Budget. The authorized officer or owner should compare actual cash receipts and disbursements with budgeted amounts and follow up if there are significant variances.

Monthly Bank Statements. The authorized officer or owner should receive monthly bank statements unopened. He or she opens and reviews the statement and canceled checks, then delivers them to the bookkeeper for reconciliation.

Payment by Check. Except for small expenditures out of petty cash (see below), all business expenses should be paid by check, electronic transfer, or credit card in order to leave a traceable trail of the transaction. Checks should be pre-numbered and should be approved by the authorized corporate officer or business owner before payment is made.

Petty Cash Fund. Petty cash is a small amount of money kept on hand for payment of incidental expenses. One person should be in charge of the petty cash and must keep records of amounts spent. These records should be reviewed by the business owner or bookkeeper before the petty cash fund is replenished.

Separation of Duties. A good system of checks and balances can be achieved by separating duties so no one individual handles an entire transaction from start to finish. Separating duties may be difficult in small businesses with few employees. In those cases, additional oversight responsibility falls on the business owner.

Signature Plates and Check Stock. Signature plates, mechanical check signers, and check stock should be kept under the custodial control of the authorized officer or owner.

As the business grows, consult with an accounting practitioner to modify internal controls to fit the volume of revenue and size of operations. It is important that the benefits achieved from these controls are worth the time and cost of applying them.

E. FINANCIAL STATEMENTS

If the accounting entries properly record business transactions and operations, the financial statements will accurately represent the financial condition of the business. This is crucial if the owner is asked to provide financial statements to lenders, bankers, vendors, or regulating agencies to verify the financial condition of the business. Financial statements for a very small company may be contained in only a few pages, whereas a medium or large company's financial statements may be lengthy.

The duration of time the financial statements cover is referred to as an "accounting period." The needs of the business dictate how often financial statements are prepared. At a minimum, financial statements are prepared annually. However, quarterly or monthly statements are recommended because project activities can change in short periods of time and affect the amounts on the financial statements.

The basic financial statements are:

- Income statement.
- Balance sheet.
- Cash flow statement.

1. INCOME STATEMENT

The income statement is sometimes referred to as the "statement of operations," or "profit and loss statement." It reports the revenue and expenses that occurred over a given time period with the resulting profit or loss.

The income statement contains the following categories:

- **Revenue.** The operating income from the normal business activity of the company. Nonoperating revenues are shown as other income.
- **Direct costs.** Include items that can be charged directly to a specific project. Materials, subcontracts, labor, equipment rentals, permits, and bonds are examples of direct costs. Included in labor are payroll taxes, insurance, and other employee benefits.
- **Indirect costs.** Include costs that cannot be traced to a single project, but apply to a number of different jobs. An example is a company vehicle and its fuel.

- **Gross profit.** This is a subtotal of the excess of revenues over direct and indirect costs. For example, a company reports a gross profit of $180,000 after subtracting direct job costs of $592,000 and indirect job costs of $28,000 from total revenue of $800,000.
- **General and administrative expenses.** Include such expenses as heat, electricity, office rent, office insurance, office supplies, furniture, telephone, legal expenses, donations, advertising, and the salaries of office employees.
- **Other income/expenses (nonoperating revenues or expenses).** Include items not directly related to the company's primary business. For example, gains or losses resulting from the sale of assets.
- **Net income or net profit**. This is the bottom line after all costs, expenses, and income taxes have been deducted from revenue.

The income statement can be summarized as follows:

Revenue – Direct Job Costs – Indirect Job Costs = Gross Profit
and
Gross Profit – General and Administrative Expenses – Taxes = Net Income

Although this information offers insight into the company's historical performance, the income statement only reflects the financial conditions for the accounting period for which the overall financial statement is generated. An example of an income statement is shown in Figure 9-1.

2. BALANCE SHEET

The balance sheet is a one- or two-page summary showing a company's assets, liabilities, and owners' equity for an accounting period. The balance sheet is like a "snapshot" of the company's financial condition at a particular point in time, while the income statement is more like a video showing activity or a period of time.

The balance sheet lists all major assets such as cash, bank accounts, equipment, property, contracts, and anything else of value owned by or owed to the company. It also lists all liabilities such as overhead expenses, debts, rental, lease, mortgage payments, and anything else that the company owes. Finally, the balance sheets show the owners' equity, or net worth, which reports owner investment into the business plus profits not yet distributed to the owners. An example of a balance sheet is shown in Figure 9-2.

The basic equation for a balance sheet is:

Assets = Liabilities + Owners' Equity

3. CASH FLOW STATEMENT

Cash flow refers to the money received by the contractor for work performed and money disbursed for expenses like office rent, materials, or payments to subcontractors. The cash flow statement summarizes the company's investing, financing, and operating activities for a specific accounting period. It shows the source of funds (where the money came from) and use of funds (where the money went). An example of a cash flow statement is shown in Figure 9-3.

Figure 9-1

SAMPLE INCOME STATEMENT
For the period ended December 31, 20XX

Revenue	$800,000	100%
Direct Costs		
Labor	224,000	28%
Materials	220,000	28%
Subcontracts	147,200	18%
Total Direct Costs	592,000	74%
Indirect Costs		
Job Overhead	28,000	3%
Total Indirect Costs	28,000	3%
Total Costs	620,000	77%
Gross Profit	180,000	23%
General Overhead		
General Office Salaries	48,000	
Advertising	1,600	
Auto/Truck - Gas and Oil	14,400	
Auto/Truck - Repairs and Maintenance	2,800	
Contributions	480	
Depreciation	8,000	
Dues and Subscriptions	480	
Insurance - General	3,000	
Interest	1,640	
Legal and Accounting	1,200	
Miscellaneous	1,200	
Office Expenses	960	
Payroll and Insurance	2,880	
Repairs and Maintenance	480	
Sales Tax	5,480	
Small Tools and Supplies	2,400	
Taxes and Licenses	2,200	
Telephone	2,400	
Travel and Entertainment	2,840	
Utilities	1,200	
Total General Overhead	$143,240	18%
Net Income Before Taxes	$36,760	5%

Figure 9-2

SAMPLE BALANCE SHEET
December 31, 20XX
Assets

Current Assets

Cash		$22,400
Accounts Receivable		73,160
Cost and Estimated Earnings in Excess of Billings on Uncompleted Contracts		16,440
Inventory		32,000
Total Current Assets		$144,000
Property and Equipment	$300,000	
Less Accumulated Depreciation	(57,000)	243,000
Total Assets		$387,000

Liabilities

Current Liabilities

Accounts Payable	$28,500
Notes Payable	72,116
Billings in Excess of Costs and Estimated Earnings on Uncompleted Contracts	204
Current Portion of Long-Term Debt	10,000
Total Current Liabilities	$110,820
Mortgages Payable	125,600
Contracts Payable	8,000
Total Liabilities	$244,420

Owners' Equity

Common Stock, $1 par Value, Issued and Outstanding	1,000
Retained Earnings	141,580
Total Owners' Equity	142,580
Total Liability and Owners' Equity	$387,000

Figure 9-3

SAMPLE CASH FLOW STATEMENT
For the period ended December 31, 20XX

Cash Flow Provided from Operating Activities:

Net Income	$ 132,450
Adjustments to reconcile Net Income to Net Cash - Non-cash adjustments for Depreciation	23,201

Changes in Balance Sheet accounts that affect Operating Activities:

(Increase) Decrease in Accounts Receivable	(92,946)
(Increase) Decrease in Inventory	14,183
(Increase) Decrease in Prepaid Expenses	(1,200)
Increase (Decrease) in Accounts Payable	28,708
Increase (Decrease) in Payroll Taxes Payable	(2,395)
Increase (Decrease) in Credit Line	6,058
Increase (Decrease) in Income Taxes Payable	236
Increase (Decrease) in Employees Payable	2,005

Net Cash (Used) Provided by Operating Activities	**$ 110,300**

Cash Flow (Used) Provided by Investing Activities

(Increase) Decrease in Fixed Assets	(28,245)
Net Cash (Used) Provided by Investing Activities	**$ (28,245)**

Cash Flow (Used) Provided by Financing Activities

Net Borrowing (Payment) on Note Payable	(122,590)
Net Cash (Used) Provided by Financing Activities	**$ (122,590)**
Net Increase (Decrease) in Cash	**$ (40,535)**
Cash, Beginning of Period	**$ 630,225**
Cash, End of Period	**$ 589,690**

ANALYZING FINANCIAL INFORMATION

Once financial statements have been prepared, this information should be thoroughly reviewed and analyzed for evaluating the financial condition of the business and for preparing future estimates and bids.

A. FINANCIAL RATIOS

Financial ratios and formulas applied to information from financial statements are used by many business managers to help evaluate the business. Financial ratios show relationships between figures on the financial statements and give information about a company's financial strengths and weaknesses. Managers in any type of business should be able to interpret financial ratios and make appropriate decisions regarding the future financial direction of their business. Comparing financial ratios over a period of time allows a company to identify potential financial problems and take appropriate action.

There are three common financial ratios computed from balance sheets:

1. **Quick Ratio (or "Acid Test")**. Measures financial "liquidity" of a business to pay current liabilities with current assets such as cash and accounts receivable, without selling inventory.

$$\frac{\text{Current Assets - Inventory}}{\text{Current Liabilities}} = \text{Quick Ratio}$$

2. **Current Ratio**. Measures a company's financial strength to pay current liabilities by only using current assets, including inventory. The higher the current ratio, the greater difference between current liabilities and a company's ability to pay them (the company is at less risk of default).

$$\frac{\text{Current Assets}}{\text{Current Liabilities}} = \text{Current Ratio}$$

3. **Debt-to-Equity**. Measures the relationship between capital contributed and invested by the owners and the funds provided by creditors. The higher the ratio, the greater the risk to a current or future creditor. A lower ratio means the company is more financially stable and may be in a better position to borrow.

$$\frac{\text{Total Liabilities}}{\text{Total Equity}} = \text{Debt-to-Equity}$$

B. OPERATING BUDGETS

An operating budget is created annually based on information gathered from previous years showing how much it cost to operate the business for a year. Operating budgets help determine how much company overhead to include when bidding projects. These costs are categorized under general and administrative expenses on the income statement.

The budgeting process includes:

- Identifying the budget items and estimating expenditures for the coming year.
- Monitoring and recording the actual expenditures when they occur.
- Comparing and analyzing the difference between the budgeted and actual amounts.
- Taking corrective action and making adjustments when needed.

By comparing budgeted and actual amounts for the same period from previous years, a business can improve budget analysis, see trends, and collect important historical information.

C. ESTIMATING WORKSHEETS

Generally, expenses from the income statement are used for estimating company overhead and an appropriate markup in pricing work when creating the job estimate. Estimating worksheets help in analyzing and comparing estimates from prior jobs. This will show how closely the estimate compares to actual time, revenue, and expenses. If the estimate was effective, it covers job costs, project and company overhead, and results in a profitable project. If the estimate was not effective, the estimator will know where to adjust pricing in future proposals.

One area that is often overlooked in the estimating process is bad debts. Accounts receivable should regularly be analyzed to obtain an estimate of uncollectable accounts. A high percentage of bad debts indicates that the company's procedures for granting credit to customers or for collecting accounts receivable need to be reviewed. The best method for estimating future bad debt losses, is to base estimates on the company's previous experience with bad debts. Accurate estimating of bad debts is required for preparation of a cash budget and for an accurate representation of the company's financial picture.

D. WORKING CAPITAL

Working capital is a measure of a business' ability to meet short-term obligations. It measures cash plus other assets that will soon result in cash (like receivables) compared to short-term debts. Bankers and other creditors look for a positive working capital amount as an indication of a business' likelihood to meet current obligations.

A company's working capital is calculated by subtracting current liabilities from current assets. "Current" is defined as within the next 12 months. The difference between the liabilities and assets gives an amount of money left over, as if the business were to suddenly pay off all current debts by liquidating current assets.

Current Assets – Current Liabilities = Working Capital

Calculating working capital helps determine how well a business will survive in the short term. Successful contractors maintain enough working capital to meet all business requirements.

E. CASH FLOW

Cash flow is the inflow of available funds to a business and the outflow of cash for paying obligations. A positive cash flow means cash received was greater than cash paid out. A negative cash flow means receipts were less than disbursements.

Inadequate cash flow is one of the major causes of failure for small construction businesses. A business must maintain enough cash to meet payroll, pay for materials, make equipment payments, and satisfy other financial obligations as they come due. This can be tricky because expenditures often must be made before cash is received from customers.

The following are some keys to effectively manage cash flow:
- Send out accurate invoices. If prices or quantities do not match what the customer expects, it could take time to straighten out the problems and for the business to get paid.
- Send invoices on a timely basis. Customers need to receive a bill before they will pay.
- Follow up with slow-paying customers on a regular basis.
- Prepare careful estimates for bids and proposals, including sufficient amounts to cover overhead and provide a profit.
- Pay bills on time and take advantage of early payment discounts.
- If bills cannot be paid on time, contact suppliers to work out a payment plan.
- If funds are limited, consider leasing or renting rather than buying equipment.

F. JOB COSTING

Job costing is the process of tracking the costs associated with a work item over multiple projects. The job-cost system should be tailored to a particular business defining costs and revenue in units as well as dollars. Revenue units refer to the kind of work that is done. A revenue unit for a drywall contractor would be boards hung or finished. A revenue unit for a paving contractor might be square feet of paving completed or tons of asphalt mix used. Cost units refer to hours of labor or equipment and quantities of material used.

When job-cost reports have been prepared, they need to be reconciled to the general ledger. To do this, the costs for all jobs are added together. This sum should equal the direct costs on the income statement. Job costing data is extremely useful to increase accuracy in project estimating. By analyzing job-costing records, a business will be able to take corrective action before a job ends. Job-costing data from previous projects can be used as the basis of the new estimate.

G. BREAK-EVEN ANALYSIS

The break-even point is the volume at which total revenue equals total costs. It is the point where the right combination of gross profit on jobs, volume of work, and fixed overhead costs are combined to show an overall net profit. The break-even point is calculated by the following formula:

$$\text{Break Even} = \frac{\textbf{Overhead Expenses}}{\text{Gross Profit Margin (GPM) \%}}$$

GPM % is calculated as follows:

$$\text{Gross profit margin \%} = \frac{\textbf{Revenue - Direct Job Costs – Indirect Job Costs}}{\text{Revenues}}$$

Break-even analysis emphasizes the importance of a well-prepared operating budget in addition to accurate job-cost data. The analysis can be used in selecting, pricing, and budgeting projects for profit. It also helps determine the gross profit needed on jobs to cover overhead.

MANAGING CONSTRUCTION COSTS

A. EQUIPMENT COSTS

Equipment is generally understood to be all tools that are purchased or rented by the contractor to complete a project. Hand tools, cords, hoses, forklifts, graders, and cranes should all be considered equipment.

Obtaining and maintaining construction equipment is expensive. Sometimes buying equipment is financially advantageous; other times renting or leasing is preferable. In addition to extent of use, the decision to purchase, lease, or rent can depend on a number of financial considerations such as interest rates, tax regulation, or a company's debt load.

In most cases, short-term renting of equipment carries significantly higher costs than longer-term leasing or ownership. Still, renting equipment has advantages. It makes little financial sense to incur the entire cost of purchasing equipment that is used only occasionally or for a short time. Renting is also effective for temporary replacement, such as when a piece of equipment is being repaired. When a project is far away, renting from a nearby source could be more cost effective than hauling equipment a long distance. Renting can also be financially prudent when highly specialized equipment is needed. In some cases, it is better to rent equipment that has high or specialized maintenance requirements. The rental company is usually responsible for maintenance and repair.

Leasing differs from renting in that leasing generally requires a longer payment contract – typically, one to five years. The popularity of equipment leasing tends to vary in relation to tax law, interest rates, and the economic climate. Equipment leasing increases when tax laws support it, interest rates are high, and/or the construction economic climate is moderate. Over the middle- to long-term, leasing can result in substantially lower costs than renting. Another advantage of leasing is that it allows a business to keep upgrading to the latest models each time the lease ends.

Leasing may also be more attractive than purchasing because leasing is usually accounted for as an operating expense rather than as a long-term liability (such as a bank loan for equipment purchase). By not being considered fixed assets, leasing frees up working capital.

A contractor should be aware that lease contracts can vary significantly. Equipment maintenance agreements, options to buy, excessive use charges, and a myriad of other clauses can lead to leasing costs nearly as low as ownership costs or nearly as high as rental costs. Each leasing agreement needs to be read carefully to understand the terms and conditions within before it is signed.

The most common means to acquire construction equipment is by purchase. Construction equipment purchases should be viewed as a significant long-term investment. Before a final decision is made to purchase equipment, a business should consider:

- Current and future need;
- Equipment suitability;
- Equipment reliability;
- Equipment features and future add-ons;
- Maintenance costs;
- Insurance costs;
- Financing terms;
- Warrantees;
- Dealer support; and
- Resale value.

Rather than being viewed as an operating expense, purchased equipment is considered a capital investment. When the purchased equipment is well utilized, appropriately financed, and amply maintained, the overall costs can be well below those incurred by renting or leasing the same piece of equipment.

1. ACCOUNTING FOR EQUIPMENT COSTS

Accounting procedures for equipment costs vary but must conform to tax regulations. Regardless of whether the equipment is rented, leased, or purchased, an internal rate for each piece of equipment is established. The rate for each piece of equipment should include all operating expenses, such as fuel, oil, filters, tires, equipment repair, storage, delivery, finance costs, insurance, and taxes. The internal rate does not include transportation costs to or from the job site, nor does it include operator costs. This rate is charged as a cost against a project depending on the time the equipment is used on the project.

Each separate equipment unit will show the projects on which it was used as well as the total hours of use. All rental, lease, purchase, maintenance, and repair costs are also accounted for in the equipment unit. By accounting for each piece of equipment in this manner, a company will be able determine whether the equipment is being adequately and profitably used. This equipment performance information can also assist in the decision to upgrade (or downgrade) to newer or differing equipment.

2. EQUIPMENT DEPRECIATION

Because of wear and obsolescence, almost all construction equipment is continually declining in value. This loss of value is called depreciation. Depreciation is a cost of doing business and a legitimate tax deduction. Depreciation costs include the initial cost of the equipment, taxes, freight, delivery, and set-up expenses. Depreciation does not include financing and interest costs.

In most cases, construction equipment does not lose all or most of its value in one year. For this reason, the Internal Revenue Service has created depreciation schedules (see MACRS below). The schedule allows the cost of depreciation to be spread across the number of years of the life of the equipment. Depreciation schedules differ according to the type of equipment. For example, automobiles and light-duty trucks have a three-year schedule; most other construction equipment has a five-year schedule.

The **straight-line depreciation method** is the simplest and most commonly used method for calculating depreciation. Under the straight-line depreciation method, the basis of the asset is written off evenly over the useful life of the asset. The same amount of depreciation is taken each year. Though equipment decreases in value more in the first year than in later years, straight-line depreciation is still commonly used by contractors for estimating purposes.

Accelerated depreciation allows for a greater proportion of equipment costs to be taken during the earlier years of an asset's life. For financial accounting purposes, accelerated depreciation is generally used when an asset is expected to be much more productive during its early years, so that depreciation expense will more accurately represent how much of an asset's usefulness is being used up each year. The Modified Accelerated Cost Recovery System is the only fully accelerated schedule approved by the Internal Revenue Service.

B. MODIFIED ACCELERATED COST RECOVERY SYSTEM

The Modified Accelerated Cost Recovery System (MACRS) is the statutory procedure used to compute cost recovery deductions for all tangible assets placed in service after 1986. MACRS is the current method of accelerated asset depreciation required by the United States income tax code. Under MACRS, all assets are divided into classes that dictate the number of years over which an asset's cost will be recovered. Different depreciation methods can be used for company management and for tax purposes. The same company may use the straight-line method for financial statements and the MACRS accelerated rates for income tax purposes.

C. MATERIAL COSTS AND ACCOUNTING

Materials are defined as anything supplied that becomes part of the final project, such as concrete, fasteners, lumber, steel, and drywall. Delivery, material inspection, and storage costs are considered part of material costs. Material costs do not include installation, service, or progress inspections.

The process of acquiring and accounting for materials is fundamental to the success of any business. Accounting and financial concerns apply to purchasing, expediting, receiving, and returns phases. For example, in the purchasing phase, the accounting system should include a systematic way to compare material prices and track purchases from ordering through delivery. Such a system can ensure that the right materials are ordered and that they are ordered at the best price.

Shipping and delivery expenses are also an area of scrutiny. Shifting of delivery costs to the contractor can add substantial amounts. The terms FOB "free on board," or FAS "free alongside the vessel" call for materials to be delivered with no expense to the purchaser. As examples, the contractor would, in such cases, stamp or write on the purchase orders: "FOB job site" if delivered by truck or train or "FAS port storage" if the materials are to be delivered by ship.

D. PAYMENT TERMS

Payment terms for materials or services can be whatever is agreed upon by both the buying and selling parties. This can vary from full payment in advance, cash on delivery, or any of several scheduled payments. The most common business method is "net 30," meaning the bill is to be paid in full within 30 days from the date of invoice – usually the date the materials were shipped.

Many vendors offer discounted payment terms in order to encourage prompt payment. For example, a "2/10, net 30" offers a 2% discount for payment in full within 10 days of the invoice date; otherwise, the full billing amount is due 30 days after the date of the invoice.

A contractor should take advantage of cash discounts not only because they can add up to substantial amounts ($1,000 for every $50,000 in materials), but also because regular failure to do so is an indication to vendors that the contractor may have cash flow problems. In cost-plus contracts, cash discounts usually go to the contractor, and are counted as contractor earned income. Other contracts recoup discounts to the project budget.

E. PROGRESS PAYMENTS

Construction contracts regularly designate partial payments to the contractor as the work progresses. Most commonly, payments are made monthly. Other projects pay following the completion of specific events, such as excavation, foundation work, etc. In either case, periodic payments are based or justified by the work accomplished since the previous payment. A retainage, usually 10%, is withheld from the payment and is paid when the project is completed.

A written request is needed for each progress payment. With each request, the contractor normally includes a lien waiver and an affidavit that the contractor's payments to subcontractors and suppliers are current. The payments are often approved by the project architect, based on adequate evidence that the work the payment covers has been adequately performed.

Late payments by the owner can be a serious problem for contractors. Before a contract is entered into, every prudent contractor will examine the owner's financial capacity – at least as it pertains to the project. Many construction contracts allow the contractor to request and receive financing and credit information about the owner.

The Prompt Payment Act requires federal agencies to make contractor payments within 14 days after receiving a progress payment application. The contractor must then pay subcontractors within seven days after being paid, unless cause can be shown to withhold the payment.

1. PROGRESS PAYMENTS FOR LUMP-SUM CONTRACTS

As with all progress payments, pay requests for a lump-sum contract are based on the percentage of work items performed. In the case of the lump-sum contract, work is estimated by the costs incurred by the contractor and by the invoices presented to the contractor by the subcontractors since the last payment. A breakdown of these costs is called a "schedule of values." The schedule of values breaks the project down into cost components. Cost components occur in sequence, in that they correspond to the sequence of work items being completed. The schedule allows the architect or owner to easily check the contractor's pay requests against the completed work.

It is not expected that the schedule of values will allow for balanced payments through the entire project. Early payments tend to be a bit higher. The initial costs associated with moving in and setting up a project, as well as a portion of general overhead, bonding, insurance, and taxes can place a substantial burden on a company's cash flow.

The process of recouping these expenses early in the project is known as "front-end loading." Front-end loading consists of figuring such expenses disproportionately into the early work items (excavation, foundation work, etc.). These costs are not shown on the cost breakdown; they are included in the listed work items.

2. PROGRESS PAYMENTS FOR UNIT-PRICE CONTRACTS

Progress payments for unit-price contracts are less arbitrary than for lump-sum contracts. Unit-price payments are based on the actual number of completed work items (cubic yards, tons, lineal feet, number of units). Because of the many separate work items, the payment request may be lengthy. The payment amount is calculated by multiplying the unit-price by the number of units completed since the previous payment.

F. PERIODIC PAYMENTS FOR COST-PLUS CONTRACTS

The one exception to the rule that payments to contractors are based on actual work performed is the cost-plus contract. Periodic payments for cost-plus contracts are based on expenses rather than work, and therefore, are not true progress payments. This, however, does not mean the contractor has any less liability to perform the work for the expenses that are paid. It simply recognizes that payments under the cost-plus contract correspond directly to costs, rather than to work. In order to justify payment, the contractor needs to submit copies of payrolls, invoices, and receipts.

Payments can be calculated in a variety of ways. Some contracts designate monthly submitting of costs. The payment will cover those costs, plus add the agreed-upon profit in proportion to the costs. Other cost-plus contracts stipulate that owners make periodic advance payments to allow the contractor to purchase materials and pay workers. In such cases, the contractor submits a payment estimate in advance for the coming month. At the conclusion of the month, the contractor reconciles the advanced payment with the actual costs and the balance is adjusted on the next month's estimate. Some cost-plus contracts designate "constant-balance" bank accounts, wherein the owner regularly deposits funds to cover spending. The contractor submits regular cost statements to account for the overall amounts.

G. PAYMENTS TO SUBCONTRACTORS

After the contractor is paid, the subcontractors are to be promptly paid. To assure that costs are in line with estimates, and to ensure the work performed by subcontractors is adequate, the contractor may use many of the same practices used by the owner. The subcontractor may be required to submit cost breakdowns. Retainage may be withheld from subcontractor pay – usually at the same rate withheld from the contractor. The subcontractor may be required to submit copies of payroll and evidence that supplier payments are current.

If it appears that subcontractors are not paying their bills, the contractor may withhold pay from the subcontractor. However, a contractor may not delay payment to the subcontractor simply to use the money for other purposes. If subcontractors feel payment is excessively tardy or inadequate, redress can be made in a number of ways, including a relief through the contractor's payment bond, by suing for breach of contract, and/or by filing a mechanic's lien.

In the construction industry, the use of joint-check agreements has become common. A joint-check agreement allows a general contractor to make payments due under a subcontract to both the subcontractor and a third party. A joint-check agreement may also be used between the owner, general contractor, and a subcontractor. Under this arrangement, the owner would issue checks jointly to the general contractor and the subcontractor. These agreements are used to avoid lien and bond claims by unpaid second-tier subs and suppliers and to maintain work progress.

H. Final Payment

After the project is completed, corrected of any deficiencies, and finally inspected and accepted, the contractor submits a request for final payment. This request comprises several documents, including waivers of any liens, an affidavit verifying that all workers, suppliers, and subcontractors have been paid, as-built drawings, written warranties, maintenance bonds, any appliance or machine operating and maintenance instructions, and authorization from the performance surety to make the final payment. Of course, the request also contains the final payment amount. This amount includes any residual payments owed to the general contractor, along with the retainage.

Summary

Tracking financial information should be a vital priority for every company. The law requires that construction contractors keep accurate business records. Tax, payroll, insurance, and other financial information must be supplied to various governmental agencies. Banking, insurance, bonding, and other private agencies also require financial information from the contractor. Additionally, the contractor needs adequate and accurate financial information in order to monitor business finances and to aid in making business decisions.

A proper financial accounting system is not limited to maintaining and producing financial records. The contractor's accounting system must provide the types and amounts of financial information that are needed to both control and direct the company toward its greatest potential.

Proper accounting is the basis for job costing, estimating, and project cost control. Additionally, a quality financial system keeps the contractor informed of cash flow and the financial condition of the business. Finally, it provides important support data for legal issues that might come up.

10

TAX LAWS

This chapter provides a general overview of federal tax laws. To get help with specific tax issues, order free publications and forms, and ask tax questions, call an IRS Taxpayer Advocate at 877.777.4778 or go to the IRS Web site at www.irs.gov. Business owners should also consider consulting an accounting practitioner for help in determining the specific forms and reporting deadlines for federal, state, and local taxes for their business.

There are certain business taxes that anyone who starts a company must pay. If the company has employees, there are additional tax-related responsibilities. There are four general taxes that a company must pay:

- Income tax.
- Self-employment tax.
- Employment taxes.
- Excise taxes (for more information on excise taxes, see IRS Publication 510).

INCOME TAX

All businesses, except partnerships, must file an annual income tax return. Partnerships file an information return. Generally, a business must pay taxes on income by making regular payments of estimated tax during the year. For nearly all taxpayers, the due date for the first estimated tax payment of each year is April 15 – the same day the *return* is due for the *previous* year. Subsequent payments are due June 15, September 15, and January 15 of the following year. Although the payments are "quarterly," they are not three months apart. The second payment is due just two months after the first one.

SELF-EMPLOYMENT TAX

Self-employment tax is a Social Security and Medicare tax primarily for individuals who work for themselves. It is similar to the Social Security and Medicare taxes that are withheld from employee paychecks and matched by equal employer contributions. The tax generally is paid quarterly. In 2010, the self-employment tax was 15.3% of net self-employment earnings with 12.4% going to Social Security and 2.9% going to Medicare. Generally, an individual must pay self-employment tax and file Schedule SE (Form 1040) if net earnings from self-employment were $400 or more.

EMPLOYMENT TAXES

Once a company hires employees, the company must pay employment taxes and file forms to report those taxes. Employment taxes include: Social Security and Medicare taxes; federal income tax withholding; and federal unemployment (FUTA) tax. The IRS Publication 15, *Circular E, Employer's Tax Guide*, available online at www.irs.gov, explains an employer's tax responsibilities.

A. Social Security and Medicare Taxes

Social Security and Medicare taxes pay for benefits that workers and their families receive under the Federal Insurance Contributions Act (FICA). These benefits include old-age, survivors, disability, and hospital insurance. Social Security and Medicare taxes are paid equally by the employer and the employee. For every dollar withheld from an employee's paycheck, the employer contributes an equal amount. Employers report Social Security and Medicare taxes withheld on Form 941, *Employer's Quarterly Federal Tax Return*.

The tax rate for Social Security has a wage base limit, which is the maximum wage that is subject to the tax for the year. The Social Security tax rate and wage base are subject to change each year. Employers should consult *Circular E* for the most current tax rates and wage base limit.

B. Federal Income Tax Withholding

Employers must withhold federal and state income taxes from employee paychecks then forward this money to the appropriate government agency. Each employee must fill out a Form W-4, *Employee's Withholding Allowance Certificate*. Employers use the filing status and withholding allowances shown on this form to figure the amount of income tax to withhold from employee wages. A Form W-4 remains in effect until the employee gives the employer a new one.

The deductions for federal withholding are determined based on the employee's Form W-4 and by using the tables provided in *Circular E, Employer's Tax Guide*. Federal income tax withholdings are reported on Form 941, *Employer's Quarterly Federal Tax Return*.

C. Federal Unemployment (FUTA) Tax

Employers report and pay *Federal Unemployment Tax Act* (FUTA), tax separately from Federal Income tax, and Social Security and Medicare taxes. FUTA, together with state unemployment systems, provides for payments of unemployment compensation to workers who have lost their jobs. Most employers pay both a federal and a state unemployment tax. Only the employer pays FUTA tax. This tax is **not** deducted from an employee's wages.

The federal unemployment tax is reported on Form 940, *Employer's Annual Federal Unemployment (FUTA) Tax Return*. The FUTA tax rate in 2010 was 6.2% on the first $7,000 of wages paid to each employee during the calendar year. Employers should read the instructions for Form 940 for the most current FUTA tax rate.

Payroll Reporting Responsibilities for Employers

Because individual circumstances for each employer vary, responsibilities for withholding, depositing, and reporting employment taxes will differ as well. The following information is an overview. A business may wish to consult an accounting practitioner to help determine the business' specific responsibilities.

Federal 941 taxes and reporting. Employers must file Form 941, *Employer's Quarterly Federal Tax Return*, to report federal income tax withholding, Social Security tax, and Medicare tax.

Federal 940 taxes and reporting. Employers must file Form 940, *Employer's Annual Federal Unemployment (FUTA) Tax Return,* annually to report Federal Unemployment Tax and deposit the balance of FUTA due by January 31.

Form W-2 Wage Reporting. Employers must furnish two copies of Form W-2, *Wage and Tax Statement*, to each employee to whom wages were paid during the year before January 31. Copies must also be sent to the Social Security Administration by the last day of February (or last day of March if filing electronically). If an employee quits before the end of the year, the Form W-2 may be given to him or her any time after employment ends but no later than January 31 of the following year. However, if the employee asks for Form W-2 when he or she quits, the form must be given to the employee within 30 days of the request or within 30 days the final wage payment, whichever is later.

The following chart provides a brief summary of an employer's basic responsibilities.

New Employees:	Quarterly (By April 30, July 31, October 31, and January 31):
☐ Verify work eligibility of employees	☐ Deposit FUTA tax if undeposited amount is over $500
☐ Record employees' names and SSNs from Social Security cards	☐ File Form 941 (pay tax with return if not required to deposit)
☐ Ask employees for Form W-4	
Each Payday:	**Annually (see *Circular E* for due dates):**
☐ Withhold federal income tax based on each employee's Form W-4	☐ Remind employees to submit a new Form W-4 if they need to change their withholding
☐ Withhold employee's share of Social Security and Medicare taxes	☐ Ask for a new Form W-4 from employees claiming exemption from income tax withholding
☐ Include advance earned income credit payment in paycheck if employee requested it on Form W-5	☐ Reconcile Forms 941 (or Form 944) with Forms W-2 and W-3
☐ Deposit:	☐ Furnish each employee a Form W-2
• Withheld income tax	☐ File Copy A of Forms W-2 and the transmittal Form W-3 with the SSA
• Withheld and employer Social Security taxes	
• Withheld and employer Medicare taxes	☐ Furnish each other payee a Form 1099 (for example, Form 1099-MISC, Miscellaneous Income)
Note: *Due date of deposit depends on your deposit schedule (monthly or semiweekly)*	☐ File Forms 1099 and the transmittal Form 1096
Annually (By January 31):	☐ File Form 940
☐ File Form 944 if required (pay tax with return if not required to deposit)	☐ File Form 945 for any nonpayroll income tax withholding

PAYROLL TAX DEPOSITS

Withheld taxes are considered to be "trust" funds that do not belong to the business and cannot be used for any other purpose. Funds withheld must be available when tax deposits are due and must be deposited into a financial institution that is an authorized depositary for federal taxes.

Deposits may be made by check, money order, or cash. Unless deposits are made electronically, they must be accompanied by a deposit coupon. All employers are allowed to file using the Electronic Federal Tax Payment System (EFTPS). Some taxpayers (whose taxes exceed certain amounts) are required to use EFTPS. These rules do not apply to Federal Unemployment Tax (FUTA).

EFTPS is a service offered free by the U.S. Department of the Treasury to help business and individual taxpayers pay all their federal taxes electronically. More information about EFTPS can be found online at www.eftps.gov.

There are monthly or semiweekly deposit schedules for determining when to deposit Social Security, Medicare, and withheld income taxes. The deposit schedule that must be used is based on the total tax liability that the business reported on Form 941. Deposit schedules are **not** determined by how often employees are paid. Employers should refer to IRS Publication 15, *Circular E, Employer's Tax Guide,* for more information about how to determine when to deposit employment taxes.

A payroll service may be helpful in meeting these requirements. However, if an employer does not use a payroll service, required tax deposits may be made as shown in the following chart.

Quarter	Period Ending	Quarterly Filing Date
Jan-Feb-Mar	Mar 31	Apr 30
Apr-May-Jun	Jun 30	Jul 31
Jul-Aug-Sep	Sep 30	Oct 31
Oct-Nov-Dec	Dec 31	Jan 31

INFORMATION RETURNS

If a business makes or receives payments, it will likely have to report the payments to the IRS on information returns. Specific instructions for each of the forms listed below can be found on the IRS Publications Web site.

- **Corporation** – Submit Form 1120 the 15th day of the third month after end of fiscal year.
- **Subchapter S Corporation** – Submit Form 1120-S the 15th day of the third month after end of fiscal year.
- **Partnership** – Submit Form 1065 the 15th day of the fourth month after end of fiscal year.
- **Sole Proprietor** – Submit Schedule C with individual income tax return.
- **W-2** – Send to each employee from whom taxes were withheld. Date Due: January 31.
- **W-3** – Send to IRS summarizing the W-2s. Date Due: Last day in February for the preceding year.
- **1099** – Send to each employee/consultant for any compensation not subject to withholding. Date Due: By January 31 for the preceding year.
- **1096** – Send to IRS summarizing the 1099s. Date Due: By February 28 for previous year.

RECORDKEEPING

Retain all records of employment taxes for at least four years after the original due date for the taxes, or the date the tax is paid, whichever is later. Records should be available to the IRS for review. Examples of records that need to be kept are:

- Employer identification number (EIN).
- Amounts and dates of all wage, annuity, and pension payments.
- Amounts of tips reported.
- Records of allocated tips.
- The fair market value of in-kind wages paid.
- Names, addresses, Social Security numbers, and occupations of employees and recipients.
- Any employee copies of Forms W-2 and W-2c that were returned as undeliverable.
- Dates of employment.
- Periods for which employees and recipients were paid while absent due to sickness or injury, and the amount and weekly rate of payments the employer or third-party payers made to them.
- Copies of employees' and recipients' income tax withholding allowance certificates (Forms W-4, W-4P, W-4S, and W-4V).
- Dates and amounts of tax deposits made and acknowledgment numbers for deposits made by EFTPS.
- Copies of returns filed, including Form 941 TeleFile Tax Records and confirmation numbers.
- Records of fringe benefits provided including substantiation.

State Tax Requirements

A. Income Tax

Employers are required to withhold state income tax from the wages of their employees. Withholding amounts are based on information provided by the employee on the New Jersey Employee's Withholding Allowance Certificate (NJ-W4) or Federal Form W-4, which has been signed by the employee. Tables for computing the amount of New Jersey income tax to be withheld are given in the *New Jersey Gross Income Tax Instructions for Employers.*

The withheld tax must be remitted to the Division of Taxation on a weekly, monthly, or quarterly basis depending on the amount of withholding tax liability. A quarterly report is required of all employers regardless of the amount of tax liability. Employers must file a New Jersey Gross Income Tax Reconciliation of Tax Withheld each year, regardless of tax withheld, on or before the end of February.

An employer's identification number must be included on filings and in all correspondence with the New Jersey Division of Taxation. Where possible, the New Jersey Identification Number will be the same as the Federal Employer Identification Number.

Employers must furnish two copies of the Wage and Tax Statement (W-2) to each employee from whom any amount of income tax was withheld or would have been withheld under the withholding tables and methods issued by the Division of Taxation. New Jersey law also requires the inclusion on the W-2 of the separate amounts deducted and withheld as worker contributions due State Disability Insurance, Workforce Development, and Healthcare.

B. Sales and Use Tax

Contractors doing business in New Jersey have special responsibilities under New Jersey's sales and use tax laws. A complete explanation of sales and use tax responsibilities is available in publication *S&U-3 Contractors and New Jersey Taxes*, which is located online at **www.state.nj.us/treasury/taxation/pdf/pubs/sales/su3.pdf**.

Generally, a contractor is required to **pay sales or use tax** on the materials, supplies, equipment, and services he or she purchases. A contractor is treated as the retail purchaser of materials and supplies used on, or incorporated into, real property, rather than as a reseller of such materials and supplies.

If a contractor chooses to separately itemize materials and labor on a customer's bill and the bill is for a taxable capital improvement, repair, maintenance, or installation service, the contractor is responsible for **collecting sales tax** from the property owner. The cost of materials may include the sales tax paid by the contractor when the materials and supplies were purchased. The remainder of the customer's bill is for labor and is subject to sales tax. If the contractor does not itemize the materials and the labor for a taxable job, the entire receipt is subject to tax.

The sales tax collected must be sent to the state either monthly or quarterly, depending on the amount of sales tax collected each month. All businesses registered to collect sales tax and remit use tax must file a New Jersey Sales and Use Tax Quarterly Return every three months regardless of whether or not any sales were made or tax due for that particular period.

Use tax is imposed on the purchase of goods and services on which sales tax was not collected, or was collected at a rate less than the New Jersey sales tax rate. A contractor pays any use tax owed on the sales tax returns.

A valid New Jersey exemption certificate allows a qualified individual or business to purchase certain goods and/or services without paying sales tax. The exemption certificates most frequently used in the construction industry are:

- Resale Certificate (Form ST-3) allows an individual to buy materials that will become part of the product being sold without being taxed.
- Exempt Use Certificate (Form ST-4) exempts certain items from sales tax if they are purchased for a particular use.
- Contractor's Exempt Purchase Certificate (Form ST-13) is issued by a contractor to a supplier when the contractor purchases of materials, supplies, or services for use in performing work on the real property of an exempt organization, a New Jersey or federal governmental entity, or a qualified housing sponsor.

The New Jersey Division of Taxation maintains regional offices throughout the state where business owners can receive assistance in person on both individual and business tax concerns. Business owners may also contact the main Division of Taxation for more information.

New Jersey Department of the Treasury
Division of Taxation
P. O. Box 281
Trenton, NJ 08695-0281
609.292.6400
800-323-4400 (Forms Request System)
www.state.nj.us/treasury/taxation/

11

CONSTRUCTION LIEN LAW

DEFINITION OF A LIEN

Webster's Dictionary defines a lien as "a claim on the property of another as security against the payment of a just debt."

A lien is a legal claim upon property that may be used by a contractor, material supplier or anyone who supplied labor or materials for improvements to the property, as a lawful remedy for securing payment for those improvements. Lien laws are based on the theory that if an owner's property has been improved, the owner should not receive the benefit of the improvements unless he or she pays for it. Lien laws give some protection to laborers and material suppliers in the event of default by a contractor or property owner.

When a lien is recorded with the appropriate governmental agency, it serves as a cloud on the owner's title to the property, and in worst cases, property may be foreclosed and sold and the proceeds used to pay laborers or material suppliers. If a lien is placed against property, it makes it difficult for the owner to sell that property or borrow against it. Lien foreclosures can happen even if the owner has paid the general contractor in full, but the general contractor has not paid laborers or material suppliers.

The *New Jersey Construction Lien Law* is a very firm expression by the New Jersey legislature to protect those who contribute labor or material to enhance the property of another.

Public property is not subject to a statutory lien in New Jersey. Refer to the chapter on risk management for a more complete discussion of methods to protect contractors on public works.

ENTITLEMENT TO FILE A LIEN

Any contractor, subcontractor, or supplier who provides work, services, material, or equipment pursuant to a contract, shall be entitled to a lien for the value of the work or services performed, or materials or equipment furnished in accordance with the contract and based upon the contract price.

LAND SUBJECT TO LIEN

The land occupied by any building or other structure, together with a convenient space around the building or other structure, is also subject to the lien. The definition of "convenient space" is determined by the court when rendering judgment on the lien. A lien claimant may record a lien upon more than one property or more than one lot owned by the same owner in the same claim, but the amount owed against each property must be stated.

PROCEDURES FOR FILING A LIEN

The following paragraphs describe a general procedure for filing a lien. A contractor should always contact an attorney before filing a lien. Make certain to allow the attorney sufficient time to act properly in filing the appropriate notices as there are usually specific timelines for filing a valid lien claim.

A. LIEN CLAIM FORM

A contractor, subcontractor, or supplier entitled to file a lien shall do so on a lien claim form. The lien claim form should include:

- Name and address of claimant (and/or partnership, corporation, or LLC);
- Name of owner of property subject to lien;
- Legal description of the property;
- The last date that services, material, or equipment were provided; and
- Lien claim amount due (as calculated for the value of the work, services, material, or equipment provided based on the contract).

The lien claim form should be lodged for record with the clerk in the county where the work took place within 90 days following the date the last work, services, material, or equipment was provided for which payment is claimed. In the case of a residential construction contract, the lien claim form should be lodged for record no later than 10 days after receipt by the claimant of the arbitrator's determination, and within 120 days following the date the last work, services, material, or equipment was provided for which payment is claimed.

B. SERVING OF LIEN CLAIM

Within 10 days following the lodging for record of a lien claim, the claimant shall serve on the owner, and, if any, the contractor and subcontractor against whom the claim is asserted, a copy of the completed and signed lien claim and marked "received for filing" or a similar stamp with a date and time or other mark indicating the date and time received by the county clerk. Service shall be by:

- Personal service as prescribed by the Rules of Court adopted by the Supreme Court of New Jersey;
- Simultaneous registered or certified mail or commercial courier whose regular business is delivery service;
- Ordinary mail addressed to the last known business or residence address of the owner or community association, contractor, or subcontractor.

If the service of the lien claim is not properly executed, it may affect the right of the lienor to enforcement of the lien.

C. PAYMENT OF LIENS

When different liens are asserted against any property, all lien claims established by judgment as valid claims will be paid as follows:

- First-tier lien claimants;
- Second-tier lien claimants;
- Third-tier lien claimants;
- If there are no first-tier lien claimants, the lien fund for second-tier lien claimants shall be allocated in amounts equal to that second tier's valid claims; and
- If there are no first- or second-tier lien claimants, the lien fund for third-tier lien claimants shall be allocated in amounts equal to that third tier's valid claims.

NEW JERSEY PERMANENT STATUTES
TITLE 2A: ADMINISTRATION OF CIVIL AND CRIMINAL JUSTICE
CHAPTER 44A: CONSTRUCTION LIEN LAW

2A:44A-1. Short title
This act shall be known and may be cited as the "Construction Lien Law."

2A:44A-2. Definitions relative to construction liens
As used in this act:

"Claimant" means a person having the right to file a lien claim on real property pursuant to the provisions of this act.

"Community association" means a condominium association, a homeowners' association, a cooperative association, or any other entity created to administer or manage the common elements and facilities of a real property development that, directly or through an authorized agent, enters into a contract for improvement of the real property.

"Contract" means any agreement, or amendment thereto, in writing, signed by the party against whom the lien claim is asserted and evidencing the respective responsibilities of the contracting parties, including, but not limited to, price or other consideration to be paid, and a description of the benefit or improvement to the real property subject to a lien. In the case of a supplier, "contract" shall include a delivery or order slip referring to the site or project to which materials have been delivered or where they were used and signed by the party against whom the lien claim is asserted or that party's authorized agent. As referenced herein: the phrase "party against whom the lien claim is asserted" means the party in direct privity of contract with the party asserting the lien claim; and the term "signed" means a writing that bears a mark or symbol intended to authenticate it.

"Contract price" means the amount specified in a contract for the provision of work, services, material or equipment.

"Contractor" means any person in the direct privity of contract with the owner of real property, or with a community association in accordance with section 3 of P.L.1993, c.318 (C.2A:44A-3), for improvements to the real property. A construction manager who enters into a single contract with an owner or a community association for the performance of all construction work within the scope of a construction manager's contract, a construction manager who enters into a subcontract, or a construction manager who is designated as an owner's or community association's agent without entering into a subcontract is also a "contractor" for purposes of this act. A licensed architect, engineer or land surveyor or certified landscape architect who is not a salaried employee of the contractor, or the owner or community association, performing professional services related to the improvement of property in direct contract with the property owner shall be considered a "contractor" for the purposes of this act.

"County clerk" means the clerk of the county in which real property to be improved is situated.

"Day" means a calendar day unless otherwise designated.

"Dwelling" means a one-, two- or three-family residence that is freestanding or shares a party wall without common ownership interest in that party wall. A dwelling may be part of a real property development.

"Equipment" means any machinery or other apparatus, including rental equipment delivered to the site to be improved or used on the site to be improved, whether for incorporation in the improved real property or for use in the construction of the improvement of the real property. A lien for equipment shall arise only for equipment used on site for the improvement of real property, including equipment installed in the improved real property. In the case of rental equipment, the amount of any lien shall be limited to the rental rates as set forth in the rental contract.

"Filing" means the (1) lodging for record and (2) the indexing of the documents authorized to be filed or recorded pursuant to this act in the office of the county clerk in the county where the property subject to the lien is located, or, in the case of real property located in more than one county, in the office of the county clerk of each such county. A document that is "lodged for record" shall mean a document that is delivered to the county clerk and marked by the clerk with a date and time stamp or other mark indicating the date and time received.

"First tier lien claimant" means a claimant who is a contractor.

"Improvement" means any actual or proposed physical changes to real property resulting from the provision of work, services, or material by a contractor, subcontractor, or supplier pursuant to a contract, whether or not such physical change is undertaken, and includes the construction, reconstruction, alteration, repair, renovation, demolition or removal of any building or structure, any addition to a building or structure, or any construction or fixture necessary or appurtenant to a building or structure for use in conjunction therewith. "Improvement" includes, but is not limited to, excavation, digging, drilling, drainage, dredging, filling, irrigation, land clearance, grading or landscaping. "Improvement" shall not include the mining of minerals or removal of timber, gravel, soil, or sod which is not integral to or necessitated by the improvement to real property. "Improvement" shall not include public works or improvements to real property contracted for and awarded by a public entity. Any work or services requiring a license for performance including, but not limited to, architectural, engineering, plumbing or electrical construction, shall not constitute an improvement unless performed by a licensed claimant.

"Interest in real property" means any ownership, possessory security or other enforceable interest, including, but not limited to, fee title, easement rights, covenants or restrictions, leases and mortgages.

"Lien" or "construction lien" means a lien on the owner's interest in the real property arising pursuant to the provisions of this act.

"Lien claim" means a claim, by a claimant, for money for the value of work, services, material or equipment furnished in accordance with a contract and based upon the contract price and any amendments thereto, that has been secured by a lien pursuant to this act. The term "value" includes retainage earned against work, services, materials or equipment furnished.

"Lien fund" means the pool of money from which one or more lien claims may be paid. The amount of the lien fund shall not exceed the maximum amount for which an owner can be liable. The amount of the lien that attaches to the owner's interest in the real property cannot exceed the lien fund.

"Material" means any goods delivered to, or used on the site to be improved, for incorporation in the improved real property, or for consumption as normal waste in construction operations; or for use on site in the construction or operation of equipment used in the improvement of the real property but not incorporated therein. The term "material" does not include fuel provided for use in motor vehicles or equipment delivered to or used on the site to be improved.

"Mortgage" means a loan that is secured by a lien on real property.

"Owner" or "owner of real property" means any person, including a tenant, with an interest in real property who personally or through an authorized agent enters into a contract for improvement of the real property. "Owner" or "owner of real property" shall not include a "community association" that holds record title to real property or has an interest in real property.

"Person" means an individual, corporation, company, association, society, firm, limited liability company, limited liability partnership, partnership, joint stock company or any other legal entity, unless restricted by the context to one or more of the above.

"Public entity" includes the State, and any county, municipality, district, public authority, public agency, and any other political subdivision or public body in the State.

"Real property development" means all forms of residential and non-residential real property development including, but not limited to, a condominium subject to the "Condominium Act," P.L.1969, c.257 (C.46:8B-1 et seq.), a housing cooperative subject to "The Cooperative Recording Act of New Jersey," P.L.1987, c.381 (C.46:8D-1 et al.), a fee simple townhouse development, a horizontal property regime as defined in section 2 of P.L.1963, c.168 (C.46:8A-2), and a planned unit development as defined in section 3.3 of P.L.1975, c.291 (C.40:55D-6).

"Residential construction" also referred to as "residential housing construction" or "home construction," means construction of or improvement to a dwelling, or any portion thereof, or any residential unit, or any portion thereof. In the case of a real property development, "residential construction" or "residential housing construction" or "home construction" also includes: (1) all offsite and onsite infrastructure and sitework improvements required by a residential construction contract, master deed, or other document; (2) the common elements of the development, which may also include by definition the offsite and onsite infrastructure and sitework improvements; and (3) those areas or buildings commonly shared.

"Residential construction contract" means a contract for the construction of, or improvement to, a dwelling, or dwellings or any portion thereof, or a residential unit, or units, or dwellings, or any portion thereof in a real property development.

"Residential purchase agreement" means a contract between a buyer and a seller for the purchase of a dwelling, or dwellings or a residential unit or units in a real property development.

"Residential unit" means a unit in a real property development designed to be transferred or sold for use as a residence, and the design evidenced by a document, such as a master deed or declaration, recorded with the county clerk in the county where the real property is located, or a public offering statement filed with the Department of Community Affairs. "Residential unit" includes a unit designed to be transferred or sold for use as a residence that is part of a multi-use or mixed use development project. "Residential unit" shall not include a unit designed for rental purposes or a unit designed to be transferred or sold for non-residential use.

"Second tier lien claimant" means a claimant who is, in relation to a contractor: (1) a subcontractor; or (2) a supplier.

"Services" means professional services performed by a licensed architect, engineer, land surveyor, or certified landscape architect, who is not a salaried employee of the contractor, a subcontractor or the owner and who is in direct privity of contract with the owner for the preparation of plans, documents, studies, or the provision of other services by a licensed architect, engineer or land surveyor prepared in connection with improvement to real property, whether or not such physical change is undertaken.

"State" means the State of New Jersey and any office, department, division, bureau, board, commission, or agency of the State.

"Subcontractor" means any person providing work or services in connection with the improvement of real property pursuant to a contract with a contractor or pursuant to a contract with a subcontractor in direct privity of contract with a contractor.

"Supplier" means any supplier of material or equipment, including rental equipment, having a direct privity of contract with an owner, community association, contractor or subcontractor in direct privity of contract with a contractor. The term "supplier" shall not include a person who supplies fuel for use in motor vehicles or equipment delivered to or used on the site to be improved or a seller of personal property who has a security agreement providing a right to perfect either a security interest pursuant to Title 12A of the New Jersey Statutes or a lien against the motor vehicle pursuant to applicable law.

"Third tier lien claimant" means a claimant who is a subcontractor to a second tier lien claimant or a supplier to a second tier lien claimant.

"Work" means any activity, including, but not limited to, labor, performed in connection with the improvement of real property. The term "work" includes architectural, engineering or surveying services provided by salaried employees of a contractor or subcontractor, as part of the work of the contractor or subcontractor, provided, however, that the right to file a lien claim for those services shall be limited to the contractor or subcontractor.

2A:44A-3. Lien entitlement for work, services, etc.; terms defined

a. Any contractor, subcontractor or supplier who provides work, services, material or equipment pursuant to a contract, shall be entitled to a lien for the value of the work or services performed, or materials or equipment furnished in accordance with the contract and based upon the contract price, subject to sections 6, 9, and 10 of P.L.1993, c.318 (C.2A:44A-6, 2A:44A-9 and 2A:44A-10). The lien shall attach to the interest of the owner or unit owner of the real property development, or be filed against the community association, in accordance with this section.

b. For purposes of this section:

(1) "interest of the owner of the real property development" includes interest in any residential or nonresidential units not yet sold or transferred and the proportionate undivided interests in the common elements attributable to those units;

(2) "interest of the unit owner" includes the proportionate undivided interests in the common elements of the real property development;

(3) "unit owner" means an owner of an interest in a residential or nonresidential unit who is not a developer of the property and acquires the unit after the master deed or master declaration is recorded, or after the public offering statement is filed with the Department of Community Affairs; and

c.   In the case of a condominium, notwithstanding the provisions of the "Condominium Act," P.L.1969, c.257 (C.46:8B-1 et seq.), or in the case of any other real property development with common elements or common areas or facilities, if the contract is:

(1) with the owner of the real property development, then the lien shall attach to the interest of the owner of the real property development;

(2) with the community association, the lien claim shall be filed against the community association but shall not attach to any real property.

In either case, if the work, services, material or equipment are performed or furnished as part of the common elements or facilities of a real property development, the lien shall not attach to the interest of the unit owner.

d.   If the work, services, material or equipment are performed or furnished solely within or as part of a residential or nonresidential unit, the lien shall attach only to the interest of the unit owner.

e.   If a tenant contracts for improvement of the real property, the lien shall attach to the leasehold estate of the tenant and to the interest in the property of any person who:

(1) has expressly authorized the contract for improvement in writing signed by the person against whom the lien claim is asserted, which writing provides that the person's interest is subject to a lien for this improvement;

(2) has paid, or agreed in writing to pay, the majority of the cost of the improvement; or

(3) is a party to the lease or sublease that created the leasehold interest of the tenant and the lease or sublease provides that the person's interest is subject to a lien for the improvement.

f.   An amount of a lien on an interest of a person other than a tenant shall be limited to the amount that person agreed in writing to pay, less payments made by or on behalf of that person in good faith prior to the filing of the lien.

g.   If an interest in real property is lawfully conveyed after work, services, material, or equipment are performed or furnished but before a lien attaches, the lien shall attach only to the interest retained by the owner or unit owner or community association, as the case may be, who contracted for the work, services, material or equipment and not to the interest previously conveyed.

h.   Nothing in this act shall be construed to limit the right of any claimant from pursuing any other remedy provided by law.

Nothing in this act shall be construed to limit the right of any claimant from pursuing any other remedy provided by law.

2A:44A-4. Lien for improvements; attachment
Liens for the following improvements shall attach to real property only in the manner herein prescribed. In the case of an improvement:

a.   Involving a dock, wharf, pier, bulkhead, return, jetty, piling, groin, boardwalk or pipeline above, on or below lands under waters within the State's jurisdiction, the lien shall be on the improvements together with the contracting owner's interest in the lots of land in front of or upon which the improvements are constructed and any interest of the contracting owner of the land in the land or waters in front of the land;

b.   Involving removal of a building or structure or part of a building or structure from its site and its relocation on other land, the lien shall be on the contracting owner's interest in the improved real property on which the building or structure has been relocated;

c.   Involving excavation, drainage, dredging, landfill, irrigation work, construction of banks, making channels, grading, filling, landscaping or the planting of any shrubs, trees or other nursery products, the lien shall be on the land to which the improvements are made, and shall not be upon the adjoining lands directly or indirectly benefited from the improvements.

2A:44A-5. Liens, certain; prohibited
No liens shall attach nor shall a lien claim be filed:

a.   For materials that have been furnished or delivered subject to a security agreement which has been entered into pursuant to Chapter 9 of Title 12A of the New Jersey Statutes (N.J.S.12A:9-101 et seq.);

b.   For public works or improvements to real property contracted for and awarded by public entity; provided, however, that nothing herein shall affect any right or remedy established pursuant to the "municipal mechanic's lien law," N.J.S.2A:44-125 et seq.;

c.   For work, services, material or equipment furnished pursuant to a residential construction contract unless there is a strict compliance with sections 20 and 21 of this act.

2A:44A-6. Filing lien claim

a.   A contractor, subcontractor or supplier entitled to file a lien pursuant to section 3 of P.L.1993, c.318 (C.2A:44A-3) shall do so according to the following process:

(1)   The lien claim form as provided by section 8 of P.L.1993, c.318 (C.2A:44A-8) shall be signed, acknowledged and verified by oath of the claimant setting forth:

(a)   the specific work or services performed, or material or equipment provided pursuant to contract; and

(b)   the claimant's identity and contractual relationship with the owner or community association and other known parties in the construction chain.

(2)   In all cases except those involving a residential construction contract, the lien claim form shall then be lodged for record within 90 days following the date the last work, services, material or equipment was provided for which payment is claimed. In the case of a residential construction contract, the lien claim form shall be lodged for record, as required by paragraph (8) of subsection b. of section 21 of P.L.1993, c.318 (C.2A:44A-21), not later than 10 days after receipt by the claimant of the arbitrator's determination, and within 120 days following the date the last work, services, material or equipment was provided for which payment is claimed. If requested, at the time of lodging for record, the clerk shall provide a copy of the lien claim form marked with a date and time received.

b.   A lien shall not attach or be enforceable unless the lien claim or other document permitted to be filed is:

(1)   filed in the manner and form provided by this section and section 8 of P.L.1993, c.318 (C.2A:44A-8); and

(2)   a copy thereof served in accordance with section 7 of P.L.1993, c.318 (C.2A:44A-7), except that every document lodged for record that satisfies the requirements of this section, even if not yet filed, shall be enforceable against parties with notice of the document. A document shall be first filed, however, in order to be enforceable against third parties without notice of the document, including, but not limited to, an owner, bona fide purchaser, mortgagee, grantee of an easement, or a lessee or a grantee of any other interest in real estate.

c.   In the case of a residential construction contract the lien claim shall also comply with section 20 of P.L.1993, c.318 (C.2A:44A-20) and section 21 of P.L.1993, c.318 (C.2A:44A-21).

d.   For purposes of this act, warranty or other service calls, or other work, materials or equipment provided after completion or termination of a claimant's contract shall not be used to determine the last day that work, services, material or equipment was provided.

2A:44A-7. Serving of lien claim by claimant

a.   Within 10 days following the lodging for record of a lien claim, the claimant shall serve on the owner, or community association in accordance with section 3 of P.L.1993, c.318 (C.2A:44A-3), and, if any, the contractor and subcontractor against whom the claim is asserted, a copy of the completed and signed lien claim substantially in the form prescribed by section 8 of P.L.1993, c.318 (C.2A:44A-8) and marked "received for filing" or a similar stamp with a date and time or other mark indicating the date and time received by the county clerk. Service shall be by personal service as prescribed by the Rules of Court adopted by the Supreme Court of New Jersey or by:

(1)   simultaneous registered or certified mail or commercial courier whose regular business is delivery service; and

(2)   ordinary mail addressed to the last known business or residence address of the owner or community association, contractor or subcontractor. A lien claim served upon a community association need not be served upon individual "unit owners" as defined in section 3 of P.L.1993, c.318 (C.2A:44A-3).

b.   The service of the lien claim provided for in this section shall be a condition precedent to enforcement of the lien; however, the service of the lien claim outside the prescribed time period shall not preclude enforceability unless the party not timely served proves by a preponderance of the evidence that the late service has materially prejudiced its position. Disbursement of funds by the owner, community association, a contractor or a subcontractor who has not been properly served, or the creation or conveyance of an interest in real property by an owner who has not been properly served, shall constitute prima facie evidence of material prejudice.

2A:44A-8. Lien claim form

The lien claim shall be filed in substantially the following form:

CONSTRUCTION LIEN CLAIM

TO THE CLERK, COUNTY OF _____:

In accordance with the "Construction Lien Law," P.L.1993, c.318 (C.2A:44A-1 et al.), notice is hereby given that (only complete those sections that apply):

1.   On (date), I, (name of claimant), individually, or as a partner of the claimant known as (name of partnership), or an officer/member of the claimant known as (name of corporation or LLC) (circle one and fill in name as applicable), located at (business address of claimant), claim a construction lien against the real property of (name of owner of property subject to lien), in that certain tract or parcel of land and premises described as Block _____, Lot _____, on the tax map of the (municipality) of _____, County of_____, State of New Jersey, (or if no Block and Lot is assigned, a metes and bounds or other description of the property) in the amount of $(lien claim amount), as calculated below for the value of the work, services, material or equipment provided. (If the claim is against a community association in accordance with section 3 of P.L.1993, c.318 (C.2A:44A-3) set forth the name of the community association and the name and location of the property development.) The lien is claimed against the interest of the owner, unit owner, or against the community association in accordance with section 3 of P.L.1993, 318 (C.2A:44A-3) or other party (circle one; if "other", describe: _____).

2.   In accordance with a written contract for improvement of the above property, dated_____, with the property owner, community association, contractor, or subcontractor (circle one), named or known as (name of appropriate party), and located at (address of owner, unit owner, community association, contractor or subcontractor), this claimant performed the following work or provided the following services, material or equipment:

   a.   _____

   b   _____

   c.   _____etc.

3.   The date of the provision of the last work, services, material or equipment for which payment is claimed is _____, 20__ .

4.   The amount due for work, services, material or equipment delivery provided by claimant in connection with the improvement of the real property, and upon which this lien claim is based, is calculated as follows:

   A.   Initial Contract Price: $ _____

   B.   Executed Amendments to Contract Price/Change Orders: $_____

   C.   Total Contract Price (A + B) = $_____

   D.   If Contract Not Completed, Value Determined in Accordance with the Contract of Work Completed or Services, Material, Equipment Provided : _____

   E.   Total from C or D (whichever is applicable): $ _____

   F.   Agreed upon Credits: $ _____

   G.   Amount Paid to Date: $ _____

   TOTAL LIEN CLAIM AMOUNT E - [F + G] = $_____

NOTICE OF UNPAID BALANCE AND ARBITRATION

AWARD

This claim (check one) does_____does not_____arise from a Residential Construction Contract. If it does, complete 5 and 6 below; if not residential, complete 5 below, only if applicable. If not residential and 5 is not applicable, skip to Claimant's Representation and Verification.

5.   A Notice of Unpaid Balance and Right to File Lien (if any) was previously filed with the County Clerk of _____ County on _____, 20 __ as No. _____, in Book _____ Page _____.

6.   An award of the arbitrator (if residential) was issued on_____ in the amount of $_____.

CLAIMANT'S REPRESENTATION AND VERIFICATION

Claimant represents and verifies under oath that:

1.   I have authority under this claim.

2.   The claimant is entitled to the amount claimed at the date of lodging for record of the claim, pursuant to claimant's contract described above.

3.   The work, services, material or equipment for which this lien claim is filed was provided exclusively in connection with the improvement of the real property which is the subject of this claim.

4.   This claim form has been lodged for record with the County Clerk where the property is located within 90 or, if residential construction, 120 days from the last date upon which the work, services, material or equipment for which payment is claimed was provided.

5.   This claim form has been completed in its entirety to the best of my ability and I understand that if I do not complete this form in its entirety, the form may be deemed invalid by a court of law.

6.   This claim form will be served as required by statute upon the owner or community association, and upon the contractor or subcontractor against whom this claim has been asserted, if any.

7.   The foregoing statements made by me in this claim form are true, to the best of my knowledge. I am aware that if any of the foregoing statements made by me in this claim form are willfully false, this construction lien claim will be void and that I will be liable for damages to the owner or any other person injured as a consequence of the filing of this lien claim.

Name of Claimant _____

Signed _____

(Type or Print Name and Title)

SUGGESTED NOTARIAL FOR INDIVIDUAL CLAIMANT:

STATE OF NEW JERSEY

COUNTY OF   ss:

On this ____ day of _____ 20___, before me, the subscriber, personally appeared (person signing on behalf of claimant(s)) who, I am satisfied, is/are the person(s) named in and who executed the within instrument, and thereupon acknowledged that claimant(s) signed, sealed and delivered the same as claimant's (s') act and deed, for the purposes therein expressed.

_____

NOTARY PUBLIC

SUGGESTED NOTARIAL FOR CORPORATE OR LIMITED LIABILITY CLAIMANT:

STATE OF NEW JERSEY

COUNTY OF   ss:

On this ____ day of _____ 20__, before me, the subscriber, personally appeared (person signing on behalf of claimant(s)) who, I am satisfied is the Secretary (or other officer/manager/agent) of the Corporation (partnership or limited liability company) named herein and who by me duly sworn/affirmed, asserted authority to act on behalf of the Corporation (partnership or limited liability company) and who, by virtue of its Bylaws, or Resolution of its Board of Directors (or partnership or operating agreement) executed the within instrument on its behalf, and thereupon acknowledged that claimant signed, sealed and delivered same as claimant's act and deed, for the purposes herein expressed.

_____

NOTARY PUBLIC

NOTICE TO CONTRACTOR OR SUBCONTRACTOR, IF APPLICABLE

The owner's real estate may be subject to sale to satisfy the amount asserted by this claim. However, the owner's real estate cannot be sold until the facts and issues which form the basis of this claim are decided in a legal proceeding before a court of law. The lien claimant is required by law to commence suit to enforce this claim.

The claimant filing this lien claim shall forfeit all rights to enforce the lien claim and shall be required to discharge the lien claim of record, if the claimant fails to bring an action in the Superior Court, in the county in which the real property is situated, to establish the lien claim:

1.   Within one year of the date of the last provision of work, services, material or equipment, payment for which the lien claim was filed; or

2.   Within 30 days following receipt of written notice, by personal service or certified mail, return receipt requested, from the owner or community association, contractor, or subcontractor against whom a lien claim is filed, as appropriate, requiring the claimant to commence an action to establish the lien claim.

You will be given proper notice of the proceeding and an opportunity to challenge this claim and set forth your position. If, after the owner (and/or contractor or subcontractor) has had the opportunity to challenge this lien claim, the court of law enters a judgment against any of you and in favor of the claimant filing this lien claim, and thereafter judgment is not paid, the owner's real estate may then be sold to satisfy the judgment. A judgment against a community association for a claim of work, services, material or equipment pursuant to a contract with that community association cannot be enforced by a sale of real estate.

The owner may choose to avoid subjecting the real estate to sale by the owner (or contractor) by either:

1.   paying the claimant and obtaining a discharge of lien claim from the claimant, by which the owner will lose the right to challenge this lien claim in a legal proceeding before a court of law; or

2.   causing the lien claim to be discharged by filing a surety bond or making a deposit of funds as provided for in section 31 of P.L.1993, c.318 (C.2A:44A-31), by which the owner will retain the right to challenge this lien claim in a legal proceeding before a court of law.

2A:44A-9. Amount of lien claim

a.   The amount of a lien claim shall not exceed the unpaid portion of the contract price of the claimant's contract for the work, services, material or equipment provided.

b.   Except as set forth in sections 15 and 21 of P.L.1993, c.318 (C.2A:44A-15 and 2A:44A-21), and subject to section 7 of P.L.1993, c.318 (C.2A:44A-7) and subsection c. of this section, the lien fund shall not exceed:

(1) in the case of a first tier lien claimant or second tier lien claimant, the earned amount of the contract between the owner and the contractor minus any payments made prior to service of a copy of the lien claim; or

(2) in the case of a third tier lien claimant, the lesser of: (a) the amount in paragraph (1) above; or (b) the earned amount of the contract between the contractor and the subcontractor to the contractor, minus any payments made prior to service of a copy of the lien claim.

c.   A lien fund regardless of tier shall not be reduced by payments by the owner, or community association in accordance with section 3 of P.L.1993, c.318 (C.2A:44A-3), that do not discharge the obligations for the work performed or services, material or equipment provided, including, but not limited to:

(1) payments not in accordance with written contract provisions;

(2) payments yet to be earned upon lodging for record of the lien claim;

(3) liquidated damages;

(4) collusive payments;

(5) use of retainage to make payments to a successor contractor after the lien claim is lodged for record; or

(6) setoffs or backcharges, absent written agreement by the claimant, except for any setoffs upheld by judgment that are first determined by: (a) arbitration or alternate dispute resolution in a proceeding conducted in accordance with section 21 of P.L.1993, c.318 (C.2A:44A-21); or (b) any other alternate dispute resolution agreed to by the parties.

d. Subject to subsection c. above, no lien fund exists, if, at the time of service of a copy of the lien claim, the owner or community association has fully paid the contractor for the work performed or for services, material or equipment provided.

e. For purposes of a lien fund calculation, the "earned amount of the contract" is the contract price unless the party obligated to perform has not completed the performance in which case the "earned amount of the contract" is the value, as determined in accordance with the contract, of the work performed and services, material or equipment provided.

f. If more than one lien claimant will participate in a lien fund, the lien fund shall be established as of the date of the first of the participating lien claims lodged for record unless the earned amount of the contract increases, in which case the lien fund shall be calculated from the date of the increase.

g. No lien rights shall exist for other than first, second, or third tier lien claimants.

2A:44A-10. Attachment of lien claim to interest of owner; amount of liability

Subject to the limitations of sections 3 and 6 of P.L.1993, c.318 (C.2A:44A-3 and 2A:44A-6), the lien shall attach to the interest of the owner from and after the time of filing of the lien claim. Except as provided by section 20 of P.L.1993, c.318 (C.2A:44A-20), no lien shall attach to the interest acquired by a bona fide purchaser as evidenced by a recordable document recorded or lodged for record before the date of filing of the lien claim. A lien claim shall not, except as provided by sections 20 and 22 of P.L.1993, c.318 (C.2A:44A-20 and 2A:44A-22), have a priority over any mortgage, judgment or other lien or interest in real estate first recorded, lodged for record, filed or docketed. A lien claim filed under this act shall be subject to the effect of a Notice of Settlement filed pursuant to P.L.1979, c.406 (C.46:16A-1 et seq.).

2A:44A-11. Amendment of lien claim, form

a. A lien claim may be amended for any appropriate reason, including but not limited to correcting inaccuracies or errors in the original lien claim form, or revising the amount claimed because of:

(1) additional work performed or services, material, or equipment provided;

(2) the release of a proportionate share of an interest in real property from the lien in accordance with section 18 of P.L.1993, c.318 (C.2A:44A-18); or

(3) the partial payment of the lien claim.

A lien claim may not be amended to cure a violation of section 15 of P.L.1993, c.318 (C.2A:44A-15).

b. The amended lien claim, which shall be filed with the county clerk, shall comply with all the conditions and requirements for the filing of an original lien claim, including but not limited to the notice requirements of section 7 of P.L.1993, c.318 (C.2A:44A-7) and shall be subject to the limitations of sections 9 and 10 of P.L.1993, c.318 (C.2A:44A-9 and 2A:44A-10). That portion of the amended lien in excess of the amount previously claimed shall attach as of the date of filing of the original lien claim. That excess amount shall also be used to calculate the lien fund pursuant to subsection f. of section 9 of P.L.1993, c.318 (C.2A:44A-9).

c. The amended lien claim shall be filed in substantially the following form:

AMENDMENT TO CONSTRUCTION LIEN CLAIM

TO THE CLERK, COUNTY OF   :

1. On (date), the undersigned claimant, (name of claimant) of (address of claimant), filed a CONSTRUCTION LIEN CLAIM in the amount of ($) DOLLARS for the value of the work, services, material or equipment provided in accordance with the contract between claimant and (name) as of (date).

2. This construction lien claim was claimed against the interest of (name) as (circle one): owner, unit owner, community association or other party; (if "other," describe: _____)" in that certain tract or parcel of land and premises described as Block   , Lot   , on the tax map of the   (municipality) of   , County of   , State of

New Jersey, for the improvement of which property the aforementioned work, services, material or equipment was provided. (If the claim was against a community association in accordance with section 3 of P.L.1993, c.318 (C.2A:44A-3), set forth the name of the community association and the name and location of the property development.)

3. This amends a lien claim which was previously lodged for record on __ _____, 20 and filed with the County Clerk of   County on   , 20__ and recorded on _____,_20__ as No.   in Book No.   , Page   . A Notice of Unpaid Balance and Right to File Lien (if any) was previously filed with the County Clerk of   on   , 20__ and recorded on   , 20__ as No.   in Book No.   , Page   .

4. Amendments to the original claim were recorded in the office of the County Clerk on   , 20 as No.   in Book No.   , Page   . (Complete if applicable)

5. Effective the date of the lodging for record of this AMENDMENT TO CONSTRUCTION LIEN CLAIM, the value of the lien is claimed to be in the total amount of ($) DOLLARS, inclusive of all prior lien claims or amendments thereof.

6. The work, services, material or equipment provided upon which this Amendment is made are:

   a.

   b.

   c.   (etc.)

7. The date of the provision of the last work, services, material or equipment for which payment is claimed is (date).

8. The reason for this amendment is _____

   CLAIMANTS REPRESENTATION AND VERIFICATION

       (Same as for lien claim)

   NOTICE TO OWNER OF REAL PROPERTY

       (Same as for lien claim)

   NOTICE TO SUBCONTRACTOR OR CONTRACTOR

       (Same as for lien claim)

2A:44A-12. Authorized withholding, deductions
Upon receipt of notice of a lien claim, the owner, or community association in accordance with section 3 of P.L.1993, c.318 (C.2A:44A-3), shall be authorized to withhold and deduct the amount claimed from the unpaid part of the contract price that is or thereafter may be due and payable to the contractor or subcontractor, or both. The owner or community association may pay the amount of the lien claim to the claimant unless the contractor or subcontractor against whose account the lien is filed notifies the owner and the lien claimant in writing within 20 days of service of the lien claim upon both the owner or community association and the contractor or subcontractor, that the claimant is not owed the monies claimed and the reasons therefor. Any such payment made by the owner or community association shall constitute a payment made on account of the contract price of the contract with the contractor or subcontractor, or both, against whose account the lien is filed.

2A:44A-13. "Construction Lien Book," "Construction Lien Index Book;" fees
   a. The county clerk shall provide a book designated as the "Construction Lien Book" in which shall be entered each Notice of Unpaid Balance and Right to File Lien, Amended Notice of Unpaid Balance and Right to File Lien, lien claim and amended lien claim, and discharge, subordination or release of a lien claim or Notice of Unpaid Balance and Right to File Lien presented for filing pursuant to this act.

   b. The county clerk shall cause marginal notations to be made upon each document filed pursuant to this act, as follows:

      (1) upon each Notice of Unpaid Balance and Right to File Lien, the date an amendment to that Notice or discharge thereof, and related lien claim or amendment thereto is filed;

      (2) upon each lien claim, the date an amendment thereto is filed; and the date a discharge, subordination or release thereof is filed; and

(3) upon the affected lien claim or amended lien claim, the date of the filing of the Notice of Lis Pendens pertaining to the real property subject to the lien claim.

c. The failure of the clerk to cause a marginal notation to be made in accordance with subsection b. of this section shall not affect the validity, priority or enforceability of any document filed pursuant to this act.

d. The county clerk shall provide and maintain an index book designated as the "Construction Lien Index Book," setting forth alphabetically, and arranged by owners' or community associations' names, and by claimants' names, each Notice of Unpaid Balance and Right to File Lien, Amended Notice of Unpaid Balance and Right to File Lien, lien claim, amended lien claim, discharge, subordination and release of a lien claim or Notice of Unpaid Balance and Right to File Lien.

e. Each county clerk shall charge fees for the filing and marginal notation of the documents authorized to be filed by this act as set forth in N.J.S.22A:2-29.

2A:44A-14. Claimant's failure to commence; forfeiture, liability

a. A claimant filing a lien claim shall forfeit all rights to enforce the lien, and shall immediately discharge the lien of record in accordance with section 30 of P.L.1993, c.318 (C.2A:44A-30), if the claimant fails to commence an action in the Superior Court, in the county in which the real property is situated, to enforce the lien claim:

(1) Within one year of the date of the last provision of work, services, material or equipment, payment for which the lien claim was filed; or

(2) Within 30 days following receipt of written notice, by personal service or certified mail, return receipt requested, from the owner, community association, contractor, or subcontractor against whose account a lien claim is filed, requiring the claimant to commence an action to enforce the lien claim.

b. Any lien claimant who forfeits a lien pursuant to this section and fails to discharge that lien of record in accordance with section 30 of P.L.1993, c.318 (C.2A:44A-30), shall be liable for all court costs, and reasonable legal expenses, including, but not limited to, attorneys' fees, incurred by the owner, community association, contractor, or subcontractor, or the total costs and legal expenses of all or any combination of them, in defending or causing the discharge of the lien claim. The court shall, in addition, enter judgment against the claimant who fails to discharge the lien for damages to any of the parties adversely affected by the lien claim.

c. (Deleted by amendment, P.L.2010, c.119).

d. Any disputes arising out of the improvement which is the subject of a lien claim but which are unrelated to any action to enforce a lien claim may be brought in a separate action or in a separate count in the same action.

2A:44A-15. Improper lodging of lien claim; forfeiture of rights; liability

a. If a lien claim is without basis, the amount of the lien claim is willfully overstated, or the lien claim is not lodged for record in substantially the form or in the manner or at a time not in accordance with this act, the claimant shall forfeit all claimed lien rights and rights to file subsequent lien claims to the extent of the face amount claimed in the lien claim. The claimant shall also be liable for all court costs, and reasonable legal expenses, including, but not limited to, attorneys' fees, incurred by the owner, community association, contractor or subcontractor, or any combination of owner, community association in accordance with section 3 of P.L.1993, c.318 (C.2A:44A-3), contractor and subcontractor, in defending or causing the discharge of the lien claim. The court shall, in addition, enter judgment against the claimant for damages to any of the parties adversely affected by the lien claim.

b. If a defense to a lien claim is without basis, the party maintaining the defense shall be liable for all court costs, and reasonable legal expenses, including, but not limited to, attorneys' fees, incurred by any of the parties adversely affected by the defense to the lien claim. The court shall, in addition, enter judgment against the party maintaining this defense for damages to any of the parties adversely affected thereby.

c. If a lien claim is forfeited pursuant to this section, or section 14 of P.L.1993, c.318 (C.2A:44A-14), nothing herein shall be construed to bar the filing of a subsequent lien claim, provided, however, any subsequent lien claim shall not include a claim for the work, services, equipment or material claimed within the forfeited lien claim.

d. For the purpose of this section "without basis" means frivolous, false, unsupported by a contract, or made with malice or bad faith or for any improper purpose.

2A:44A-17. Lien claims unabated by death of party in interest

No lien claim under this act or right thereto shall abate by reason of the death of any party in interest and the right to the lien claim may be asserted by the personal representative of a deceased contractor, subcontractor, or supplier against the personal representative of a deceased owner, contractor or subcontractor.

2A:44A-18. Calculation of proportionate share under residential construction

This section shall solely apply to work, services, material or equipment furnished under a residential construction contract. If a lien attaches to an interest in real property, the lien claimant shall release a proportionate share of the interest in real property from the lien upon receipt of payment for that proportionate share. This proportionate share shall be calculated in the following manner:

    a.   If there is a contract between the lien claimant and the owner or other writing signed by the parties which provides for an allocation by lot or tract, or otherwise, that allocation of the proportionate share shall be binding upon the lien claimant. Absent a contract between the lien claimant and the owner or other writing signed by the parties, any allocation made shall be proportionate to each lot if subdivision approval has been granted or to each tract if no subdivision approval is required or has been granted.

    b.   If the work performed by the lien claimant was for a condominium in which a master deed is filed before the lien attaches, or for work performed for a cooperative in which a master declaration is filed before the lien attaches, then the proportionate share shall be allocated in an amount equal to the percentage of common elements attributable to each residential unit, subject to the limitations of subsections b. and c. of section 3 of P.L.1993, c.318 (C.2A:44A-3).

    c.   If subsection a. or b. of this section does not apply, then the lien shall not be released as to any portion of the interest in real property.

    d.   If a lien claimant receives payment of the proportionate share but refuses to discharge its lien claim, then upon application to a court having jurisdiction thereof, the court shall order the discharge of the lien claim to the extent of that proportionate share. The lien claimant shall be further subject to section 30 of P.L.1993, c.318 (C.2A:44A-30), and any amounts to be paid shall be paid from the amount due the claimant.

2A:44A-20. Notice of Unpaid Balance and Right to File Lien, form

    a.   All valid liens filed pursuant to this act shall attach to the interest of the owner from the time of filing of the lien claim, subject to this section and sections 3, 6, and 10 of P.L.1993, c.318 (C.2A:44A-3, 2A:44A-6 and 2A:44A-10).

    b.   A lien claim validly filed under this act shall have priority over a prior conveyance, lease or mortgage of an interest in real property to which improvements have been made, only if a Notice of Unpaid Balance and Right to File Lien is filed before the recording or lodging for record of a recordable document evidencing that conveyance, lease or mortgage. The Notice of Unpaid Balance and Right to File Lien shall be filed in substantially the following form:

TO THE CLERK, COUNTY OF _____ :

NOTICE OF UNPAID BALANCE AND RIGHT TO FILE LIEN

In accordance with the "Construction Lien Law," P.L.1993, c.318 (C.2A:44A-1 et al.), notice is hereby given that:

1. (Name of claimant), individually or as a partner of the claimant known as (Name of partnership), or an officer/member of the claimant known as (Name of corporation or LLC) (Please circle one and fill in name as applicable) located at (Business address of claimant) has on (date) a potential construction lien against the real property of (name of owner of property subject to lien), in that certain tract or parcel of land and premises described as Block _____, Lot _____, on the tax map of the (municipality) of _____, County of _____, State of New Jersey, in the amount of ($_____), as calculated below for the value of the work, services, material or equipment provided. (If claim is against a community association in accordance with section 3 of P.L.1993, c.318 (C.2A:44A-3), set forth the name of the community association and the name and location of the property development.) The lien is to be claimed against the interest of the owner, unit owner, or other party, or against the community association (circle one; if "other", describe: _____).

2. The work, services, material or equipment was provided pursuant to the terms of a written contract (or, in the case of a supplier, a delivery or order slip signed by the owner, community association, contractor, or subcontractor having a direct contractual relation with a contractor, or an authorized agent of any of them), dated _____ , between (claimant) and owner, unit owner, community association, contractor or subcontractor (circle one), named

or known as (name of contracting party) and located at (address of other contracting party), in the total contract amount of ($) together with (if applicable) amendments to the total contract amount aggregating ($).

3.   In accordance with the above contract, this claimant performed the following work or provided the following services, material or equipment:

      a.   _____

      b   _____

      c.   _____ etc.

4.   The date of the provision of the last work, services, material or equipment for which payment is claimed is (date.)

5.   The amount due for work, services, material or equipment provided by claimant in connection with the improvement of the real property, and upon which this lien claim is based is calculated as follows:

      A.   Initial Contract Price: $ _____

      B.   Executed Amendments to Contract Price/Change Orders: $_____

      C.   Total Contract Price (A + B) = $ _____

      D.   If Contract Not Completed, Value Determined in Accordance with the Contract of Work Completed or Services, Material, Equipment Provided: _____

      E.   Total from C or D (whichever is applicable): $ _____

      F.   Agreed upon Credits: $ _____

      G.   Amount Paid to Date: $ _____

      TOTAL LIEN CLAIM AMOUNT E - = $_____

6.   The written contract (is) (is not) (cross out inapplicable portion) a residential construction contract as defined in section 2 of P.L.1993, c.318 (C.2A:44A-2).

7.   This notification has been lodged for record prior or subsequent to completion of the work, services, material or equipment as described above. The purpose of this notification is to advise the owner or community association and any other person who is attempting to encumber or take transfer of said property described above that a potential construction lien may be lodged for record within the 90-day period, or in the case of a residential construction contract within the 120-day period, following the date of the provision of the last work, services, material or equipment as set forth in paragraph 4 of this notice.

CLAIMANT'S REPRESENTATION AND VERIFICATION

Claimant represents and verifies that:

1.   I have authority to file this Notice of Unpaid Balance and Right to File Lien.

2.   The claimant is entitled to the amount claimed herein at the date this Notice is lodged for record, pursuant to claimant's contract described in the Notice of Unpaid Balance and Right to File Lien.

3.   The work, services, material or equipment for which this Notice of Unpaid Balance and Right to File Lien is filed was provided exclusively in connection with the improvement of the real property which is the subject of this Notice of Unpaid Balance and Right to File Lien.

4.   The Notice of Unpaid Balance and Right to File Lien has been lodged for record within 90 days, or in the case of a residential construction contract within 60 days, from the last date upon which the work, services, material or equipment for which payment is claimed was provided.

5.   The foregoing statements made by me are true, to the best of my knowledge.

      Name of Claimant _____

      Signed _____

      (Type or Print Name and Title)

SUGGESTED NOTARIAL FOR INDIVIDUAL CLAIMANT:

STATE OF NEW JERSEY

COUNTY OF   ss:

On this _____ day of _____ 20___, before me, the subscriber, personally appeared (person signing on behalf of claimant(s)) who, I am satisfied, is/are the person(s) named in and who executed the within instrument, and thereupon acknowledged that claimant(s) signed, sealed and delivered the same as claimant's (s') act and deed, for the purposes therein expressed.

_____

NOTARY PUBLIC

SUGGESTED NOTARIAL FOR CORPORATE OR LIMITED LIABILITY CLAIMANT:

STATE OF NEW JERSEY

COUNTY OF   ss:

On this _____ day of _____ 20__, before me, the subscriber, personally appeared (person signing on behalf of claimant(s)) who, I am satisfied is the Secretary (or other officer/manager/agent) of the Corporation (partnership or limited liability company) named herein and who by me duly sworn/affirmed, asserted authority to act on behalf of the Corporation (partnership or limited liability company) and who, by virtue of its Bylaws, or Resolution of its Board of Directors (or partnership or operating agreement) executed the within instrument on its behalf, and thereupon acknowledged that claimant signed, sealed and delivered same as claimant's act and deed, for the purposes herein expressed.

_____

NOTARY PUBLIC

c.   A claimant electing to file a Notice of Unpaid Balance and Right to File Lien as described above need not serve a copy upon any interested party.

d.   After the filing of a Notice of Unpaid Balance and Right to File Lien, any person claiming title to or an interest in or a lien upon the real property described in the Notice of Unpaid Balance and Right to File Lien, shall be deemed to have acquired said title, interest or lien with knowledge of the anticipated filing of a lien claim, and shall be subject to the terms, conditions and provisions of that lien claim within the period provided by section 6 of P.L.1993, c.318 (C.2A:44A-6) and as set forth in the Notice of Unpaid Balance and Right to File Lien. A Notice of Unpaid Balance and Right to File Lien filed under this act shall be subject to the effect of a Notice of Settlement filed pursuant to P.L.1979, c. 406 (C.46:16A-1 et seq.).

e.   The Notice of Unpaid Balance and Right to File Lien shall be effective for 90 days or in the case of a residential construction contract claim for 120 days from the date of the provision of the last work, services, material or equipment delivery for which payment is claimed as set forth in paragraph 4 of the Notice of Unpaid Balance and Right to File Lien.

f.   The lodging for record or filing of a Notice of Unpaid Balance and Right to File Lien shall not constitute the lodging for record or filing of a lien claim nor does it extend the time for the lodging for record of a lien claim, in accordance with this act.

g.   Failure to file a Notice of Unpaid Balance and Right to File Lien shall not affect the claimant's lien rights arising under this act, to the extent that no conveyance, lease or mortgage of an interest in real property occurs prior to the filing of a Notice of Unpaid Balance and Right to File Lien or lien claim.

h.   A Notice of Unpaid Balance and Right to File Lien may be amended by the filing of an Amended Notice of Unpaid Balance and Right to File Lien in accordance with this section.

2A:44A-21. Legislative findings, additional requirements for filing of lien on residential construction

a.   The Legislature finds that the ability to sell and purchase residential housing is essential for the preservation and enhancement of the economy of the State of New Jersey and that while there exists a need to provide contractors, subcontractors and suppliers with statutory benefits to enhance the collection of money for goods, services and materials provided for the construction of residential housing in the State of New Jersey, the ability to have a stable marketplace in which families can acquire homes without undue delay and uncertainty and the corresponding need of lending institutions in the State of New Jersey to conduct their business in a stable environment and to lend money for the purchase or finance of home construction or renovations requires that certain statutory provisions as related to the lien benefits accorded to contractors, subcontractors and suppliers be modified. The Legislature further finds that the construction of residential housing generally involves numerous subcontractors and suppliers to complete one unit of housing and that the multiplicity of lien claims and potential for minor monetary disputes poses a serious impediment to the ability to transfer title to residential real estate expeditiously. The Legislature further finds that the purchase of a home is generally one of the largest expenditures that a family or person will make and that there are a multitude of other State and federal statutes and regulations, including "The New Home Warranty and Builders' Registration Act," P.L.1977, c.467 (C.46:3B-1 et seq.) and "The Planned Real Estate Development Full Disclosure Act," P.L.1977, c.419 (C.45:22A-21 et seq.), which afford protection to consumers in the purchase and finance of their homes, thereby necessitating a different treatment of residential real estate as it relates to the rights of contractors, suppliers and subcontractors to place liens on residential real estate. The Legislature declares that separate provisions concerning residential construction will provide a system for balancing the competing interests of protecting consumers in the purchase of homes and the contract rights of contractors, suppliers and subcontractors to obtain payment for goods and services provided.

b.   The filing of a lien for work, services, material or equipment furnished pursuant to a residential construction contract shall be subject to the following additional requirements:

(1)   As a condition precedent to the filing of any lien arising under a residential construction contract, a lien claimant shall first file a Notice of Unpaid Balance and Right to File Lien by lodging for record the Notice within 60 days following the last date that work, services, material or equipment were provided for which payment is claimed in accordance with subsection b. of section 20 of P.L.1993, c.318 (C.2A:44A-20), and comply with the remainder of this section.

(2)   Upon its lodging for record, a Notice of Unpaid Balance and Right to File Lien, shall be served in accordance with the provisions for the service of lien claims in section 7 of P.L.1993, c.318 (C.2A:44A-7).

(3)   Unless the parties have otherwise agreed in writing to an alternative dispute resolution mechanism, within 10 days from the date the Notice of Unpaid Balance and Right to File Lien is lodged for record, the lien claimant shall also serve a demand for arbitration and fulfill all the requirements and procedures of the American Arbitration Association to institute an expedited proceeding before a single arbitrator designated by the American Arbitration Association. The demand for arbitration may be served in accordance with the provisions for the service of lien claims in section 7 of P.L.1993, c.318 (C.2A:44A-7) along with: (a) a copy of the completed and signed Notice of Unpaid Balance and Right to File Lien; and (b) proof by affidavit that the Notice of Unpaid Balance and Right to File Lien has been lodged for record.

If not yet provided at the time of service of the demand for arbitration, a copy of the Notice of Unpaid Balance and Right to File Lien marked "filed" by the clerk's office shall be provided by the claimant to the parties and the arbitrator, as a condition precedent to the issuance of an arbitrator's determination.

All arbitrations of Notices of Unpaid Balance and Right to File Lien pertaining to the same residential construction shall be determined by the same arbitrator, whenever possible. The claimant, owner, or any other party may also request consolidation in a single arbitration proceeding of the claimant's Notice of Unpaid Balance and Right to File Lien with any other Notice of Unpaid Balance and Right to File Lien not yet arbitrated but lodged for record by a potential lien claimant whose name was provided in accordance with section 37 of P.L.1993, c.318 (C.2A:44-37). The request shall be made in the demand for arbitration or, in the case of a request by a person other than the claimant, by letter to the arbitrator assigned to the arbitration or, if none has been assigned, to the appropriate arbitration administrator, within five days of when the demand for arbitration is served. The arbitrator shall grant or deny a request for a consolidated arbitration proceeding at the arbitrator's discretion.

(4)   Upon the closing of all hearings in the arbitration, the arbitrator shall make the following determinations: (a) whether the Notice of Unpaid Balance and Right to File Lien was in compliance with section 20 of P.L.1993, c.318 (C.2A:44A-20) and whether service was proper under section 7 of P.L.1993, c.318 (C.2A:44A-7); (b) the earned amount of the contract between the owner and the contractor in accordance with section 9 of P.L.1993, c.318 (C.2A:44A-9); (c) the validity and amount of any lien claim which may be filed pursuant to the Notice of Unpaid Balance and Right to File Lien; (d) the validity and amount of any liquidated or unliquidated setoffs or counterclaims to any lien claim which may be filed; and

(e) the allocation of costs of the arbitration among the parties. When making the above determination, the arbitrator shall also consider all determinations made by that arbitrator in any earlier arbitration proceeding pertaining to the same residential construction.

(5) If the amount of any setoffs or counterclaims presented in the arbitration cannot be determined by the arbitrator in a liquidated amount, the arbitrator, as a condition precedent to the filing of the lien claim, shall order the lien claimant to post a bond, letter of credit or funds with an attorney-at-law of New Jersey, or other such person or entity as may be ordered by the arbitrator in such amount as the arbitrator shall determine to be 110% of the approximate fair and reasonable value of such setoffs or counterclaims, but in no event greater than the amount of the lien claim which may be filed. This 110% limitation for any bond, letter of credit or funds shall also apply to any alternative dispute resolution mechanism to which the parties may agree. When making the above determinations, the arbitrator shall consider all determinations made by that arbitrator in any earlier arbitration proceeding pertaining to the same residential construction.

(6) The arbitrator shall make such determinations set forth in paragraphs (4) and (5) of this subsection and the arbitration proceeding shall be completed within 30 days of receipt of the lien claimant's demand for arbitration by the American Arbitration Association unless no response is filed, in which case the arbitrator shall make such determinations and the arbitration proceeding shall be deemed completed within 7 days after the time within which to respond has expired. These time periods for completion of the arbitration shall not be extended unless otherwise agreed to by the parties and approved by the arbitrator. If an alternative dispute mechanism is alternatively agreed to between the parties, such determination shall be made as promptly as possible making due allowance for all time limits and procedures set forth in this act. The arbitrator shall resolve a dispute regarding the timeliness of the demand for arbitration.

(7) Any contractor, subcontractor or supplier whose interests are affected by the filing of a Notice of Unpaid Balance and Right to File Lien under this act shall be permitted to join in such arbitration; but the arbitrator shall not determine the rights or obligations of any such parties except to the extent those rights or obligations are affected by the lien claimant's Notice of Unpaid Balance and Right to File Lien.

(8) Upon determination by the arbitrator that there is an amount which, pursuant to a valid lien shall attach to the improvement, the lien claimant shall, within 10 days of the lien claimant's receipt of the determination, lodge for record such lien claim in accordance with section 8 of P.L.1993, c.318 (C.2A:44A-8) and furnish any bond, letter of credit or funds required by the arbitrator's decision. The failure to lodge for record such a lien claim, or furnish the bond, letter of credit or funds, within the 10-day period, shall cause any lien claim to be invalid.

(9) Except for the arbitrator's determination itself, any such determination shall not be considered final in any legal action or proceeding, and shall not be used for purposes of collateral estoppel, res judicata, or law of the case to the extent applicable. Any finding of the arbitrator pursuant to this act shall not be admissible for any purpose in any other action or proceeding.

(10)   If either the lien claimant or the owner or community association in accordance with section 3 of P.L.1993, c.318 (C.2A:44A-3) is aggrieved by the arbitrator's determination, then the aggrieved party may institute a summary action in the Superior Court, Law Division, for the vacation, modification or correction of the arbitrator's determination. The arbitrator's determination shall be confirmed unless it is vacated, modified or corrected by the court. The court shall render its decision after giving due regard to the time limits and procedures set forth in this act and shall set time limits for lodging for record the lien claim if it finds, contrary to the arbitrator's determination, that the lien claim is valid or the 10-day requirement for lodging for record required by paragraph (8) of this subsection has expired.

(11)   In the event a Notice of Unpaid Balance and Right to File Lien is filed and the owner conveys its interest in real property to another person before a lien claim is filed, then prior to or at the time of conveyance, the owner may make a deposit with the county clerk where the improvement is located, in an amount no less than the amount set forth in the Notice of Unpaid Balance and Right to File Lien. For any deposit made with the county clerk, the county clerk shall discharge the Notice of Unpaid Balance and Right to File Lien or any related lien claim against the real property for which the deposit has been made. After the issuance of the arbitrator's determination set forth in paragraphs (4) and (5) of this subsection, any amount in excess of that determined by the arbitrator to be the amount of a valid lien claim shall be returned forthwith to the owner who has made the deposit. The balance shall remain where deposited unless the lien claim has been otherwise paid, satisfied by the parties, forfeited by the claimant, invalidated pursuant to paragraph (8) of this subsection or discharged under section 33 of P.L.1993, c.318 (C.2A:44A-

33). Notice shall be given by the owner in writing to the lien claimant within five days of making the deposit.

(12)   Solely for those lien claims arising from a residential construction contract, if a Notice of Unpaid Balance and Right to File Lien is determined to be without basis, the amount of the Notice of Unpaid Balance and Right to File Lien is significantly overstated, or the Notice of Unpaid Balance and Right to File Lien is not lodged for record: (a) in substantially the form, (b) in the manner, or (c) at a time in accordance with this act, then the claimant shall be liable for all damages suffered by the owner or any other party adversely affected by the Notice of Unpaid Balance and Right to File Lien, including all court costs, reasonable attorneys' fees and legal expenses incurred.

(13)   If the aggregate sum of all lien claims attaching to any real property that is the subject of a residential construction contract exceeds the amount due under a residential purchase agreement, less the amount due under any previously recorded mortgages or liens other than construction liens, then upon entry of judgment of all such lien claims, each lien claim shall be reduced pro rata. Each lien claimant's share then due shall be equal to the monetary amount of the lien claim multiplied by a fraction in which the denominator is the total monetary amount of all valid claims on the owner's interest in real property against which judgment has been entered, and the numerator is the amount of each particular lien claim for which judgment has been entered. The amount due under the residential purchase agreement shall be the net proceeds of the amount paid less previously recorded mortgages and liens other than construction liens and any required recording fees.

2A:44A-22.   Priority of mortgages over liens; conditions

a.   Every mortgage recorded before the filing of a lien claim or the filing of a Notice of Unpaid Balance and Right to File Lien in accordance with section 20 of P.L.1993, c.318 (C.2A:44A-20), shall have priority as to the land or other interest in real property described and any improvement wholly or partially erected or thereafter to be erected, constructed or completed thereon, over any lien established by virtue of P.L.1993, c.318 (C.2A:44A-1 et al.) to the extent that:

(1)   the mortgage secures funds that have been advanced or the mortgagee is obligated to advance to or for the benefit of the mortgagor before the filing of the lien claim or Notice of Unpaid Balance and Right to File Lien in accordance with section 20 of P.L.1993, c.318 (C.2A:44A-20); or

(2)   the mortgage secures funds advanced after the filing of a lien claim or the filing of a Notice of Unpaid Balance and Right to File Lien in accordance with section 20 of P.L.1993, c.318 (C.2A:44A-20), and the funds are applied in accordance with paragraphs (1) through (7) of subsection b. of this section.

b.   Every mortgage recorded after the filing of a lien claim or the filing of a Notice of Unpaid Balance and Right to File Lien in accordance with section 20 of P.L.1993, c.318 (C.2A:44A-20), shall have priority as to the land or other interest in real property described and any improvement wholly or partially erected or thereafter to be erected, constructed or completed thereon, over any lien established by virtue of this act to the extent that the mortgage secures funds which have been applied to:

(1)   The payments of amounts due to any claimants who have filed a lien claim or a Notice of Unpaid Balance and Right to File Lien;

(2)   The payment to or the securing of payment by, the party against whose interest the lien claim is filed of all or part of the purchase price of the land covered thereby and any subsequent payment made for the improvements to the land, including but not limited to any advance payment of interest to the holder of the mortgage as required by the mortgagee as a condition of the loan;

(3)   The payment of any valid lien or encumbrance which is, or can be established as, prior to a lien provided for by this act;

(4)   The payment of any tax, assessment or other State or municipal lien or charge due or payable at the time of, or within 60 days after, such payment, as required by the mortgagee as a condition of the loan;

(5)   The payment of any premium, counsel fee, consultant fee, interest or financing charges, or other cost related to the financing, any of which are required by the lender to be paid by the owner, provided that the total of same shall not be in excess of 10 percent of the principal amount of the mortgage securing the loan upon which they are based;

(6)   The payment to the owner of that portion of the purchase price of the real property on which the improvements are made or to be made which have previously been paid by the owner, exclusive of any

interest or any other carrying costs of such real property, provided, however, that at the time of the payment of such funds to the owner, the budget upon which the loan was made indicated that the amount of the loan is not less than the total of: (a) the purchase price of the real property, (b) the cost of constructing the improvements, and (c) any cost listed in paragraphs (3), (4), and (5) of subsection b. of this section; or

(7) An escrow in an amount not to exceed 150% of the amount necessary to secure payment of charges described in paragraphs (1), (3), (4) and (5) of subsection b. of this section.

c. Nothing in P.L.1993, c.318 (C.2A:44A-1 et al.) shall be deemed to supersede the mortgage priority provisions of R.S.46:9-8 or diminish the effect of a Notice of Settlement filed pursuant to P.L.1979, c.406 (C.46:16A-1 et seq.).

2A:44A-23. Payment of claims; pro rata payment

a. The amount due a lien claimant shall be paid only after the lien claim has been established by judgment, or, in the case of an execution sale, only to those lien claimants whose lien claims were filed before application was made to the court for distribution of the sale proceeds. All lien claims established by judgment are valid claims that shall be concurrent and shall be paid as provided in subsection c. of this section.

b. The sheriff or other officer conducting an execution sale authorized by section 24 of P.L.1993, c.318 (C.2A:44A-24) shall pay the proceeds to the clerk of the Superior Court and the Superior Court shall provide proper disposition of sale proceeds to the persons entitled thereto under P.L.1993, c.318 (C.2A:44A-1 et al.).

c. The Superior Court shall order the distribution of a lien fund, after its calculation in accordance with section 9 of P.L.1993, c.318 (C.2A:44A-9), in the following manner:

(1) If there are first tier lien claimants, the lien fund shall be allocated in amounts equal to their valid claims. If the total of those claims would exceed the maximum liability of the owner or community association as provided by section 9 of P.L.1993, c.318 (C.2A:44A-9), the allocations shall be reduced pro rata so as not to exceed that maximum liability;

(2) From the allocation to each first tier lien claimant, amounts shall be allocated equal to the valid claims of second tier lien claimants whose claims derive from contracts with that first tier lien claimant. If the total of the claims is less than the allocation to that first tier lien claimant, the first tier lien claimant shall be paid the balance. If the total of the claims exceeds the allocation to that first tier lien claimant, the second tier claimants' allocations shall be reduced pro rata so as not to exceed that first tier lien claimant allocation;

(3) From the allocation to each second tier lien claimant, amounts shall be allocated equal to the valid claims of third tier lien claimants whose claims derive from contracts with that second tier lien claimant. If the total of the claims is less than the allocation to that second tier claimant, the second tier lien claimant shall be paid the balance. If the total of the claims exceeds the allocation to that second tier lien claimant, the allocation to the third tier lien claimants shall be reduced pro rata so as not to exceed that second tier lien claimant allocation;

(4) If there are no first tier lien claimants, the lien fund for second tier lien claimants shall be allocated in amounts equal to that second tier's valid claims. If the total of the claims of any group of second tier lien claimants exceeds the lien fund for that group of claimants as provided by section 9 of P.L.1993, c.318 (C.2A:44A-9), the allocations shall be reduced pro rata so as not to exceed that lien fund; and

(5) If there are no first or second tier lien claimants, the lien fund for third tier lien claimants shall be allocated in amounts equal to that third tier's valid claims. If the total of the claims of any group of third tier lien claimants exceeds the lien fund for that group of claimants as provided by section 9 of P.L.1993, c.318 (C.2A:44A-9), the allocations shall be reduced pro rata so as not to exceed that lien fund.

2A:44A-24.1 Lien claims enforced by suit

a. Subject to the requirements of section 14 of P.L.1993, c.318 (C.2A:44A-14), and in the case of lien claims arising from residential construction contracts the additional requirements of sections 20 and 21 of P.L.1993, c.318 (C.2A:44A-20 and 2A:44A-21), a lien claim arising under P.L.1993, c.318 (C.2A:44A-1 et al.) shall be enforced by a suit commenced in the Superior Court within one year of the date of the last provision of work, services, material or equipment, payment for which the lien claim was filed. Venue shall be laid in the county in which the real property affected by the lien claim is located.

b. A lien claimant shall join as party defendants the owner or community association, if applicable, in accordance with section 3 of P.L.1993, c.318 (C.2A:44A-3), contractor or subcontractor alleged to have failed to make payments for which the lien claim has been filed and any other person having an interest in the real property that would be adversely affected by the judgment. The court shall order joinder of necessary parties or determine if it is appropriate for the suit to proceed if party defendants are not joined.

c.   The court shall stay the suit to the extent that the lien claimant's contract or the contract of another party against whose account the lien claim is asserted provides that any disputes pertaining to the validity or amount of a lien claim are subject to arbitration or other dispute resolution mechanism.

d.   Upon commencement of the suit, the lien claimant shall cause a Notice of Lis Pendens to be filed in the office of the county clerk or register pursuant to N.J.S.2A:15-6 et seq.

e.   A party to a suit to enforce a lien claim shall be entitled to assert any defense available to any other party in contesting the amount for which a claimant seeks to have the lien reduced to judgment.

f.   The judgment to be entered in a suit to enforce a lien claim shall (1) establish the amount due to the lien claimant; and (2) direct the public sale by the sheriff or other such officer as the court may direct of the real property and improvement affected by the lien. The proceeds of the sale shall be distributed in accordance with section 23 of P.L.1993, c.318 (C.2A:44A-23). If funds are realized at the sale in an amount greater than the lien fund, the surplus funds shall be distributed in accordance with law.

g.   Nothing in this act shall bar recovery of money damages pursuant to a lien claim arising under P.L.1993, c.318 (C.2A:44A-1 et al.).

h.   A judgment obtained against a community association that is unpaid may be enforced by assessment against unit owners as they would be assessed for any other common expense, after reasonable notice, and in a manner directed by the court. In ordering assessments, the court shall be guided by the master deed, bylaws or other document governing the association. A judgment shall not be enforced by the sale of any common elements, common areas or common buildings or structures of a real property development.

i.   Upon resolution of the suit other than by the entry of final judgment in favor of the plaintiff in accordance with subsection f. of this section, a cancellation or discharge of lis pendens should be filed, by the party who filed the enforcement action, in the office of the county clerk or register where the notice of lis pendens is filed.

2A:44A-25. Issuance of writ of execution

If judgment in an action to enforce a lien claim under this act is entered in favor of the lien claimant, a writ of execution may issue thereon, in accordance with the judgment.

2A:44A-27. Interest in residential property, priority to all subsequent liens

The interests in real property set forth in section 21 of this act shall have priority to all subsequent liens under this act upon the land and upon the improvements thereon, except such as may be removable as between landlord and tenant, which may be sold and removed by virtue of any lien for the erection, construction or completion of the same, free from the prior encumbrances.

2A:44A-30. Filing of certificate to discharge lien claim of record

a.   When a lien claim has been filed and the claim has been paid, satisfied or settled by the parties or forfeited by the claimant, the claimant or claimant's successor in interest or attorney shall, within 30 days of payment, satisfaction or settlement, or within 7 days of demand by any interested party, file with the county clerk a certificate, duly acknowledged or proved, directing the county clerk to discharge the lien claim of record, which certificate shall contain:

(1)   The date of filing the lien claim;

(2)   The book and page number endorsed thereon;

(3)   The name of the owner of the land, or the community association, if applicable, named in the notice;

(4)   The location of the property; and

(5)   The name of the person for whom the work, services, equipment or materials was provided.

b.   If the claimant shall fail or refuse to file this certificate, as set forth in subsection a. of this section, then any party in interest may proceed in a summary manner by filing an order to show cause in accordance with the Rules of Court adopted by the Supreme Court of New Jersey. A judge of the Superior Court may, upon good cause being shown, and absent receipt of written objections and grounds for same, order the lien claim discharged on the return date of the order to show cause. The county clerk shall thereupon attach the certificate or order to the original notice of lien claim on file and shall note on the record thereof "discharged by certificate" or "discharged by court order," as the case may be and any lien foreclosure action shall be dismissed with prejudice.

c. Any party in interest may proceed to discharge a lien claim on the ground that it is without factual basis by filing an order to show cause in the same manner as set forth in subsection b. of this section.

d. In those circumstances in which the lien claim has been paid in full, the lien claimant has failed to file a lien claim discharge pursuant to this section, and at least 13 months have elapsed since the date of the lien claim, the owner or community association may, in accordance with section 33 of P.L.1993, c.318 (C.2A:44A-33) submit for filing a duly acknowledged discharge certificate substantially in the form provided by subsection a. of this section accompanied by an affidavit setting forth the circumstances of payment as set forth below:

OWNER (OR COMMUNITY ASSOCIATION) AFFIDAVIT OF PAYMENT TO DISCHARGE LIEN CLAIM

TO THE CLERK, COUNTY OF

The undersigned, being duly sworn upon the undersigned's oath, avers as follows:

1. I am an owner of real property located at (address of property subject to lien), in that certain tract or parcel of land and premises described as Block ____, Lot ____, on the tax map of the (municipality) of _____, County of _____, State of New Jersey (In the case of a community association, I am an (officer/manager/agent) of the community association, (name of community association) for property located at (location of property development).)

2. On or about (date), I caused to be sent to (name of contractor or subcontractor to whom payment was made), located at (address designated for payment by the filed lien claim form), the final payment in the amount of ($) in full satisfaction of a certain lien claim dated (date) which was filed by (name of lien claimant) against the real property designated in paragraph 1, on (date) in the office of the county clerk of the County of (name of county) in Construction Lien Book ___, Page ____.

3. At least 13 months have elapsed since the date of the lien claim and 90 days before filing this affidavit, I mailed or caused to be mailed by certified mail to the last known address of the lien claimant as set forth in the filed lien claim form written notice of my intention to file a discharge certificate with respect to the lien claim. To the best of my knowledge and belief, no written communication denying or disputing payment in full of the lien claim has been received from the lien claimant (name).

4. Wherefore, the undersigned directs the county clerk of the County of (name of county) to cause to be filed the discharge certificate accompanying this affidavit, and further directs the county clerk to cause a notation of the discharge of the lien to be endorsed upon the margin of the record of the original lien claim, stating that the discharge is filed, and setting forth the date, book and page number of the filed discharge.

Name of Owner/Community Association

Signed _____

(Type or Print Name and Title)

NOTARIAL FOR INDIVIDUAL OWNER

STATE OF NEW JERSEY

COUNTY OF   ss:

On this ____ day of _____ 20___, before me, the subscriber, personally appeared (name of owner/community association) who, I am satisfied, is/are the person(s) named in and who executed the within instrument, and thereupon acknowledged that the owner/community association signed, sealed and delivered the same as the owner's/community association's act and deed, for the purposes therein expressed.

_____ _____

NOTARY PUBLIC

NOTARIAL FOR CORPORATE OR LIMITED LIABILITY OWNER/COMMUNITY ASSOCIATION:

STATE OF NEW JERSEY

COUNTY OF 9 (   )   ss:

On this ____ day of _____ 20__, before me, the subscriber, personally appeared (person signing on behalf of owner/community association) who, I am satisfied is the Secretary (or other officer/manager/agent) of the Corporation (partnership or limited liability company) named herein and who by me duly sworn/affirmed, asserted authority to act on behalf of the Corporation (partnership or limited liability company) and who, by virtue of its Bylaws, or Resolution of its Board of Directors (or partnership or operating agreement) executed the within instrument on its behalf, and thereupon acknowledged that the owner/community association signed, sealed and delivered same as owner's/community association's act and deed, for the purposes herein expressed.

_____

NOTARY PUBLIC

e.   Any lien claimant who fails to discharge a lien claim of record pursuant to this section shall be liable for all court costs, and reasonable legal expenses, including, but not limited to, attorneys' fees, incurred by the owner, community association, the contractor, or subcontractor, or any combination of owner, community association, contractor and subcontractor, as applicable, to discharge or obtain the discharge of the lien, and in addition thereto, the court shall enter judgment against the claimant for damages to any or all of the parties adversely affected by the failure to discharge the lien.

f.   Upon discharge of record in all cases, the party who filed the enforcement action shall cause the Notice of Lis Pendens to be cancelled or discharged of record pursuant to N.J.S.2A:15-6 et seq. Any party who filed the enforcement action who fails to cancel or discharge the lis pendens of record pursuant to this section shall be liable for all court costs, and reasonable legal expenses, including but not limited to, attorneys' fees, incurred by the owner, community association, the contractor, or subcontractor, or any other interested party, or any combination thereof, as applicable, to obtain the cancellation or discharge of the lis pendens, and in addition thereto, the court shall enter judgment against the claimant for damages to any or all of the parties adversely affected by the failure to cancel or discharge the lis pendens.

2A:44A-31. Filing of surety bond, deposit

a.   When a lien claim is filed against any improvement and land under this act, the owner, community association in accordance with section 3 of P.L.1993, c.318 (C.2A:44A-3), contractor or subcontractor may execute and file with the proper county clerk a bond in favor of the lien claimant, with a surety company, duly authorized to transact business in this State, as surety thereon in an amount equal to 110% of the amount claimed by the lien claimant. The amount of the bond shall be equal to 110% of the amount claimed by the lien claimant but in the case of a lien claim arising from a residential construction contract, no greater than the earned amount of the contract between the owner and the contractor as determined by the arbitrator in accordance with paragraph (4) of subsection b. of section 21 of P.L.1993, c.318 (C.2A:44A-21). The bond shall be filed in accordance with the language set forth in subsection d. of this section, along with payment in the amount of $25, conditioned upon the payment of any judgment and costs that may be recovered by the lien claimant under this claim. Any form of bond proffered that contains language inconsistent with the language set forth in subsection d. of this section shall be the basis for a cause of action to strike such language from the form of bond.

b.   As an alternative, the owner, community association, contractor or subcontractor may deposit with the clerk of the Superior Court of New Jersey, funds constituting an amount equal to 110% of the amount claimed by the lien claimant, but in the case of a lien claim arising from a residential construction contract, no greater than the earned amount of the contract between the owner and the contractor as determined by the arbitrator in accordance with paragraph (4) of subsection b. of section 21 of P.L.1993, c.318 (C.2A:44A-21). The deposit shall be made along with payment in the amount of $25, conditioned upon the payment of any judgment and costs that may be recovered by the lien claimant under this claim. The deposit may be made without the necessity of commencing any legal action. The written receipt provided by the court clerk for the deposit made may be filed with the county clerk as evidence of that deposit.

c.   Any surety bond filed with the county clerk under this section shall be discharged, and any deposit with the clerk of the Superior Court shall be returned to the depositor, without court order, upon presentment by the owner, community association, contractor or subcontractor of any of the following:

(1) a duly acknowledged certificate as provided in paragraph (2) or (3) of subsection a. of section 33 of P.L.1993, c.318 (C.2A:44A-33);

(2) an order of discharge as provided in paragraph (4) of subsection a. of section 33 of P.L.1993, c.318 (C.2A:44A-33);

(3) a judgment of dismissal or other final judgment against the lien claimant; or

(4) a true copy of a Stipulation of Dismissal, with prejudice, executed by the lien claimant or its representative in any action to foreclose the lien claim which is subject to the surety bond or deposit.

d.   The bond shall be filed in substantially the following form:

(Name of Bond Company)

(Bond No.   ) Bond Amount $_____

BOND DISCHARGING CONSTRUCTION LIEN

WHEREAS, on the (date), (name of claimant) (hereinafter "Lienor") filed a Construction Lien for the sum of (amount written out)   ($), in the office of the Clerk of the County of (name of county where lien claim was filed), (hereinafter "Clerk"), against the real property of owner, (name of owner), or community association (or name of community association) and the tenancy interest of Lot (#), Block (#), (address of property or name and location of the property development in the case of a community association) on the Tax Map of Township of (name of municipality), County of (name of county), State of New Jersey as more fully set forth in the notice of lien, a true copy of which is attached hereto, and which lien was filed (date lien claim was filed) in book (#), page (#).

WHEREAS, in accordance with the "Construction Lien Law," P.L.1993, c.318 (C.2A:44A-1 et al.), the Principal is permitted to file a bond for 110% of the lien amount, which would be a total bond penalty of (amount written out) ($) (hereinafter "Penal Sum").

NOW THEREFORE, in consideration of the discharge of said lien by the Clerk, the Principal and (name of bond company) as surety, having an office at (address of bond company) and authorized to do business as a surety, do hereby pursuant to the statute provided, in such case made and jointly and severally undertake and become bound to the Clerk in an amount not exceeding the Penal Sum, ($) conditioned for the payment of any and all judgments that may be rendered against said property in favor of the Lienor, its successors or assigns, in any action or proceedings to enforce the alleged lien as described.

Sealed with our seal and dated the day of (month), (year)

Witness:_____   (Name of principal)

By:(Signature)

Title:(Printed name and title of signatory)

Witness:_____   (Name of Bond Company)

By: (Signature)

Title:(Printed name and title of signatory)

2A:44A-32. Release, discharge from claim

When the bond, deposit or any combination thereof, authorized by section 31 of this act, is properly filed or deposited, the improvements and land described in the lien claim shall thereupon be released and discharged from the claim and no execution shall issue against the improvements and land. The words "released by bond" or "released by deposit of funds," as applicable, and a reference to the time and place of filing of the bond or deposit shall be entered by the county clerk upon the record of the lien claim.

2A:44A-33. Discharge of record of lien claim

a.   A lien claim may be discharged of record by the county clerk:

(1) Upon the execution and filing with the county clerk of a surety bond, or the deposit of funds with the clerk of the Superior Court of New Jersey, in favor of the claimant in an amount equal to 110% of the amount of the lien claim; or

(2) Upon receipt of a duly acknowledged certificate, discharging the lien claim from the claimant having filed the lien claim, or the claimant's successor in interest, or attorney; or

(3) Pursuant to the filing of an owner's or community association's discharge certificate in accordance with section 30 of P.L.1993, c.318 (C.2A:44A-30), provided that 90 days prior to the filing of the affidavit, substantially in the form set forth in section 30 of P.L.1993, c.318 (C.2A:44A-30), the lien claimant is notified by certified mail at the lien claimant's last known address of the owner's or community association's intent to file a discharge certificate and no written communication from the lien claimant denying or disputing payment in full of the lien claim is filed with the county clerk and served on the owner or community association; or

(4) Pursuant to an order of discharge by the court.

b.   When judgment of dismissal or final other judgment against the lien claimant is entered in an action to enforce the lien claim under this act and no appeal is taken within the time allowed for an appeal, or if an appeal is taken within the time allowed for an appeal, or if an appeal is taken and finally determined against the lien claimant, the court before which the judgment was rendered, upon application and written notice to the lien claimant as the court shall direct, shall order the county clerk to enter a discharge of the lien claim.

c.   If an appeal is taken by the claimant, the claim shall be discharged unless the claimant posts a bond, in an amount to be determined by the court, to protect the owner or community association from the reasonable costs, expenses and damages which may be incurred by virtue of the continuance of the lien claim encumbrance.

d.   Upon discharge of record of the lien claim, unless the action for enforcement also involves claims, by way of counterclaim, cross claim or interpleader, arising out of or related to the improvements that are the subject of the lien claim in which the owner or community association is an interested party, the court shall also order that the owner or community association no longer be a party to an action to enforce the lien claim, and the surety issuing the bond shall be added as a necessary party.

2A:44A-34. Book, page number of original record of lien claim necessary for release, discharge

A discharge, subordination or release of a lien claim or Notice of Unpaid Balance and Right to File Lien, a receipt of payment of a lien claim, or any order of the court discharging or releasing a lien claim, shall recite the book and page number of the original record of the lien claim, and a full description of the property discharged or released. The county clerk may refuse to discharge, release or satisfy a lien claim or file a receipt of payment of a lien claim unless the provisions of this section have been satisfied.

2A:44A-35. Discharge, subordination, release of lien claim

A discharge, subordination or release of a lien claim or Notice of Unpaid Balance and Right to File Lien shall be duly acknowledged or proved, and recorded in a properly indexed book for that purpose. A notation of the record of the discharge of a lien claim or Notice of Unpaid Balance and Right to File Lien shall be endorsed upon the margin of the record in the book where the original lien or Notice of Unpaid Balance and Right to File Lien is recorded stating that the discharge is filed, giving the date of filing and setting forth the book and the page number where the discharge, or receipt of payment of the lien or order or owner's or community association's discharge certificate discharging the lien, is recorded.

2A:44A-36. Liability for fraud

A person who fraudulently deprives a person entitled to the benefits of this act shall be liable to that person for any damages resulting therefrom.

2A:44A-37. Furnishing of list of subcontractors, suppliers

a.   If required in a contract or upon written request from an owner or community association to a contractor, a subcontractor, or both, the contractor or subcontractor shall, within 10 days, provide the owner or community association with an accurate and full list of the names and addresses of each subcontractor and supplier who may have a right to file a lien pursuant to this act.

b.   If required in a contract or upon written request from a contractor to a subcontractor, the subcontractor shall, within 10 days, provide the contractor with an accurate and full list of the names and addresses of each subcontractor or supplier who may have a right to file a lien pursuant to this act.

c.   Any list provided pursuant to subsection a. or b. of this section shall be verified under oath by the person providing same.

d.   Reliance upon the verified list shall be prima facie evidence establishing the bona fides of payment made in reliance thereon and shall constitute an absolute defense to any claim that the party making such payment should have made additional inquiry to determine the identity of potential claimants.

e.   Any person to whom a written request has been made pursuant to subsection a. or b. of this section who does not provide a list in compliance with this section shall be liable in damages to: (1) the party requesting the list; or (2) the owner or community association, including, but not limited to, court costs and the reasonable legal expenses, including attorneys' fees, incurred by any or all of them, in defending or causing the discharge of a lien claim asserted by a party whose name is omitted from the list.

2A:44A-38. Waivers of construction lien rights

Waivers of construction lien rights are against public policy, unlawful, and void, unless given in consideration for payment for the work, services, materials or equipment provided or to be provided, and such waivers shall be effective only upon and to the extent that such payment is actually received.

12

GLOSSARY

Acceleration: The advancement of a project ahead of its regular schedule.

Acceptance Period: A period of time, usually referred to in bidding documents, during which the owner may review bids to determine which, if any, are to be accepted. The term usually relates only to public contracts. The owner or agency may hold each bidder's bond or security deposit throughout the acceptance period, after which they are replaced by payment and performance bonds in the case of the successful bidders, and are returned to all other bidders.

Accident: An unplanned event, whether or not the accident results in loss or injury.

Accounting: The system of recording and summarizing business and financial transactions and analyzing, verifying and reporting the results, primarily to be used in making economic decisions.

Accrual Method: A basis of recordkeeping and a method of accounting whereby all income is recorded at the time it is earned, regardless of when it is received. Expenses are recorded at the time they are incurred, regardless of when they are paid.

Acid-Test Ratio: A calculation of a firm's liquidity position; that is, the ratio of its "quick" assets (current assets less inventory) to current liabilities.

Acts of God: Highly unusual or catastrophic events (hurricanes, tornadoes, etc.) that cause damages or delays that could not have been reasonably foreseen.

ADA: *Americans With Disabilities Act.* Statute that prevents unreasonable discrimination based on personal disability.

Addendum (pl. Addenda): Modifications to the contract documents issued before the bid date for consideration by the plan holders in preparing bids. Addenda become official parts of the contract documents and are legally binding on the signers of the contract.

Agent: A person authorized to act for another; one who is employed to represent another in business and legal dealings with third persons. In a typical agency relationship, three parties are involved: a principal, an agent, and a third party. The agent represents the principal in dealing with the third party or parties.

Agreement: A written or verbal contract between two or more parties, an understanding regarding common interests.

Allowance: A sum of money set aside by the owner to remove a particular portion of work from competitive bidding. This is typical of government-subsidized institutions with work that must be competitively bid and with projects in which certain portions of the work are proprietary and, therefore, must be removed from competitive bidding. It is also used where the owner wishes to personally select construction components and it is impractical to write specifications for such items.

Arbitration: The submission of a dispute to a third party (individual or party), known as an arbitrator(s), whose judgment is final and binding. Decisions at arbitration hearings, unlike those in judicial cases, do not establish precedents.

Asbestos: A mineral (magnesium silicate) that has been processed and used to fireproof buildings, insulate electrical wires, and make brake linings in cars. Asbestos has been proven to have serious, long-term health consequences. The primary risk comes from breathing airborne asbestos particles. Diseases caused from asbestos exposure include asbestosis, mesothelioma, and lung cancer.

As-Built Drawings: The final drawings submitted by the contractor to the owner illustrating how a project was actually built.

Assets: Resources owned by the company that create value for the business. Assets are divided into current assets and noncurrent assets.

Balance Sheet: A statement of the financial condition of a business at a point in time that indicates the assets, liabilities, and owners' equity of the business.

Bar Chart: A series of bars plotted to a horizontal time scale used to schedule a construction project. Each bar represents the beginning, duration, and completion of a designated segment of the total project.

Bid: An offer to perform a contract for work and labor or for supplying materials at a specified price. In the construction industry, a bid is considered an offer by the contractor to the owner. The bid becomes a contract after the other party accepts the bidder's offer with all other contractual requirements.

Bid Bond: A form of security that ensures the bidder will enter into a contract for the amount bid if an award is made to the bidder.

Bond: An insurance contract by which a bonding agency guarantees payment of a specified sum in the event of a financial loss. Bond requirements depend on the size, risk, and liability of the work a contractor does. In the construction industry, there are different kinds of bonds. (See Bid Bond and Surety Bond.)

Building Code: A set of rules that specify the minimum acceptable level of safety for constructed objects. Building codes are developed by standards organizations through a network of development committees with representatives from the various affected entities. The building code becomes law of a particular jurisdiction when formally enacted by the appropriate authority.

Certificate of Occupancy: A document issued by the building inspector certifying that the structure conforms to all relevant code sections and is, therefore, safe for use. An owner must obtain a certificate of occupancy before a building can be used. A new building cannot be considered complete until a certificate of occupancy has been issued. In some instances, a partial certificate of occupancy will be issued for portions of the building to be occupied.

Certificate of Substantial Completion: The document issued by the architect when the building, or a portion thereof, is compete to the degree that the owner can use the building, or a portion thereof, for its intended purpose.

Change Order: A document signed and dated by both the owner and contractor acknowledging that the contract has been modified to reflect a change in the scope of work. A change order generally reflects the change in the contract price and/or time that has been agreed upon as a result of the changed scope of work. The change may be requested by the architect, owner, or contractor.

Claim: A demand, an assertion, a pretense, a right or title to. An action initiated by one of the parties of a contract against the other party. This action may be in the form of a written letter, a legal document, or some instrument establishing the difference between the two parties.

Codes: Regulations, ordinances, or statutory requirements of a governmental unit relating to building construction and occupancy, adopted and administered for the protection of public health, safety, and welfare.

Competitive Bidding: A process whereby sealed proposals are submitted to the owner for consideration. Competitive bidding is mandatory on public work projects. A private owner may choose to use competitive bidding in securing the most economical contractor for the construction of the project. However, a private owner is not legally bound to the competitive bidding process.

Completed Contract Method: An accounting method of earnings recognition in which all costs and revenues on a construction project are deferred until the project is completed. Then, both costs and revenues are recognized at the same time. Contrast this method with the "Percentage of Completion" method of earnings recognition.

Construction Management: The process of professionally managing a construction project from start to finish for the purpose of controlling time, cost, and quality. Ideally, construction management is linked to the owner as an agent and thereby places itself in a fiduciary relationship with the owner. In this relationship, the construction manager can properly represent the owner to both the design professional and the contractors without concern regarding conflict of interest on his part.

Contract: A mutually understood agreement that has a legal purpose and is made by two or more parties, each party having legal capacity. In order to render a contract valid, it must include an offer, acceptance, and consideration on the part of both parties, the ability of both parties to contract, and mutual assent.

Contract Price: The amount agreed upon by the contracting parties for performing all labor and furnishing all materials contemplated by their contract.

Contractor: A person who, for compensation or with the intent to sell, arranges or undertakes or offers to undertake or submits a bid to construct, alter, repair, add to, subtract from, improve, move, wreck, or demolish for another, any building, highway, road, excavation or other structure, building, or improvement attached to real property.

Corporation: A legal entity separate from the persons who formed it. Corporations are owned by individual stockholders. If a corporation fails, shareholders normally only stand to lose their investment and employees will lose their jobs. Generally, neither will be further liable for debts that remain owing to the corporation's creditors.

Cost Control: Management procedures that monitor and track project costs for purposes of performing within the estimate.

Cost-Plus-Fee Contract: An agreement under which the contractor is reimbursed for direct and indirect costs and in addition is paid a fee for services. The fee is often tied to other incentives, such as cost reductions, completion date, or attainment of project milestones.

Credit: The term used in a double-entry accounting system. An entry on the right-hand side of an account constitutes an addition to revenue, net worth, or liability account. Correct accounting procedures require that debits equal credits for each entry. For example, if a note receivable is collected, the company will debit cash for the amount of the note and credit the notes receivable account in the same amount.

Critical Path Method (CPM): A planning and scheduling method that uses arrow diagrams to show the connection between work activities or tasks in the construction process. It determines the relative significance of each activity and establishes the sequence and duration of operations.

Current Assets: Assets that can be converted into cash within one year or one operating cycle.

Current Liabilities: Liabilities currently payable or scheduled to become payable within one year or one operating cycle. Examples are notes payable, accounts payable, unpaid wages, payroll taxes, and sales taxes due.

Damages: In the context of a construction contract, damages are losses suffered by a party to a construction contract as the result of a breach by another party, for which a court will provide a remedy.

Damages, Actual: Real, substantial, and just damages, or the amount awarded to a complainant in compensation for his actual and real loss or injury, as opposed to "nominal" or "punitive" damages.

Damages, Consequential: Damage, loss or injury that does not flow directly from the act of the party but only from some of the reasonably foreseeable consequences or results of the wrongful act.

Debit: The term used in a double-entry accounting system. To debit is to record an entry on the left side of a ledger account. Debits represent increases in asset and expense accounts, and decreases in liability, capital, and revenue accounts. Correct accounting procedures require that debits equal credits for each entry. For example, if a note receivable is collected, the company will debit cash for the amount of the note and credit the notes receivable account in the same amount.

Depreciation: The amount of expense charged against earnings by a company to write off the cost of an asset over its useful life, giving consideration to wear and tear, obsolescence, and salvage value. A portion of depreciation expense is apportioned to each accounting period.

Design-Build (or Design-Construct): A method of organizing a building project in which a single entity does the design and construction of the structure at a set fee negotiated in advance. In a conventional construction contract, an owner hires both an architect and a contractor separately. In the design-build contract, the owner negotiates only one contract with one organization.

Detailed survey (lump sum) contract: A contract where the contractor agrees to perform a project for a predetermined lump sum payment amount. The contractor is obliged to satisfactorily complete the project regardless of whether the contractors makes a profit or suffers a financial loss.

Direct Costs: In construction, those costs that can be directly identified as belonging to a specific project.

Drawings: Illustrations that show the physical description of the project to be constructed. They include the type, quantity, size, and location of each item in the project.

EEO: *Equal Employment Opportunity Act* of 1972. Provides power to courts to rule against employment discrimination regarding race, color, religion, sex, national origin, or age.

Employee: Anyone who is involved in "work" or its equivalent by physical or mental exertion, as controlled or required by the employer, and done for the primary benefit of the employer and the business. Neither partners nor volunteers are considered employees. An employee generally works under the direction and control of a supervisor or owner, typically for an hourly wage or by piecework.

Employer: Any person acting directly or indirectly in the interest of an employer in relation to an employee.

Estimating: A process of analyzing and compiling the cost of labor and material needed to complete a given project. It involves calculating the amount of labor and equipment needed to do the work and multiplying the volume by costs per unit or measurement.

Expense: A cost of doing business, including direct cost, indirect cost, general and administrative expense, and other expenses.

Extension: Extra time granted to complete the project.

Fast-Track Method: A method that allows the contractor to begin construction on earlier phases of the project before all the plans are completed for the entire project. Caution must be exercised in the signing of a contract using this method. Many changes may result when going from phase to phase, and provisions must be included in the initial contract to compensate the contractor for additional work.

Field Order: A minor change in the contract that is not expected to result in any appreciable extra cost or time.

First Aid: Initial care given immediately to an injured person.

Fixed Assets: Tangible property, used in the operation of a business, that does not fall into the category of current assets. It often includes land, equipment, buildings, furniture, and fixtures.

Float Time: In project scheduling, the difference between the amount of time available to accomplish an activity and the time necessary to accomplish the activity.

Friable: Compounds or particles that can be crumbled by hand (often referring to asbestos).

Front-End Loading: The practice of overpricing items of work done at the beginning of a job and underpricing those at the end so that the contractor or subcontractor can receive disproportionately larger payments at the beginning of the contract.

General Conditions: Those portions of the contract documents that set forth many of the rights, responsibilities, and relationships of the parties involved. Conditions can be either expressed, which are stated in the contract, or implied, which are not set forth in words but arise out of the intentions of the parties to the contract.

General Contract: Under the single contract system, the contract between the owner and the contractor for construction of the entire work. Under the separate contract system, it is the contract between the owner and the contractor for construction of architectural and structural work.

General Overhead: A company's general and administrative expenses that are not directly related to project costs, such as accounting costs, computer costs, rent, utilities, and similar operating costs.

Gross Profit: The excess of company revenues over direct costs and indirect costs.

Hazardous Material: Any substance that can cause injury or death.

Income Statement: Financial document that illustrates a company's financial status over a given period of time. Sometimes called profit and loss statement, operating statement, or statement of earnings. The income statement reports only the financial condition of the company covered during the accounting period, and does not reflect the current financial situation.

Indemnification: To hold harmless against liability. Owners include indemnity or hold-harmless clauses in contracts with contractors.

Indirect Costs: In construction, costs that apply directly to construction earnings but to more than one job.

Injunction: A legal order to refrain from doing a specified act.

Insurance: A contract whereby, for a stipulated consideration, one party undertakes to compensate the other for loss on a specified subject by specifying perils. The party agreeing to make the compensation usually is called the insurer or underwriter; the other is the insured; the agreed consideration is the premium; the written contract is the policy; the events insured against are risks or perils; and the subject, right, or interest to be protected is the insurable interest. Bonding is not a form of insurance, even though surety bonds are frequently sold by insurance agents and insurance companies often act as sureties.

Invitational Bid: A private project that is open for bid only from invited contractors.

Job Costing: The process of tracking the costs associated with a work item over multiple projects. Job costing information is used to increase accuracy in project estimating. It includes direct and indirect costs.

Job Log: A daily record of all work, deliveries, accidents, and unusual events that take place at the job site.

Joint Venture: Created when two or more firms join together on a particular project. A joint venture contract requires a common purpose and equal control among parties. Though the joint venture itself becomes a separate business entity, the companies maintain their individual business types.

Laborer: Any person who, under properly authorized contract, personally performs labor for improving real property.

Liability: A legal term signifying legal or financial responsibility.

Liabilities: A financial term referring to the obligations, debts, and claims against the assets of a business.

Lien: A legal right to take or hold property as payment or security for payment of a debt.

Lien, Mechanics': A claim created by law for the purpose of securing priority of payment of the price value of the work performed and materials furnished in erecting or repairing a building or other structure and, as such, attached to the land as well as to buildings and improvements erected thereon.

Lien, Partial Waiver of: In the construction industry, a document used to certify that a portion of the total amount due to a subcontractor has been paid and, therefore, that portion or amount of money cannot be used as a basis for a lien against the property.

Lien Waiver: To deny the right expressed in the lien. In the construction industry, it is a certificate issued upon completion of the work, signifying that all monies have been paid and that the right to the lien against the property is removed.

Liquidated Damages: A dollar amount stipulated in the contract and agreed upon at the time the contract is formed as to the amount of damages to be recovered by either party for a breach of the agreement by the other. It is written in the contract as an amount established to be withheld by the owner on a daily basis for every day past the stipulated completion date of the contract. A "liquidated damages" clause in the contract differs from a "penalty" clause in that the purpose of a "penalty" clause is to secure performance, while the purpose of a "liquidated damages" clause is to fix the amount to be paid in place of performance. Liquidated damages are enforceable if they represent a reasonable effort to forecast, at the time of contract formation, the actual damages the owner might incur as a result of the delay of the project.

Long-Term Debt: That portion of a debt to be paid later than the current operating cycle or one year, whichever is later. It relates to the principal portion of notes, bonds, or other securities payable and is part of long-term liabilities.

Long-Term Liabilities: Liabilities of a business that are due in more than one year.

Markup: The amount added to a bid to cover overhead and profit. In an estimate, the markup is often calculated as a percentage of project costs.

Material Supplier: A person or organization under contract to the owner, contractor, subcontractor, or sub-subcontractor who supplies materials or equipment to the site of the improvement. The material supplier performs no labor or installation of the materials.

MSDS: Material Safety Data Sheet. A document that describes the properties and hazards of a chemical.

Negligence: Failure to exercise the degree of care that a reasonable and prudent party would exercise under the same circumstances. Negligence occurs when a professional standard of care is not met. An architect's failure to show the existence of an electric power line on a set of plans, which the architect knew was in the construction area, is an example of negligence.

Net Income: The amount of revenues of a business remaining after costs, expenses, and taxes on income have been deducted.

Net Working Capital: The excess of current assets over current liabilities.

Nonconforming Work: Work that does not fulfill the requirements of the contract documents.

Notice of Award: The formal document from the owner informing the winning contractor that the bid has been accepted.

Notice to Bidders: Also called the Invitation to Bid, the notice to bidders is the formal document that contains information needed to bid on an upcoming project.

Notice to Proceed: Written communication issued by the owner that authorizes the contractor to proceed with work and establishes the date when work begins. This also applies to a notice from the general contractor to the subcontractor to proceed, although such communication is often a verbal notice to proceed.

OSHA: Occupational Safety and Health Administration. A federal agency that regulates and enforces safety in workplaces. Also *Occupational Safety and Health Act* – the law that defines safety in workplaces.

Overhead: Company administrative and project-related costs that are not directly related to project costs, such as safety costs, accounting costs, sanitation costs, computer costs, etc.

Owners' Equity - Net Worth: The residual interest in assets that remains after deducting liabilities.

Partnership: A relationship between two or more persons based upon a written, oral, or implied agreement, to combine their resources and skill in a joint enterprise and to share profits and losses jointly.

Payment Bond: A legal instrument that guarantees payment for labor and materials used or supplied in the performance of the contract. The payment bond protects the owner, developer, and contractor against liens filed by unpaid parties to the work. A payment bond is sometimes known as a labor or material payment bond.

Percentage of Completion Method: A method of recognizing earnings in an accounting system that is designed to match revenues and expenses of a job in the same proportion over the length of the entire job. It is based on an estimate, revised periodically throughout the construction period, of the total cost to complete the project. At the end of a given accounting period, the ratio of costs to date to total estimated costs is determined. This ratio is the percentage of completion.

Performance Bond: A performance bond insures completion of the project by the contractor, guaranteeing that if the contractor defaults, the bonding company will step in and finish the work. A performance bond also is applicable between a general contractor and its subcontractor, assuring the general contractor that the subcontractor will perform or pay.

Prequalification: The process of proving, before a bid is awarded, that a contractor has the capacity to fulfill a contract.

Preventive Maintenance: Any action or program designed to prevent damage to equipment or machinery.

Progress Payment: Payment for work completed by measuring the work in place and applying a previously agreed unit cost to the measured amount to determine the total payment.

Project Overhead: Costs that directly relate to the project but are not included as construction labor or materials. These costs, incurred on the job site, might include electricity, cleanup, security forces, and travel expenses.

Quantity Survey: Also called a Takeoff. A complete listing of all the materials and items of work needed for a project.

Release of Lien: When the debt is fully paid, a release of the lien is provided by the party in which it exists or to which it accrues. In the construction industry, it is a document releasing the signer's (contractor and/or subcontractor) right to a mechanics' lien on the project. The lien is then removed from the records and a clear title issued.

Respirator: A personal protection device that prevents airborne contaminants from being inhaled.

Responsive Bid: A bid that complies in all material respects with the request for bid or the request for proposal.

Retainage: The hold back by a property owner or general contractor of a part of the price to be paid for work until conditions specified in a contract are satisfied. The amount withheld is usually a fixed percentage of the total contract price.

Schedule of Values: A statement furnished by the contractor to the architect or lender reflecting the portions of the contract sum allotted for the various parts of the work and used as a basis for reviewing the contractor's applications for progress payments.

Set-Asides: Public projects that can only be bid on by designated companies led by minority or socially disadvantaged persons. (See Allowances.)

Sole Proprietorship: A business entity or form of business that is usually unincorporated, owned, and controlled exclusively by one person. It is the simplest and least expensive business entity to set up.

Specifications: Documents that contain the detailed, written descriptions and instructions about a project.

Subcontract: An agreement between the general contractor and another contractor or supplier.

Subcontractor: Any person who performed services for the construction, alteration, or repair of a residence at the request or direction of a contractor.

Subrogation: The right of an insurance company to recover losses from the party whose negligence caused the damages.

Substantial Completion: The state of completion whereby the building, or a part thereof, is rendered complete to the degree that the owner can use the building, or a part thereof, for its intended purpose.

Surety Bond: A surety bond is a promise by a bonding agency to provide limited restitution to a consumer if a contractor fails to pay an arbitration award. If required for licensure, a licensed contractor must provide and maintain a surety bond in the full amount that is required by the licensing authority.

Unit Price Contract: A contract used when each unit of work is bid with its own price. The unit price contract guarantees prices for each unit even though the finished project may result in fewer or more units than originally estimated. The owner is contractually obligated to pay for all those units.

Value Engineering: A proposal that if accepted results in a savings that is shared 50-50 between the owner and contractor. The proposal usually is a change in how a portion or aspect of a contract is accomplished differently from the original contract and equals or exceeds the specifications.

Warranty: A promise that if a claim is not true, a consideration (such as replacement or repair) will be granted. An express warranty is written; an implied warranty is assumed based on the warrantor's actions or words.

Workers' Compensation Insurance: A form of insurance, adopted in all 50 states, in which employees are paid for injuries suffered on the job. Employers pay into a fund (with no portion of the payment being paid by the employee) that is reserved for employee claims.